ISRAEL'S ETHNOGENESIS

Avraham Faust

ISRAEL'S ETHNOGENESIS:

Settlement, Interaction, Expansion and Resistance

Avraham Faust

Equinox Publishing Ltd

London   Oakville

Published by

UK: Equinox Publishing Ltd., Unit 6, The Village, 101 Amies St., London SW11 2JW
USA: DBBC, 28 Main Street, Oakville, CT 06779

www.equinoxpub.com

First published 2006

Library of Congress Cataloguing-in-Publication Data
A catalogue record for this book is available from the Library of Congress

ISBN 1904768989
ISBN 9781904768982

Typeset by Forthcoming Publications Ltd.
www.forthcomingpublications.com

Printed and bound in Great Britain by Antony Rowe Ltd, Chippenham, Wiltshire

To my parents

Yosef (Yosh) and Ya'el Faust

CONTENTS

Part I
INTRODUCTION

Part II
AN ARCHAEOLOGICAL EXAMINATION
OF ISRAELITE ETHNICITY

LIST OF FIGURES

FOREWORD

Many articles and books have been devoted to Israel's emergence in Canaan, and have attempted to identify the earliest Israel in the archaeological record. While the equation of the settlers in the Iron Age I highland villages with the Israelites seems to have been quite straightforward in the past, this identification has become one of the hottest debates in the archaeology of ancient Israel and even in biblical studies; views regarding the timing of Israel's emergence as an ethnic group and the processes which led to it and accompanied it vary greatly. The present book attempts to trace Israelite ethnic markers and ethnically specific behaviors, and to identify the historical contexts in which they became such; it concludes that Israel's emergence was a long and complex process, which covers the entire Iron Age I (with ethnic negotiations continuing even later).

While many advances were made in recent years, the present monograph differs from most previous works by a combination of several factors: Its scope, it's focus on the archaeological record, its position as part of a wider study of Iron Age society, and, consequently, its research questions.

Most recent treatments of ancient Israel have been carried out in articles. Yet ethnicity is one of the most problematic topics in archaeology in general, while the question of ethnogenesis is even more obscure. Articles, therefore, cannot adequately deal with such a complex issue, and will always leave much unanswered, particularly when dealing with such a difficult case-study. Furthermore, even the majority of the books published recently on the topic differ greatly from the present work—not only are many textually oriented, but almost all of them deal with Israelite ethnicity as part of an interest in Israel's 'political history'. They focus on ethnicity mainly because it became a major issue in determining questions such as the historicity of the Bible, or of various narratives within it. I believe ethnicity cannot be studied in isolation from other aspects of society, and that such an 'isolationist' approach is part of the reason for the dead-end we have presently reached in this area of study.

This book is part of large-scale examination of Iron Age society of ancient Israel, and ethnicity is therefore analyzed within what I believe is a more appropriate framework. Moreover, the scope of the book and the discussion of various elements enables us to examine each of the interpretations suggested to the observed patterns within the period's context (cf. Hodder's contextual archaeology), thus strengthening its probability. While the written sources serve mainly as a second fiddle, usually only at the second stage of the analysis, they also provide a context against which to examine the likelihood of the proposed explanations.

The written sources, and especially the Bible, are indeed invaluable sources that can give us insights into the society that produced them. The mere existence of these texts gives the study of Israelite ethnicity an advantage over the study of other ethnic groups in antiquity. However, due to the fragmentary nature of the texts and their debated historicity, they typically were used here as a secondary source only, although in a few chapters they merited a central role. In most cases, the discussion is decisively archaeological in orientation. That is, Iron Age archaeological data was thoroughly examined, and its social significance was studied. While only aspects seemingly relevant for the study of ethnicity were discussed in this book, this procedure ensured that the research agenda was for the most part dictated by the archaeological evidence; the texts were incorporated only within an archaeologically established research framework. And this holds true for even the more 'biblical' chapters, such as the one on circumcision—the biblical data was incorporated within a larger framework based on the archaeological data. With this, I have reversed the traditional relationship between the two sources of information in most biblical archaeological studies.

It should be noted that such is not meant to undervalue the texts—many discussions could not have proceeded without the insights gained by an examination of them. But I believe that after over a hundred years of archaeological research, it was worthwhile to reverse the usual scientific procedure and give the archaeological evidence an opportunity to set the agenda. This resulted in new questions and vistas in the study of ancient Israel.

It is my belief that the different approach of the book is one of its strengths, as is its scope. Even if some of the historical reconstructions and interpretations presented will not be accepted by all readers, I hope that the approach, at least, will be accepted as appropriate and worthy of developing. The same goes for the scope of the monograph. While some of the discussions might be speculative, and some of the arguments will surely not be accepted by all readers, the overall scenario presented here is not to be undermined by a challenging of some of my interpretations, or by the omission of a few debatable details.

And finally, the database available from ancient Israel is unparalleled. Hundreds of planned excavations and thousands of salvage excavations have been carried out within a relatively limited geographic region, which has also been extensively surveyed. This data is accompanied by texts, which, despite their problematic nature as historical sources, can give valuable insights into the society that produced them. If used appropriately, the existing data from ancient Israel can serve as an archaeological laboratory. The issue of ethnogenesis is, to a very large extent, still shrouded in mystery in the anthropological literature, and I hope that by using the rich and varied database available from ancient Israel, the present study will contribute to an understanding of the processes that lead to the creation of ethnic consciousness. It will, I hope, exemplify the potential the large database from ancient Israel has to contribute to anthropological archaeology.

The first draft of this monograph was written during my post-doctorate research at Harvard University as a Fulbright scholar in 2002. My warmest thanks to Professor Larry Stager, of the Department of Near Eastern Languages and Civilizations at Harvard, for inviting me to conduct the research at his department, and for his time and help. I would also like to thank Professor Ofer Bar-Yosef of the Department of Anthropology at Harvard for his great assistance, without which I could not have completed the writing of this book then. Many friends and colleagues have commented on earlier drafts of the monograph or parts of it, or discussed some of the ideas expressed in the book. I would like to thank, first and foremost, Dr Shlomo Bunimovitz of Tel Aviv University and Professor Aren Maeir of Bar Ilan University. Thanks are also due to Professors Elizabeth Bloch-Smith, Mark Smith, David Schloen, Daniel Master, Ryan Byrne, Anson Rainey, Joshua Schwartz, Zeev Safrai, Eyal Regev, Aaron Demsky, Hanan Eshel and Shimon Cooper. I would also like to thank numerous colleagues, including Shlomo Bunimovtiz, Zvi Lederman, Zvi Gal and Yardena Alexander, Karen Covello-Paran, Gabriel Barkay, Alon de-Groot, Zvi Greenhut, David Amit, Amihai Mazar, Aren Maeir, and Lily Singer-Avitz, who supplied me with unpublished information. I would also like to thank Yulia Rudman for redrawing the plans and Shimon Hai for redrawing the maps. I would also like to thank Ben Gordon for meticulously editing the manuscript, and Duncan Burns for his careful copy-editing.

I would also like to thank the Fulbright program for granting me the scholarship for my post-doctorate research, and to the Ingeborg Rennert Center for Jerusalem Studies and the Koschitsky fund, both at the Martin (Szusz) department of Land of Israel Studies and Archaeology, Bar-Ilan University, for their Help.

My deepest appreciation goes to my family—my children, Kama, Marvah and Yannai, who had to 'give up' a father even when I was technically at home—and especially my wife, Iris, who took on an unfair share of the daily tasks at home while I worked on the book. I am so grateful to all of them.

Avraham Faust
Ramat-Gan, Israel, May 2005

ABBREVIATIONS

AA	*American Antiquity*
ABD	David Noel Freedman (ed.), *The Anchor Bible Dictionary* (New York: Doubleday, 1992)
ADAJ	*Annual of the Department of Antiquities of Jordan*
AJA	*American Journal of Archaeology*
ARA	*Annual Review of Anthropology*
ASOR	American Schools of Oriental Research
AASOR	*Annual of the American Schools of Oriental Research*
BA	*Biblical Archaeologist*
BAR	*Biblical Archaeology Review*
BASOR	*Bulletin of the American Schools of Oriental Research*
CA	*Current Anthropology*
EB	*Encyclopaedia Biblica*
EI	*Eretz-Israel*
ESI	*Excavations and Surveys in Israel*
IEJ	*Israel Exploration Journal*
JAA	*Journal of Anthropological Archaeology*
JBL	*Journal of Biblical Literature*
JESHO	*Journal of the Economic and Social History of the Orient*
JSOT	*Journal for the Study of the Old Testament*
JSOTSup	Journal for the Study of the Old Testament Supplement Series
JNES	*Journal of Near Eastern Studies*
NEA	*Near Eastern Archaeology*
NEAEHL	E. Stern (ed.), *New Encyclopedia of Archaeological Excavations in the Holy Land* (4 vols.; Jerusalem: Israel Exploration Society)
OEANE	E.M. Meyers (ed.), *The Oxford Encyclopedia of Archaeology in the Near East* (New York: Oxford University Press)
OJA	*Oxford Journal of Archaeology*
PEQ	*Palestine Exploration Quarterly*
RB	*Revue Biblique*
SHAJ	*Studies in the History and Archaeology of Jordan*
SJOT	*Scandinavian Journal of the Old Testament*
TA	*Tel Aviv*
UF	*Ugarit Forschungen*
ZAW	*Zeitschrift für die Alttestamentliche Wissenschaft*
ZDPV	*Zeitschrift des Deutschen Palästina-Vereins*

Part I

INTRODUCTION

1

INTRODUCTION

The question of Israel's origins has been discussed intensively in biblical-historical and archaeological research. Many studies have questioned the foreign origin of the Israelites, or have been devoted, as of recent, to the issue of when the inhabitants of the highland of ancient Israel began to see themselves as Israelite. Much has also been written on the possible contribution of archaeological research to this discussion.

Until recently, it had been taken for granted in most studies that the Israelites were in existence during the Iron Age I. The hundreds of sites identified in the central highlands of ancient Israel—mainly in the region stretching from the southern Hebron hill country to northern Samaria, but also in the Galilee—were assumed to be Israelite, as was their material culture. For various reasons discussed below, this view is no longer widely accepted, and today scholars use caution when referring to the identity of the settlers in the highlands during the Iron Age I. Consequently, one of the most interesting and hotly debated issues today is identifying when the Israelites came into being as an ethnic group, and thus at which point, if at all, it is justified to refer to sites as 'Israelite'. These questions are at the heart of this study.[1]

Ethnicity and the Study of Society

As ethnicity is but one aspect of social life, and probably the most illusive of them (see Renfrew 1993: 20), it cannot be studied separately from other aspects of society. Likewise, it should only be tackled after such issues as economic structure, inequality, class, gender, social organization, cosmology, and worldviews have been adequately dealt with. Unfortunately, much of the

---

1. Notably, while we would attempt to answer many of the questions surrounding Israel's emergence in Canaan, it is not our aim to discuss the origin of the Israelites (in the sense of descent). This question, though interesting and important, is of little relevance to the issue of Israel's ethnogenesis, as will be shown below. The issue will be discussed briefly in Chapter 18.

study of Israelite ethnicity has been conducted only as a by-product of studies by scholars more focused on the reconstruction (or deconstruction) of political, or biblical, history. Whereas they correctly understood that the general history of ancient Israel is inseparable from the issue of ethnicity, many of these scholars did not pay attention to other aspects of Israelite society and thus did not have a good chance of gaining a real insight into Israelite ethnicity.

The present study deals with ethnicity as part of a more comprehensive look at Israelite society, of which ethnicity is but one aspect (e.g. Faust 2005b). While this monograph is not intended to treat all aspects of the society—only those of the Israelite social and cognitive life that are of importance for the study of ethnicity will be discussed in detail—the examination is carried out within the framework of a larger study of the Israelite society, hence providing a context against which to examine the interpretations suggested.

The Study of Ancient Israel: Current Approaches

All studies of ancient Israel are based to some extent on two types of data: historical, which is mainly biblical, and archaeological. In an approach typical of most studies conducted until the 1970s, the biblical-historical data were given a prominent position while the archaeological finds were used mainly to supplement a historically based reconstruction, or, in other words, to 'illustrate' the texts. Several archaeologists, most notably W.G. Dever, have become frustrated by this approach to the archaeological record and called for a full separation, even 'liberation', of the archaeological discussion from that of the texts. Influenced by the advances of New Archaeology, they objected to the methods and approaches of traditional Biblical Archaeology, and called for the foundation of a secular 'Syro-Palestinian Archaeology'.[2] During the 1970s and the 1980s these two distinct approaches coexisted.

In the 1990s, however, Dever modified his approach. Realizing that the texts, as problematic as they are, still give a wealth of information regarding various aspects of Israelite life, he called for a new approach to the study of ancient Israel, which he termed 'New Biblical Archaeology' (1993a). Unlike the older methods of Biblical Archaeology that 'preferred' the texts over the finds, his new approach gives equal weight to both types of data. With some modifications, the present work aims at developing the research of Israelite ethnicity in this spirit.

---

2. Although calling for a dialogue with biblical scholars. For an overview, see Dever 1985, 1993a.

Archaeology and Israelite Society: The Way Forward

A similar situation exists regarding the state of research of the archaeology of society in ancient Israel, particularly of the Iron Age II, which has not received a great deal of scholarly attention at all (e.g. Bunimovitz 2001). While Israelite society was discussed by many, in this area also the vast majority of scholars have used the written sources, mainly the Bible, as their guide, with the archaeological finds functioning usually only as an illustration to a textually derived analysis (e.g. de Vaux 1961; Reviv 1993). Moreover, the relatively few studies that did pay close attention to the material record had at their base an agenda derived from presupposed textually supported knowledge.

Archaeology, however, is well equipped to deal with ancient society, as can be seen in most archaeological studies in other parts of the world. The present study proposes an approach to the study of the Iron Age society where the archaeological record will, in most cases, be examined by itself. This will result in an agenda uninfluenced by the written sources.[3]

There are several clear advantages in using the archaeological record in place of historical sources as the principal database (cf. McGuire 1982: 161-62). The texts we have are extremely problematic on issues of dating and redaction, and therefore cannot be easily used. They also demonstrate, as with all written sources, extreme partiality and bias. Archaeological finds, however, in addition to providing a fresh look at the problems at hand, can reflect the entire society with all its sub-groups; while these finds are also partial in the sense that they only represent the part of a society's material culture that survived, they are much less biased.

The main research questions should be delineated based on an exhaustive examination of patterns in the material record.[4] The attempt to find answers to these questions should proceed using all evidence possible: archaeological finds should be scrutinized for similar patterns, and anthropological methods should be used to explain them. Only then can the data provided by the

---

3.   One can claim that the interest in ethnicity, or any other subject for that matter, is biblically driven. While I do not wish to go into a detailed discussion of this issue, suffice it to state that the proposed procedure will at least ensure that the research questions that would compose such a study (i.e. the study of ethnicity) will be based on the archaeological finds and derived from it, and not *dependant* on texts.

4.   Everything on the archaeological record should be examined as part of a general study of society: house size, internal division, changes in this division, settlement patterns, pottery distribution, etc. While, as we shall see later, ethnicity is not the totality of traits, the examination must be comprehensive in determining what should be connected to ethnicity and what should not.

written sources come into consideration.[5] These sources are of major importance in examining a period that is, after all, historical, and they can provide
significant insights into the society that produced them. 'Written sources' in
this context and for our purposes refer mainly not to grand historical narratives, but rather to more mundane information that can be learned from the
texts. It is worth quoting King and Stager, although the historical texts will
be used much less frequently in this work then in theirs:

> For our purposes, then, it matters little whether the biblical accounts are 'true'
> in the positivistic sense of some historians and biblical scholars. It is enough
> to know that the ancient Israelites believed them to be so. The stories must
> have passed some test of verisimilitude, that is, having the appearance of
> being true or real. In this sense the biblical account and many other ancient
> accounts, however, self-serving and tendentious, become grist for the cultural
> historian's mill. (2001: 7)

The texts' value lies not in their being 'true' in an absolute sense, but in
what they can tell about the society that, in the words of Murray, 'believed
them to be true' (1998: xxxi). Burckhardt applied a similar approach to the
Greeks in the nineteenth century (1998: 5). Much insight can also be gained
even by the society's spoken language, the knowledge of which is an
important step in understanding its world, material and spiritual alike (see
also Faust 2001a).

   As an instructive example of this approach, we can outline here issues
surrounding the four-room house, a plan identified archaeologically and to
be discussed at length in Chapter 9 of this volume. The house can be interpreted by archaeological and anthropological analysis as reflecting, for
example, maximal privacy and/or an egalitarian ethos. Texts seem to indicate that this was indeed the case in the society under discussion. They are
used here as no more than an illustration of the reality reflected in the
archaeological record, and while they should be examined critically, findings
of biblical criticism regarding dating of texts cannot be used to discredit the
archaeologically derived conclusions.

   Historical archaeologists such as James Deetz (1996), Henry Glassie
(1976), Ann Yentsch (1991), and Randall H. McGuire (1982) have combined the archaeological record with texts in such a manner. It seems that
historical archaeology is thus the closest sub-field to Dever's New Biblical

---

5.   Such an approach to the use of historical sources in archaeology runs contrary to
the prevalent approach in the Near East, which has frequently used archaeology to illustrate history. The current approach 'places texts and maps in the same role as anthropological descriptions or natural scientific laws… Unlike these sources, as products of the
society under study, they enable us to give interpretation from within that society. That is,
they may enable us to give the same interpretation to archaeological material as people
from within that society would have given' (Dark 1995: 57).

Archaeology. In a study of ethnicity, McGuire sees the use of documentary and archaeological data together as a means of overcoming the limitations of both (1982: 162). It is this approach that will be adopted in most chapters of the present book.

Admittedly, the textual sources are underused in most parts of the present work, for two reasons. First, the use of the texts as a main source for our research questions and agenda has proven somewhat futile over the years. An emphasis of archaeology, even at the expense of other sources of information, is therefore required in order to bring fresh insights and move research forward. Only after this is established can the texts receive, again, a primary role in the discussion. Second, the current debate on the emergence of Israel is interwined with the debate on the historicity of the Bible. Relying too heavily on the latter will result in many scholars doubting the existence of the former. In the present scholarly atmosphere (cf. Chapter 3) it is therefore better to 'err on the side of caution', and to use the Bible only as a secondary source—one that is not crucial for the arguments raised—otherwise those who doubt the historicity of the various texts will *a priori* disregard the conclusions of such a study.

The Archaeology of Ancient Israel and Anthropology

There is hardly another region in the world that has been excavated and surveyed so intensively as the Land of Israel. The thousands of salvage excavations and probably hundreds of planned excavations along with extensive surveys that have taken place in this small area have provided the basis for a very strong foundation for archaeological inquiry. Combine this with the large amount of texts available for the Iron Age onward and the wealth of data is immense, and could have led to exceptionally detailed anthropological studies of the ancient human societies of the region. Due to historical reasons, however, Near Eastern Archaeology developed a different agenda, and the region with so much potential was left almost completely outside the realm of anthropology.

The study of ethnogenesis, the formation of ethnic groups, can serve as an example. This is an important issue, one that has generally not received a great deal of attention due to the fact that the nature of pre-ethnic grouping is difficult to decipher, as discussed below. With regard to ancient Israel, however, we possess a huge body of archaeological data regarding both the periods before and after that in which there is a consensus regarding Israel's existence. This abundance of material, combined with at least a number of texts pertaining to the period, present us with a database large enough to tackle the question of Israel's ethnogenesis.

It is my hope that the present monograph will contribute both to the study of ancient Israel in the spirit of the New Biblical Archaeology and to the study of ethnogenesis in general, if only in exemplifying the importance and potential of the archaeology of ancient Israel to such a study.

The Structure of the Book

The book has five major parts, each composed of several chapters. Part I includes introductory and summarizing chapters. Following this introduction, Chapter 2 presents a brief overview of the study of ethnicity in general archaeological and anthropological literature, and the advances made in scholarship regarding this complex issue. Chapter 3 critically summarizes past research on Israelite ethnicity.

Part II investigates Israelite ethnicity through an analysis of specific features, primarily archaeological. Chapter 4 presents an overview and explication of the research methodology. Archaeological means (based on the discussion in Chapter 2) are employed to identify specific traits that appear to reflect Israelite ethnicity, or have emerged as a result of ethnically specific behaviors. The study focuses on the Iron Age II, when it is agreed that there was an Israelite ethnicity. The relevant traits are traced back in time, in order to identify the context in which they became meaningful. Chapter 5 discusses pork consumption and avoidance, a feature that seems to have had particular significance during the Iron Age I, emerging from interactions with the Philistines. Chapter 6 discusses the absence of decoration on Israelite pottery during the Iron Age II, apparently a function of both an ethos of egalitarianism and simplicity, whose roots may be traced to the Iron I, and of ethnic negotiations with other contemporaneous groups that used highly decorated pottery. Chapter 7 examines the absence of imported ceramics in most Iron II Israelite sites, the complex explanation of which may be partially traced to the aforementioned ethos, with apparent roots in the Iron I, or perhaps as a result of interactions with the Philistines and/or Canaanites and their pottery. Chapter 8 draws attention to the fact that although Iron I pottery forms show significant continuity with Late Bronze Age forms, the repertoire is much more limited, which too may be interpreted as representing an egalitarian ideology and ethos. Chapter 9 discusses the complex design of the four-room house. An analysis of the movement within these structures, the perception of space they reflect, and their status in Israelite society shed light on several societal values, including conceptions of order, privacy, and egalitarianism. The house seems to have embodied the Israelite ethos and way of life. Chapter 10, unique in this section in its discussion of non-archaeological finds, focuses on another emblem of Israelite ethnicity: circumcision. Although the custom cannot be identified archaeologically, its discussion in the context of other archaeological traits, juxtaposed with ethnographical data, is illuminating. While circumcision was practiced by many Near Eastern societies prior to Iron Age I, it apparently developed as an ethnic marker as a consequence of the interaction of the highlanders with the Philistines at the time, and is therefore consistent with the aforementioned archaeological traits in terms of its timing and the factors underlying its emergence as an ethnic marker. Chapter 11, the last chapter of Part II, discusses the ethos of egalitarianism and simplicity, one of the basic characteristics of Israelite identity as emerging from the previous discussion. This ethos, ostensibly reflected in many traits, seems to be the product of interactions and negotiations with other more hierarchical groups.

Part III discusses the impact of the Philistines on Israelite ethnicity. Chapter 12 deals with settlement patterns during the late Iron Age I and early Iron Age II. The finds, such as the lack of tenth-century rural settlements, seem to indicate that the highland society faced a serious external threat during this period, posed probably from the Philistines. This threat served as a prime catalyst of the urbanization and state formation processes that characterized the late Iron I and the early Iron Age II. Chapter 13 discusses the vital importance of statehood and/or contacts with states for the development of ethnicity in general, and in regards to ancient Israel in particular. Chapter 14 briefly discusses the Philistines' status in Iron I society, and their impact on the formation of Israelite ethnicity, as reflected in the Israelite traits discussed above. Chapter 15, the last chapter of Part III, draws heavily on the concepts of totemic and ethnic identities of Comaroff and Comaroff in discussing the processes by which the highland villagers of the twelfth century BCE, whose identity was probably relatively 'totemic', transformed into 'ethnic' Israelites. In contrast to previous chapters, which discuss the reasons for the emergence of various ethnic markers, this section also focuses on processes and modes of adoption of these traits.

Part IV of the book deals with Merenptah's Israel, and discusses the range of evidence which supports the existence of some type of Israelite identity prior to the interaction with the Philistines. Chapter 16 discusses the existence of Israel earlier in the Iron I. Several of the archaeological traits which we showed to be ethnically meaningful emerged *prior* to the interactions with the Philistines and are thus better explained in the context of the late thirteenth century and the interaction of the highlanders with the Egyptio-Canaanite system, rather than of the eleventh century. Their earlier development is considered here. Chapter 17 discusses the reality of the late thirteenth-century highland as a background for the emergence of early Israelite identity. The processes and changes occurring during Iron Age I are also discussed, up to the point of interactions with the Philistines, which provided final shape to the Israelite identity. Chapter 18 re-examines the issue of Israel's origins. A unique aspect of the present monograph lies in its isolation of the question of Israel's origins—whether their ancestors were slaves in Egypt, semi-nomads from Transjordan, semi-nomads from Cisjordan, or revolting sedentary Canaanites—from the study of their emergence as a distinct group in the Iron Age. Israelite ethnicity need not be dependent on the ancestry of the Israelites, but rather on what they considered *themselves* to be. A discussion of Israel's ethnicity together with its origins may cause confusion, and is therefore dealt with separately in this chapter in light of the insights presented in previous chapters.

Part V examines in more detail some aspects of distribution. Chapter 19 examines traits such as the collared rim jar and Philistine pottery, which were associated by earlier scholarship with ethnicity, yet have recently been discounted as ethnically insignificant. A closer examination of the distribution of these traits, however, reveals that they must represent symbolic behavior and shows them to be ethnically sensitive, although in a manner much more complex than previously believed. Chapter 20 focuses on Transjordan, and revisits various features of that region whose association with Israel have been disregarded. An in-depth examination of the finds proves that the case is more complex. This is followed by a summary in Chapter 21 and a postscript in Chapter 22, pointing to some ironic aspects of the present debate.

2

ARCHAEOLOGY AND ETHNICITY

Identifying ethnic groups in the archaeological record is notoriously difficult. In the words of Renfrew, 'the most problematic of all the concepts which we have tended to use is that of "a people"' (1993: 20). It is my aim in the present chapter briefly to review some central themes in the archaeological study of ethnicity. Rather than to summarize the entire discussion or cover all major topics of this area of study, my aim is to point, very briefly, to several major developments and issues that may be of importance for the discussions in the following sections of this work.

Ethnicity in Archaeology:
Previous Research and Existing Approaches

The Culture History School
Archaeologists have always made attempts to identify ethnic groups in the archaeological record. This endeavor was more or less the main agenda of the Culture History school, the dominant archaeological approach during most of the twentieth century. Archaeologists working in this tradition equated 'archaeological cultures', identified by their material culture, with ethnic groups (e.g. Jones 1997; McNairn 1980). Childe succinctly explains the rationale for this approach: 'We find certain types of remains—pots, implements, ornaments, burial rites and house forms—constantly recurring together. Such a complex of associated traits we shall term "cultural group" or just a "culture". We assume that such a complex is the material expression of what today would be called a "people"' (1929: v-vi). This approach was based on a normative understanding of culture, i.e., that norms or rules of behavior prescribe the practices and behaviors of members of any given group, as a result of shared ideas, worldviews, and beliefs (e.g. Jones 1997: 24; Johnson 1999: 16-17).

With the advent of New Archaeology, the methodological foundations of the Culture History school and its normative approach to culture were heavily criticized and fell into disfavor (Binford 1962, 1965; see also Jones 1997;

Trigger 1989; Ryman, O'Brien, and Dunnell 1997).[1] As we shall see below, it is clear today that a material culture is also shaped by influences such as ecology, economy, and gender, and thus cannot be simplistically equated with ethnicity.

The New (Processual) Archaeology
The New Archaeology, which evolved in the 1960s and later came to be known as 'Processual Archaeology', generally failed to direct much attention to the identification of ethnic groups (see Jones 1997: 5, 26-27, 111; de Boer 1990: 102). This school grew out of the dissatisfaction of the 'unscientific' nature of the Culture History school, specifically its inductive approach, its lack of rigorous scientific procedures, its descriptive nature, and, most important for our purposes, its normative approach to culture (Binford 1962, 1965). The new school believed that archaeological remains were the product of a range of complex processes and not 'simply a reflection of ideational norms' (Jones 1997: 26).

Moreover, adherents of the New Archaeology school were interested in generalizations and laws, and disregarded the specific and the unique. This attitude is summarized by Trigger:

> Its emphasis on nomothetic generalizations was accompanied by the obvious implication that the study of any national tradition as an end in itself was of trivial importance. Richard Ford called into question the legitimacy of 'political archaeology' and of any correlation between archaeology and nationalism, asking archaeologists instead to embrace a 'universal humanism'. By denying the worth of such studies the New Archaeology suggested the unimportance of national traditions themselves… (1989: 314-15)[2]

Studies of differences and uniqueness were consequently inconsistent with their scientific agenda (Trigger 1989: 312-19). It is further likely that the disinterest in discussions of ethnicity also resulted from the horrifying outcome of the racial archaeology that was so prevalent in Europe (e.g. Hall 1997: 1-2). This so-called archaeology collaborated with the justification of the Nazi claims of racial superiority and, as a consequence, contributed to the extermination of millions. Ethnicity was relegated to a minor role as a part of discussions on style, which were in themselves not of great concern. De Boer, for example, pointed out that the New Archaeology tended to

---

1. Childe himself was aware of some of the limitations. According to him, 'perhaps we might call its members a people, but we should have no right to assume that this people as a whole spoke a single language or acted as a political unit, still less that all its members were related physiologically' (1951: 40).

2. This view seems to be also 'nationalistic' (or 'imperialist') in a way, since it supported American interests, if unintentionally. The above quotation ends: 'and of anything that stood in the way of American economic activity and political influence'.

disfavor stylistic studies leaned toward cultural and historical reconstructions, which became in some circles a 'virtual pariah' (1990: 102).

The New Archaeologists, interested mainly in function, viewed only style, implicitly or explicitly, as being of any importance for the study of ethnicity. They classified three types of artifacts and assemblage variations according to the type of social domain in which the artifacts usually function: technomic, socio-technic, and ideo-technic (Binford 1962: 219; Jones 1997: 110). Binford notes that common to these classes of artifacts are stylistic qualities (i.e., of a nature not dictated by raw production materials or technology), which functioned to promote group solidarity and identity, and are likely most relevant for the study of ethnic origins, migrations, and interaction between groups (1962: 220). Vessel forms, for example, were seen as created by strictly utilitarian considerations while decoration was seen as stylistic (Jones 1997: 111). Ethnicity, then, was viewed as being expressed only in such non-functional traits.

Therefore relatively few studies on ethnicity and related issues were produced by scholars of the New Archaeology school, who perceived such questions as unimportant or even inconsistent with the school's generalizing spirit.

Changes in Anthropological Approaches to Ethnicity
At about the same time, however, revolutionary changes were occurring in the anthropological approach to ethnicity.

The most important development in the study of ethnicity in general came with the publication of *Ethnic Groups and Boundaries*, a volume edited by Barth (1969). In his Introduction to the book, Barth criticizes the conventional view of ethnic groups as 'culture-bearing units' (1969: 10-13), by which he means groups sharing core values that find representation in cultural forms (1969: 10-11). (Note the similarity with the above-mentioned Culture History approach championed by Childe). Barth defines ethnic groups as, in essence, a form of social organization; its critical criterion is an ability to be identified and distinguished among others, or in his words, allowing 'self-ascription and ascription by others' (1969: 11, 13). Ethnic identity here is not determined by biological or genetic factors but is subject to perception and is adaptable. Barth's views had an immense impact in the social sciences, so much so that in Emberling's overview of the study of ethnicity in archaeology, works on the subject are referred to as 'B.B.' (before Barth) or 'A.B.' (after Barth) (1997: 295; see also Jones 1997: 60).[3] With his work, emphasis shifted from the shared elements or characteristics of a group to the features that distinguish it from others. It was the contact

3. Archaeologists were even more influenced by his work than social/cultural anthropologists. See, e.g., the evaluation of Banks (1996: 12-17).

between groups that was seen as essential for the formation of the self-identity of a group (see also Cohen 1985), which is thus clearly manifested in its material culture.

Following these developments in anthropology and sociology, archaeologists have also come to understand that ethnicity is too complex to be merely identified with a material or an archaeological culture (see, e.g., Hodder 1982a); it is fluid, it is merely one of several attributes of an individual's complete identity, and it is subjective (e.g. Shenan 1989, 1991; Emberling 1997; Schortman, Urban, and Ausec 2001; Jones 1997, and bibliography there). This new understanding of ethnicity also seemed appropriate for several post-processual approaches to archaeology that were beginning to develop (e.g. Hall 1997: 142; Jones 1997: 5-6).

Archaeology and Ethnicity: The Response
As observed in existing groups, the subjective nature of ethnicity has led some scholars to question the ability of archaeologists to identify ethnic groups in the material record of extinct societies (see Jones 1997: 109-10, 124; with regard to the Levant, see Herzog 1997).[4] Yet in most cases, clear relationships between material culture and ethnicity can be identified, however complicated they may be (McGuire 1982; Kamp and Yoffee 1980; Emberling 1997, and others; see also Howard 1996: 239-40), and the potential of archaeological inquiry to deal with such issues should not be underestimated.

The new anthropological approaches to ethnicity were propagated at a time of change in archaeological thinking. New/Processual Archaeology, at least in its original orthodox version, was the target of increasing criticism, primarily by what came to be known as Post-Processual Archaeologies. Such scholars pointed to its failure to isolate any universal laws of human behavior (which, after all, had been one of its main aims; see Flannery 1973), its neglect of cognitive aspects, and its disregard for the individual (Trigger 1989; Hodder 1991, 1992, and others). The post-processual approach reinstated a different, yet normative approach to culture, which did not seek to desert older approaches entirely (Hodder 1991: 1; Bunimovitz 1999: 147-48).[5] Today archaeology is much more responsive to the study of ethnicity, acknowledging its subjective nature. Unlike the old Processual

4. Note that some claim that ethnicity is modern, and that there were no ethnicities in the past (based on works such as Anderson 1983; Gellner 1983). This view, which is based on studies of modern nationalism, is unfounded (e.g. Hall 1997; A. Smith 1986, 1994; Banks 1996; Atkinson 1994; Comaroff and Comaroff 1992, and many others; see also Grosbi 2002), and need not be discussed here.

5. Note that Hodder's own criticism of the normative approach differs greatly from that of the New Archaeology, and includes the lack of treatment of the individual, etc. (1991: 156-61).

Archaeology, today's approaches feel comfortable in tackling problems concerning ideology and worldviews and in dealing with symbols. And this is true regarding both post-processual approaches and the new Cognitive/ Processual Archaeology, as championed by Renfrew (1994).

The recovery of 'normative archaeology' in post-processual approaches is also evident in the resurging interest in style.[6] It is clear today that function and style cannot be separated, so that the form of the artifact can reflect both, and therefore is potentially important for the study of identity (e.g. Wiessner 1990, and references). Furthermore, it is widely accepted today that style is not only a passive reflection of various modes of behavior, but is actively used to convey messages concerning one's identity and status, which ultimately influence the actions or attitudes of others (see Jones 1997: 110- 17, and references). Wiessner (1990) refers to two types of styles: emblemic and assertive. Assertive style is the way by which people actively use material items to convey messages relating to their social status and position, for example, to send messages of 'I'm richer', or 'I'm better than everyone else'. Such messages are transmitted, for example, by wearing an expensive watch, which clearly sends a message or even messages on its user/owner. Emblemic style, on the other hand, is used to convey messages regarding one's identity and group membership. By wearing a yarmulke, for example, Jewish people send a clear message on their group identity. It should be stressed that while the two types of messages are seemingly contradictory, they can be expressed simultaneously by the same item, at times confound- ing the ability to distinguish between the two types of messages.

Archaeology and Ethnicity:
Identifying Ethnic Groups in the Archaeological Record

It is accepted today that groups define themselves in relation to, and in con- trast with, other groups (Barth 1969; see also R. Cohen 1978a: 389; A.P. Cohen 1985: 558). The ethnic boundaries of a group are not defined by the sum of cultural traits but by the idiosyncratic use of specific material and behavioral symbols as compared with other groups (McGuire 1982: 160; see also Kamp and Yoffee 1980: 96; Emberling 1997: 299; Barth 1969: 14, 15; J.M. Hall 1997: 135). McGuire points out that overt material symbols of ethnic identity (ethnic markers) are the clearest evidence of the maintenance of an ethnic boundary (1982: 163). However, such markers are scarce in the archaeological record. Furthermore, grasping the symbolic significance of

---

6.   Summarizing the various approaches to style, let alone their developments, is well beyond the scope of the present work. See, e.g., Sacket 1977, 1985, 1986; Plog 1980, 1983; Wiessner 1983, 1985, 1988; Pollock 1983; Wobst 1977; Washburn 1989; Jones 1997; see also various papers in Conkey and Hastrof 1990.

artifacts can be extremely difficult. While all groups may communicate mes-sages of identity through material culture, the vehicles used differ by group, message, and context. Which artifact can express a boundary of a group depends on the ideas people in that society have about what 'an appropriate artifact for group marking' is (Hodder 1991: 3), but the selection may seem arbitrary to outside observers (as well as to many group members). One group might choose elements of clothing, while another might choose ceramics. Pinpointing those elements of material culture that were meaning-ful to any particular group, and determining when to attribute significance to an observed variation in the distribution of certain artifacts is, therefore, a complicated endeavor.

However, in addition to such markers, ethnicity can also be identified by 'ethnically specific behavior', or more accurately, by the material correlates of such behavior. Such behavioral differences might include, in McGuire's words, 'variations in rubbish disposal patterns…or differences in floor plans of dwellings, which reflect differing behavioral requirements for space' (1982: 163). This ethnic behavior is much easier to identify than ethnic markers. As an instructive example one can consider the 'Parting Ways' site in Plymouth, Massachusetts, which was inhabited by freed African slaves following the American revolution (Deetz 1996: 187-211). Excavations at the site revealed a material culture generally similar to that of contemporary sites, but as observed by Deetz, there existed real differences in house con-struction, trash disposal, and community arrangement as compared to these sites—differences that could have been overlooked based on an analysis of the artifacts themselves (1996: 210). So it is not the artifacts themselves that necessarily carry any ethnic importance, but the use made of these artifacts that is potentially important.

Furthermore, social dimensions such as economic status, prestige, relig-ion, occupation, urban or rural setting, and other factors may all affect the symbolic content of artifacts (McGuire 1982: 164; see also Kamp and Yoffee 1980: 97; London 1989; Skjeggestand 1992: 179-80; Orser and Fagan 1995: 215-16; Emberling 1997: 305-306, 310-11; see also Finkelstein 1996a: 204). Contradictions between different kinds of symbols may confound interpreta-tions even further, such as when a member of an ethnic group characterized by a low economic status attains a higher status, or in elite dwellings, when the finds might include both symbols of solidarity with the local group along with symbols of solidarity with its peers. The latter message might at times contradict the former (see below).

In order to differentiate between the various 'combinations of effects', a full examination of the society should be undertaken to identify all the social dimensions relevant to material culture production and symbolization (see Kamp and Yoffee 1980). Only after the other elements have been identified can we attribute ethnic labels to some traits of material culture. The second step, of course, should be to find the tangible connection between those material traits and the ethnic group under discussion. The difficulties inherent in any attempt to identify symbolic traits in the archaeological record require that attention be given also to written sources. Although sometimes quite problematic, a careful examination of these sources is needed in order to extract maximum information and gain insights to the society in question (see also J.M. Hall 1997: 142).

Another consideration is that boundary maintenance varies greatly in time and space. An object symbolizing ethnicity of a certain group in one context might be of less importance in another contemporaneous one (see Hodder 1982a). Some boundaries might, therefore, be represented with sharp falloffs in distribution patterns of certain traits, while others may be more blurred (see de Boer 1990: 102). Moreover, in some cases, differences can exist between different areas of interaction of the same groups (Hodder 1982a: 27-31). Unfortunately, the highly important issue of variations in the degree of boundary maintenance of the same groups has received insufficient attention in past research (see also Bunimovitz and Faust 2001).

The Formation and Persistence of Ethnic Groups

In an analysis of the archaeological evidence of ethnic groups in Arizona in the second half of the nineteenth century, and in light of the historical record and anthropological and sociological research, McGuire demonstrated three main variables that influence the formation and adaptation of ethnic groups: competition, ethnocentrism, and the differential distribution of power (1982). What follows is an expanded discussion of these.

Comeptition

Many scholars have addressed the central role played by competition in ethnic boundary maintenance. McGuire asserts that it is a common theme in all theories (1982). Hodder's works on the Baringo region (e.g., Hodder 1979a, 1979b, 1982a; but see de Boer 1990: 103) serve as a good illustration of its importance.[7] Here, material, social, and psychological rewards are affected by the level of ethnic boundaries maintenance in the context of individual and group competition. Competition, however, does not explain why formation is channeled along ethnic lines (McGuire 1982: 169-70).

Ethnocentrism

Ethnocentrism, in the words of Seymour-Smith, refers 'to the habit or tendency to judge or interpret other cultures according to the criteria of one's own culture. It is a universal tendency, though...we may observe greater and

---

7. For a similar study on Iron Age Israel, see Bunimovitz and Faust 2001.

lesser degrees…' (1986: 97). Members of other groups are therefore seen as somewhat inferior, and the respect accorded to them usually depends on their degree of similarity to the group of reference (McGuire 1982: 170). Ethnocentrism explains why the effects of competition are manifest along ethnic lines. However, after the primary contact between groups, ethnocentrism can no longer be considered an independent variable, and is later shaped by the action of other forces, such as power relations (*ibid.*).

Differential Distribution of Power
Differential distribution of power is the key variable in explaining changes in ethnic boundary maintenance. Power determines the distribution of most, if not all, of the wealth possessed by a society, and is significant from the perspective of the individual as a strategy for gaining access to material, social, and psychological rewards. From an inter-group perspective, if the disparity between two ethnic groups is great, then strong boundary mainte-nance can be expected to deny members of the weaker group access to higher prestige or wealth. Yet within the weaker group individual members can compete for power on a smaller stage. It should be noted that in some cases ethnic identity has been used as a state-endorsed instrument of politi-cal control (Ucko 1988: xi; see also Small 1997: 279-81; Patterson 1991: 79; Emberling 1997: 304). Notably, it seems as if ethnic groups are arranged in hierarchical relationships, although this is not an essential feature (Ember-ling 1997: 303). The issue of the relations between ethnicity and state, as well as that of ethnicity and social hierarchy (see Comaroff and Comaroff 1992) will be developed below.

In his summary of the relationship between these three components he outlined, McGuire claims, 'competition provides the motivation for group formation, ethnocentrism channels it along ethnic lines, and the differential distribution of power determines the nature of the relationship' (1982: 173). This hypothesis is supported by the measuring of two variables: the degree of ethnic boundary maintenance by examination of food refuse, ceramics and architecture, which he believes are proven to be more ethnically sensi-tive, and the disparity of power between ethnic groups through group size and control over resources, which is reflected in wealth and military strength, among others.

While a promising and instructive line of research (see also Faust 2000a), one issue that seems to have been neglected in McGuire's work, in its emphasis on the importance of ethnocentrism, is that of its formation. His study focused on a specific historical reality in which the existence of groups such as Anglos, Mexican Americans, and Chinese might be taken for granted, but such is not always the case. Therefore, the last theoretical issue we address here is that of 'ethnogenesis'.

Ethnogenesis

Ethnogenesis has been largely disregarded as a research topic (Emberling 1997: 308; A. Smith 1986: 41), possibly due to its highly problematic nature. Yet this is a central question in the study of ethnicity, and one that lies at the heart of the present monograph.

Seymour-Smith defines ethnogenesis as 'The construction of group identity and resuscitation or persistence of cultural features of a people undergoing rapid and radical change. It may also be used to refer to a new ethnic system emerging out of an amalgamation of other groups' (1986: 97). Patterson asserts: 'Ethnogenesis is the historical creation of a people with a sense of their collective identity...' (1991: 31). Emberling, after establishing the connection between ethnicity and states (see more below), argues that ethnogenesis is closely connected with state formation processes and with state control, citing as an example the creation of new ethnic identities when a state or empire conquers independent groups; in this sense, ethnicity can be seen as a form of resistance (1997: 308). These issues, which received relatively little attention in the past, will be discussed at length below.

3

ISRAELITE ETHNICITY: STATE OF RESEARCH

In the late 13th–12th cents. B.C. there occurred a major influx of new settlers into the hillcountry, especially from Jerusalem northward to Shechem. Hundreds of small villages were now established, not on the remains of destroyed or abandoned Late Bronze Age Urban Canaanite sites, but de novo. These villages are characterized chiefly by their hilltop location and lack of defensive walls; densely arranged 'four-room' or courtyard houses of very stereotyped plan; an abundance of cisterns and silos for storage of water and foodstuffs; intensive cultivation of nearby terraced hillsides; a ceramic repertoire that is basically derived from Late Bronze Age Canaanite pottery types, but contains some new elements that are characteristic of isolated and poor rural areas; the increasing use of iron implements; and, above all, an 'egalitarian' material culture that shows little sign of social stratification. (Dever 1994: 215-16)

During the Late Bronze Age Canaan was an Egyptian province. The locations and material remains of the Iron I agricultural villages indicate a rather different lifestyle from that of the Late Bronze Age, the settlements of which were concentrated mainly in the valleys and plains and were highly stratified. The Iron Age settlements were rural and concentrated in an area that was relatively uninhabited in the preceding centuries (see Finkelstein 1988; Dever 1994, 1995a: 204). Their inhabitants lived in a new type of building, called the three- or four-room house. The finds from the Iron Age hill country villages were poor and rudimentary (Fig. 3.1). While pottery forms had Late Bronze Age antecedents, the assemblages typically included a limited pottery repertoire, consisting of cooking pots, bowls, and storage jars, which were mainly of the collared rim type.

Until the 1990s, scholarly consensus held that these settlers constituted 'early Israel', corresponding to the period of the Judges in the Hebrew Bible (Albright 1961; Aharoni 1979: 193-94; see Finkelstein 1988). This concept was based on the reasonable assumption that the settlement of the Israelite tribes as mentioned in the Hebrew Bible was synonymous with the Iron I material remains uncovered by archaeologists, a seemingly secure identification in light of the mentioning of Israel as an ethnic group in the Merenptah stele, dating to the end of the thirteenth century BCE (Stager 1985a; Na'aman 1994b: 247-49; Bloch-Smith and Alpert Nakhai 1999: 77).

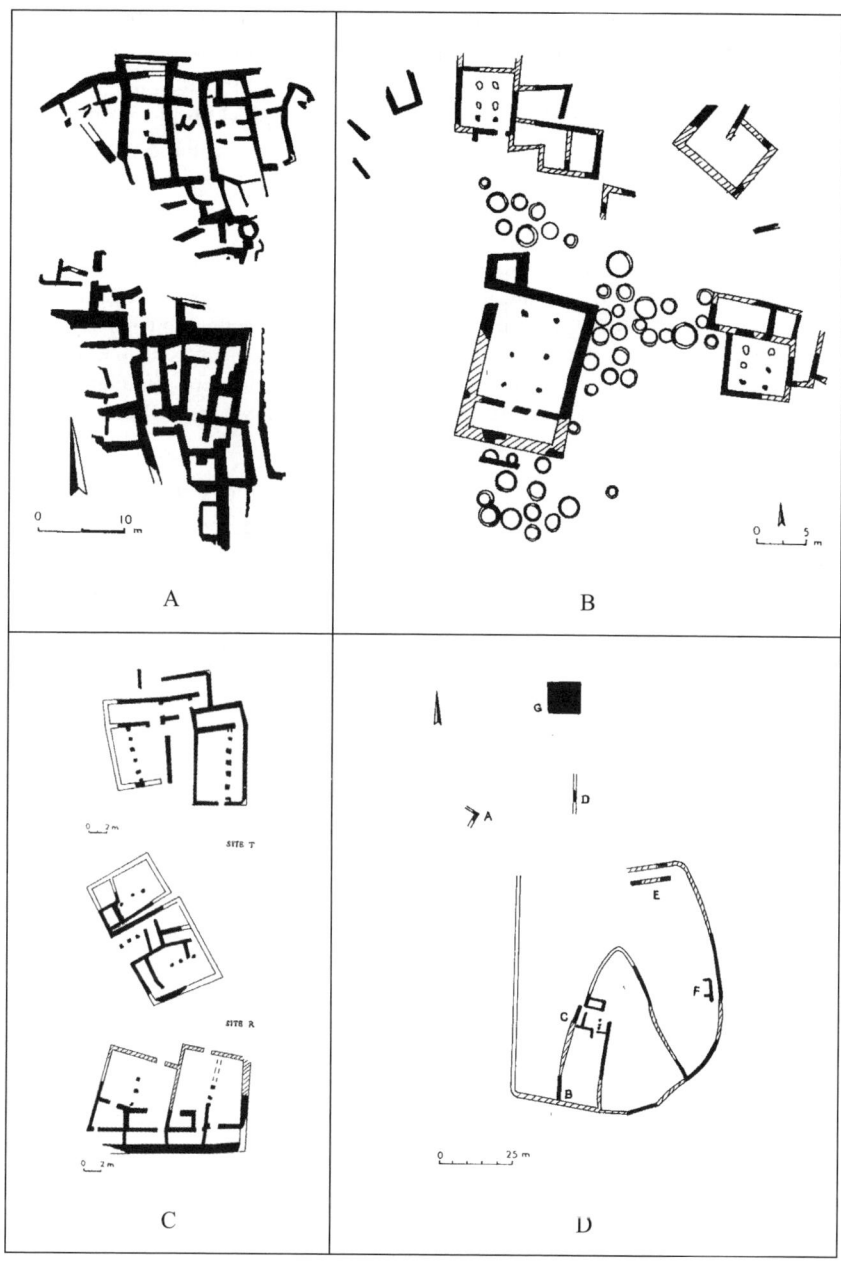

Figure 3.1. *Plans of Several Iron I Villages in the Highlands.*
A: 'Ai (after Finkelstein 1988: Fig. 85); B: 'Izbet Sartah (after Finkelstein
1988: Fig. 21); C: Khirbet Raddana (after King and Stager 2001: 10);
D: Giloh (after A. Mazar 1994: Fig. 4).

Therefore material culture of these sites was understood, in the tradition of the dominant Culture History school, as representing the Israelites (e.g. A. Mazar 1992b: 287-95). This approach can be exemplified by the various attempts made to deduce the Israelite character of Megiddo Stratum VI from the presence of several characteristics, mainly the collared-rim jar (see Albright 1937; Aharoni 1970; Esse 1991, 1992, and references). According to Aharoni:

> ...Megiddo VI is no longer a Canaanite city. It contains no evidence for Philistine domination. It is an unwalled settlement in which the ceramic tradition continues in large measure that of the local Canaanite culture in company with an abundance of collared-rim jars so typical of Israelite occupation. Its buildings are entirely different, and Megiddo's venerable sacral tradition is unequivocally terminated. Does all this not indicate that Megiddo VI was the first Israelite settlement founded there? (1970: 265)[1]

Gradually, however, serious doubts arose on the direct equation of these material remains with the Israelites. Criticism focused on the discrepancy between the territories supposedly inhabited by Israelites, and the distribution of their assumed material markers. According to Ibrahim, for example, the presence of both four-room houses and collared rim jars in Transjordan outside of the area of the Israelite settlement (Ibrahim 1975; 1978; see Chapter 20) is clearly problematic evidence. Ibrahim believes that the appearance of the collared rim jars in the Jordan Valley, the Ammonite region, and north of this area poses a problem for those who accept the proposal that these jars were associated with the Israelites (Ibrahim 1978: 123). He concludes: 'The presence of the collared-rim jar during the late 13th–12th centuries cannot be attributed to one single ethnic group. The origin and the long use of the type under discussion, whenever and wherever, ought to be considered in connection with a social-economic tradition' (1978: 124).[2]

Similar discrepancies were observed in the distribution of the four-room house. These houses have been uncovered both in Transjordan and in the coastal plain (e.g. Ibrahim 1975; A. Mazar 1980: 74-75; Finkelstein 1996a: 204-205), leading many scholars to conclude that the unique connection between this building type and the Israelites is incorrect, and that the four-room house, as well as collared rim jars, should be explained by their functionality and suitability for life in highland farming communities. These explanations were in implicit accordance with the adaptation spirit of the New Archaeology.[3]

1. This issue will be discussed in detail in Chapter 19.
2. Yet, Ibrahim did not offer any specific explanation for the distribution or longevity of the collared rim jar.
3. Since artifacts can be both functional and symbolic, the division between the two is of course artificial (Hodder 1991: 53-55; see also below).

The observation of these issues was also accompanied by a more cautious approach to the issue of identifying ethnic groups in the archaeological record—what has been called 'pots and peoples' (e.g. Parr 1978; but see already Engberg 1940). While a cautious and even negative approach was typical of the New Archaeology (e.g. Renfrew 1993; Jones 1997: 5, 26-27), it had only an indirect influence on Syro-Palestinian archaeology. However, although these two lines of criticism—the problematic distribution of traits on the one hand and the indirect impact of the skepticism of the New Archaeology toward the study of ethnicity on the other—occurred together, it should be stressed that they are not complementary, if not contradictory, as we shall see below. Both, however, have gradually raised doubts over the once popular identification of the Israelites with these material traits.

Various scholars have pointed to the heterogeneity of Iron Age I society in the region, and to the fact that there is no evidence that the highland's 'material culture' was distinctively Israelite, as opposed to being Jebusite, Hivite, Moabite, etc. (Miller and Hayes 1986: 85), or of any other group which, according to the Bible, inhabited the region at the time. The texts indicated that, although the area was inhabited only by Israelites during the Iron Age II, there were other groups in the region during the Iron Age I (e.g. the Gibeonites, Josh. 9; the Jebusites, Judg. 19.10-11; 2 Sam. 5.5-7; and many others). Since the attempts to identify more than one 'archaeological culture' in the region failed, most scholars concluded that the Israelites could not be identified.

Indeed, the problems with Iron I ethnic labels initially concentrated on this question of how to distinguish an Israelite from a member of any other group inhabiting the region at the time—e.g. Gibeonite, Pherazite, or Kenite, as mentioned in the Bible (B. Mazar 1981; Ahlstrom 1984; A. Mazar 1994: 90-91; Finkelstein 1988: 28, 65; see also Skjeggestand 1992: 165, 176, 177, 185; Stager 1998: 137; Kempinski 1995: 60).[4] However, not only were the basic concepts of the Culture History school never questioned, but they were directly responsible for the dissatisfaction with the identification of the Israelites with the highland material culture. The inapplicability of the term 'Israelites' was based on our inability to differentiate between Israelites and others in the archaeological record, and was therefore still in the spirit of the Culture History school.

In 1989, London published a more sophisticated solution to this problem. She suggested that the distinction between the so-called 'Israelite' and other settlements should be viewed as resulting from socio-economic differences, i.e., rural vs. urban. Variations, therefore, reflect diverse cultural elements within the same ethnic group. This is a more sophisticated solution since it is

4. For various attempts to identify other groups, see, e.g., B. Mazar 1964; Kempinski 1981; and others.

based on the understanding that material culture is not a direct and simple representation of an ethnic group and requires the consideration of other factors.[5]

Solutions and Problems

With these challenges hanging, the Israelite ethnic label on the settlers in the highlands became increasingly problematic. At the time, Finkelstein suggested that we should treat all groups living in the Iron I highlands as Israelites (1988: 27-28) on the rationale that regardless of their ethnic affiliation during the Iron I, they became Israelite from the tenth century BCE onward after the formation of the monarchy (see also A. Mazar 1990b: 95-96).

Finkelstein's solution was a subject of criticism, particularly by Skjeggestand (1992). The critics based much of their argumentations on Finkelstein's misleading conclusion that the Iron Age pottery from the highlands was very different from its Late Bronze Age predecessor (Skjeggestand 1992: 170 n. 24; Dever 1995a; 2000: 69 n. 21; see also Chapter 8 of this volume). The assumption was that the similarity in pottery forms (and perhaps in other traits as well) between the Late Bronze Age and the Iron Age I indicates continuity in population and culture, therefore invalidating the applicability of the term 'Israelite' for these (Canaanite) settlers. As we shall see below, however, this criticism was much less important for the present discussion than is usually thought, and led it in a wrong direction.

In order to avoid the problem, Dever suggested calling the highland's Iron I population 'Proto-Israelite' (1991: 87; 1992a, 1995a: 206-207; see also Williamson 1998: 147). Dever's rationale seems to have been based on his awareness that this population had indeed constituted an ethnic group, and that this, together with the mentioning of Israel in the Merenptah stela and the continuity of material culture from Iron I to Iron II in the hill country (when there is no doubt about the identity of the population), is sufficient justification to use the term. Like Finkelstein, he partially used the consensus on the Iron Age II reality as a basis for conclusions on a previous period.

At the same time, however, the minimalist school was established,[6] and attempted to undermine the relevancy of the term 'Israel' to Iron Age society, beginning with the Iron I, but continuing well into the Iron II (see, e.g., Whitelam 1996a; Thompson 2000).[7] Thompson's approach is repre-

---

5.   As we shall see later, however, this theoretical suggestion was based on lack of familiarity with the data from lowland villages.

6.   The school is also referred to as the nihilistic, deconstructionist, destructionist, and Copenhagen school, and is led by Lemche, Thompson, Whitelam, and Davies. Although they differ on some matters, their views are similar enough to label them as a school.

7.   And even later. Thompson (1999; 2000: 155-57), for example, had attempted to deny the ethnic identity of Second Temple period Jews.

sentative; he claims that his study leaves no room for ethnic unity within the highland regions (2000: 156; see also P.R. Davies 1992: 69). The very existence of ancient Israel has been questioned (despite denials, e.g., by Lemche 1998c: 63), thus dragging the debate to other grounds. This is not the place for a detailed discussion of this political school and its political-ideological views (as has been detailed by many, e.g., Dever 1998: 50; Pasto 1998; Rendsburg 1999),[8] but it should be emphasized that these scholars have usually offered no new evidence or even new insights into the discussion. None are archaeologists,[9] and generally their writings show inaptitude in both archaeological theory and even archaeological data (see Dever 1998: 46).[10] Moreover, as noted by many scholars, many demonstrate a lack of textual knowledge, and perhaps also of Hebrew/paleography (see, e.g., the debate over Tel Dan and Siloam inscriptions).[11] As we shall see below,

8. See also Rainey 1994 and various papers in Levine and Mazar 2001; a short discussion of one aspect will be conducted below.

9. This fact, by itself, does not of course say anything about their ability to master the literature and data. As we shall see below, however, this is not the case.

10. It is clear that they know the archaeological evidence only from secondary and tertiary sources, and even these are not always understood fully. Ahlstrom, for example, refers to four-room houses in 'Afula, Tel Keison, etc. (1993: 339; note that he is not the only one to make this mistake). This claim does not fit the archaeological finds, and seems to result from the fact that some of the houses contained four rooms and some had pillars. As we shall see below, however, the distinguishing feature of the four-room house lies not in the number of rooms, which is rarely four, but in their unique arrangement. When mentioning 'Afula, Ahlstrom refers to Dothan (1978: 35), who described four rooms, one of which was divided by monoliths, and a courtyard. It seems as if these features misled Ahlstrom into concluding that the house is of the four-room house category; however, most houses with four rooms are not necessarily 'four-room houses' (in Hebrew the name of the house better translates into 'four spaces', which is a much better term). In addition, many minimalists do not always discuss the finds in details to support their assertions, and this also hinders appropriate criticism of those assertions. Examples can be seen in Chapter 9. As for the lack of familiarity with archaeological theory, compare Lemche's (wishful) statement regarding the importance of writings in early states: 'It is rather immaterial whether we accept one scribe as the sole and lonely administrative officer in ancient Jerusalem and maintain that an ancient state did not need more scribes to run business. The important thing is whether this scribe fulfills the duties and obligation which are part of a society properly called a "state"' (1996: 108), with Flannery's comment at the beginning of the summary of his paper on archaic states: 'we cannot rely on textual information to identify the earliest archaic states, since most had no writing (e.g. Moche) or only limited writing (e.g. Uruk)' (1998: 54). While the issue of statehood relates only indirectly to the present discussion (see Chapter 13), this can serve as a random example of the minimalists' awareness of the relevant literature.

11. See, e.g., Rogerson and Davies's paper on the Siloam Tunnel (1996), and the harsh criticism it received on all grounds (e.g. Hendel 1996; Cahill 1997; see also the replies by J.A. Hacket, F.M. Cross, P.K. McCarter, A. Yardeni, A. Lemaire, E. Eshel, and A. Hurvitz, which were published together under the general title: 'Defusing

however, they have greatly influenced academic discourse, especially in their denial of Israelite ethnicity (e.g. Thompson 2000: 156).

Within this new intellectual environment, Finkelstein re-examined the archaeological evidence for Israel's existence in the highland during the Iron Age I and took a more critical stance. Referencing earlier papers by Dever (1995b, 1995c), whose title included the phrase, 'Will the Real Israel Please Stand Up?', he wrote a paper whose title included the question 'Can the Real Israel Stand Up?' There, he claimed that since the pottery forms continue Late Bronze Age antecedents and the characteristic architectural forms of the highlands are found in the lowlands and Trans-Jordan, these cannot be seen as Israelite (Finkelstein 1996a). He concluded that the only criterion that can be used to infer the presence of Israelites at the time is the absence of pig bones (1996a: 206). Yet, despite this he concluded that the Israelites cannot be recognized in the Iron Age I archaeological record, but only in that of the Iron II (1996a: 209).

A Summary of the Current State of Research into Israelite Ethnicity

Today, the prevalent attitude toward the study of ethnicity is one of skepticism (see also Edelman 2002; for more optimistic assessments, see Bloch-Smith 2003; R.D. Miller 2004). Although those dealing with the archaeology of ancient Israel still work to a large extent in the tradition of the Culture History school, ironically, it seems that the evaluation of ethnicity—the center of this approach—has changed. This is not so much a result of methodological changes, since, as noted above, the methodologies and approaches of the New Archaeology and subsequent schools did not have a direct impact on the archaeology of the Land of Israel (for sophisticated recent treatments, see Bloch-Smith 2003; Dever 2003; R.D. Miller 2004; Killebrew 2005). But it is more a result of what seems to be a failure of the conservative cultural history approach to account for the variability and distribution of the finds, which was strengthened by the indirect influence of the negative views of the New Archaeology to the study of ethnicity. Yet, as we shall see below, this current skeptical approach is unwarranted. An updated study of the old

Pseudo-Scholarship', in *BAR* 23.2 [1997], pp. 41-50, 68). It is especially worthwhile to quote Cahill, as it is the only archaeological comment and it pertains to the earlier discussion regarding the minimalists' inability to use the archaeological data. Cahill writes: 'Rogerson and Davies' arguments…bespeak their unfamiliarity with the archaeological record, the nature of the archaeological accumulation in Jerusalem, and the natural characteristics of the Gihon spring…' (1997: 184). (Note that the above relate only to the 'debate' over the Siloam Inscription; for the Tel Dan inscription, see, e.g., Rainey 1994). This is not the place for a detailed discussion of the minimalist school.

material in light of the advances in the study of ethnicity mentioned in Chapter 2 can certainly give some new insights into the study of Israelite ethnicity, and also lend support to some of the old ideas.

A Methodological Note: Studying Ethnicity on the Site Level

Most studies of Israelite ethnicity base their analysis on a site level, i.e., identifying the inhabitants of a particular site as members of one group. The heated debate over the ethnic identity of Megiddo VI is a particularly telling example.

Following the finding of a relatively large number of collared rim jars in Megiddo VI, Albright concluded that it was an Israelite settlement (1937). Engberg raised several objections to this characterization, and suggested that the site became Israelite only during the period represented by Stratum V (1940). Albright was seemingly convinced (1940), although the debate continued and Aharoni, for example, raised similar claims (1970; see above, and see also Fritz 1994: 232).

Notably, they all addressed the question of whether Megiddo VI was an Israelite settlement. The possibility that the site was inhabited by a population which belonged to more than one ethnic group was not usually discussed, although such a theory could have explained what these scholars regarded to be contrasting evidence (based on the archaeological findings, i.e., 'Israelite collared rim jars' together with 'Canaanite assemblages and/or traditions'). Such a theory was raised by Kempinski on the basis of architectural remains, but did not receive much discussion (1989: 78-90).

Megiddo is only one example, to be discussed in greater detail below (Chapter 19), of the difficulty in simply referring to a site as 'Israelite', 'Philistine', 'Canaanite', etc., as many ancient sites were inhabited by members of more then one ethnic group. (The proximity of several groups at a single site often tended even to increase boundary maintenance between them; e.g. Olsen and Kobylinski 1991: 7; Barth 1969: 9-10; Kamp and Yoffee 1980: 93; A. Cohen 1974b: xi). In such a case, treating the entire site as the unit of analysis will distort the evidence, as symbols of more then one ethnic group will be grouped together (cf. Bunimovitz 1990, who mentioned a similar problem in a different historical context). Consider, for example, a situation in which pottery decoration was highly sensitive to ethnic messages, and several distinct types of bowl decorations were used by various groups, while many other traits of material culture at the site were not ethnically meaningful. In such a case it is highly unlikely that the excavator would have correctly identified as meaningful these isolated traits which appear only in a few houses each. It is much more likely that it would go unnoticed, just like other classes of data that are expected to be found incidentally in one house and not in another. The finds would have most likely been published on the site level only,[12] therefore preventing the possibility of even later correctly identifying the pattern. Moreover, this tendency might even distort our ability to identify ethnic behavior. It should be stressed that several recent reports do not fall into the abovementioned trap, as they supply adequate data regarding where pottery was found, therefore enabling later studies to identify the pattern; however, recent excavations tend be on a very small scale, therefore preventing any pattern from being identified due to the size of the sample.

Moreover, since many recent reports do not give enough consideration to social questions including ethnicity, relevant information is often not presented. Bones are often reported in groups for each stratum, without a subdivision.[13] As a result, even if two groups living contemporaneously at the same site had different food habits easily identifiable in the zoo-archaeological finds, we would not be able to differentiate between them today. It is clear, therefore, that ethnicity must be examined at the household level.[14]

Ethnicity and Israelite Origins

While the question of Israelite origins in the sense of descent is, of course, interesting, it is, contrary to the prevalent view, irrelevant to the issue discussed here and to the understanding of the nature and formation of Israelite ethnicity. As the vast anthropological (and now also archaeological) literature clearly indicates, from the moment the Israelites began to see themselves as distinct they became so, and should be treated accordingly by modern scholarship (e.g. Barth 1969; Emberling 1997: 304). The question of their origin—whether their ancestors were slaves in Egypt, semi-nomads in Transjordan or in the central highlands, Canaanite peasants, or a combination of some or all of the above, is of lesser importance for the present discussion, as interesting and important as it may be.[15] This is true not only

12.   As in most relatively old publication reports, and even in many modern preliminary ones. Modern reports are expected to be different, but these are still rare.

13.   See, e.g., Hesse and Wapnish 1997: 251. Hesse and Wapnish criticized this tendency, claiming that within-site variation could be more important. At times, however, results are examined with attention for within-site variation; see Horwitz 1986–87.

14.   For some excellent examples, see Stein *et al.* 1996. The importance of 'within-site variation' for the study of status and function, for example, was recently exemplified by Loyet (2000); see also Hesse and Wapnish 1997: 251.

15.   The only exception is if one accepts the view that all Israelites came from Egypt —in which case their ethnogenesis was, of course, earlier, making the study of their ethnogenesis in the present context, including this monograph, obsolete. The issue of 'origins' will be discussed in detail in Chapter 18.

in regard to larger historical schemes (see Whitelam 1996b: 38-39), but also to more mundane aspects, such as the history of artifacts (in contrast to the frequent assumption; see Skjeggestand 1992: 172, 175, 177). In the words of A. Cohen, 'the history of a cultural trait will tell us very little about its social significance within the situation in which it is found at present' (1974a: 3).[16]

It seems that much of the debate has concentrated on issues whose relevancy to the problems of ethnic identification is very partial or even minimal. The present book will seek to demonstrate that by a close examination of the archaeological record we can trace Israel's ethnogenesis to the Iron Age I.

16. Consider, in light of this statement (see also Hodder 1982b: 204-207), the potential unimportance of the abovementioned continuities in pottery forms from the Late Bronze Age to Iron I. See more below.

Part II

AN ARCHAEOLOGICAL EXAMINATION
OF ISRAELITE ETHNICITY

4

Israelite Markers and Behavior

Since we know that not all aspects of material culture are necessarily seen as ethnically meaningful by any society at a given time, I will not attempt to equate and differentiate all aspects of life of the Israelites and their neighbors. After all, even if most of the traits are similar, the remaining differences could prove to be quite meaningful. I will, therefore, focus on several aspects, some already observed and discussed in the past and some new, which I believe were meaningful at the time, and hence of importance for the study of ethnicity. Notably, there is one theme that repeats itself in many traits, probably as a result of its importance for the group's ethos and ideology, and it will receive a separate and detailed treatment in its own right.

Aside from a few chapters where the nature of the evidence requires a focus on the Iron Age I in examining cultural traits, the discussion will for the most part concentrate initially on Israelite ethnic markers and behavior during the Iron II, as there seems to be a consensus among archaeologists that during this time there was an Israelite ethnos (e.g. Finkelstein 1988: 27-28; Dever 1992a, 1995a: 206-207; Joffe 2002; Alpert Nakhai 2003: 140; see also, from a different perspective, Grosbi 2002). The second step will entail a reaching back in time with these traits in an attempt to identify when they were formed as symbols and markers of identity, or when the behavior of which they were a result was formed. This is to say that we are not searching for the first appearance of these traits, but for the time at which they could have become ethnically meaningful. The Jewish *Hassidim*, for example, wear a *shtreimel*, a fur hat that we could, theoretically, trace in the historical and archaeological record; but its first appearance will not present us with the first *Hassid*, and actually not with a *Hassid* at all. The same is true for many cultural traits. What is important is their meaning in a given context, not their time and place of invention, or when they first appeared. What we are searching for is, therefore, the historical context in which the different traits could have become meaningful, and from which they were bestowed with additional and new meaning.

   Chapters 5–10 will discuss several traits or behaviors that can be related
to the Israelites, all of which, with the exception of circumcision, appear on
the archaeological record. Chapter 11 will discuss a more general mode of
behavior, characteristic of the Israelites, which seems to be behind much of
these specific traits; this chapter will also survey several additional patterns
that seem to have resulted from this behavior.

A Note on Pottery and Ethnicity

Several of the features to be discussed are associated with pottery, and an
introductory note is in order. Pottery is so often associated with ethnicity
that the entire debate over identification of ethnic groups in the archaeological record is, as we have seen, sometimes referred to as one of 'pots and
peoples' (e.g. Kramer 1977; Parr 1978; Kalentzidou 2000, to name only a
few; note that the term was originally negative). Its ubiquity in archaeological excavations naturally makes pottery the most studied of archaeological
finds, and allows it to be used as a statistical tool. Its use in daily life adds to
its attractiveness as an index of ethnicity. The study of pottery, however, can
be subdivided into many aspects, of which a few are form, decoration,
function, and repertoire. Although there can be a correlation between
messages conveyed by these aspects, some can be transmitted by only one;
an ethnic marker, for example, is often manifested in pottery decoration, but
not necessarily in form or function. Similarly, pottery decoration might be
insignificant ethnically while function (at times denoting behaviour) carries
meaning (see Chapter 2; see more below).
   The discussion of pottery as an ethnic index of the Israelites has recently
concentrated on continuity in forms, overshadowing other aspects which
were regarded to be of significance in the past (e.g. most recently, Bunimovitz and Yasur-Landau 1996). Yet despite this, form need not be such a
central issue, and ethnicity could very well be expressed through decoration
or repertoire (see Chapters 6–8). The fact that pottery forms show continuity
is not necessarily of significance. As can be seen in Chapter 18, the common
interpretation of such continuity is misleading, as ethnicity could be
expressed through other channels. Moreover, despite the importance of
pottery for archaeological analysis, it is quite possible that at times no aspect
of pottery will prove to be ethnically meaningful at all; ethnicity can just as
likely be transmitted through other channels.[1] In the present study, however,
such is not the case, and those ethnically meaningful aspects of pottery are to
be discussed below.

---

   1.   For a summary and analysis of a large number of studies, see Clark 2001: 19-22.

5

MEAT CONSUMPTION

It is already widely known and well established that the avoidance of pig meat is an important cultural, and even ethnic, trait in Iron Age Israel (see Hesse 1990; Finkelstein 1996a: 206; Stager 1995: 344). The significance of pork consumption was identified during the 1980s once the faunal remains of various Iron Age I sites and a pattern in the distribution of pork consumption and avoidance were observed (see Hesse 1986, 1990). The analysis clearly showed that sites that can be regarded as Israelite did not yield pig bones, while Philistine sites had them in abundance. The near consensus regarding the significance of this trait[1] allows us to use it as a good starting point.[2]

The Finds: Pork Consumption in the Iron Age I[3]

Pig remains were almost entirely absent at Iron Age I sites in the highlands and at others believed to be inhabited by Israelites/proto-Israelites, as demonstrated by the analysis of reported faunal remains (see Stager 1995: 344; Finkelstein 1996a: 206; 1997: 228-29). In Shiloh pig bones were reported to be only 0.1% of the faunal assemblage (Hellwing *et al.* 1993: 311, 316). They constitute 0.4% at 'Izbet Sartah (Hellwing and Adjeman 1986: 142, Table 8.2[4]), and were absent from the assemblages of Mt Ebal (Horwitz 1986–87: 185), Raddana, and 'Ai (Stager 1995: 344). They were also absent at Dan (Ilan 1999: 55), and in the Beersheba valley, where they were completely absent from Arad (Hellwing *et al.* 1993: 348, Table 15.50), and constituted only 0.23% at Beersheba (Hellwing 1984: 106), 0.1% at

---

1. For the reservations that do exist, see below.

2. Note that according to Clark (2001: 17), food preferences are ethnically sensitive.

3. Since the discussion of this trait in the research literature concentrates almost exclusively on the Iron Age I, this chapter will begin by discussing this period, and will refer to the situation during the Iron Age II only later, in order to reach a fuller and more comprehensive picture.

4. Note that this figure is composed of 5 bones (out of 1203), all of which had been found in mixed loci.

Tel Masos (Hellwing *et al.* 1993: 348, Table 15.50), where, according to Tchernov and Drori, only one pig bone was found the site (1983: 218). Pig bones were also absent from Beth-Shemesh (0.1%; Bunimovitz and Lederman 1997: 48-49).

The abovementioned data stand in sharp contrast to those of many coastal sites inhabited by Philistines. Pig constitutes some 23% of the faunal assemblage at Ashkelon (Stager 1995: 344), 18% of the assemblage at Miqne/ Ekron (Hesse 1986: 23), and 8% at Tel Batash (biblical Timnah). Stager claims that the Philistine preference for swine and pork, a popular food in the diet of the Mycenaeans and Greeks, was brought with them to Canaan in the twelfth century BCE (1995: 344).

Since the contemporaneous Philistine sites in the coastal plain exhibit a large amount of pig remains, the custom of restraining from pork consumption is seen by many as the hallmark of the Israelites (e.g. Hesse 1990; Stager 1995: 344). Even Finkelstein, who takes a rather minimalist stance regarding the issue in question, states: 'pig taboos, are emerging as the main, if not only avenue that can shed light on ethnic boundaries in the Iron I. Specifically, this may be the most valuable tool for the study of ethnicity of a given, single Iron I site' (1996a: 206; see also Finkelstein and Silberman 2001: 119-20).[5] Finkelstein is driven to this conclusion because the dichotomy cannot be attributed to ecology and/or setting. Pigs are found not only in the Iron Age I coastal sites, but in both highland and lowland, rural and urban sites during the Bronze Age.

Pork Consumption in the Bronze Age

Evidence that the absence of pig meat in the Iron I highland sites is not a result of ecological conditions can be seen by their discovery, sometimes in large quantities, in Bronze Age sites in the highlands and lowlands. During

---

5. As already mentioned, this assertion is puzzling (see also Finkelstein 1997: 230). If Finkelstein identifies the Israelites in the Iron I, his claim that other traits such as collared rim jars and four-room houses were mistakenly attributed to the Israelites (see Chapters 9 and 19) does not deprive this group of its identity. What one should look for is not the totality of traits, but rather those which are meaningful, and since Finkelstein agrees that pig taboos were significant, then according to his own rationale he should have declared that while he corrected some past mistakes (i.e. concerning the collared rim jars and the four-room houses) he has identified the Israelites archaeologically during the Iron I. (It should be stressed that I believe that some of the traits he rejects are also meaningful; see more below.) Another comment relates to the fact that if Finkelstein is correct about the importance of pig taboos, then, as mentioned above, examining the finds from a site as a whole might obliterate two distinct groups living in the same site. It is possible, for example, that Tel Batash's (Timnah; see above) population was composed of both pig consumers on the one hand, and people who avoided pork on the other, therefore resulting with the percentage that is somewhat low for a Philistine site.

the intermediate Bronze Age, pigs constituted some 15.2% of the faunal assemblage of 'Emeq Refaim in the highlands (Horwitz 1989: 46). During the Middle Bronze Age they formed 6.3% of the assemblage at coastal Tel Michal (Hellwing and Feig 1989: 246), 6.2–9.0% at Tel Aphek in the Sharon Plain (Hellwing 2000: 294, table 15.4), 8% at 'Emeq Refaim in the highlands (Horwitz 1989: 46), 3.1% and 0.1% at Lachish in the Shephelah (excavation seasons I–VI and XI, respectively; Hellwing *et al*. 1993: 346, Table 15.44), 31%–45% at Tell el-Hayyat in the northern valleys (Falconer 1995), and 3.5% at Middle Bronze II Shiloh in the highlands (Hellwing *et al*. 1993: 311, 313, 314; no such bones were found in the Middle Bronze III level there). Pigs were seemingly found in the Late Bronze Age strata of Tel Dan in the northern valleys (Ilan 1999: 55), and were abundant at Tel Miqne\Ekron in the Shephelah (8%; Hesse 1986: 23). They were rare, however, in contemporaneous levels at Shiloh (0.17%; Hellwing *et al*. 1993: 311), Tel Michal (0.3%; Hellwing and Feig 1989: 246) and Tel Lachish (0.2%; Hellwing *et al*. 1993: 347, Table 15.47).

In this light, the absence of pig bones cannot be explained by ecological explanations and must be meaningful, therefore leading Finkelstein to the above conclusion. The fact that some of the Bronze Age sites are villages precludes any claim that pigs are not suitable for a rural setting and thus are absent from the Iron I highland villages.

The Scope of Pig Avoidance

Hesse and Wapnish recently claimed that many groups in the ancient Near East did not consume pig meat and therefore its avoidance cannot be seen as proof of the existence of Israelites (1997). While there is no doubt that this is true, it should be stressed that since Israelites obviously did not consume pig meat, as is clear from the evidence from Iron Age II sites, places where such bones were found in relatively large quantities can be regarded as non-Israelite, a conclusion that stems even from their argument (see also Faust 2000a). The presence of pigs could, theoretically, be of some significance (indirectly at least) for the study of ethnicity, even according to them. This formulation seems, as we shall see below, to be sufficient in the present context, and helps us to identify some of the various groups that were in existence at the time.

The Importance of the Trait in the Iron Age II

Though most of the discussion concentrated, naturally, on Iron I, it is important to stress that pig avoidance is also typical of Israelite sites in Iron II (see Finkelstein 1997: 228-29). This can be seen at the 'Ophel (0%;

Horwitz and Tchernov 1989: 150), Beth-Shemesh (less than 1%; Hesse and Brown 2000), and Tel 'Ira (0.35% and 0%; Dayan 1999; Horwitz 1999; note that during the Byzantine period pigs constituted some 20% of the assemblage, therefore precluding ecology as a factor). Shiloh, with 2%, is an exception (Hellwing *et al.* 1993: 311, 316).[6] Israelites clearly did not consume pork during the Iron Age II.

The remarkable fact is, however, that according to Hesse and Wapnish, the Philistines consumed a large amount of pig meat only for a short period of time, during the Iron Age I (1997: 263); by the Iron Age II at Miqne/ Ekron, for example, only 10% of the faunal assemblage was composed of pig bones, a much lower figure than that of the Iron Age I (Hesse 1986: 23, see also Lev-Tov 1997). This, along with their interpretation that consumption of pig meat is associated with the non-elite (which is irrelevant for the present discussion), is used by them as an argument against the identification of communities which did not consume pork as Israelite, and to caution against a simplistic equating of pig avoidance with an ethnic group. While caution is indeed in order, I believe that the issues raised by them and particularly the short period of great popularity of pork at Philistine sites leads to a contrary conclusion. Not only does the discussed pattern of pig avoidance in this case relate to the Israelites, but it also gives us the *Sitz im Leben* of their taboo. As mentioned above, groups choose their markers and behaviors in relation, or in contrast, to other groups. It is reasonable to assume that pig avoidance was chosen in contrast to the Philistine custom of consuming large amounts of pork,[7] and since this is relevant only to the Iron Age I, then behavior that contrasts this custom could have only been formed then. It is probable that pig avoidance was practiced to at least some extent earlier (and by various groups),[8] but became canonical following contact with the Philistines. And whatever the reasons may be for the later changes in Philistine eating habits,[9] it need not affect the above conclusion regarding the date of the canonization of the Israelites' pig avoidance. In Stager's words, 'probably at that time during the biblical "Period of the Judges", the pork taboo developed among the Israelites as they forged their identity partly in contrast to their Philistine neighbors. Thus during the Iron Age 1 the pig becomes a distinctive cultural marker...between Philistine and Israelite' (1995: 344).

6.   Note that the late date of Iron II Shiloh makes it unclear as to who the inhabitants of the site were at the time.

7.   Similar to other patterns that were a result of the interaction with the Philistines. The issue will be developed in Chapter 15.

8.   Thus, in light of both the early date of this avoidance on the one hand (e.g. at Mt Ebal), and the long history of this pattern in the ancient Near East on the other (Hesse and Wapnish 1997).

9.   This issue will be touched upon in Chapters 10 and 14.

A Note on Canaanites and Pigs

Though to a lesser degree, the food habits discussed here are also relevant in regard to the third important 'ethnic group' which existed at the time—the 'Canaanites'.[10] The data presented above seem to indicate that Canaanites did not usually practice pig avoidance, as evidenced by the existence in relatively large numbers of pigs in most Bronze Age sites (though usually smaller than these of Philistine sites; in any event the figures in Canaanites sites vary greatly), and also from the finds in Iron Age Tel Qasile and Tel Qiri (Davis 1987: 249; 1985: 148; see also Faust 2000a: 16). Also of interest in this regard are the finds from Iron I Tell Hesban (see Hellwing *et al.* 1993: 348, Table 15.50).

Although the amount of pig remains at Bronze Age sites varies greatly, it was only rarely avoided (particularly during the Late Bronze Age). Since, as stated earlier, it is safe to say that the Israelites did avoid pork, this trait seems to be meaningful, to a certain degree, in relation to the reality in the entire region during the Iron Age. That is to say that when a site indicates pork consumption, but only to a small degree, it can be identified as both non-Israelite and non-Philistine—leaving us with what we loosely called 'Canaanites'. In summary, though no coherent picture can be established, Canaanite pork consumption is somewhere in between that of the Israelites, who avoided it, and the Philistines, who consumed it in large quantities during the Iron Age I.

Summary

The importance of the pig taboo for the Israelites is well known, and likely received much of its importance due to interaction with and in contrast to the pork-eating Philistines. The height of Philistine pork consumption according

10. Admittedly, referring to the Canaanites as an ethnic group is somewhat misleading and problematic (see also Lemche 1991, 1998a; Na'aman 1994a; Hess 1999; Rainey 1996, 2003, and references). It is clear that by using this name for the entire population of Canaan during the Middle and Late Bronze Age (as well as to some of the population during the Iron Age), we ignore the fact that there were probably several identity groups at the time, and apparently not all of the population was Canaanite, if at all. Still, our inability at the present stage of research to identify the ethnic complexity in the Bronze Age should not lead us to ignore groups which were obviously not Israelite or Philistine. Furthermore, it seems as if this is how the Israelites later treated these groups. In any event, we need to address this population, and the expression 'Canaanites', with all the reservations, is sufficient for our purpose, which here is to identify the Israelites. (Identifying identity subtleties within what we call the 'Canaanite society' is well beyond the scope of the present study.

to the archaeological record was during the Iron Age I, thus giving us a clear indication of the time and context in which pig avoidance could have become so ethnically important.

It is likely, as Hesse and Wapnish indicate (1997), that various groups did not consume pork in the Near East even prior to the arrival of the Philistines, some of which would perhaps later become Israelites. Yet this 'totemic' behavior did not become canonized until interaction with the Philistines.[11]

11.   The process in which mundane, daily activities become loaded with meaning will be discussed in Chapter 15.

6

DECORATED POTTERY

The absence of painted decoration on the local pottery of Israel's highlands during the Iron Age I has received some discussion (e.g. Dever 1995a: 205; A. Mazar 1985b: 69; 1992b: 290; Bloch-Smith and Alpert Nakhai 1999: 76; King and Stager 2001: 139), and is usually explained by the low standards of living in the highland at the time.[1] A phenomenon that seems to be widely known, but is hardly discussed, is the conspicuous absence of decoration on the pottery manufactured in the kingdoms of Israel and Judah during the Iron Age II (Barkay 1992: 354; Aharoni 1982: 177; Franken and Steiner 1990: 91; Dever 1997b: 465; Lapp 1992: 442). Such stands in sharp contrast to both the contemporary pottery of the nearby regions of Cyprus, Phoenicia, Philistia,[2] Midian, Moab, and Edom (e.g. Barkay 1992: 325, 326, 336-38, 354, 358; E. Mazar 1985; Ben-Shlomo, Shai and Maeir 2004), and the second-millennium BCE tradition (Franken and London 1995) (Fig. 6.1). Unlike the situation in the Iron Age I, it cannot be claimed that a low standard of living is responsible for the lack of decoration in the Iron Age II, as this was in some cases extremely high.[3] This absence must be meaningful, and can be explained only on ideological, cognitive, and symbolic levels.

1. This argument is very problematic, as even many 'simple' societies (much more simple than that of the Iron I) do decorate their pottery.

2. It is possible that during the seventh century BCE Philistia did not produce decorated pottery (e.g. at Ashkelon and Ekron). Since, however, it seems as if earlier decorated pottery ('Ashdod pottery', or the 'Late Philistine Decorated Pottery', of the tenth–ninth, and perhaps even eigth centuries; Ben-Shlomo, Shai, and Maeir 2004) was manufactured in this region, then it can be contrasted with Judah. The reality in the seventh century should be examined as part of a study of changes in the Philistine society of that time.

3. As already claimed, a functional explanation does not negate a social or cognitive one, and the dichotomy is artificial; see Hodder 1991: 53-54; Jones 1997: 110-27. For example, cosmological explanations could be given to various types of behavior that could also be explained along functional lines (see Hodder 1991: 53). The presence of a functional explanation for past behavior makes it very difficult for scholars to ascribe it to any other kind of explanation. The absence of a functional explanation, however, makes the need for another form of explanation more apparent.

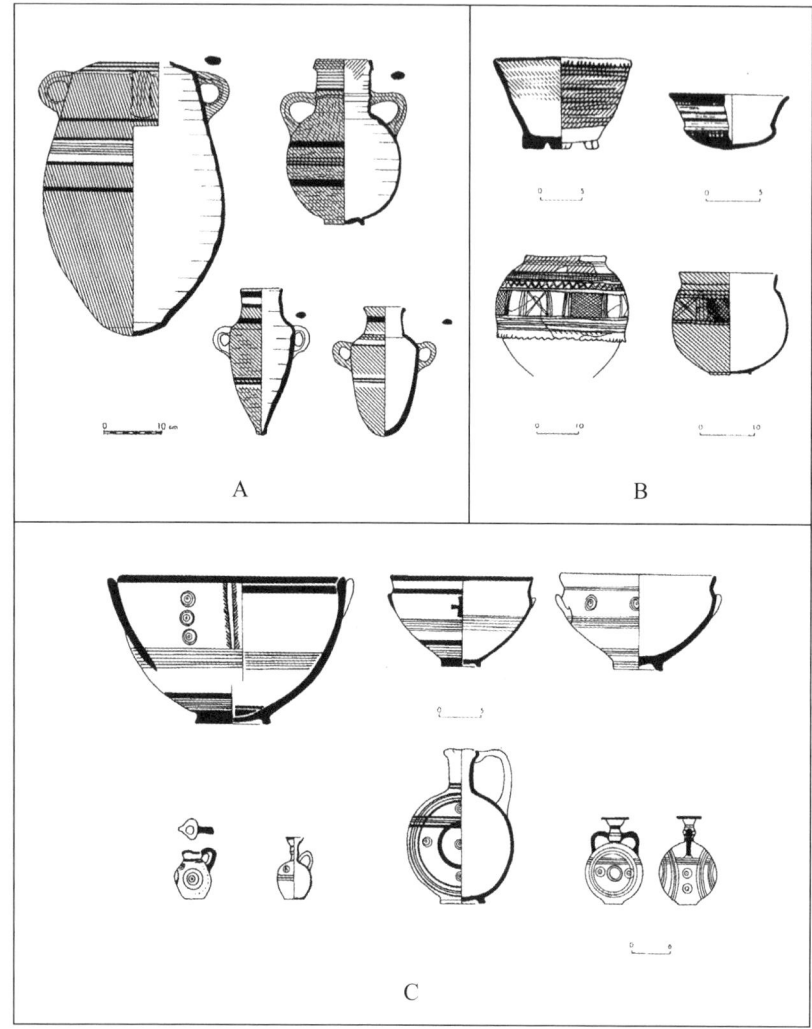

Figure 6.1. *Examples of Iron II Decorated Pottery from Selected Regions.*
A: Iron II 'Philistine' pottery (based on Ben Shlomo, Shai, and Maeir 2004:
Fig. 2); B: Edomite pottery (based on E. Mazar 1985); C: Cypro-Phoenician
pottery (based on Barkay 1992: Fig. 9.28).

Why are Pots Decorated?

Decoration is used to convey various messages (David *et al.* 1988; Hodder
1991; Braun 1991; see also Conkey and Hastrof 1990; Faust 2002). On
pottery it has usually been regarded as meaningful, even by the New

Archaeology school. As we have seen in Chapter 2, scholars of this school did not typically pay a great deal of attention to ethnicity, but many regarded stylistic characteristics, in the words of Jones, 'as residual formal variation, a frequently quoted example being decoration on pottery' (1997: 111). As such, stylistic variation was seen by many processual archaeologists as an indication of ethnic variation (e.g. Binford 1962; 1965; Sacket 1977). Variation in decoration, not seen as functional, was therefore regarded by these scholars as a means of studying ethnicity, if not the most effective of them (e.g. David *et al.* 1988). Not surprisingly, the importance of decoration received much more attention by later, post-processual studies. Shanks and Tilley claim that 'style may be actively used to mark out boundaries of different social groups when there is intense interaction between them' (1987: 87; see also Bunimovitz and Faust 2001).[4] It is thus clear that if variation in decoration is meaningful and conveys messages, its absence in an environment where pottery is decorated is at least of equal importance. In an environment in which pottery is often decorated, not decorating pottery at all is much more conspicuous than a different style of pottery (e.g. David *et al.* 1988).

Following Wiesner, messages conveyed by decoration/style can be divided into two coexisting types: emblemic and assertive (e.g. 1990; see also Chapter 2). The first involves messages concerning our identity as part of a group, for example, with which group we identify ourselves, or to which group we belong. The second involves messages on the individual, for example, 'I'm richer or better than everyone else'. While messages of difference and conformity within the group might appear contradictory, they coexist. We should be aware of the second type of message, but our interest here is in the first: emblemic style. Societies use various kinds of artifacts, such as clothes, utensils, house design, and pottery to convey messages concerning identity. As observed by many, pottery, and especially decoration on pottery, was used in many periods and in various cultures, whether directly or indirectly, as a major vehicle for such messages.

Several ethnographical studies have found that stylistic differences are the best indicators of ethnicity (see below). This can also be seen, for example, in Uruk, where Hamrin Polychrome (Jemdat Nasr) pottery comprised as much as 25% of the ceramic assemblage in one neighborhood, whereas it was absent in other excavated areas of domestic occupation (Emberling 1997: 323); it is likely that the Philistine pottery was also meaningful, a topic to be discussed in great detail below.

---

4.   These messages are not necessarily connected with ethnicity, and could relate to practically every aspect of life.

Internal and External Messages

While it is clear that decoration on pottery could convey messages regarding ethnicity, and that the absence of decoration should also be examined in this light, deciphering the actual message and establishing its relation and importance to ethnicity (if there is any) is much more complex.

Notably, messages carried by decoration are in many, if not most, cases directed to the group itself (e.g. Hodder 1991: 109-19; David *et al.* 1988; de Boer 1990: 103-104). In such cases pottery decoration (like other elements) could be used as a means, for example, to affirm the social order, send messages concerning relations between ages or sexes, and reaffirm society's values and ethics. As stated by David *et al.*, 'Designs on pottery, far from being "mere decoration", art for art's sake, or messages consciously emblemic of ethnicity, are low-technology channels through which society implants its values in the individual—every day at mealtimes' (1988: 379).

Hodder, for example, presents a detailed discussion of the importance of calabashes decoration in the Ilchamus (Njemps) society, which he interprets as relating to male–female relations inside the groups (1991: 109-19). It is interesting that, apart from simple beaded items, the Ilchamus are the only cultural group that produces decorated artifacts in the region (1991: 109, 118). Hodder explains this uniqueness by the fact that the calabashes are manufactured for tourists, and the income that they bring the women further changes gender relations in Ilchamus society (1991: 118-19). However, this practice also is of importance for the study of ethnicity, as a good example of the way in which messages that are primarily internal also carry external messages, if only as a by-product. After all, decorated items were manufactured only by the Ilchamus.

The situation described by Hodder is not unique. In summarizing their study on pottery decoration among several groups in Cameroon, David *et al.* write that the Mafa and Bulahay peoples engage in pottery decoration as a means for transmitting messages within the group. They continue:

> Mafa society is characterized by a high degree of order in social relations and by considerable social pressure on the individual by the group…we find that respect for roles is the cardinal virtue; the body is assimilated to the social body… In such societies…decoration and the persistence of designs through social time and space are to be explained by their mnemonic visual expression of underlying structures of belief and thought that most distinctively constitute the societies' unique identities. This being the case…, pottery decoration and, indeed, the structured system of ceramic types are likely to offer not only good but the best evidence of 'ethnicity' generally preserved in the archaeological record. (1988: 378)

In this respect, pottery decoration and even forms can be seen as resulting from an ethnically specific behavior or from a 'mind-set' (see Deetz 1996).

The resulting pattern is, therefore, unique to a certain ethnic group. Indeed, according to David *et al*., 'what the outsider reads as 'ethnicity' is the incidental by-product of the interplay of Mafa and Bulahay cognition and society' (1988: 378; see also Hodder 1982a: 54).

Deciphering the Message

The almost complete lack of decoration on pottery manufactured during the Iron Age II in the kingdoms of Israel and Judah, and earlier in the territories presumably inhabited by Israelites or Proto-Israelites, must therefore be very meaningful. Its mere absence is a powerful statement, which might be directed to within the group or in relation with the outside world. Deciphering it is a complex endeavor.

What were the messages transmitted by a lack of decoration? Internally, the lack of decoration could indicate an ideology of simplicity and egalitarianism, one which accords well with other Israelite traits to be presented below.[5] A similar phenomenon of lack of decoration, though in a completely different time and place, was observed by Noel Hume (1974: 108). He noticed that the earliest English delftware (in London) was usually elaborately decorated. After the civil war, potters began to produce undecorated plain vessels. Only after the restoration in 1660 did decorated pottery become popular again. Deetz (1996: 81) summarized this trend: 'Puritans attitudes toward decoration of everyday objects might have had an effect on the delftware industry in the London area in the form of reduction of the amount of decorated pottery before the Restoration'. He, furthermore, attributes the lack of decoration on various artifacts in Anglo-America to Puritan attitudes (1996: 81-82).

It seems as if part of the explanation for the discussed phenomenon in Iron Age Israel lies in the same direction. The 'inside' messages that were transmitted by 'Israelite' ceramics are very complex, and went through certain changes over time (e.g. Faust 2002). Whereas a complete discussion of the topic is far beyond the scope of the present book, it is important to stress that in this case too, there is an overlap between the various kinds of messages. While the Israelite ethos of simplicity and egalitarianism played, no doubt, a part in the internal structuring of Israelite society, it remained different from other groups (see below); and since the lack of decoration is, at least partially, a by-product of this behavior, it therefore is also of importance for identifying ethnicity, and not only for learning intra-group messages. The issue will be discussed at length later in Chapters 11, 15, 17,

---

5. Such accordance between various facets of culture is expected; see Deetz 1996; David *et al*. 1988: 378; Hodder 1991.

but it is important to stress that the ethos of egalitarianism could be, in itself, a result of ethnic conscience, which *was* created as part of ethnic negotiations with other groups (see below, Chapters 15, 17).

When did Simple and Undecorated Pottery Become Meaningful?

The absence of decoration on Iron Age II pottery in Israel and Judah is indeed remarkable when examining the reality in nearby societies; it must have been meaningful at the time. Directly or indirectly, it clearly reflected Israelite ethnicity in the period of the monarchy. Since, however, we are interested in the *formation* of Israelite ethnicity, it is important to ask: When did producing undecorated pottery become significant? As the Iron Age I pottery in the highland was not decorated, it is more than likely that the Iron II custom is part of the Iron I heritage, and that using undecorated pottery had already turned into a meaningful trait then.

The Philistine Connection

There are clear indications that Philistine pottery, both monochrome and bichrome, was regarded as a meaningful ethnic trait by the Philistines, Canaanites, and Egyptians, as seen in the distribution of both monochrome and bichrome vessels (Bunimovitz and Faust 2001; see also below, especially Chapter 19). The absence of monochrome (Myc. 3C1b) pottery in various Egyptio-Canaanite sites in the Shephelah (e.g. Gezer, Beth-Shemesh, Lachish) should be explained by its being ethnically meaningful, and not by a chronological gap (Bunimovitz and Faust 2001; see also Stager 1995). The same is true of the bichrome pottery (Fig. 19.3), which is abundant in one quarter of Tel Qasile (Stratum X), while it is practically absent from a nearby quarter (the complex mechanisms that influenced the distribution of the bichrome pottery will be discussed in detail in Chapter 19). Since the Philistine pottery seems to have carried ethnic messages for the Philistines, Canaanites, and Egyptians, it is extremely likely that it was seen as such by other groups, including the Israelites, or proto-Israelites, or whatever other groups that lived in the highlands at the time. The absence of bichrome Philistine pottery in the Iron Age I highland sites (see Chapter 7 and, especially, Chapter 19) indicates that this was indeed the case. Cleary, this was a significant trait.[6]

We have already seen the importance of the Philistines as the Israelites' 'other', and a similar picture will emerge from many of the following chapters. Since the Philistine pottery was highly decorated, it is possible that the

---

6. Due to the proximity between Philistia and the highlands, such pottery was expected to be found there (see the detailed discussions in Chapters 7 and 19).

Israelites chose not to decorate their pottery as part of their ethnic negotia-tion with the Philistines, and that this tradition continued into the Iron II. It would suffice for now to say that this element should be dated, in light of the above, to some point during the Iron I, when the Israelites closely interacted with the Philistines and with their 'meaningful' decorated pottery. The typical 'Philistine' decoration disappeared after the Iron I; and therefore, if it indeed was the cause for Israelite avoidance, this must have been a result of the Iron I interaction (see more below).

If this is correct, then simple and undecorated pottery was not *only* a result of internal messages (as suggested earlier), but could also be a direct reflection of ethnicity.[7] The two, however, are not necessarily contradictory, since it is likely that the abovementioned ethos 'responsible' for the internal messages is also a result of ethnic negotiations (see below).[8]

A reality in which a group defines itself in contrast to another in such a way is not without ethnographic parallels. In his study, de Boer refers to 'mainstream groups' and 'backwoods groups'. In his case, 'mainstream groups produce elaborate and complex art; by comparison, backwoods groups display a severely limited decorative repertoire'. De Boer, however, stresses that 'this is not to say that backwoods folk an uncreative stylists whose aesthetics are limited by an impoverished interfluvial environment' (1990: 103). A similar situation, in which a group defines itself by using 'simple' material culture, was also observed in Mexico (Levy 1998). It is likely that Israelite–Philistine relations should be viewed in this light.

An Alternative Explanation
While there is not doubt that interaction with the Philistines is an appropriate context for the emergence of a behavior that avoided decorated pottery, one should remember that the absence of decoration is typical of the highland pottery even before the highlanders interacted with the Philistines. Later (Chapter 15) we shall see that it is possible that some traits that resulted from functional reasons became meaningful because of other causes, and it is possible that this is the case here. Perhaps, for example, the highlanders did not decorate their pottery because of functional reasons, and due to the interaction with the Philistines this behavior became canonized. Still, the Late Bronze Age pottery was very much decorated, and it could also have been an appropriate context for the development of such a custom. We are not yet in a position to develop this alternative explanation; it will be further evaluated below (Chapters 16, 17).

7. See below, Chapter 19, for differences in boundary maintenance between groups.
8. The ethos and its development will be discussed in Chapter 11. The way in which all traits were 'chosen' is discussed throughout the book, but see especially Chapter 15.

Summary

It is possible that the hardship of life in the highlands during the Iron Age I resulted in simple and undecorated pottery. But hardship cannot explain the lack of decoration on Iron Age II pottery. Therefore, it seems clear that plain pottery must have been 'canonized' at some point as an Israelite marker (or resulted from an Israelite behavior, or a combination of the two; see more below). It is possible that this was a result of interaction with the Philistines during the Iron Age I, or the Egyptio-Canaanite culture of the closing years of the Late Bronze Age.

The above discussion seems to have explained 'when' (i.e. Iron Age I) and 'why' (i.e. as a combination of being different from the 'other's' decorated pottery and as a reflection of an egalitarian ethos) the tradition of leaving pottery undecorated developed and became a significant attribute of Israelite pottery. The process through which such behavior is canonized will be discussed mainly in Chapters 15 and 16.

7

IMPORTED POTTERY

An interesting feature of the finds at Iron Age II Israelite sites is the almost complete absence of imported pottery (e.g. Dever 1997b: 465; Lapp 1992: 442). Since the Iron Age II is a period of intensive trade in this region (e.g. Sherratt and Sherratt 1993: 363; Elat 1979; Niemeyer 1993; Finkelstein 1996b: 120-26, 144-53; Holladay 1995: 382-86, Katz 1979: 88; see also Singer-Avitz 1999), this absence is conspicuous. In the first part of this chapter I will demonstrate that such is the case, and in the latter part I will attempt to explain it.

Trade and Ceramics during the Iron Age II

There seems to be a consensus that the kingdoms of Israel and Judah participated in the flourishing trade in the Mediterranean and the Levant in the Iron Age II, in no small part due to their proximity to and likely close relations with the Phoenicians. Archaeological discoveries in many sites in Israel and Judah have uncovered various indications for trade, some of which will be discussed below.

The most obvious archaeological manifestation of this trade is ceramics. Imported pottery of various foreign origins is found in many sites throughout the Mediterranean and the Levant,[1] with types uncovered in Israel including the Bichrome, Black on Red, and Akhziv Wares (e.g. Barkay 1992: 325, 338; A. Mazar 1990a: 514; Katz 1979; see now also Schreiber 2003). The distribution of various types of ceramics, especially those associated with the Phoenicians trade, along with other kinds of artifacts, usually serve as an indication of this widespread commercial activity (e.g. Katz 1979; Sherrat and Sherratt 1993). However, as will be shown below, imported pottery is extremely rare at most sites in the kingdoms of Israel and

---

1. For the importance of ceramics as an indicator of trade, see various papers in Zerner, Zerner, and Winder 1993.

Judah (see Dever 1997b: 465),[2] while, strangely, other indications of trade are present. Several ancient sites, particularly Jerusalem and Beersheba, can be examined in exploring this question.

An analysis of the large selection of fish bones found in the City of David of Jerusalem and in the 'Ophel indicate an intensive trade with the Mediterranean and the southern coastal plain; the archaeological evidence suggests that the fish trade was well organized in the city, and several fish types were eaten there (Lernau and Lernau 1992: 136; see also Lernau and Lernau 1989; Borowoski 1998: 172-76). Similarly, the analysis of shells uncovered in the City of David—with shells originating in the Mediterranean Sea, the Red Sea, and the Nile—indicated intensive trade between those areas and the inhabitants of the city (Mienis 1992: 129). An examination of a small collection of wood remains found in the 'Ophel reveals that about 8% were imported from relatively long distances (Lipschitz 1989). Several inscriptions might indicate trade with South Arabia (Shiloh 1987a) and even Greece (Sass 1990). Auld and Steiner conclude:

> The new city quarters were mainly inhabited by rich merchants and artisans with their families and servants… Several inscriptions…may signify Arab traders living in the city… Luxury goods were imported into Judah. Excavations in and around the city have revealed the following imports: wood or wooden furniture from North Syria, ivory from Mesopotamia, decorative shells from the Red Sea, wine jars from Greece or Cyprus, fine pottery bowls from Assyria, scarabs from Egypt, and fish from the Mediterranean. Bronze ingots must have been imported from either Transjordan or Cyprus. (1996: 63-64; see also Franken and Steiner 1990: 123-25)[3]

Of special importance in this regard are the fish bones, as they indicate daily routine trade with Mediterranean—if not more distant—sites (see Borowski 1998: 174-76).

2.   It should be noted that in most cases the published data are not quantified or even quantifiable, noted exceptions including the works of Bikai (1978), Hunt (1985, 1987), and Singer-Avitz (1999), therefore making it impossible to carry out detailed statistical research on various types of pottery. Imported pottery, however, is recorded much more often than local pottery, even if the amount is insignificant. Since detailed statistics are not provided, I had to rely on the excavators' impressions and the data given by them on this basis (see Waldbaum 1994: 62 n. 4). Fortunately, however, the data concerning the absence of imported pottery, which stand at the base of the present chapter, are in most cases unambiguous.

3.   It should be noted that some of the evidence which they quote is quite meager. The Assyrian bowls mentioned above refer probably to those which were found a few kilometers from Jerusalem at the Palace of Ramat-Rachel and were probably manufactured locally (e.g. Bloom 1988: 169-78). The wine jars from Greece or Cyprus refer, to the best of my knowledge, only to one fragment of such a find (Auld and Steiner 1996: 70).

Pottery, however, indicates otherwise. In summarizing his analysis of Jerusalem's pottery forms based on hundreds of vessels found in Caves II and III, Eshel writes: 'As far as the international commercial relationships are reflected, there are some clear contacts with the old Israelite centres of Samaria and Hazor and a lower rate with Megiddo, Beth-Shean and Far'ah. Our analysis also reflects a low rate of contacts with the homeland area of Phoenicia...as well as with its cultural satellite regions of South Jordan... and the Philistine areas' (1995: 62). Franken and Steiner also mention the absence of luxury objects and imported pieces in these caves, a situation reflected also in Cave I and the entire extramural quarter analyzed by them (1990: 5, 125, 128). Kathleen Kenyon was similarly impressed regarding the poverty of finds of her excavations (1974: 132, 135). A similar picture is revealed by the finds in other excavations in Jerusalem, for example, the excavations in the City of David and the Jewish quarter (De Groot, Geva, and Yezerski 2003: 15); the very few imported pieces found in other excavations, as at Ketef Hinom (Barkay 1984: 104), does not alter this reality.[4]

Another instructive site is Beersheba, one of the most extensively excavated in Israel. Lipschitz and Biger have analyzed wood remains from this site, and counted 22 fragments of cedars which were found in the Iron Age strata (1991: 171). Furthermore, in their work on other Iron Age Negev sites, they found that cedar constitutes 10% of the wood assemblage in the seventh century BCE, and thus can be seen as a marker of widespread commerce and wealth, given that its regime imported such expensive goods for monumental constructions (1991: 172). Singer-Avitz concluded that Beersheba had an important part in South Arabian trade, maintaining that it was a 'gateway community' along this route,[5] as based on various finds at the site and in spite of the petrographical analysis, to be discussed below (1999).

Yet, concerning pottery, the conclusions are radically different. In summarizing her analysis of several unique kraters which were found in Beersheba II, G. Bachi writes:

4. I am aware of the fact that in some cases I refer to vessel form (e.g. in quoting Eshel's study of Jerusalem's pottery), while in other cases I discuss the origin of the pottery (e.g. Beersheba, below). This is a result of the lack of data. In most cases I refer only to stylistic differences, as these are more readily available, and perhaps also more significant (as they were easily observable in antiquity). As Eshel has indicated for Jerusalem, and as Singer-Avitz found regarding Lachish and Beit-Mirsim (1999: 12), the pottery was usually composed of shapes which were different from vessels found at contemporary coastal sites. However, as the data from Beersheba indicate, even when there are more similarities in forms, which is a rare phenomenon, the vessels were manufactured locally and were not imported. See also Stark *et al.* 2000.

5. Cf. Gunneweg, Perlman, and Meshel 1985 on Kuntillet 'Ajrud.

> Few vessels of the black on red ware have been found in Beersheba, and no
> examples have as yet been unearthed of the ware with the red slip, so typical
> of the coastal sites. It seems reasonable to assume that the local potter had
> little opportunity to see these types of pottery in the Beersheba market place.
> In all likelihood, he saw vessels in the coastal area and returned home to
> reproduce them in local clay… (1973: 42)

Bachi's impression is substantiated by a scientific analysis of the pottery.
Although Singer-Avitz, after an examination of some 900 vessels—roughly
half of Beersheba's pottery—concluded that a relatively large percentage of
the pottery consists of coastal and Edomite forms (1999), the petrographical
analysis by Y. Goren revealed that the vessels, with the exception of three
Egyptian wares, were not imported, but were manufactured in various parts
of Judah (Singer-Avitz 1999).[6]

The same is seen at many sites in kingdoms of Israel and Judah (Fig.
7.1[7]). The mound of Beth-Shemesh was excavated almost entirely by three
expeditions, and very few imported vessels were reported by Mackenzie and
Grant (see Katz 1979: 40); the recent excavations yielded only a handful of
Iron II imported sherds among the thousands of sherds from this period that
were uncovered (Shlomo Bunimovitz and Zvi Lederman, personal communication). At Gibeon (Pritchard 1962), Moza (Alon de-Groot and Zvi
Greenhut, personal communication), Hebron (Alon de-Groot, personal
communication), Kh. Marjameh (A. Mazar 1995: 114), Kh. Jemein (Dar
1986: 38), Beit Aryeh (Riklin 1997: 12), Kh. Jarish (David Amit, personal
communication), Kh. Malta (Covello-Paran, personal communication), Kh.
Rosh Zayit (the village; Gal 2001; Gal and Alexandre 2000), and Tel Mador
(Gal 1992a: 36-43) the same is apparent; in many of these sites not a single
imported sherd was discovered.

This stands in sharp contrast to sites in the coastal plain and the northern
valleys, where imported pottery is much more abundant (Fig. 7.1). Almost
every excavated coastal site yielded such pottery, from Rukeish (Culican
1973; Hestrin and Dayagi-Mendels 1983) in the south, through Ashkelon
(Stager 1993: 107; Master 2003), Mesad Hashavyahu (Naveh 1962), Azor

---

6.   Note that there seem to be a few imported vessels in the other half of Beersheba's
pottery (that was not studied by Singer-Avitz; Singer-Avitz, personal communication).

7.   Figure 7.1 is a schematic map showing the prevalence of imported pottery at
various sites. I have attempted to refer to all excavated sites, in instances in which the
published material enabled a conclusion regarding the presence or absence of imported
pottery. Notably, quantifying the finds is problematic, and in most cases I followed the
excavators' impression. In order to overcome some of the shortcomings of distribution
maps, this map attempts to show both the presence and absence of imported pottery. Note
that not all the sites are contemporaneous. Furthermore, the percentage of imported
pottery could change over time at a site, or could vary among different contemporaneous
parts of sites. For the problematic nature of such maps, see in the text. Indeed, due to the
many subtleties involved, the map should not be used without a close reading of the text.

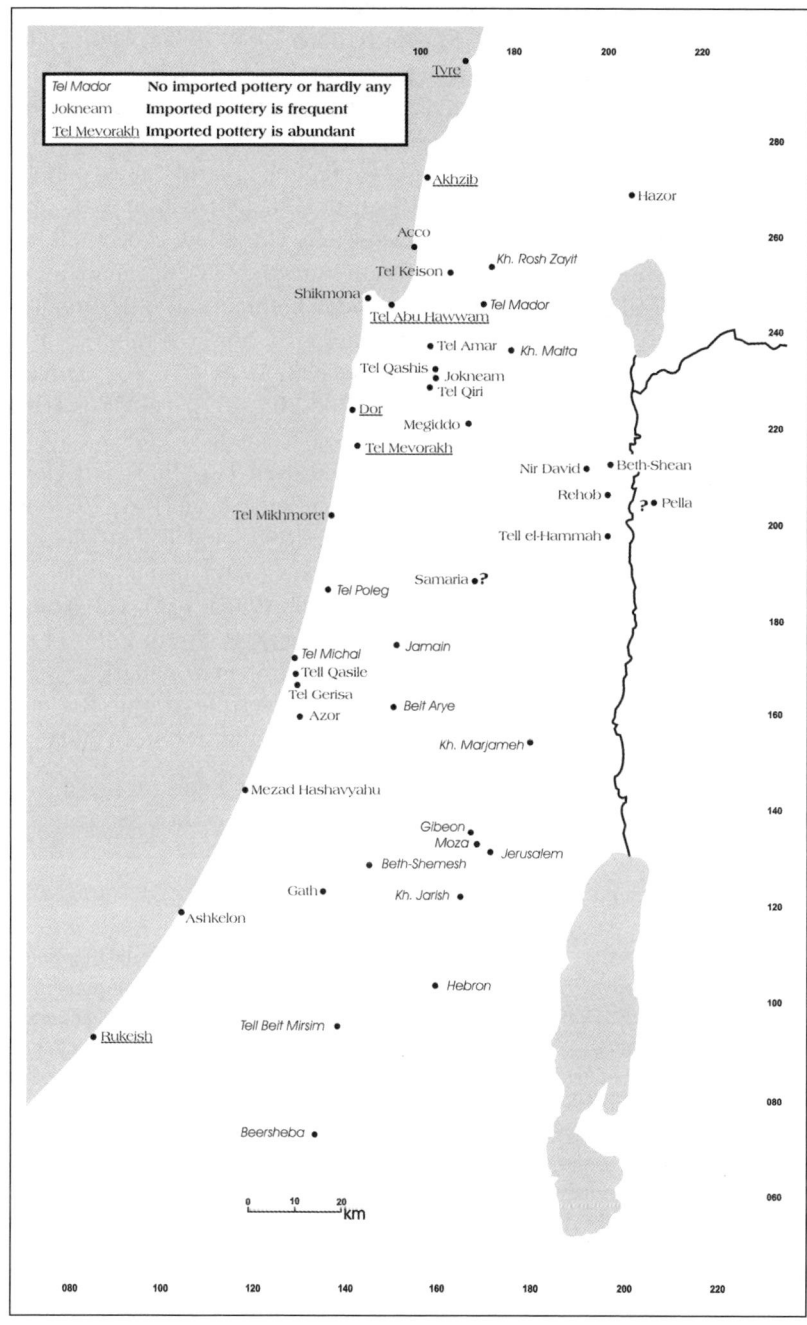

Figure 7.1. *Distribution Map of Imported Pottery
in the Land of Israel in the Iron Age II.*

(Dothan 1993c: 129), Tel Mikhmoret (Porath, Paley, and Stieglitz 1993: 1044), Tel Mevorakh (Stern 1978), Dor (Gilboa 1989, 1998a; Stern 1996), Shiqmona (Elgavish 1994), Tell Abu Hawwam (Ballensi, Herrera, and Artzy 1993: 9-10; Katz 1979: 49), Tel Keisan (Humbert 1993), Acco (Dothan 1993a: 21; Katz 1979: 46), and Akhziv (Prausnitz 1993; E. Mazar 1993), to Tyre (Bikai 1978) in the north. Though, as mentioned earlier, most publications do not give quantitative data or statistics, such pottery appears to be generally not rare in the sites mentioned above (for a few exceptions, see below). In addition, imported pottery is not infrequent in some more inland sites, such as Tell es-Safi (A. Maeir, personal communication).[8] Imported pottery seems to be frequent also in most sites in the northern valleys,[9] urban and rural alike; examples are Tell Amar (see Katz 1979: 48), Yoqneam and Tel Qiri (Hunt 1985: 143-53; 1987: 181, 202-203, 209), Tel Qasis (Hunt 1985: 143-53), Megiddo (see Katz 1979: 44-45; Kempinski 1989: 88-89, 94-95, 98, 220), Hazor (Yadin *et al.* 1958, 1960; Ben-Tor 1989), Nir David (Edelstein undated; Levy and Edelstein 1972) Beth-Shean (Katz 1979: 40; James 1966: 123, 129), Tel Rehov (A. Mazar 1999), and Tell el-Hammah (Cahill and Tarler 1993).[10] Imported pottery was found also in some sites across the Jordan, such as Tell es-Say'idia (Tubb 1998a: 115), Tell Abu al-Kharaz (Fischer 1994: 130; 1996: 103) and Pella (R.H. Smith 1993: 1178), though apparently in much smaller quantities. Imported pottery in small quantities was also found in the Negev 'fortresses' and the Aravah (R. Cohen 1986: 374, 377; Meshel 1974: 26; Bienkowski and Van der Steen 2001: 28; Levy, Adams, and Najjar 2004).

8. A few sites in the coastal plain also exhibit a pattern similar to that of Israel and Judah. According to Singer-Avitz, imported wares are notably absent from the Iron II level at Tel Poleg (1989a: 377). Though imported pottery was reported in the Iron II level at Tel Michal (Singer-Avitz 1989b), the excavators refer to the 'dearth of imports in Tel Michal' (Singer-Avitz 1989b: 87). Since, however, they compare it to the contemporaneous site of Tel Mevorakh, which yielded large quantities, it is possible that this statement should, with the lack of detailed statistics, be treated somewhat cautiously, particularly in light of the finds from the later Iron II level. The picture at the contemporaneous and adjacent Tel Qasile is also not clear (but see A. Mazar 1985a: 81-82). In any event, the pattern in this region requires a more detailed study, both spatial and diachronical.

9. Although the northern valleys were, to a large extent, within the boundaries of the kingdom of Israel, it was also populated by a non-Israelite population (see, most recently, Finkelstein 1999: 44, 48; see also the detailed discussion in Faust 2000a).

10. Schreiber had recently analyzed the Cypro-Phoenician pottery found in the Levant. She claimed that Black on Red juglets, for example, were found in 'relatively small quantities throughout the region west of the Jordan' (2003: 28). Still, when she discusses the finds, one can clearly see that hardly any pottery was found in the highlands (see the discussion on pp. 85-169, 186-212).

Trade and the Distribution of Imported Pottery in the Kingdoms of Israel and Judah

The most reasonable explanation for the difference between the finds in the highlands and the coastal area and the valleys is economical, that is, trade related. Imported pottery is more likely to be found near trade routes, the important of which crossed the coastal plains and the valleys. While there is no doubt that economy would explain part of the pattern ('fall off analysis'; see Renfrew and Bahn 1996: 354; see also Hodder 1979b), it cannot be the sole explanation. After all, since Beersheba and Jerusalem exhibit much evidence indicating that they participated in large scale trade, the fact that such is not manifested in ceramics does not indicate that a lack of commerce should be an explanation for the absence (or rarity) of imported pottery in Judah and Israel. This is especially true for Beersheba, as it was located on what many scholars consider to be one of the most important trading routes, to Arabia (see Singer-Avitz 1999; Finkelstein 1996b: 114, 120-23; Holladay 1995: 383-86).

Moreover, there is no geographic logic in attributing the distribution only to trade. A fine example of the phenomenon can be seen at the Iron II village of Kh. Malta in the lower Galilee. In spite of its proximity to the area where abundant quantities of imported pottery were found, only a single Iron II imported sherd was discovered at the site (Covello-Paran, personal communication), therein suggesting an anomaly in the distribution map if examined only from an economic perspective. This is particularly true in light of large quantities found in the eastern site of Tell el-Hammah, for example. The Iron II village at Kh. Rosh Zayit, located immediately above the coastal plain, also contained only a minor amount of Cypro-Phoenician pottery and Akhziv wares, in sharp contrast to an earlier fort excavated at the site and to most coastal plain sites (Gal 1992b: 13; 2001: 137; see also Gal and Alexandre 2000).[11] No imported sherds were reported also from the soundings at Tel Mador (Gal 1992a: 36-43). The rural nature of at least two of these three sites cannot explain this phenomenon, as rural sites in the northern valleys much farther away from the Phoenician coast yielded larger quantities of imported pottery (e.g. Tel Qasis, Tel Qiri, and Nir David).

---

11. Note that the statistics published in this final report are somewhat problematic, as most vessels were recorded only when indicative pieces such as rims were found, while any body sherds of *imported* pottery were counted. The data should therefore be examined in relation to the pottery that had actually been reported in each stage. In any event, the finds indicate a huge decline in the percentages of imported pottery when one compares the fort and village.

The Inadequacies of the Economic Explanation

In light of the data presented above, several factors emerge showing that the economic explanation is insufficient, and indicating that the distribution is non-random (cf. Hodder 1979b: 7, 14):

1.   The contradictory evidence in Beersheba and Jerusalem, where various non-ceramic evidence indicates intensive trade, while imported pottery is almost absent.

2.   The lack of imported pottery in settlements which are adjacent to sites or areas where such pottery is abundant, a pattern particularly conspicuous in the Galilee (Beth-Shemesh might also serve as an example). Such sharp fall-offs cannot be explained simply as being a result of 'distance-decay falloff' or similar explanations (Hodder 1979a: 452). It is important to reemphasize that even if imported pottery is expected to be present in somewhat higher percentages in the valleys due to the trade routes which crossed this region, its almost complete absence in the Lower Galilee, so close to the Phoenician coast, must still be of significance.

3.   The fact that the absence of imported pottery correlates with the distribution of other traits (discussed in other chapters of this work) indicates that this trait too is important. This seems to represent a reality where, to use Hodder's words, 'regional plateaus of similar frequencies of some traits in assemblages may be found with sharp falloffs at the edges…that cannot be explained by normal distance-decay falloff or by environmental, functional adaptation' (1979a: 452; see also 1979b: 12).

As distance and location cannot account for this distribution, it becomes increasingly clear that the solution to the discrepancy between the various types of evidence belongs, at least partially, to the socio-cultural realm (see also Hodder 1979b).

Value and Attitudes toward Imported Pottery

Orser outlines three kinds of value. Exchange value is the market value of a commodity; esteem value is an additional, sometimes emotional, value which could be added to an artifact; use value involves the utilitarian usage of the artifact (1996). Any artifact or commodity can therefore be seen in a number of ways, whether it be understood as having high exchange or esteem value and thus is desired, or it be used as an everyday object. Yet there is even another dimension of value to objects; as Wood claimed, all vessels should be 'culturally accepted' (1990: 88). Artifacts that are not might be avoided.

While it is quite obvious that the pottery vessels discussed here were manufactured either as containers or as commodities in their own right (e.g. W.P. Anderson 1990: 50; Sherratt and Sherratt 1993: 370; see also 1991: 362-63), I would suggest that the inhabitants of Jerusalem and Beersheba, as well as many other sites in the kingdoms of Israel and Judah, viewed these pottery vessels differently than their contemporaries in Tyre, Tell Abu Hawwam, Megiddo, and Tell el-Hammah. While Jerusalem and Beersheba have indeed participated in interregional and even international trade, this is not manifested in pottery, since imported pottery was not culturally accepted in these sites. This is not surprising considering that stylistic similarities and differences are not merely a result of interaction, which has been well established following studies by scholars such as Plog (1980) and Hodder (1979a, 1982a).

An example from the New World can demonstrate that negative attitudes toward foreign pottery is both not unique to Israel's Iron Age and can have a great impact on distribution. Brian Thomas examined two late eighteenth-century sites in North Carolina—Salem, a Moravian site, and Richmond, the central city in the region. According to Thomas, 'the results of the ceramic analysis illuminate clear differences in the distribution of ceramic categories from Richmond and Salem… The identifiable ceramics recovered at Richmond consisted of 58 percent British styles (49 imported British ceramics and 9 percent British copies). Salem, by comparison, had only 21 percent British styles' (B.W. Thomas 1994: 25).[12] Given Richmond's significance as a local center, its high percentage of British styles need not seem unordinary; yet why was Salem, a center of pottery importation that even produced imitations of imports if the need arose (p. 26), so radically different? Thomas suggests that the population of Salem wanted outsiders, on the one hand, to view them as part of the region. Their importation and imitation of 'foreign' artifacts, and even symbols, sent this message to all other communities. Yet, on the other, they truly did not want to be part of the 'outside world', and their desire to maintain clear boundaries with it led to an avoidance of daily use of this ceramic (p. 26). Furthermore the disparity between Salem and Richmond is far smaller than that between sites in Iron Age Israel with imports, usually in the lowlands, and those without. From this perspective the Iron Age pattern is indeed very significant.

Another feature of Israel and Judah of the Iron Age that accords well with the absence or rarity of imported pottery is the lack of decoration on pottery, as discussed in the previous chapter, suggesting a general propensity to avoid other kinds of pottery. Another line of supportive evidence has to do with perceptions of trade in Israelite society; though the Bible is a problematic

12. One should note that the dig was on a small scale, and the results should therefore be regarded with caution.

source, its language is most revealing. The most common term in Biblical
Hebrew for a trader is a 'Canaanite', as in Hos. 12.8: 'A Canaanite, in whose
hands are false balances, he loves to oppress' (see also Isa. 23.8; Job 40.30;
Prov. 31.24; Zeph. 1.11; see also Elat 1977: 203; 1979: 529; Liver 1962:
204; EB 1968: 161, 163; King and Stager 2001: 189-90). Canaanites were
obviously not viewed positively in the Iron Age society that produced much
of the Bible.[13] The term indicates that the trading profession too was viewed
negatively, whether most traders were Canaanites or not. As stated by King
and Stager, 'at least in their propaganda the Israelites were condescending
toward traders and commerce' (2001: 190).

Possible Explanations for Negative Attitudes
towards Imported Pottery

But why did such an attitude develop? Though a full analysis of ancient
Israel's worldviews is beyond the scope of the present work, I would like to
mention several possible explanations.[14] A simple one is that ethnocentrism,
or a general negative view of foreigners and thus foreign goods, lies behind
this phenomenon (see Jary and Jary 1995: 207). Another involves the
manipulation of the local elite; following Appadurai, the negative attitude
could be a result of 'the antagonism between "foreign" goods and local
sumptuary...structures' which 'is probably the fundamental reason for the
often remarked tendency of primitive societies to restrict trade...' (1986:
33). Though Appadurai discusses a different situation, the manipulation of
the elite could be behind an ideology that leaves trade under their monopoly.
Smith-Kipp and Schortman also state, 'Chiefdoms or early states would
have been tempted to protect if not monopolize trade whenever possible...'
(1989: 379; see also Sherratt and Sherratt 1991: 359). Indeed, the abovementioned pattern, in which pottery was not imported while cedars and other
goods were, indicates that during the period discussed here international
trade in Israel and Judah was a state-controlled endeavor.[15] However, even if
the manipulation of the elite is involved in the development of the discussed

13. E.g. Eissfeldt 1966; Friedman 1987; Clines 1993; see also Wenham 1979: 8-13.

14. Theoretically, avoidance could also be seen as a form of resistance (see Joyce,
Bustamante, and Levine 2001). Since, however, a certain degree of avoidance of
imported pottery seems to have been present among all segments of Israelite society,
(internal) resistance cannot be the explanation for the phenomenon.

15. There are various lines of argument that make this interpretation plausible (see
also Sherratt and Sherratt 1991: 359), especially in light of pottery's low price in the
ancient world (e.g. Vickers and Gill 1994; Sherratt and Sherratt 1991: 363; Faust 1999b:
181; *contra* Hunt 1987: 202, 209; Quesada 1998: 88-89), which makes it a suitable
vehicle for such messages.

ethos, it could not have been its initiator. Such an attitude would have had to be in alignment with existing ideas or approaches.

It is also possible that the absence of imported pottery, as well as of decoration on pottery, resulted from an ideology of egalitarianism and simplicity. This ideology has been previously proposed regarding ancient Israel (e.g. Gottwald 1979; Gordis 1971; see also Chapter 11), and though it received much criticism (see Lemche 1985), it corresponds with other elements in the society's material culture. Its possible roots will be discussed in detail below (Chapter 11).

Another explanation also relates to a worldview. The anthropologist Mary Douglas, who studied some aspects of Israelite society on the basis of texts, presented in 'Deciphering a Meal' a diagram in which the human and non-human (or animal) realms are divided into those under the covenant, namely Israelites and their livestock, and all others (1972: 75, Fig. 6).[16] If this classification is correct, then it is inevitable that such a system operated in all realms of life, including others not considered by Douglas. For example, if we divide the non-human category into animals and artifacts, we would arrive at a classification where wares also would be divided into those 'under the covenant' and all others, and thus one that could account for the observed phenomenon, as it necessitated a dichotomy between local and 'other' artifacts. Moreover, there is some indication in the Bible[17] that artifacts were indeed classified in a similar manner, as in Num. 31.20-24, where purification is required of booty taken from non-Israelites (see also Licht 1995: 115; and also Ben-Shamai 1958: 392).[18] Pottery, however, cannot be

16. It should be stressed that in this work (here and in Chapter 9) I am referring only to the ideas Douglas developed during the 1960s and '70s. Though she still uses some of concepts (e.g. the concept of the covenant; see, e.g., Douglas 2000), she changed her ideas significantly over the years (see the discussion in Fardon 1999: 185-205). This is not the place to discuss her new ideas and interpretations, but I should like to stress that in my opinion the ideas expressed in her earlier works, like the one discussed here, seem to fit the archaeological record (and hence, I believe, the period's reality).

17. While the following passages do supply a good illustration of this reality (and their relevance is examined), and it is likely that they are related, the archaeological-anthropological discussion is not dependent upon them. Therefore, any claim regarding their date can, at most, question the validity of the illustrative material, but not of the main argument.

18. Many scholars interpret the purification of booty to stem from previous contact with corpses (e.g. Licht 1995: 115) and not necessarily from non-Israelite ownership (for a short survey of biblical attitudes toward the impurity of non-Israelites, see Klawans 1995: 288-93). The dating of this paragraph from Numbers is problematic. It is attributed to the P-source, probably even to a late phase (see Gray 1906: 419; Licht 1995: 116). The dating of the P-source, however, is not clear. The traditional view dates it to the Persian period (Wenham 1979: 9-11; see also Eissfeldt 1966: 207-208, who mentions both fifth and sixth centuries BCE as probable); recently, however, there seems to be a growing

purified, and perhaps this is the cause for its avoidance (Lev. 6.21; 11.33; 15.12).[19] The reasons for the development of such a classification system (see Douglas 1975: 306-14) were probably, as Douglas claimed, part of the Israelites' extensive boundary maintenance (1972: 77), the roots of which should be sought in Israel's ethnogenesis.

The exact scenario is not yet clear, and any of the explanations presented above could be plausible; all of them, however, should first be considered as part of a more general study of the worldviews and ideology of Israelite society (in this regard, see also Pedersen 1926: 307), much of which was established during its ethnogenesis. Before assessing any of them, it should be reiterated that only a socio-cultural explanation can fully account for the discussed pattern; it must come at least as a supplement to any economic-related explanation. A negative view toward imported pottery, shared by many members of the society discussed here, correlates well with the prevalent view of trade in ancient Israel, where 'domestic commerce per se' is seen as unimportant (A. Mazar 1990a: 510; see also Elat 1979: 546). It did not, of course, prevent massive trade likely organized by the state, as was already observed by some scholars (e.g. Elat 1979: 545-46; see also Elat 1977: 203; McNutt 1999: 158); such comes in contrast to the situation in most contemporary centers, where 'merchants enterprise, rather than state-controlled exchange, became the dominant mode of trading activity' (Sherratt and Sherratt 1993: 362; see also 1991: 376). Nor did it likely prevent some use of imported objects by members of the elite and by others (e.g. some of the inhabitants of Samaria, and perhaps other urban centers; this is not surprising in this specific historical setting; see, e.g., the various texts relating to the relationship between the kingdom of Israel and Tyre).

consensus to date it to the Exilic period, while maintaining that some or much of the data are earlier in origin (see Clines 1993: 580). While this seems sufficient to allow us to relate to these data in this context, I would like to mention that a growing number of scholars tend to date the P-source to the eighth and seventh centuries (therefore returning to the initial dating of de Wette); see, e.g., Wenham 1979: 13; Schwartz 1999: 32-33; Friedman 1987; Weinfeld 1979; Hurvitz 1974; Milgrom 1991: 12-13, and many others. Leviticus, quoted in the next sentence, is also attributed to the same source. In addition, as we are dealing here with some of Douglas's ideas, it is interesting that Douglas (1975: 315-16) also claimed that an earlier date for the P-source suits her thesis.

19.   For the dating of the texts, see the preceding footnote. By the end of the Second Temple period similar ideas and interpretations, among other things, led to the avoidance of imported pottery in general, and to intensive use of stone vessels by those concerned with purity, namely, priests (see Ariel and Strikovsky 1990). The problem with the idea presented here, which attributes similar ideas to the Iron Age, lies in the fact that the later sources do not indicate historical precedent; if they could, they would have probably preferred to cling to any such sign of continuity.

The Case for an Elite Monopoly

It may be that we must search for a combination of some or all of the above explanations in arriving at what is responsible for the discussed pattern. Since the elite monopoly is the only explanation that pertains only to the Iron Age II, we shall begin by evaluating it. We recall that it suggests that the ideology against contact with foreigners and foreign goods was a result of a manipulation of the elite, which aimed at maintaining a monopoly over trade, and that due to other factors rooted earlier in the Iron I it suited the broader Israelite worldviews. There are several interrelated clues that indicate that this indeed was the case.

First, it should be stressed that pottery of all sorts, including imported vessels, was probably relatively cheap (e.g. Vickers and Gill 1994; see also Sherratt and Sherratt 1991: 363; Faust 1999b: 181, and references) and thus abundant in all segments of society. An ideology that prevented its purchase and use was the most effective means to abate trade amongst the entire population. This in turn emphasizes the relevance of pottery in propogating such an ideology.

Second, it is clear that the classification has been modified over time; the basic categories probably referred only to 'foreign' vs. 'local'. During later phases of the Iron II, at least, there was also differentiation between pottery and, for example, cedars, whose treatment was different. This indicates a much more complex system of classification, which must be a result of a later development, possibly instigated by the elite.

Third, according to Sherratt and Sherratt, 'it was to the advantages of the elite that the added value should be monopolised through the concentration of manufacturing in centres rather than at farms and villages. Such a system always contained the potential for conflict, and was dependent both on religious sanction and—in the last resort—on force' (1991: 359). Though Sherratt and Sherratt discuss a different period (and concentrate on the manufacturing process, rather than on consumption), some archaeological evidence might support a similar scenario in the beginning of the Iron II in ancient Israel. As we shall see in Chapter 12, although villages and hamlets were abundant during the Iron Age I (e.g. Finkelstein 1988) and from the ninth century BCE onward (Faust 2000b), during the eleventh century BCE and the early decades of the tenth, they gradually disappeared from the archaeological record (Faust 1999a, 2003a[20]). Such a phenomenon can be partially explained as a result of forced settlement. Yet it also accords well with the above explanation by Sherratt and Sherratt, and thus could be a

20. The few villages that existed at the time were seemingly vassal villages owned by the crown; see Faust 2000a.

result of the elite's attempt to concentrate the manufacturing process in its hands. The ideology of an avoidance of foreign goods correlates with the 'religious sanctions' mentioned by Sherratt and Sherratt, though in this case the focus was placed on consumption, and was used as an easier substitute to the use of force to keep this monopoly. The reappearance of 'independent' villages in the later stages of the Iron Age could be a result of the weakening power of the Israelite state(s), while the ideology discussed had already been well established and absorbed.

The above scenario, however, leaves unanswered the question of how such an ideology and worldview developed, and what made it acceptable. A closer look at the reality during the Iron Age I might be worthwhile in attempting to answer this question, as it is there that the other three explanations offered above appear to have been rooted.

Imported Pottery during the Iron Age I

An ideology against the use of imported pottery could have indeed suited the Iron Age II emergent elite's needs quite well, but its effectiveness must have been dependent on an agreement with other pre-existing facets of Israelites' worldviews. A similar absence of imported pottery can be identified in the Iron I (e.g. Dever 1995a: 204; 1997c: 79; Meyers 1988: 144; Bloch-Smith and Alpert Nakhai 1999: 76). Theoretically, this should not come as a surprise, as this period is characterized by the cessation of the international trade; the lack of imported pottery in the highland is, therefore, expected. Still, as we shall see later (mainly Chapter 19), the fact that Philistine pottery is practically absent from the highland is most conspicuous, as this pottery 'traveled' to other far more remote parts of the country. Philistine pottery is indeed the only import that one would expect to find in an Iron I context, and its absence begs an explanation. Again, it could be argued that the poor conditions in the highlands at the time and the self-sufficiency of the Iron I highland communities (see Meyers 1988: 144) explains the lack of imported and decorated pottery, but it is also possible that this behavior was canonized as part of ethnic negotiation and boundary maintenance.[21]

---

21. It should be reiterated that the dichotomy between functional and other lines of explanations (e.g. stylistic and structural, or, in more general terms, social and cognitive explanations; see Hodder 1991: 53-54; Jones 1997: 110-27), is somewhat misleading. In the present case, however, we can see how a behavior whose roots could have been functional becomes symbolic. It is not necessary, therefore, to 'wait' until the formation of the monarchy, when the functional explanation is completely irrelevant, in order to raise the ideological explanation. It is likely that this behavior was canonized earlier; otherwise it would not have been easily accepted by the population (if the elite had indeed adopted it for purposes suggested above).

The Philistines and Onward

Several converging processes can be examined in understanding why negative views toward imported pottery developed. First, as we have already claimed, the lack of Philistine pottery in Iron I highland settlements is significant. This pottery was ethnically meaningful at the time (see the extended discussion in Chapter 19), and perhaps the negative attitudes toward Philistine pottery of the Iron I were later transferred to all types of imported pottery. A connection with the negative views toward decorated pottery discussed above is also likely, as much of the period's imported (Philistine and later Phoenician) pottery at nearby sites was decorated.

Second, the lack of imports seems to reflect an ethos of simplicity, which rejected the display of such 'luxuries' or 'exotic' items. This ethos is reflected in many facets of Israelite society, and in most cases, like the present one, its roots can be traced to the Iron I. As we shall see in Chapter 11, however, the ethos itself seems to have resulted from ethnic negotiations.

Third, a reality in which one groups defines itself in contrast to other groups is also a good environment for the development of ethnocentrism and a classification system that dichotomized 'us' and 'them', as observed by Douglas (above).

Finally, as already suggested, it is possible that following the formation of the monarchy (statehood) the negative attitude toward imports was manipulated by the new elite, helping it to keep a monopoly over trade.

These factors seem to be in accord with the settlement pattern of the time, which involved the massive relocation of populations, the egalitarian worldview, and the strict boundary maintenance that began during the Iron Age I (below). Such an account views the interaction with the Philistines as a prime mover to which other explanations and processes should be attached; Philistine pottery was regarded as foreign, and it transferred its negative association to all foreign pottery.

An Alternative Explanation

There remains, however, the option that the negative views toward imported pottery were born even earlier in the Iron I. The Late Bronze Age is a unique period of international relations and influences (e.g. various papers in Cline and Harris Cline 1998); imported pottery is found everywhere during this period, including in the most sparsely settled regions of the country (e.g. Gonen 1992b: 236-40), and inevitably played a role in various types of ceremonial/symbolic behaviors (e.g. van Wijngaarden 1999). In fact, there is probably no other period when imported pottery played such a crucial rule in so many symbolic aspects of life. This 'international' environment seems even a better background for the development of such a cultural avoidance from the Philistine pottery, and the thirteenth-century context is therefore the most appropriate for the initial development of such attitudes. The possible reasons for such a development will be discussed below, but it should be stressed that even if this 'early' scenario will turn out to be the most persuasive, it does not negate all of the above. It simply indicates that the initial meaningfulness of the trait should be looked for at the transitional period from the Late Bronze to the Iron Age. The Philistine pottery, in this case, was therefore viewed negatively from the beginning, and helped to channel the interaction between the highlanders and the Philistines along negative lines.[22]

The exact process by which such an ethos was chosen will be discussed later. Here it is sufficient to say that while it is possible that it was expanded in the tenth century BCE, it clearly existed earlier, during the Iron Age I.

Summary

Although the lack of imported pottery in the Iron I might theoretically be explained on the basis of the poor conditions and the closed economy of the highland settlements, the conspicuous lack of imported pottery in most Iron II sites in Judah and large parts of Israel cannot. This avoidance must therefore be seen as ethnically meaningful. It is likely that interaction with the Philistines resulted in negative attitudes toward their highly symbolic pottery, or that the 'international' character of the Late Bronze Age caused such an avoidance as a response to the use of various imports at the time. The ideology of simplicity and egalitarianism that evolved during the Iron Age I as part of the same process further contributed to an environment in which all imported pottery came to be viewed negatively. During the early Iron Age II this attitude may have been adopted and encouraged by the state as a means of protecting a monopoly over trade. But it was in the Iron I that the avoidance of imported pottery became a factor in the structuring of the highland society, one more indicator that Israel's ethnogenesis occurred then.

---

22. Those relations were on negative terms due to other factors, of course (see Chapters 12, 14), but following this scenario it is clear why the qualities of Philistine pottery helped make the Philistines' 'otherness' more prominent from the beginning.

8

POTTERY FORMS AND REPERTOIRE

Iron Age I Pottery Forms

Much research has concentrated on the Iron I ceramic repertoire, particularly following the publication of Finkelstein's (1988) seminal work. Finkelstein observed that Israelite Iron Age pottery was very much different from that of the Late Bronze Age (1988: 274). His assessment received much criticism, and as a result of the heated debate, it has become commonly accepted that there is much continuation in pottery forms onward from the Late Bronze Age (e.g. Dever 1992b: 551-52; 1993b; 1994: 216; 1995a; A. Mazar 1985b; 1992b: 292; see also Finkelstein 1992: 65).[1]

Indeed, this continuity is easily observable in various forms. The typical Iron I cooking pots, for example, have received a great deal of discussion. Dever stated:

> I note simply (a) that all the Iron I [cooking pot] forms are clearly descendent from the Late Bronze II forms. They exhibit only the normal, indeed predictable, evolution from short, sharp, triangular thirteenth-century BCE to a more rounded characteristic rim. (b) These 'new' cooking pot rims are typical of *all* sites by the early-mid twelfth-century BCE sites—'Canaanite', 'Philistine', and my 'Proto-Israelite' sites… (c) These rims *may* serve as *fossiles directeurs* for 'early Israelite' sites, since they are especially common in the hill-country villages. But the fact that they do not have a distribution exclusive to these areas cautions us against relying on these cooking pots *alone* as 'ethnic markers' (as also with the so-called 'Israelite collar-rim' jars)… (1995a: 205; see also Dever 1993b: 27*-30*; A. Mazar 1985b: 69)

The same continuity has been shown in most pottery forms (Dever 1995a: 205-206); the collared rim jar appears to be the only exception (despite Wengrow 1996). Pottery forms, however, are not necessarily the important issue, for as was mentioned earlier, continuity is irrelevant for group self-

---

1. This fact is used, erroneously, by many to disprove the connection of Iron Age pottery with the Israelites (see Skjeggestand 1992; see also Chapter 3, and the extended discussion in Chapter 18).

identification; members of a group can adopt a symbol as their marker for many reasons, but the origins and development of this symbol may tell us nothing on its importance at any given time (e.g. A. Cohen 1974a: 3; Hodder 1982b: 204-207; see also the discussion in Chapter 18).

The Iron Age I Repertoire

Although Finkelstein stresses that much of the difference between the Iron I and the Late Bronze Age pottery involves repertoire, this issue has received much less discussion (see Dever 1995a: 206). Despite the continuity in forms found in the highlands, not all Late Bronze Age forms are continued, and the Iron I repertoire is much more limited (e.g. Albright 1961: 119; Bunimovitz and Yasur-Landau 1996: 96; Esse 1991: 109; 1992: 94-95; Dever 1995a: 204-205; Finkelstein 1992: 65; A. Mazar 1985b: 68; 1992b: 290-92; Bloch-Smith and Alpert Nachai 1999: 76; King and Stager 2001: 139) (see Fig. 8.1). Mazar, for example, refers to a 'limited number of components' in the period's repertoire, 'which reflects a poor material culture that limits itself only to the most basic forms'; noticeably, certain forms and decorated pottery are absent from the highland repertoire (1992b: 290-92).

This fact was observed a long time ago. As early as 1934, following the excavations at Bethel, Albright wrote: 'if collared store-jars and cooking pots were eliminated, the number of the remaining types would be insignificant' (1934: 12). Indeed, Albright's initial observation is confirmed by various ensuing excavations at highland sites. In Giloh, for example, about 80% of the assemblage is composed of cooking pots and storage jars, the majority of which are collared rim jars (A. Mazar 1981: 31). A large percentage of cooking pots and storage jars, though on a smaller scale, was found at other highland sites such as Mt Ebal (Zertal 1986–87) and 'Izbet Sartah (Finkelstein 1986: 46); these sites also yielded a relatively large number of bowls (including kraters), jugs, and juglets (see Esse 1992: 93). In the contemporaneous lowland sites in the northern valleys, however, a much larger repertoire is found. At Megiddo (VI), for example, to cooking pots, storage jars, bowls, kraters, jugs, and juglets were added pyxides, lamps, pilgrim flasks, and chalices, which form 18.3% of the repertoire. None of these latter vessels were found at Giloh and Ebal (Stratum II), and only chalices and pilgrim flasks were discovered at 'Izbet Sartah (Strata III–II), forming only 4.2% of the assemblage there (Esse 1992: 93). The repertoire of other sites in the northern valleys is similar to that of Megiddo, as at Tel Yoqneam and Tel Qiri (Hunt 1987: 208-209; Esse 1991: 109; 1992: 94-95), and Tel Keisan (Esse 1992: 95).

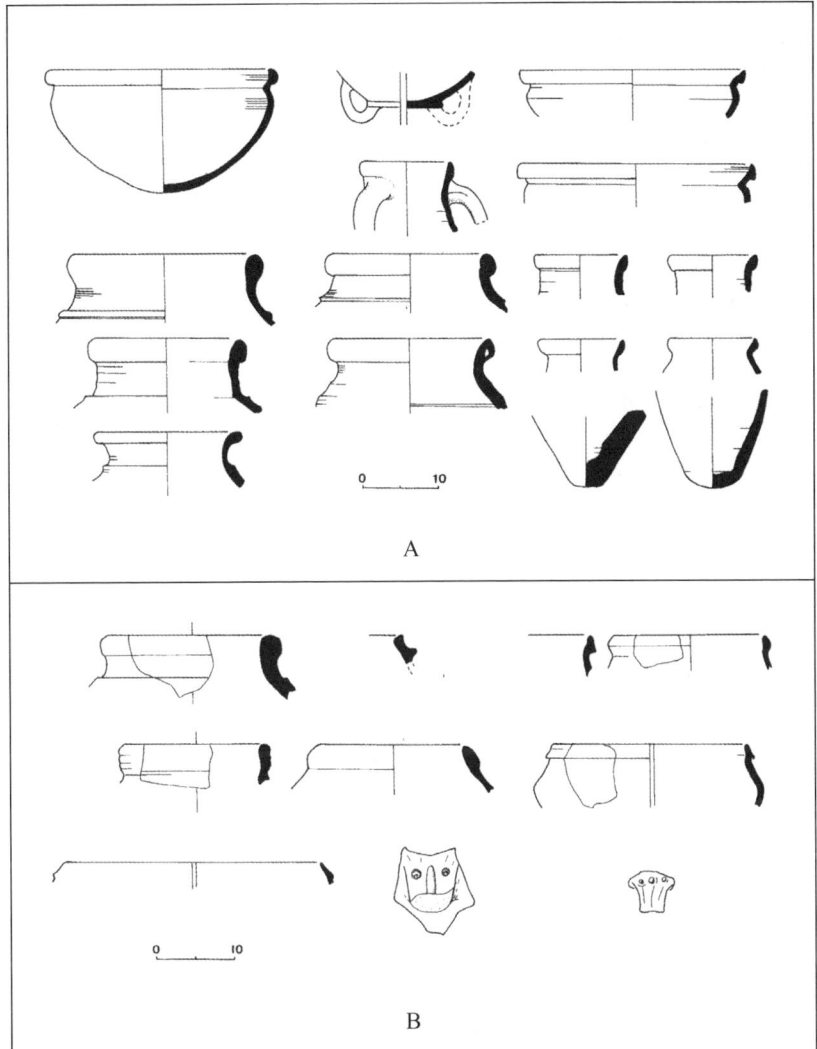

Figure 8.1. *Typical Pottery of Iron I Highland Villages.*
A: An assemblage from Giloh (after Finkelstein 1988: Fig. 9); B: Typical
vessels from southern Samaria (after Finkelstein 1988: Fig. 53).

The differences cannot be attributed to the nature of the settlements, as a
variety of forms is found in both urban and rural sites in the lowland (Esse
1991: 109; 1992: 94-95; see also Hunt 1985, 1987). The dichotomy is
between highland and lowland.[2] 'Izbet Sartah is located on the edge of the

___

2.   This claim is in contrast to London 1989; see also Esse 1992: 95 n. 70.

hill country and is thus, both literally and figuratively, on middle ground between the two.[3] Furthermore, the difference cannot be attributed mechanistically to 'ecology', as this simply cannot explain ceramic repertoire; in both the Iron Age II and the Late Bronze Age populations in the same ecological surroundings used a much wider repertoire.

The limited repertoire, as with other aspects of the period's pottery, is usually explained by the hardship in these highland villages, and of differences in social and economic background (e.g. Finkelstein 1988: 274; London 1989; see also Dever 1995a: 205; A. Mazar 1985b: 68). Mazar, for example, claims that the 'minimal range of pottery types, together with the nature of the sites themselves, is the best indication of the economic situation and the nature of the society involved. We are dealing here with a poor, self-sufficient and introverted society' (1985b: 68). We have already seen that such differentiations are problematic; as Dever observed, 'even if... these ceramic distinctions denote largely the functional differences between urban and rural "life styles", they nevertheless have socio-economic implications and thus may constitute ethnic markers' (1995a: 205).

Therefore, it is possible that in contrast to pottery forms, the limited repertoire of highland pottery is ethnically meaningful. According to Bunimovitz and Yasur-Landau, the 'poorness and isolation reflected in the Israelite assemblage' needs an explanation, and they raised the possibility that these 'hint at *ideological* behavior' (1996: 96). A similar view was presented by Albright in his famous introductory book *The Archaeology of Palestine*; there he was struck by the 'extraordinary simplicity and lack of cultural sophistication' in the archaeology of 'the period of the Judges' (1961: 119).[4] Later he raised the possibility that this resulted from the fact that 'the Israelites were in a quasi-democratic, patriarchal stage of clan life', i.e., he gave an ideological reason (the issue will be discussed in detail in Chapter 11). This trait, too, therefore, indicates that 'simplicity' can be regarded as a component of the Israelite worldview (see also Dever 1995a: 205).

Yet none of the above has attempted to *explain* the exact connection between this ideology and the finds. Perhaps these words from Goody will be helpful: 'since differences in cuisine parallel class distinction, egalitarian and revolutionary regimes tend, at least in the initial phases, to do away with the division between the *haute* and the *basse cuisine*' (1982: 147). While we are not in a position to know much about the Iron Age I cuisine, it is quite clear that the limited ceramic repertoire restricted the ability to prepare

---

3. For the ethnic and political background of the population of 'Izbet Sartah, see Faust 1999a, 2003a; see also Chapter 12.

4. Note that he contrasts it with the Late Bronze Age finds in the highlands, eliminating any ecological explanations for this difference.

elaborate meals, or at least the likelihood of complex ceremonies of consumption. It must reflect a simple cuisine, or in other words, a society which did not exhibit such distinctions.

It seems, therefore, that this limited repertoire sent internal messages concerning the society's values, namely, simplicity and egalitarianism. As a by-product of this ethnically specific behavior, it probably also reflected ethnic boundaries. The work of David *et al.* on the Mafa and Bulahay societies is recalled: 'what the outsider reads as "ethnicity" is the incidental by-product of the interplay of Mafa and Bulahay cognition and society... Far from being the product of intentional messaging directed at outsiders, Mafa and Bulahay engage in pottery decoration...in order to transmit collective messages to themselves' (David *et al.*, 1988: 378). This also appears to be the case here.[5]

The Iron Age II Repertoire

The discussion in this chapter has concentrated from the outset on the Iron Age I, yet from the tenth century BCE onward drastic changes in pottery production and forms took place. These changes included greater standardization in pottery production (e.g. Aharoni 1982: 239; Dever 1997a: 229; Barkay 1992: 325; see also Zimhoni 1997: 179), and a much richer repertoire (Aharoni 1982: 239; Zimhoni 1997: 170; see also Kelso 1968: 50). It is quite clear that such changes are not just economic, but are also related to other aspects of society, including worldviews and ideology (Dever 1997a: 229-30; see also Franken and London 1995: 221). They indicate new social complexities and internal messages (Faust 2002; in prep.), while not negating the continued existence of an egalitarian ideology and ethos.

The issue will receive a detailed discussion in Chapter 11, but a few words are in order at this stage: a clear differentiation should be made between an egalitarian ethos and egalitarian practice. The latter never truly exists, and only relatively so in regard to some simple societies. An egalitarian ethos, however, can exist even in extremely hierarchical societies. Let us recall the United States, where until a few decades ago African-Americans and other minorities were not fully equals, but a democratic ethos was still quite present (see Remini 1988: 96-102, 110; see also Macionis 1999: 69). The same can be said on Classical Athens, where the majority of the population did not enjoy the benefits of the Athenian democracy (e.g. Morris 1997: 95-97; see more below). Such was the case in Israel during the Iron Age II—egalitarianism in ethos, not in actuality (e.g. Faust 2004a).

---

5. This issue was discussed in Chapter 6. I will return to the subject later in Chapter 19.

Summary

In 1985, Amihai Mazar wrote the following: 'Thus, the ethnicity is reflected in the assemblage as a whole, while the individual pottery types appearing at the Israelite sites should not be defined as limited to any particular group' (1985b: 68). While not supplying the reasons behind this pattern (and perhaps withdrawing from this statement later), it seems as if Mazar grasped the importance of the assemblage (though not as a totality of traits), and, with some reservations, the observation is essentially correct.

The limited repertoire of the Iron I pottery reflects an ethos of simplicity and egalitarianism. The claim that it is solely the result of economic hardship is not sufficient; rather, the two explanations should be viewed as complementary rather then contradictory. This is to say that while it is likely that the limited repertoire originated from the reality of life in the highlands at the time, it became meaningful over time (cf. Hodder 1991: 54), an explanation that is particularly convincing if we consider various processes that took place in the highlands then. The course by which this 'functional' behavior became important will be discussed in detail in Chapters 11 and 15.

9

THE FOUR-ROOM HOUSE

Another trait that is of importance for the study of Israelite ethnicity is the four-room house, the dominant feature of Iron Age domestic architecture (Fig. 9.1 [next page]). The term 'four-room house' is used here, as elsewhere, as a generic term, as the majority of such houses do not have four rooms, but three. A house of this type has a few long spaces and a broad space in the back, all of which can be subdivided. The number of rooms thus varies, even greatly. Typically, the entrance is in the center of the short wall, and in many cases pillars are used to divide the long spaces, although this is neither a necessity nor a characteristic feature, as many four-room houses do not have pillars and houses of other types also use them.

While most Iron Age II houses follow the above paradigm rather closely, the Iron Age I examples are less orthodox. Determining which house should be regarded as part of this family is usually easy, though in Iron I contexts some flexibility is needed. The minimum requirements seem to be the presence of long rooms and a broad room at the back.[1]

Summary of Previous Research

Hundreds of four-room houses are known today from Iron Age sites throughout the Land of Israel, from the Galilee to the Negev highlands, and from the Transjordanian plateau to western Samaria, and even to the coastal plain (e.g. Shiqmona and Tel Qasile). The houses first appear during the Iron Age I, usually in an irregular form, but quickly crystallized into the well-known three- and four-room house forms that characterize them until they disappear in the late Iron Age (sixth century BCE).

The four-room house and its subtypes—the three- and five-room houses —have been discussed intensively in archaeological literature. Various studies examined its origins, whether they be in the nomad's tent (e.g. Kempinski 1978; Fritz 1977), or in the Late Bronze Age architecture of the Shephelah

---

1. The presence or absence of other characteristics should also be considered, but this cannot be done in a mathematical way.

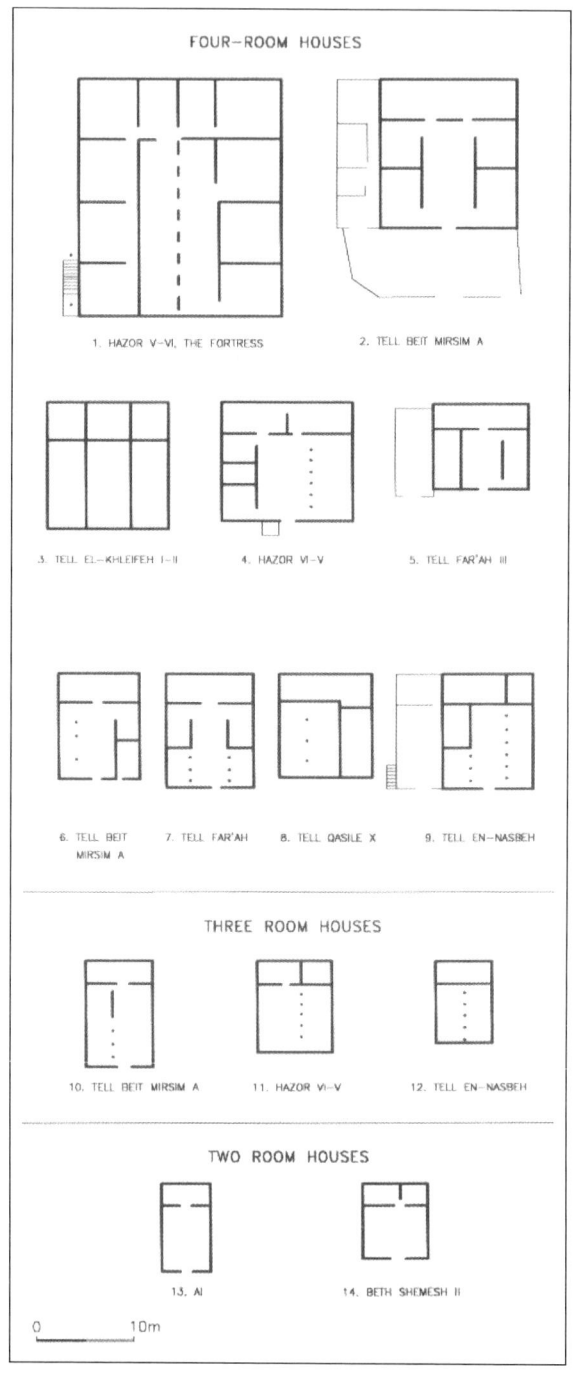

Figure 9.1. *Four-Room Houses* (based on Barkay 1992: Fig. 9.24).

(e.g. A. Mazar 1985b; Givon 1999; but see Finkelstein 1996a: 201). Other studies, based on ethnoarchaeological data, have attempted to decipher the use of space within the house (e.g. Stager 1985c; Holladay 1992, 1997).

Many studies have attempted to identify the people who used this house type. Shiloh, whose seminal works are still widely referred to today (e.g. 1970, 1973, 1978; see also 1987b), concludes, on the basis of the house distribution in space and time, that this was an 'Israelite house'. According to him: '(I)n the light of the connection between the distribution of this type and the borders of Israelite settlement, and in light of its period of use and architectural characteristics, it would seem that the use of the four-room house is an original Israelite concept' (1970: 180).

While this was supported by other scholars and is still accepted today by some (e.g. Holladay 1992; 1997), the ethnic label of this house came under steady criticism. Ibrahim, who mistakenly thought he uncovered a similar house at Sahab (see below), claimed 'that the examples found within the Ammonite and Edomite regions do not fit with the conclusion of Shiloh' (1975: 73). Other scholars, following Ibrahim's discovery as well as similar finds in other regions that were not associated with the Israelites (some, indeed, are four-room houses), have also criticized this label (see, e.g., Finkelstein 1996a; see also Ahlstrom 1993: 339-40). These discoveries gradually convinced many scholars that the classification of the four-room house as an Israelite type is unwarranted. Finkelstein's words are representative of this view; after stating that houses do sometimes reflect ethnicity, he continues: 'Unfortunately, this is not the case in the Iron Age. Y. Shiloh described the four-room house as an Israelite house type, but it has later been found also in the lowland and Transjordanian Iron I sites. Its popularity in the central hill country must be linked to environmental and social factors, rather than to the ethnic background of the communities' (Finkelstein 1996a: 204, 205; for negative assessments, see recently also Edelman 2002: 44-45; London 2003; Bloch-Smith 2003: 406-408). Once the ethnic 'explanation'[2] fell into disfavor, most scholars tried to explain the wide distribution of the house by its functionality, and such is the dominant explanation of the four-room house today.[3]

The functional analysis of daily life within the four-room house, best exemplified by the seminal studies of Stager (1985c) and Holladay (1992;

---

2. Note that the 'ethnic explanation' discussed so far is not really an explanation. Rather, it is only a description of the accordance between the distribution of the house and the distribution of an ethnic group. No one has attempted to explain the qualities of the house that made it Israelite. In any event, as we have already seen, the two explanations ('ethnicity' and 'functionality') are not necessarily contradictory.

3. Whether the label 'Israelite' is attached to it (Holladay 1992) or not (Ahlstrom 1993: 340).

1997), is based first and foremost on ethnographic and ethnoarchaeological data. It is worth noting in passing that thus far virtually no systematic research on functionality and synthesis of the archaeological finds from the many excavated four-room houses have been presented in research litera- ture. The exemplary analysis of household activities at Beersheba by Singer- Avitz (1996) is an important exception (see also Hardin 2001; Cassuto 2004). In any event, the ethnographic analogies to the four-room house have led to a consensus regarding its functionality. As clearly maintained by Stager:

> The pillared house takes its form not from some desert nostalgia monumen- talized in stone and mudbrick, but from a living tradition. It was first and foremost a successful adaptation to farm life: the ground floor had space allocated for food processing, small craft production, stabling, and storage; the second floor was suitable for dining, sleeping, and other activities… Its longevity attests to its continuing suitability not only to the environment…but also for the socioeconomic unit housed in it—for the most part, rural families who farmed and raised livestock. (1985c: 17)

Holladay's conclusions, almost echoing Stager's, are also worth mentioning:

> From the time of its emergence in force until its demise at the end of Iron Age II, the economic function of the 'Israelite House' seems to have been centered upon requirements for storage and stabling, functions for which it was ideally suited… Furthermore, its durability as preferred house type, lasting over 600 years throughout all the diverse environmental regions of Israel and Judah, even stretching down into the wilderness settlements in the central Negeb, testifies that it was an extremely successful design for the common—probably landowning—peasant. (1992: 316)

While the functional analysis of the four-room house and its ramifications for the suitability of the building to peasant daily life in ancient Israel is highly compelling, it still seems far from conveying the full story behind the structure's exceptional dominance as an architectural form during the Iron Age, and beyond this, its significance as a cultural phenomenon. Its sudden disappearance from the archaeological record in the sixth century BCE (Shiloh 1973: 281; Holladay 1997: 337; Faust 2004b, and references), for example, cannot be explained by the functional explanation. While the crystallization of the house was a long process, beginning probably in the late thirteenth century BCE and ending only during the eleventh century, its sudden disappearance is striking given that no changes in subsistence patterns (changes that could have influence the use of the structure, if it was indeed dictated by functionality) are known to have taken place during the sixth century BCE. If the house was so suitable for peasant life in the Iron Age, why wasn't it suitable for peasant life during the Neo-Babylonian and Persian periods?

The house's dominance and longevity also indicate that its form is not rooted in functionality only. There were functional houses in other periods, but none achieved such a dominant position, and perhaps more important, none were so uniform. The archaeological finds from within these houses are also telling. If the great uniformity of the house type were a result of its supreme functionality, one would expect to find at least some uniformity in the use of the various spaces within the houses, but this is entirely not the case (Cassutto 2004: 133-34). In some houses the finds in the back room indicate daily activities (Singer-Avitz 1996; Riklin 1997: 10), while in others this room was used for storing hundreds of storage jars of various kinds (e.g. Feig 1996: 3; Herr and Clark 2001: 45). The houses also appear in both urban and rural contexts and were utilized by both the rich and poor (Faust 1999c; 2005b, and references). There is even a similarity between the house and the tomb (e.g. A. Mazar 1976; Barkay 1994: 147-52; 1999), and the same concept was used in many instances for the construction of public structures (e.g. Hazor).

Another path should be sought to explain this intriguing phenomenon. Possible answers to these questions have been discussed recently (see Faust 1999c, 2000a; Bunimovitz and Faust 2002, 2003; Faust and Bunimovitz 2003), and here I would like briefly to summarize them. However, before attempting to decipher the four-room house, a few words regarding its distribution are in order.

Distribution of Four-Room Houses

As already mentioned, Shiloh (1970, 1973), Wright (1978), Holladay (1992, 1997), and many others, relying on the spatial and temporal distribution of the four-room house, argued for a close relationship between the house and the Israelites. Other scholars were opposed to this idea, pointing to many examples of four-room houses outside Israelite territory, including at 'Afula, Tel Sippor, Tel Keisan, Sahab, Tel Qasile and many others (e.g. Ibrahim 1975; Ahlstrom 1993: 339-40; Finkelstein 1996a: 204-205; A. Mazar 1985a: 75; 1985b: 68). (See Fig. 9.2 [next page] for the distribution of four-roomed houses.[4]) The appearance of the house type at these sites should be discussed at several levels.

---

4. This schematic map that is Fig. 9.2 is intended to show the main distribution of the four-room house, and not to locate every single structure. Note that in order to overcome some of the shortcomings of distribution maps, this map attempts to show both the presence and absence of this type of dwelling. I have also commented on the frequency of the four-room houses in various sites and regions. Note that not all sites are contemporaneous. Furthermore, at times there were architectural changes over time within sites, and possibly also among different contemporaneous parts of sites. Notably, due to the many subtleties involved, the map should not be used without a close reading of the text.

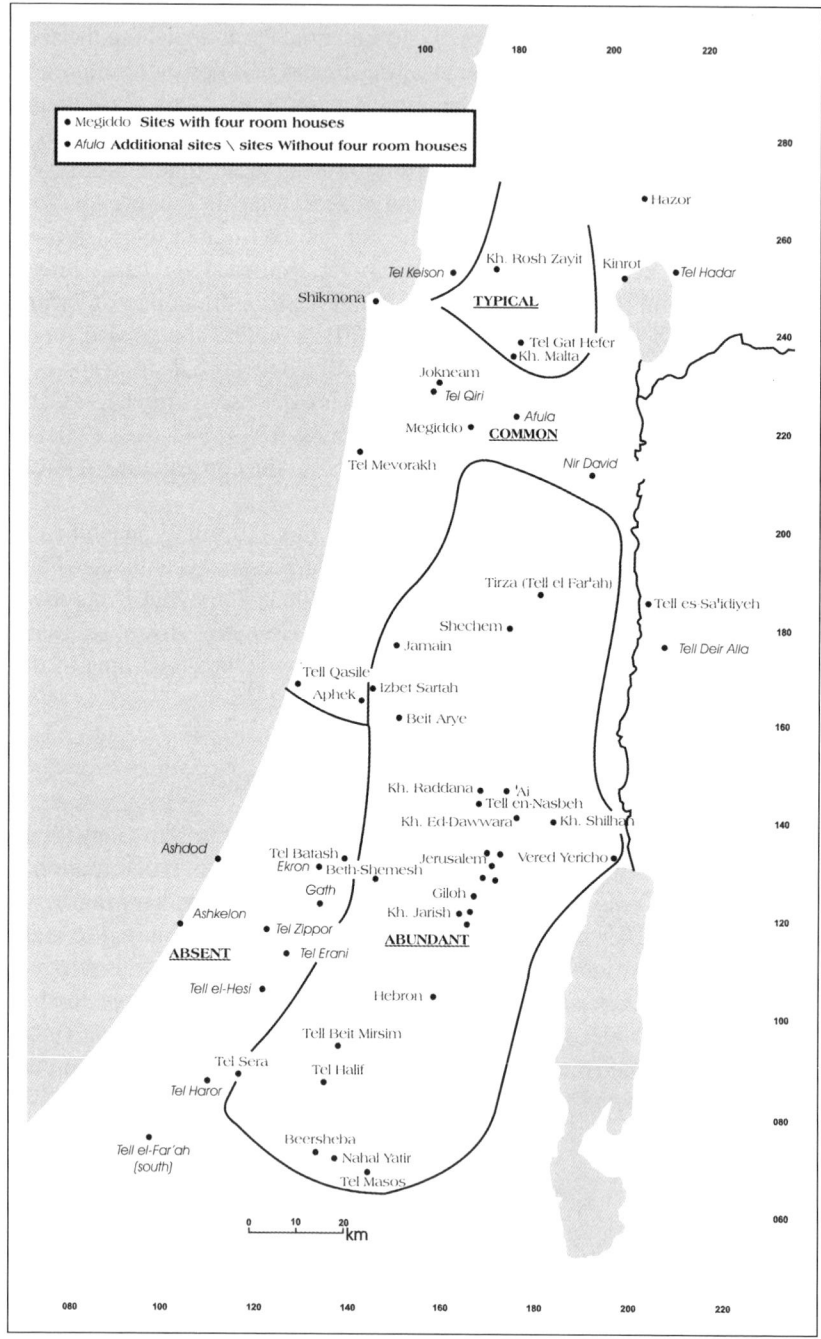

Figure 9.2. *Distribution Map of Four-Room Houses*.

First, it should be emphasized that most of these examples (e.g. 'Afula, Tel Keisan, Sahab, Tel Sippor) lack the typical characteristics of the four-room house, and thus based on a more careful examination, cannot be regarded as such. In some of these cases, the houses do have four rooms, but their configuration is completely different from that of the type. At 'Afula, for example, nothing in the plan resembles a four-room house, although there are pillars and probably four rooms (M. Dothan 1978: 35). Ahlstrom refers to Dothan (1978) as his source for the existence of a four-room house there (1993: 339), but Dothan did not report a four-room house, rather a house with four rooms. The two are not identical or even similar. It should be reiterated that the four-room house does not necessarily contains four rooms—the Hebrew term that should be translated as 'four spaces' seems much more accurate. A similar situation is evident at Sahab, where no four-room houses were found, but one room in a complex structure is divided by columns (Ibrahim 1975: 70-73, see especially Figs. 1–2). The same seems to be true also in Tel Keisan, where some houses contained four rooms and pillars, but in a completely different configuration, as acknowledged explicitly by the excavators who wrote that the houses were not four-room houses (Humbert 1993: 865-66).[5] At Tel Sippor, too, no four-room house is evident (Biran and Negbi 1966: Fig. 4). Finally, there also seems to be some confusion between four-room houses and pillared buildings, as the two are unjustifiably referred to interchangeably (see, e.g., the often quoted Ibrahim 1975; see also Ji 1997a: 394).[6] Both the number of rooms and the presence of pillars are not sufficient as indicators of the four-room house, and therefore their number in non-Israelite regions is much smaller than commonly thought.

Second, some of the houses were unearthed in territories originally thought to be outside of the Israelite realm, but on second thought can quite reasonably be regarded as Israelite, particularly in Transjordan (see Herr 2000: 178; Ji 1995, 1997a, 1997b); the issue will be discussed in detail in Chapters 19 (regarding Tel Qasile) and 20 (regarding Transjordan)

Third, examples of true four-room houses outside the supposed Israelite territory mainly date to the Iron Age I (e.g. Kautz 1981; Daviau 1999: 132),

5.   The excavator writes: 'the building consisted of four units, but it cannot be defined as a "four-room house"; the rooms formed by the partition of the courtyards were too narrow for that'. The lack of resemblance to the four-room house is clear upon examining the plan of the houses (Humbert 1993: Structure 501).

6.   An excellent example for the confusion can be seen in the identification of certain Late Bronze Age structures at Tel Batash and Tel Harasim as belonging to the four-room type (e.g. A. Mazar 1985b; Givon 1999; see also Bloch-Smith and Alpert Nakhai 1999: 103). These houses do have three rooms, and pillars; they lack, however, a broad room. In any event, this identification is completely irrelevant to the study of ethnicity, as we shall see below.

prior to the final crystallization of ethnic groups in the region and the house itself. During the Iron Age II, when the house is more readily identified and many examples are known, the number of exceptions is very few in number, and most come from Transjordan (e.g. Ghrareh; Hart 1988: 92). Therefore, definitive examples of four-room houses outside Israelite territory are very few indeed, especially during the Iron Age II; they should be explained as representing ephemeral use by non-Israelites or by Israelites living in non-Israelite regions.[7]

There appears, therefore, to be a near complete correspondence between the presence of Israelites and four-room houses. The questions are, therefore, when did this correspondence come into being, and why. We shall start with a discussion of the house's qualities.

Explaining the Four-Room House

It can be supposed that this house plan and its subtypes are related to the Israelite mind, and while conceived by it, the use of the four-room plan in daily life reflexively structured that very mind. The significance of the structure in this light can be deciphered by a close examination of several of its characteristics.

In the spirit of the work of Hillier and Hanson concerning the social logic of space (1984; see also Foster 1989; Banning and Byrd 1989; Blanton 1994: 24-37), a building plan can be analyzed and compared for its space syntax, a term refering to spatial configuration within a built structure and the hierarchy of accessibility or passage from one room to another. Its social meaning lies in the potential contact between a building's inhabitants and its guests, as well as among the inhabitants themselves. Different syntaxes hint, therefore, at different systems or codes of social and cultural relations. When properly analyzed, the syntax of the four-room house and its subtypes turn out to be conspicuously different from those of other house types known from ancient Israel. An access analysis of the house (Fig. 9.3) produces a very shallow tree, where all the branches have only one node, or room, and thus are all of equal importance. Two implications of this analysis to be illuminated below, together with other factors, are potentially of great importance for the present study; they involve an egalitarian ideology, and a concept termed 'purity and space syntax'.

---

7. As was mentioned in Chapter 3, most studies did not consider the possibility of more than one ethnic group inhabiting a site. As we shall see later (Chapter 19), Tel Qasile seems to be a good example of the co-existence of more then one ethnic group in a single settlement.

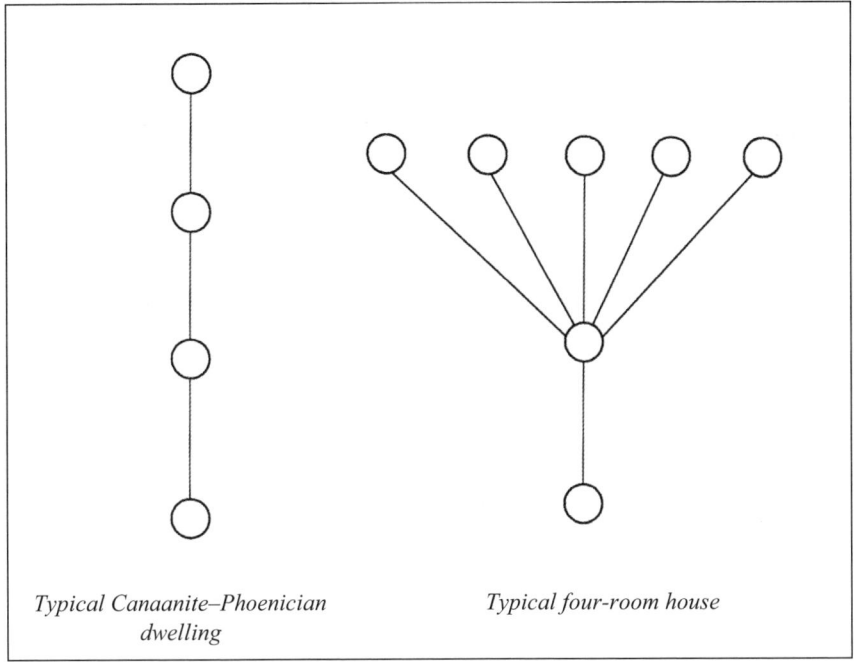

Typical Canaanite–Phoenician dwelling

Typical four-room house

Figure 9.3. *Access Analysis of a Typical Four-Room House,
as Compared to a Typical Canaanite–Phoenician House.*

Egalitarian Ideology

An intriguing implication of access analysis of the four-room house is the correspondence between its non-hierarchical configuration and the 'democratic' or egalitarian ethos of Israelite society, an ethos that has already emerged from the analysis of various traits (and will be discussed in detail in Chapter 11).

Relying on a cross-cultural sample of houses and households, Blanton recently demonstrated that large households with multiple families display a complex and hierarchically structured arrangement of living and sleeping spaces that reflect their complex social structure (1994: 64). This is often manifested as a hierarchical grading of accessibility and structural depth of spaces within the house, as related to generational and in some cases gender-based status distinctions. Special living and sleeping areas are frequently set aside for married children, as opposed to the *ad hoc* sleeping arrangements or shared sleeping spaces often seen in societies with simpler houses. Since four-room houses, particularly in the rural setting and among the elite, usually contain multiple rooms created by the division of the four main spaces, it is clear that established arrangements for space usage were part and parcel of daily life within these houses. Yet, as mentioned above, the

four-room plan lacks 'depth' or access hierarchy and expresses a more egalitarian spirit than the contemporaneous or previous house plans in ancient
Israel. It seems to have been in line with Israelite ideology and social perception more than other house plans, and thus was adopted as the main type
of building, both large and small, and of the poor and wealthy (Faust 1999b,
1999c, 2005b).

Purity and Space Syntax
The examination of movement within the house also shows that its plan is
extremely useful for a society that considered privacy to be of importance,
or that required a regulation of contact in a manner due to factors other than
status and hierarchy, thus differentiating it from the abovementioned houses
whose plans express hierarchy. Because the branches on the access analysis
contain one node, or room, each, the crossing of one room to get to another
was not necessary. The only room used as a junction is the central one, thus
allowing the regulation of contact among inhabitants.

   If purity matters were crucial for the conduct of Israelite daily life,[8] then
the unique plan of the four-room house more than enabled it.[9] Notably, most
of the biblical purity laws (e.g. those of the P-source), while imposing
restrictions on them, do not require menstruating women to leave the house,
unlike other ancient Near Eastern societies (Milgrom 1991: 952-53) and
many others throughout the world (e.g. Galloway 1997). Yet restrictions
imposed by these laws probably required them to spend some of their time
in a separate room. Since each room could be entered directly from the central space without passing through other rooms, purity could be strictly kept
even if an unclean person resided in the house. As will be discussed later,
the possible connection between the four-room plan and a specific ethnic
behavior as that related to purity laws may suggest that the former was
adapted or developed to accommodate the latter, but it is even more likely
that the conducts of behavior were structured by the house plan (e.g.
Giddens 1979, 1984).

---

   8. From the written sources we know that this society had many purity laws, although
this is not the place to discuss the dating of the various laws. It should be noted, however,
that while there seems to be a near consensus regarding the dating of some of the laws to
the Iron Age (the D-source), there is a debate regarding the date of the P-source, as
discussed above.
   9. M. Weinfeld was the first to suggest that both the correspondence of the dispersal
of the four-room house with the areas settled by the Israelites and its high popularity
throughout most of the Iron Age have to do with the ideological/cognitive realm (Netzer
1992: 199 n. 24). More than a decade ago he insightfully, though tentatively, commented
that the house plan might have resulted from the Israelite tribe's way of life, namely, that
its plan enables the separation of purity and impurity—such as the avoidance of a woman
during menstruation.

Non-verbal Communication

Houses, like other features and artifacts, participate in a society's non-verbal communication. They can be used to communicate several types of messages, including what Blanton calls 'canonical' and 'indexical' messages (1994: 8-13). A canonical message 'pertains to the meaning of enduring symbols reflecting concepts held in common by the people participating in a common cultural system' (1994: 10). Typically, symbolic communication through the medium of the dwelling involves the creation of a built environment that manifests social divisions based on gender, generation, and rank, linked to cosmological schemes that express categorical oppositions such as order vs. disorder, elite vs. non-elite, and purity vs. danger. In these instances, the house as *habitus* is a medium of communication primarily among the occupants of the house itself, providing a material frame that structures not only day-to-day interactions, but also the more infrequent formal household rituals. In this sense, the form of the house embodies taxonomic principles specific to a cultural system; by living in the house, its occupants are constantly made aware of these principles, which are thus inculcated and reinforced.

On the other hand, in an indexical message as defined by Blanton, the communication is with the outside world. In Blanton's words, 'information is communicated concerning the current status of a household…in terms… such as wealth' (1994: 10-11). While the canonical messages lie primarily within the inner parts of the house, the indexical communicative role of the house involves its more public areas and elements that provide information about costliness and taste to outsiders. The two are seemingly contradictory: 'one could predict that the goals of social linkage communication (which says, "we're part of the community") could come into conflict with the goals of indexical communication (which might contain the message: "we're better than everybody else")'; in reality, however, it is not always easy to distinguish between the two, and it seems as if both can be transmitted simultaneously from the same house (1994: 13).

Four-room houses, by the very uniformity of their plans, the egalitarian ethos reflected by them, and their dominant position within the society discussed, were used to reinforce the community's values and ideology, and to strengthen the sense of togetherness of the population; by building a house according to the traditional code of the society, the inhabitants transit of a message of 'we are part of the community', and therefore enhance the coherence of that community. At the same time, however, the differences in size and quality of the houses sent indexical messages of superiority and wealth (Faust 1999b, 2005b; Singer-Avitz 1996).

Order and Dominance

Undoubtedly, the most puzzling issue concerning the four-room plan is its ubiquity. As emphasized above, the functional interpretation falls short of explaining why this plan was applied not only in peasants' dwellings but also in public buildings outside of the rural sphere. One may suspect, therefore, that behind this extraordinary cultural phenomenon again lie cognitive aspects.

According to Douglas, many of the biblical laws, mainly those related to holiness, are at their heart about order (1966). In an insightful analysis of the abominations of Leviticus (relevant also to certain passages in Deuteronomy), she developed the idea that holiness is exemplified by wholeness and completeness. Many of the laws—covering aspects of life from war to sexual behavior, from social conduct to dietary rules—are related to sets of precepts stemming from that basic principle, all of which embrace the idea of holiness as order and sin as confusion. Holiness requires completeness in a social context—an important enterprise begun must not be left incomplete. It requires that individuals conform to the class to which they belong, and that different classes of things not be mixed with each other. To be holy is to be whole, to be one; holiness is unity, integrity, perfection of the individual and of the kind. Hybrids and other confusions are abominations.

In light of this ideology, the astonishing dominance of the four-room plan on almost all levels of Israelite architectural design becomes intelligible. If the Israelites were deeply engaged with unity and order as a negation of separateness and confusion, then these concepts must have percolated through all spheres of daily life, including material culture. Thus, it can be surmised that once the four-room house took shape and was formalized as the container and embodiment of the Israelite lifestyle and symbolic order, then other architectural schemes must have been considered a deviation, if not in violation of it.

Discussion: The Four-Room House and Israelite Ethnicity

The suitability of the four-room house plan to the Israelites' way of life does not necessarily suggest that people of other ethnicities did not utilize it, although this was in practice very sporadic. What it does suggest is that upon finding a site with no such houses, it would be very difficult to ascribe it to the Israelites. But it is not my goal merely to demonstrate that this house was used by Israelites, as important as this may be; rather, our investigation has shown that the plan of the four-room house resulted to a large extent from an ethnically specific behavior, and thus a central issue for our purposes is to find when this developed. The answer to this question appears to be quite secure.

The four-room house, or its prototype, appears as early as the late thirteenth and early twelfth centuries BCE,[10] and was crystallized by the eleventh century BCE (see A. Mazar 1990a: 486; see also Ji 1997a: 396-97).[11] Its first appearance can be explained by its functional qualities, as suggested by many scholars mentioned above. At this time the plan was not yet completely fixed, nor was the house so dominant, but was rather just one type of house among many. It is very likely that during the thirteenth to eleventh centuries BCE these houses (and, mainly, their prototypes) were used, not very frequently, by several or all the ethnic groups in the region. Only during the twelfth and mainly the eleventh centuries did the plan gradually became more and more uniform, with this house style being used dominantly by the Israelites, as it suited their emerging ways of life. The resulting pattern is that from sporadic use throughout the area during earlier stages of Iron I, it became very dominant in the settlements of what became Israel, and its use in other areas, which was sporadic to start with, decreased even more.

Once the house-plan crystallized, functional explanations cannot explain the house's dominant position in society; other factors, as briefly described above, were operating. To the extent that the development of the house was a result of its being 'chosen' by the Israelites, its plan can be seen as a result of an ethnic behavior. Other groups could, of course, continue to use this plan, but we see that such a use was never more than sporadic. Perhaps its heavy use by the Israelites conveyed messages that discouraged others from using it. The canonization of the four-room house is, therefore, an important point in time, as it indicates when this trait became ethnically significant.[12]

10.   As we have seen, Mazar claimed that the four-room house might have originated from a large three-room structure he excavated in Tel Batash (A. Mazar 1985b), a claim further supported by Givon (1999) following his excavations at Tel Harasim. Such is a problematic argument because the earlier structures lack the broad room at the back, which seems to be a major characteristic of the four-room house; there is no direct link between these two types of structures; and, methodologically, even if a link would have been established, and the earlier houses did resemble the four-room house, two examples are not sufficient for such a conclusion. For the purposes of the present work, however, Mazar's argument is irrelevant, as the origin of the house does not necessarily bear direct connection to its significance in a later stage (see Chapter 18).

11.   There are some houses that seem quite 'typical' already earlier (e.g. Herr 2000: 173-74), which is not to say that their form had already been canonized; this would occur only later. Note that the number of such sites is small and that none, even the abovementioned from Tell al-'Umayri, is as typical as some of the Iron II houses.

12.   Notably, if only part of the arguments presented here are accepted, it is sufficient to establish some sort of a unifying ethnicity for Israel and Judah, in contrast to some recent claims; cf. P.R. Davies' assertion that 'certainly it seems unlikely that there was any original connection between the settlers of Judah and these of Israel' (1992: 69; see also Thompson 2000: 156).

Notably, the destructions brought about by the Assyrians and Babylonians violently eliminated the *raison d'être* of this omnipresent ethnic symbol. Following the collapse of Judah in the early sixth century, the four-room house disappears from the archaeological record (for detailed discussion, see Faust 2004b).

10

CIRCUMCISION AND ETHNICITY

The present chapter will discuss male circumcision, another apparent marker of Israelite ethnicity. Unlike the other traits discussed above, this trait is not related to material culture, and thus the following should be seen as supplementing the previous, more archaeological, discussions. It is, however, of great importance, as the textual evidence we possess regarding circumcision as an ethnic marker is very instructive, in light of our knowledge of this custom in general and when compared to the processes the Philistines went though during the Iron Age. It can provide insight into the formation of Israel's self-identification.

Circumcision and the Bible

Overview of Research
This is not the place to summarize the entirety of research conducted by biblical scholars on the role of circumcision in the Bible (e.g. de Vaux 1961: 46-48; Isaac 1964; Fox 1974; Goldberg 1996; R.G. Hall 1992; Eilberg-Schwartz 1990, and references). Circumcision in various societies throughout the world has drawn much interest, and several explanations have been offered for the fact that what is so widespread elsewhere is in the Hebrew Bible the sign of the covenant between God and the Israelites (see the summary in Eilberg-Schwartz 1990: 141-76). Many scholars have used the comparative data in order to understand the background for circumcision in ancient Israel, such as, for example, its significance as an initiation rite. Other scholars, however, tend to lessen the importance of the comparative data, and concentrate on the role circumcision had in ancient Israel, stressing, for example, the fact that Israelite circumcision was conducted on the eighth day after birth, therefore precluding explanations such as an initiation rite or preparation for marriage which are typical interpretations of this rite in most 'traditional' societies.

Today there are many scholars who, mainly on the basis of the significance of circumcision as it appears in the Pentateuch, adopt such factors as fertility, initiation, and education as explanations for circumcision in ancient Israel (e.g. Fox 1974; Eilberg-Schwartz 1990; R.G. Hall 1992: 1026; Goldberg 1996). Heightening tribal consciousness was also mentioned in this regard, but for many it was seen only as a secondary effect (Fox 1974: 595; see more below). Other scholars, however, view circumcision as an ethnic marker, mainly on the basis of the many references to it in the historical books of the Bible (e.g. R.G. Hall 1992). These include: 'is there no woman among your cousins or in all our own people? Must you go and marry one of the uncircumcised Philistines?' (Judg. 14.3); 'Then David turned to his neighbors and said, "what is to be done for the man who kills the Philistine and wipes out our disgrace? And who is he, an uncircumcised Philistine, to defy Israel"...' (1 Sam. 17.26); 'Proclaim it not in the streets of Ashkelon, lest the Philistine women rejoice, lest the daughters of the uncircumcised exult' (2 Sam. 1.20; and others, see below). The claim that circumcision was viewed as an ethnic marker in these cases is certain indeed. But before assessing the presumed discrepancy between the two approaches (and the two 'sources' on which they are based), we should have a brief look on the place of circumcision in the region.

Circumcision in Ancient Israel and the Ancient Near East
Circumcision was seemingly widespread in the ancient Near East, at least from the third millennium BCE onward (Licht 1962: 896, 899; R.G. Hall 1992: 1025; Isaac 1964: 450). If, however, many groups practiced it, how could it serve as a marker in ancient Israel? In such a case its mere emergence seems illogical. Indeed, although not the only reason (e.g. Fox 1974: 591), this fact was used to reject the view that circumcision was a 'tribal mark'. Fox, for example, claimed that 'it is not an identity sign designating one as belonging to the covenanted people, for first of all no one would see it. Anyway, it would not be of much use in distinguishing the Israelites from their neighbors because many of them were also circumcised'. He admitted that 'for practical purposes circumcision could at most distinguish the Israelites from the Philistines' but claims that the latter was 'not an issue for P' (1974: 595). Whether it was or could have been an issue for P is a different matter to be discussed below, but Fox seems to have pointed in the right direction here, although he later ignored the implications of his own insight. He mainly studied circumcision in the Pentateuch, while other scholars studied additional texts, and viewed them differently.

Hall, for example, writes: 'although many of the surrounding nations practiced it (Jer 9.25-26), circumcision gave Hebrews a sense of national identity' (1992: 1026). According to him: 'This usage peaked when the Hebrews confronted "uncircumcised" nations, the Philistines (Judges 14.3; 15.18; 1 Sam 14.16; 17.26, 36; 31.4 [cf. 1 Chr 10.4]; 2 Sam 1.20), the

Babylonians and the Greeks' (1992: 1026). Most of Hall's references relate specifically to the Philistines. Licht stresses that the Philistines are the only ones called 'uncircumcised'—*'arelim*—as, for example, in 2 Sam. 1.19 (1962: 897). Isaac gives a similar assessment: 'the opprobrious epithet "uncircumcised" was applied apparently only the Philistines in the Bible' (1964: 450; see also Dothan and Cohn 1994: 63; Machinist 2000: 67-68). Thus, circumcision is referred to as an ethnic marker in parts of the Bible. As such, it is mentioned in reference to the Philistines, and was probably developed as a marker only as part of the Israelites' interaction with them, as they were uncircumcised.

Circumcision as an Ethnic Marker
The idea that circumcision could have had such an importance, as portrayed in the Bible, is not without parallels. Hodder observed that circumcision rites in Africa served to enhance ethnic solidarity among a group that conducted it, as the Mbunda or Wiko, against their main 'other' that did not, the Lozi (1982a: 116-17). According to Gluckman, the behavior of the Wiko in the lodge—where novices are circumcised and reside before and after the rite— was markedly hostile towards their Lozi and Kwangwa neighbors. Gluckman described how his Lozi attendants, the 'true' uncircumcised, were treated: 'The men delighted in threatening my Lozi with "cutting", and told us stories on how they frightened Lozi intruders into tears'.[1] Consider, in this light, the stories of David bringing 'a hundred foreskins of the Philistines' (1 Sam. 18.25). Without going into discussion about the historicity of the biblical narratives, Gluckman's description demonstrates that when two such groups—one that practices circumcision and one that does not—are in a state of hostility, such stories are likely to develop (and perhaps also occur). Gluckman summarized, 'Wiko circumcised probably glorify the lodge additionally against the uncircumcised foreigners because they live among these who despise them' (1949: 152). According to him, 'the lodge definitely assert Wiko pride and culture against the dominant group among whom they have settled...'

Again, an examination of this cultural trait in this light clearly indicates, as with other traits, that the Israelites defined themselves in relation to, and contrast with, the uncircumcised Philistines. But when and how did this interaction take place? A closer examination might give us a more precise date and context for the rise of circumcision as a marker.

---

1. At times, circumcision (and the accompanying ceremonies) was used for political reasons. E.R. Wolf, for example, refers to the fact that 'Dingiswayo forbade the circumcision schools that united the members of related homesteads under the jurisdiction of their chief's son' (1982: 349).

The Uncircumcised in the Bible
The biblical traditions might help us understand the function of circumcision and place the relevant stories in their historical setting. As mentioned above, most studies that have dealt with the issue have mainly considered the relevant texts in the Pentateuch, which have usually been interpreted as being unrelated to ethnicity. Yet the term uncircumcised is used quite often as a pejorative and an ethnically loaded term in several of the historical books of the Bible (mainly Judges, 1 and 2 Samuel and 1 Chronicles).

In the vast majority of these texts, the term refers to the Philistines (Judg. 14.3; 15.18; 1 Sam. 14.6; 17.26, 36; 31.4; 2 Sam. 1.20; 1 Chron. 10.4; see also 1 Sam. 18.25, 27; 2 Sam. 3.14), although it also can describe other peoples (e.g. Gen. 34.14-24), and even all the 'gentiles' (e.g. Jer. 9.25; see also Ezek. 44.9). The striking element is that they refer to the Philistines in such a negative manner *only* in texts that are meant to describe the reality during the late Iron I. This not only supports the claim that circumcision was stressed because the Israelites were facing a group which did not practice it—the Philistines—and is, therefore, an ethnic marker, but also, as we shall see, can date the importance of circumcision as an ethnic marker to the late Iron Age I.

Furthermore, *none* of the texts referring to later than the Iron I mention the uncircumcised in reference to the Philistines specifically (cf. Halpern 2001: 457). In Ezekiel 32, the prophet's list of circumcised and uncircumcised peoples includes Assyria, Elam, and some others among the latter, but no mention is made of the Philistines. Some saw this as an indication that the Philistines were ethnically and politically in decline, and were thus not important enough to be mentioned in such a prophecy (Haran 1996: 167). This, however, does not correspond with the overall picture which emerges from the texts, as there are quite a few prophecies against the Philistines in the eighth to sixth centuries BCE, indicating that they still existed and were important enough to warrant such attention. None of these prophecies, furthermore, refer to them as uncircumcised.

In summary, while there is agreement that the discussed texts are later than the Iron Age I, there is an interesting dichotomy: texts that refer to the Iron I use the term 'uncircumcised' to describe the Philistines, in contrast to texts that refer to the Iron II, which do not use the term for such purposes (see more below).

Philistine Circumcision
The disappearance of the term 'uncircumcised' as a designation for the Philistines in the Iron Age II reflects, I believe, an interesting but simple fact: the Philistines started to circumcise during this time.

It is widely known that Philistine material culture was altered significantly throughout the Iron Age. Trude Dothan's seminal work *The Philistines and their Material Culture*, deals with the Iron Age I only, and an explanation for this is posited in the last paragraph of the book. After describing the events of the eleventh century, T. Dothan writes: 'the material culture of this phase is characterized by its many local variations. It should be stressed that it was during this period of greatest expansion that Philistine culture lost its uniqueness and vitality and slowly became assimilated into the surrounding Canaanite culture...' (1982: 296). The changes that took place in the Philistine material culture have also been used by other scholars as an indication of their assimilation (see also Bunimovitz 1990: 219; A. Mazar 1986: 27; Dothan and Dothan 1992: 85-86). It is more likely, however, that what we are witnessing is simply a weaker form of acculturation (Stone 1995),[2] as it seems that the Philistines, while adopting cultural traits of other peoples and losing much of their own culture, retained their identity at least until the late Iron Age (B.J. Stone 1995; Eph'al 1997; Kempinski 1986, 1987).

In any case, there seems to be a consensus that the Philistines lost many of their cultural traits as time progressed, particularly from the tenth century onward. Therefore, when the Philistines ceased to manufacture their unique ceramics, adopted the local Phoenician script, and reduced the amount of pork they consumed, they also started to practice circumcision, like their neighbors. This is seen in the biblical texts, and direct support for this is found in Herodotus (II.104), who claimed that the 'Syrians in Palestinaea' were circumcised, and that they adopted it from the Egyptians. Herodotus was familiar with the inhabitants of the coast, and most likely referred to the Philistines, as the term Palestinaea indicates.[3]

This process can explain why the later texts, whose historicity is usually not questioned, cease to use the pejorative term 'uncircumcised' to describe

---

2. Note, in this regard, the decrease in pork consumption during the Iron Age II, mentioned in Chapter 5.

3. In their interpretation of Herodotus here, it is likely that various scholars have been misled by the assumption that the Philistines were always uncircumcised. Jacobson (1999: 67; see also Eph'al 1997: 35*), for example, seems to believe that this reference indicates that the term 'Palestinaea' includes more than Philistia, since the Philistines were *the* uncircumcised, and Herodotus could not have referred to them (some claimed that this referred to the Jews [see already Josephus, *Ant.* 8.262; also Jacobson 1999: 67] or the Arabs [M. Stern 1976: 3-4]). Since, however, I believe that at the time to which Herodotus refers the inhabitants of Philistia were circumcised, there is no need to reach these conclusions on the basis of this reference. It is therefore likely that Herodotus referred to Philistia, and that the Philistines had indeed learned it from other peoples, although whether these were the Egyptians or not is less secure; Sasson claims that the origin of this custom is Syrian (1966: 476). Notably, if Herodotus referred to the Phoenicians, then there was certainly no need to look for the circumcised beyond the coastal plain; in this case the reference is irrelevant for discussing the Philistines of course.

the Philistines—they were simply not 'uncircumcised' anymore.[4] And, again, such a situation is not without an ethnographic parallel. Hodder refers to the Elmolo, who in the past 'did not circumcise males or have *moran*, but by 1958 they had begun to adopt both these traits from the Samburu'; this was accompanied by the adoption of some other Samburu customs (1982a: 101).

Discussion

To summarize, three main implications derive from the above discussion. First, the Philistines were uncircumcised only during the first phase of their settlement. This phase is the only possible background for the development of circumcision as an ethnic marker among the Israelites. At no other time, and in the face of no other group, could this custom have developed in such a manner among the Israelites. Second, as a result, the importance of the Philistines as Israel's main 'other' is exemplified again. Third, as a by-product it is likely that the above speaks on the credibility of the texts. In the following I do not wish to summarize biblical scholarship on these texts, but rather to stress that those which described the Iron Age I seem to have some historical background, although they were written hundreds of years later than the events they describe. The mere fact that the term 'uncircumcised' is not used to refer to the Philistines during the Iron Age II is important.

If this term was used to designate the Philistines throughout the Iron Age, then its usage when the texts refer to the Iron Age I would have been mean-ingless for our purposes, since it could have been seen as an anachronism. However, the term was *not* used to designate the Philistines in any text per-taining to the Iron Age II, probably because they were no longer uncircum-cised. Its usage in relation to the Iron I must mean that the author had some ancient texts or other reliable sources in front of him, from which he drew the stories and the term. In light of the accepted view regarding the author's date (e.g. Eissfeldt 1966; Friedman 1987; Rofé 1994), it appears that he used a term that was not used in his own time to refer to the Philistines. This can be supported by the fact that the first book of Chronicles—written during the Persian period—uses the term 'uncircumcised' only once, while 1–2 Samuel uses it quite often, although the stories told in these works are similar. The editor of Chronicles must have used his own language when rewriting the stories, therefore reducing the usage of this old term significantly. Therefore,

---

4. The fact that the Philistines are missing from Jer. 9.24, which appears to list cir-cumcised people (de Vaux 1961), can be interpreted as either resulting from their unimportance at the time of the prophecy at the very end of the Iron Age (an argument I have just rejected), or from a later editorial correction. I must admit that the latter, while possible, is a problematic argument. The silence of Jeremiah is intriguing, but the overall argument as presented here fits the evidence at hand much better than all previous views.

it is reasonable from this to claim that the stories relating to the Iron I in 1–2 Samuel are at least very old, and could not have been invented during the Iron Age II, without debating whether they really happened or not.[5]

Another conclusion that can be drawn from this discussion is that some biblical scholars have underestimated the significance of circumcision as an ethnic marker, despite its being unseen. Whatever the exact date of the writings of the P-source may be, it is, as we have already seen, later than the Iron I. When it was composed the Philistines were not a burning issue, thus P developed other reasons for this long-established tradition, which, by then, had become customary among nearby peoples and probably even the Philistines. This explanation goes well with the biblical view, which uses circumcision in certain (earlier) contexts as an ethnic marker.

There is, however, another possibility. Circumcision was, as noted above, widely spread in the ancient Near East long before the Israelites, so that it is likely that at least some of the various groups that slowly developed into Israelites practiced circumcision from the beginning. When faced with an 'other' that did not practice it, the behavior became canonized. Thus the origin of the custom cannot be attributed to the formation of ethnic boundaries but to other reasons, perhaps even those attributed to the P-source by some scholars, as discussed above.[6] This practice, however, was chosen as an ethnic behavior because of the Philistines. The mechanisms through which certain traits were chosen to transmit ethnicity while others were not will be discussed in Chapter 15.

Summary

It is quite clear that the term 'uncircumcised' is used in the Bible mainly as an ethnic marker, and since most of the local population of the region practiced circumcision, the trait could have served as a marker only in relation to the Philistines. The pejorative term 'uncircumcised' is used only in texts that relate to the Iron Age I; thus it appears that the Philistines adopted circumcision during the Iron Age II as part of their acculturation process. In other words, circumcision may have been practiced earlier but became ethnically significant only as a result of relations with the Philistines, and this could have occurred only during the late Iron Age I.

---

5. Notably, Finkelstein had claimed recently that the traditions regarding the Philistines can be dated to the late Iron Age (2002b). While it is possible that some of the traditions are late, the above shows that some of the traditions could not have been invented that late, and must have been either written closer to the time they describe or based on reliable information (see also Maeir 2004).

6. This is a problematic suggestion due to the accepted low date for the P-source. It is, however, possible that the source recorded more ancient traditions.

11

HIERARCHY AND EQUALITY:
THE ROOTS OF THE ISRAELITE EGALITARIAN ETHOS

Several of the material traits that are connected with the Israelites have been shown to stem from or represent an ideology and ethos of egalitarianism, 'primitive democracy' and/or simplicity.[1] This has been reflected in the limited repertoire of Iron I pottery, the four-room house plan, and the lack of painted decoration on Iron Age 'Israelite' pottery; it is probably also connected to the lack of imported pottery in Israelite sites, and with several other material traits that will be discussed shortly.

While the development of many of these can be easily connected to interaction with the Philistines, such is not the case with all of them, and it is possible that they stemmed from other reasons. Moreover, the roots of the egalitarian ethos itself have not yet been discussed, and it seems that here too there is a good case that it results, at least partially, from interaction with other groups. Before we can discuss the roots of this ethos, however, I would like to draw attention to several additional traits that seems to exhibit it.

Israel's Egalitarian Ethos: Additional Archaeological Data

Israelite Burials

There are virtually no Iron Age burials known from the highlands dating to prior to the ninth–eighth centuries, an issue discussed at length recently by Kletter (2002) and myself (see Faust 2004a for an extended discussion; see also Tappy 1995: 65-66; Ilan 1997a: 385; 1997b: 220; Barkay 1994: 160 n. 211; Dever 2003). This stands in sharp contrast to the Late Bronze Age in all parts of the country, highlands and lowlands (e.g. Gonen 1992a; 1992b:

---

1.   In this chapter I refer to an ethos of egalitarianism, simplicity, and even democracy. The three are by no means the same. Due, however, to the early stages of research on the subject, and to the fact that this is of importance here only because of its relevance to the study of ethnicity, the differences between the three will not be discussed here, and I will refer to them as different facets of the same ethos. This is clearly an oversimplification, and a more detailed discussion will be conducted elsewhere.

240-45), and to the Iron Age I in the lowlands (Bloch-Smith 1992; Kletter 2002). Tombs and burials are an important channel for the transmission of messages of social difference and status, and they certainly served this purpose in the Late Bronze Age (e.g. Bunimovitz 1995: 326). While there was a variety of burials in Late Bronze Age Canaan, which could result from several reasons of which social hierarchy is but one, the Iron I lacks even the 'multiple cave burials' that characterized the highland throughout most of the second millennium BCE (Gonen 1992b: 245), therefore breaking a continuity that prevailed through wide segments of Canaanite society for almost 800 years (Bunimovitz 1995: 331). Even if a few Iron I burials are identified in the highlands (Bloch-Smith 2004), the general pattern is striking: during the Late Bronze Age the highlands were only sparsely settled but many tombs are known (Gonen 1992a; 1992b: 240-45; see now also Eisenstadt, Arabas, and Ablas 2004; Peleg 2004; Peleg and Eisenstadt 2004), while during the Iron Age the area was filled with settlements, but such burials are practically absent.

It is probable that all individuals during this period were buried in simple inhumations;[2] the lack of any observable burials is a clear reflection of an egalitarian ideology, and exhibits a sharp contrast to Late Bronze Age Canaanite traditions. As burials have an important social role, they are a chief vehicle through which such an ideology can be channeled or expressed.[3]

Israelite Temples
The issue of Israelite religion has received a great deal of attention by many scholars, and it deserves a separate discussion. Within the scope of the present work, however, it can only be briefly touched upon. Temples are abundant in the Late Bronze Age (Gonen 1992b: 222-32; A. Mazar 1992a) and in lowland Iron I sites (e.g. A. Mazar 1992a, 2000). Although the Late Bronze Age sites have been excavated to a relatively small extent only, temples were found at almost every site, with some sites having more than one. Conversely, despite the fact that Iron Age sites were excavated to a relatively large extent, real temples are practically absent from most sites that can be labeled as Israelite (both in the Iron Age I and Iron Age II; for the few exceptions, see A. Mazar 1992b; see also Alpert Nakhai 2001: 161-200). Dever, for example, refers to the lack of indications of 'elaborate cult or organized religious personnel' (1995a: 205), and Mazar writes that the

2. A full discussion of this issue is conducted elsewhere (Faust 2004a).
3. For an example where burial is used to exemplify egalitarian ethos, although the society is highly stratified, see Metcalf and Huntington (1991: 134) regarding Saudia Arabia, and Parker Pearson (1982) regarding England. For a detailed discussion, see Faust 2004a.

'archaeological evidence for Israelite cult practices during the settlement period is meager' (1992b: 298).[4]

The difference is very obvious in the Iron Age II, when any site that can be safely labeled as Israelite shows no signs of an organized or public cult.[5] This stands in contrast to several villages that, on other grounds, can be identified as Canaanite–Phoenician and exhibit similarity to Bronze Age Canaanite villages, where an organized cult is present (Faust 2000a: 6, 14, and references; cf. Faust 2005a). The tradition of a lack of a public/organized cult in Israelite villages should then be traced to the Iron Age I highland villages mentioned above, where it contrasted both Bronze Age tradition, and Iron Age traditions in Philistine and Canaanite regions (A. Mazar 1992b: 279-80; Faust 2000a: 14).

Religion is an important factor that can be used to enhance ethnicity (Stager 1998: 142, 149), and the absence of temples could have been used to send a message of difference in regard to both Canaanite and Philistine societies. For our purposes, the lack of elaborated cult is also of importance for the identification of an egalitarian ethos.

Israelite Royal Inscriptions
The absence to date of an Israelite royal inscription is an interesting phenomenon (in the Iron Age II of course).[6] The number of archaeological digs and the amount of finds in the areas of the kingdoms of Israel and Judah greatly exceed those in most neighboring regions, including Aram, Ammon, and Moab. The same is true in regard to amounts of written finds in general.[7] Yet despite this, monumental royal inscriptions were found in Philistia (Gitin, Dothan, and Naveh 1997), Moab (e.g. McCarter 1996: 90-92; Ahituv 2003), Ammon (McCarter 1996: 93), and Aram (Biran and Naveh 1993; 1995; see also McCarter 1996: 84-96), yet not in Israel and Judah (e.g. Na'aman 2002: 94; Hallo 2003: xxiii-xxvi; Avigad 1979). Even the Siloam inscription is not an exception, as it lacks any reference to the king, the kingdom, and even God.[8] Given the difference in intensity of research of these regions, one could expect Israel and Judah to produce several dozens of such

4. See also Dever 2001: 113; 2003: 126; Bloch-Smith and Alpert Nakhai 1999: 76; note that the 'Bull Site' and Mt Ebal are good examples of what is to be found: neither is a real temple, and even such sites are extremely rare.

5. The only Iron Age temple was found in Arad; even cultic indications, as at Dan, are rare; cf. A. Mazar 1992b; Alpert Nakhai 2001.

6. This seems to have been a problematic issue to some historians, such as Hoffman (2001: 31).

7. The spread of literacy can bee seen as an additional factor; see Demsky 1997: 367-68.

8. And the same goes for the discussion in Cross 2001.

inscriptions. The absence cannot be a result of mere chance, but should be attributed to an egalitarian ethos (Avigad 1979: 22; Hallo 2003: xxvi),[9] where such a direct display of royal power would not be looked upon favorably.[10]

Israel's Egalitarian Ethos—Summary of Previous Research[11]

The existence of such an ethos was observed already a long time ago by both biblical scholars and archaeologists.

Israel's Egalitarian Ethos in Biblical and Historical Studies
Biblical scholars, belonging to all schools, have long emphasized the 'democratic' and egalitarian character of Israelite society as portrayed by the biblical narratives, to a large extent following studies of other ancient Near Eastern societies.[12] C.U. Wolf, for example, writes that the term democracy 'may be applied rather freely to any state of social organization in which the mass of the people posses the whole sovereignty, that is to a society in which every free, adult male citizen, without distinction of fortune and class, is entitled to an equal share in the entire life.' He goes on, 'the period of the "Judges" in Israel may reflect not so much complete anarchy as decadent democracy, when "every man did which was right in his own eyes" (Judg. 17.9)' (1947: 98). He claims that some of this notion existed also in a later period, and follows with a discussion of the institutions of the 'elders' (*zqenim*) and the assembly (*'edah*), of the appointments of kings, and of *'am ha'ares* (1947: 98-107). He summarizes, 'thus the evidence of checks and balances, of parallel terms, of mythological projection, and of vestigial remains is such that the conviction cannot be avoided that some sort of democracy prevailed in ancient Israel. These traces for primitive democracy are sufficient' (1947: 108). Gordis also discusses some of ancient Israel's institutions, such as the *'edah* and *qahal*, and writes, 'the collective assembly

9. For a similar interpretation in a different context, see Stein 1994; Blanton 1998: 162.

10. It is likely that a few inscriptions will be found in the future, especially in the lowlands, where much of the population was non-Israelite and the ethos was probably weaker, and perhaps also within royal compounds. Still, such future discoveries would not change the overall pattern.

11. Most scholars who referred to these 'democratic' or 'egalitarian' societies stated from the outset that its 'egalitarian' aspects referred only to 'free adult male citizens', and does not usually include women and children (Jacobsen 1943: 159; see also C.U. Wolf 1947: 98; Boehm 1993: 229, 248; Barclay 1993: 241; Knauf 1993: 244). Developing this issue is beyond the scope of the present paper (see also Kent 1993).

12. This is not the place to discuss the texts themselves, as it is usually not sufficient simply to quote a few verses. The importance lies with the social contexts of the institutions that are mentioned, and this can be understood only by a comprehensive discussion.

of ancient Israel was never formally abolished. New conditions led to the diminution of its function so that ultimately it convened only in hours of critical importance. But the positive democratic spirit which actuated in its earliest period never died in Israel and through the Bible, it entered the fabric of western civilization' Gordis (1971: 56-57). Speiser stresses the difference between Israel (and the ancient Near East) and Egypt. The king in the former was mortal (1971: 283-84), which led to a different type of relationship between ruler and ruled. The public—'all Israel'—is responsible for appointing the king. He writes, 'the actual king-makers were the leaders of the people; and such authority on the part of people is literary "democracy". "The People" made Saul king... The men of Judah...anointed David...' (1971: 284). Similar views were expressed by Weisman (1984: 94), Shapira (1998), Lods (1962), and many others. Humphrey, in discussing the importance of 'political assemblies and freedom of speech' in his book, *Anthropology and Greeks*, writes:

> ...here it will be enough to emphasize two elements which particularly characterize Hebrew political institutions. The contractual character of leadership is a notion which underlies much biblical thinking about judges and kings and has its counterpart in the notion of the covenant between Yahweh and Israel. This implies that divine kingship which modern scholars have tried to introduce into the ancient Hebrew thinking can only be a marginal phenomenon. Prophecy is one of the essential channels for the maintenance and reassertion of the covenant between Yahweh and Israel. It is also the most powerful expression of freedom of speech among the Jews. (1978: 182-83)

Over the last generation, Israel's egalitarian ethos was discussed by Mendenhall (1962) and mainly by Gottwald (1979). Mendenhall and Gottwald treat this subject as part of their hypotheses concerning the origins of the Israelites and their establishment of a 'new (egalitarian) society',[13] an idea that stands at the heart of Gottwald's most influential monograph.

Gottwald's ideas received a great deal of criticism (e.g. Lenski 1980; Lemche 1985; Finkelstein 1988).[14] Lemche's observation that, 'instead of speaking of egalitarian societies it would be more appropriate to speak of societies which are dominated by an egalitarian ideology' (1985: 223) is surely in place. In the case of Israelite society, Lemche claims that 'this would allow for the fact that a society whose ideology is egalitarian need not

13. Later Gottwald modified the term, and instead of egalitarian society spoke of 'communitarian mode of production' (1992).
14. This is not the place to discuss Gottwald's thesis and its critique in detail (some of which will be discussed in Chapter 18); only several points which are relevant for the study of Israel's egalitarian ethos will be discussed here.

in fact be egalitarian' (1985: 223).[15] While the Bible reflects an egalitarian ethos, daily life in Iron Age Israel must have been very different in social terms. Objections were also raised by others; Lenski, for example, while not rejecting Gottwald's idea of 'revolution', adds the concept of 'frontier society'. According to him,

> the interesting thing about frontier societies is that they share many of the social and cultural patterns Gottwald attributes to ancient Israel. All of them exhibit an antagonism toward the traditional centers of power and toward the institutional arrangements that supported those centers. Populist and democratic ideologies developed and often acquired a quasireligious status. Small farms tend to be the rule, especially in the early stages of frontier expansion. (1980: 276)

Moreover, Lenski observes that most such societies had a short life span, and after a while reverted to 'more traditional ways of life, though not entirely' (1980: 276). Gottwald, however, rejects the relevance of this model to ancient Israel. He claims that the frontier in America (one of the examples discussed by Lenski), was one of expansion and that those who expanded exploited the former inhabitants of the new territories in which they settled (1983: 13). If the concept of the frontier is to be of relevance, he argues, then one should find a frontier that produced a revolution. Since this did not happen in America, he believed that the example is irrelevant; after all, in Iron Age Israel we are not witnessing a situation in which the Canaanite city-states colonized and exploited the highlands. Yet in one way or another Lenski's paper remains an important contribution, and the concept of frontier society is widely accepted today in relation to ancient Israel. It is surely also an appropriate context for our egalitarian ideology.

In any event, it is important to emphasize that many did not criticize the existence of such an ethos, even if, like Lenski, they rejected some or most of Gottwald's arguments. Cross, after rebuffing most of Gottwald and Mendenhall's reconstruction, writes: '...on the other hand, there is a strong anti-Canaanite, Patriarchal-egalitarian, anti-feudal polemic in early Israel, which appears to be authentic, grounded in history. The theses of Mendenhall and Gottwald cannot be wholly dismissed' (1988: 62; see also Halpern 1983: 248-49).

Moreover, while Gottwald came to be identified with the attribution of an egalitarian ethos to the Israelites, and there is no doubt that he developed the idea and brought to it new dimensions, we have seen that it has much earlier roots in modern scholarship. Therefore, rejection or refutation of Gottwald's ideas does not necessarily mean the rejection of the idea that the Israelites

---

15.   In fact, Lemche doubts the existence of an egalitarian ideology in Israelite society (1985: 277, 407); see more below.

had an egalitarian/democratic ethos.[16] More general criticism of the notion of an egalitarian ideology in the ancient Near East will be discussed below.

Israel's Egalitarian Ethos: Archaeological Observations
Several archaeologists have identified clear markers of an egalitarian ethos in the material record. Albright writes:

> if we survey the archaeology of the period of the Judges, we cannot help but be struck by the extraordinary simplicity and lack of cultural sophistication which we find in the twelfth and eleventh centuries. The contrast between the well-constructed Canaanite foundations and drainage systems of the thirteenth century and the crude piles of stone, without benefit of drainage, which replace them in the twelfth century, especially in Bethel, can scarcely be exaggerated. (1961: 119)

Albright suggested two reasons for this decline. In the first he claims that the Israelites 'were a wild, semi-nomadic horde'. The second, however, is much more of interest; in it he states: 'the Israelites were in a quasi-democratic, patriarchal stage of clan life…' Kelso also, following the poor character of Iron Age I finds at Bethel, refers to a 'democratic' society (1968: 48). Dever writes about 'an "egalitarian" material culture' (1994: 216), and adds, 'at all levels, however, one is struck by the lack of any evidence for elites in the Iron I villages' (1997c: 80). He concludes, 'there does appear to be a kind of primitive democracy reflected in the settlement and the remains of their material culture' (1992a: 54; see also Dever 2003).

　　While the above quotations clearly indicate that there are enough archaeological data to enable such research, not many archaeological studies have paid attention to these qualities, or developed these lines of research. After all, as Lamberg-Karlovsky claimed, 'archaeologists burdened by their occupational hazard with a materialist bias have too frequently concentrated upon economic forces…' (1985: 23).

Equality and Freedom in the Ancient Near East
The above discussion of Israel's egalitarian ethos was stimulated initially by the evidence for the existence of such an ethos in other ancient Near Eastern societies. The most well-known of these discussions is Jacobsen's paper on 'primitive democracy in ancient Mesopotamia'. Jacobsen writes:

> our material seems to preserve indications that prehistoric Mesopotamia was organized politically along democratic lines, not, as was historic Mesopo-

----

16.　In this sense, Gottwald did the supporters of the idea that ancient Israel had an egalitarian ethos a disservice. By identifying this ethos with his theory, many who rejected his theory—the majority of scholars—came to dislike this part of his thesis too, without necessarily examining it in detail.

tamia, along autocratic. The indications which we have, point to a form of government in which the normal run of public affairs was handled by council of elders but ultimately sovereignty resided in a general assembly comprising all members—or perhaps better, all adult free men—of the community. (1943: 172)

While such discussions have been dismissed as unfounded, they seem to be supported by additional studies. Diakonoff, who discusses the society at Sumer, notes that 'the village and the "nome"—communities had their own organs of self-government—popular Assemblies and Councils of Elders'. He goes on to divide the population of the Sumerian state into three segments: (1) the nobility of the communities; (2) common members of the communities; and (3) clients of various types. According to him the nobility were probably represented in the Council of Elders, while the common members, likely composing at least half of the population, were represented by the Assembly. The Council of the Elders and Assembly continued to play a role even at the time of Hammurabi, 'but now there were no more than organs of the local administration' (1974: 8, 9, 11). He summarizes:

> it seems that in principle the source of authority of the ruler was his election by community organs, though in practice his authority was hereditary. It is possible that the same organs had the right to depose the ruler. As late as in the Enūma Eliš/epic (dating from post-Hammurabian times) which was recited at the temple in connection with the ritual of investment of the king with royal power, the authority of the king of the gods, Marduk, is pictured as emanating from his election by the Council, the functions of the king being clearly defined in terms of real state practice of the II millennium B.C. (leadership of the army, questions of strategy, presiding in the Council, consultation with community organs). (1974: 11)

Humphrey, who discusses the Greek world, also explicitly refers to the fact that some of the important institutions originated in the ancient Near East (1978: 181-82). Lamberg-Karlovsky also refers to a 'social contract' between rulers and ruled, and, like most others scholars discussed above (both in regard to ancient Israel and the ancient Near East), views modern democracies as resulting from a long process whose roots should be sought in the ancient Near East, with ancient Israel playing a special role in the process (1985: 23). He rejects the view of the Mesopotamian kings as 'oriental despot', and stresses that 'in practice royal power was held in check…by an assembly of elders as well as by the priesthood'. He goes on to show that many of the biblical ideas are derived from the ancient Near East (1985: 11). According to him, archaeologists had 'too frequently concentrated upon economic forces' because of their 'materialistic bias'. However, following Habermas, he claims that ' "moral obligations" rather than economic forces have prompted or permitted the successive re-ordering of economic relationships associated with the evolution of civilizations'. Yet not all ancient societies held to these ideas. Lamberg-Karlovsky claims that 'as certain as these concepts are pivotal to Western Civilization, they are foreign to the political ideology of ancient Egypt, China and India' (1985: 23).

That such ideas were important in the ancient Near East seems well established in light of the above (see also Postgate 1992: 80-81; E. Stone 1997), and will be further demonstrated by other archaeological studies to be presented below.

A Note on Egalitarian Behavior and Corporate Rule in Recent Anthropology
Not only are there enough data from the ancient Near East that support the idea that a notion of an egalitarian ethos is realistic, a few anthropologists have recently presented evidence for the wider scope of what can be called 'egalitarian behavior'. Boehm, for example, used a large sample of ethnographic case studies to develop the idea that many simple societies followed what he called a 'reversed dominance hierarchy'.[17] According to his basic formulation, such behavior was typical of small-scale societies, and was 'reversed' to an orthodox hierarchy at some point prior to the emergence of the state (1993: 236-38). Yet it is clear that there are many complex societies also, including modern states, which have an 'egalitarian ideology', an observation noted by some who commented on his paper (Dentan 1993: 241; see also Hill 1993: 242), and seemingly acknowledged by him (Boehm 1993: 246; see more below).

Boehm was followed by Blanton, who developed a model of 'corporate rule'. According to Blanton, there are five elements that promote corporate political economy: assembly government, corporate regulation of sources of power, reflexive communication, ritual sanctification of corporate cognitive code, and semi-autonomy of lower order subsystems (1998: 154-70). Blanton identifies this type of 'corporate rule' in various states and claims that it is an important type of political formulation, while not asserting that *all* states were built along these lines (1998: 160, 171-72). The question of how widespread this type was will be briefly discussed below, but it is clear that, as noted by Blanton, it is not typical of all societies (it did not exist, for example, in ancient Egypt, China, or India; see Lamberg-Karlovsky 1985:

---

17. According to this hierarchy the leaders were led by the public. Boehm in his study 'looks to egalitarian behavior as an instance of domination of leaders by their own followers, who are guided by an ethos that disapproves of hierarchical behavior in general and of bossiness in leaders in particular' (1993: 227). It would also be of interest to compare Boehm's description of the leaders' qualities (1993: 233) with the biblical description of the formation of the monarchy. If the biblical description reflects only later, monarchic traditions, then it would indicate the strength of the discussed ethos even at that period.

23; Blanton 1998: 160). It does seem at this stage that it did exist at least in parts of the ancient Near East in general, and in ancient Israel in particular.

Between Egalitarian Ethos and Egalitarian Practice

An ethos can be referred to as, in the words of Kroeber, 'what would constitute disposition or character in an individual... The ethos includes the direction in which a culture is oriented, the things it aims at, prizes and endorses...' As such, the ethos is similar to systems of values, and it 'deals with qualities that pervade the whole culture' (1948: 294). Following Kroeber, Boehm believes that an ethos 'is directly reflected in idealized statements about how people should or should not behave or be' (1993: 233).

Before developing the discussion any further, we must remember that a differentiation should be made between ethos and practice, or in other words, between social ideology and social reality. While anthropology teaches us that 'equality is a social impossibility' and that 'there is no such thing as a society composed of exactly equal members' (Fried 1967: 27, 28), it is quite clear that some societies are more equal than others, even in actuality. We are reminded of Lemche's remark, mentioned above, which states that in place of egalitarian societies one should think of societies dominated by an egalitarian ideology (1985: 223). Therefore, while some complex societies may either be more egalitarian than others, believe themselves to be relatively egalitarian, or at least have an egalitarian ethos, none can truly be egalitarian. Dentan notes that 'both China and the United States have strongly egalitarian ideologies, Daoist–Maoist and Enlightenment respectively' (1993: 241). Yet indeed, both societies are clearly very hierarchical in reality, irrespective of their egalitarian ethos.

This discrepancy can be observed in the material record. In some very hierarchical societies, for example, simple burials reflect a social ideal of egalitarianism that is not effectively put into practice in everyday life (Metcalf and Huntington 1991: 134; Trigger 1989: 348; Parker Pearson 1982). While this observation is made on a living society, others have explained 'contrasting' archaeological data in a similar vein (e.g. Stein 1994: 39-40; see also Faust 2004a, and references).

Discussion

As we have seen, various scholars have attributed 'democratic' qualities to many ancient societies, including ancient Israel, and some have expanded the idea of corporate rule to refer to many archaic states. This idea was not left without objections. In an important paper on early state formation, Flannery refers to the issue at stake. Following a study of several 'agents' of state formation, he produced 'a list of instructions for creating early states', the tenth strategy of which is to 'solidify your position by power-sharing, even if it is little more than a gesture' (1999: 14, 15). While power-sharing is reminiscent of the ideas discussed above, Flannery's views are quite different. He speaks only of a 'pretence of power-sharing' and adds:

> because power-sharing is present to varying degrees in all states, it is sometimes confused with egalitarian, corporate, or democratic rule. More than half a century ago, Jacobsen (1943) took the existence of a council of elders and a popular assembly to mean that the Sumerian had a 'primitive democracy'. Today we know better. In the words of Diakonoff (1974), Sumerian society was an 'aristocratic oligarchy' in which the king and other oligarchs struggled for supremacy. The Sumerian council, like the council of elders who chose the Aztec *tlatoani*, was composed of aristocrats. The Sumerian Assembly gave commoners a place to complain, but they had no more say in crucial decisions than the commoners who listened to the Merina *kabary*.

Flannery goes on:

> I stress this point because some of my Mesoamerican colleagues are in danger of repeating Jacobsen's error. Scholars like Pasztory (1992) note that some Mesoamerican states, like the Maya, put the names and images of individual rulers—agents—on stone monuments; other states, like Teotihuacan, did not. This dichotomy has led to suggestions that some early states had corporate rule (Blanton et al. 1996) or even 'egalitarian behavior' (Blanton 1998).
>   Lack of individualized monuments, however, does not imply corporate rule. No such monuments were erected by any of our five agents [i.e. the rulers he discussed in his paper], although all were revered posthumously. Among the world's pristine states, many seem more interested in depicting vanquished enemies than in naming their own rulers…. Given how states are forged from chiefdoms, we can be confident that all pristine states were created by strong agents rather than committees. And those agents ruled autocratically— perhaps with councils and assemblies, but certainly not with democracy. (1999: 15)

While Flannery's criticism is compelling, I believe it does not completely refute the abovementioned concepts.[18] First, what was identified above is only an egalitarian or democratic ethos—it is not an egalitarian reality. Flannery's observations reject the idea that egalitarianism, or democracy, was prevalent in archaic societies; it does not negate the existence of such an *ethos*. While, as Flannery showed, the Sumerian were not democratic as Jacobsen had suggested, it is more than likely that they maintained a

---

18.   In addition to the arguments to be listed here, one should also remember that, as we have just seen, Jacobsen's idea is not completely abandoned in Mesopotamian archaeology, in contrast to what might be understood from Flannery (cf. Lamberg-Karlovsky 1985).

democratic ethos (see, e.g., Diakonoff 1974, quoted above). The fact that many scholars used the ethos as an indication of what actually occurred in society is problematic, but discarding the evidence we have for an egalitarian ethos only because it was erroneously used as proof of egalitarian practice is also wrong. As Flannery himself observed, agents who founded states needed support, and they received it partially on a 'pretence of power-sharing'. This pretence directly reflects the discussed ethos, while the ensuing practice, or the ways in which the ethos took form, varies from one culture to another. In the critical period of state formation discussed by Flannery it is more likely that such power-sharing behavior would be more widespread, as rulers would need more legitimacy under such circumstances. This is likely the reason for the pattern observed by him. Whether this behavior would later become an ethos depends on the society's values prior to state formation, as well as the processes which accompanied it; this cannot be determined cross-culturally. The fact that some states did not have such an ethos seems to support the relevance of the data from those who had.

Moreover, as we have seen, an examination of modern democracies can also demonstrate the clear difference between ethos and custom. Flannery's criticism may help clarify the situation in many archaic states, but by no means should it negate the existence of an egalitarian ethos in all of them.

Clearly, some of the discussion of ancient 'democracies' was unfounded, but the evidence does seem to indicate that a sort of democratic, or an egalitarian, ethos existed in many instances. Such may have been minimal, or brief; but to the same degree it could have been deeply rooted in society. And while power may have been in the hands of an autocracy, such an ethos could not have been completely overlooked by rulers and certainly found expression in their mode of rule. My intention is not to oversimplify, or to imply that by this formulation a democratic ethos can be found in each and every society. As has been shown by various scholars mentioned above, many rulers do not even pay lip-service to such concepts, so this idea is by no means universal. For those societies that do have it, it is of utmost importance in understanding their social and ideological life.

In summary, there appear to be several types of societies in regard to the question addressed here. There are those that exhibit no pretence of democracy at all, such as Egypt. The king can have divine status, and the ruler need not even maintain a façade of popular consent. There are those where such consent is necessary, however, and these likely embrace an egalitarian ethos, even if governance is autocratic. And still others may even be relatively democratic or egalitarian in practice, although it is clear that true egalitarian behavior would be much rarer than any society's rhetoric would suggest (and no society would be truly so). It should be stressed that these differences lie along a continuum and cannot be broken down into categories. Yet I believe that, in light of the above, ancient Israel was a society with a clear egalitarian and democratic ethos. Furthermore, for some time this found expression, if only to a relative extent, in its social reality.[19]

The Development and Importance of the Ethos in Ancient Israel

But how did the discussed ethos evolve in ancient Israel? It is likely that part of Israel's egalitarian ethos is derived from the people's ancient Near Eastern roots. There is, however, more to it than this. As we shall see below, ancient Israel evolved from an Iron Age I 'tribal' or 'totemic' society. Such a society is much more egalitarian, usually both in practice and in values, than most other ancient Near Eastern societies where an egalitarian ethos was observed. The reasons why this 'egalitarianism' survived state formation to a larger extent than in other Near Eastern contexts will be discussed below.

Moreover, as we have seen, the highlands of the Iron I can be defined as a 'frontier society' (Lenski 1980; see also Stager 1985c; Dever 1995a: 205; 2003; *contra* Gottwald 1983), and such societies are very likely to develop an egalitarian ethos. Lenski observed that they all exhibit antagonism toward the traditional centers and the institutions that supported them,[20] and that 'populist and democratic ideologies developed and often acquired a quasireligious status' (1980: 275-76). The nature and attributes of a frontier society seem to reinforce the society's ancient Near Eastern heritage and its relative simple social structure, and to enhance the egalitarian ethos of the highland tribal society.

Lenski stressed that frontier societies are temporary, and their egalitarianism changes. He is probably right in this assessment, but to whatever extent changes may occur in society, an ethos could be much more lasting. His case of America, for example, is in my opinion a good illustration of a society where the ethos remained despite the fact that it long ago ceased to be practiced.

---

19. Institutions relevant to the topic seem to have existed well into the period of the monarchy, and several stories indicate more than a mere ethos (e.g. Naboth's vineyard; 1 Kgs 21). However, as already mentioned, a detailed discussion of biblical texts is well beyond the scope of the present chapter.

20. Egalitarianism may indeed be seen as emerging from a dichotomy between the system and the people interacting with it. Rayner observed that 'many egalitarian societies...exist as a consequence of withdrawal from contact with or participation in hierarchical systems' (1993: 245). This observation is relevant for both the 'frontier society model' examined here and the discussion below.

When the totemic/tribal societies of the highlands were forged into 'Israel', the egalitarian ethos became much more important, as it stood in contrast to their highly stratified 'other', whether this be the Philistines or those of the Egyptio-Canaanite city-state system (cf. Rayner 1993: 245; see more below). Moreover, since it is clear that the Philistines played such a significant role in the formation of Israel's identity, negotiations with them would have elevated this ethos to an even more important position in its being contrasted with a foreign (Aegean) society that did not share the Near Eastern egalitarian heritage (cf. Wedde 1995; Crowly 1995). The processes themselves will be discussed later, mainly in Chapters 15, 16, 17, and 21.

Additional support to the notion that this ethos had indeed contrasted with 'non-Israelite' behavior can be seen in Portugali's analysis of the Israelites' terminology of settlement patterns (1999: 70-73). According to this analysis, the Israelites used two sets of terminology for different settlement systems: when they referred to the Philistine–Canaanite system it was described as very hierarchical, while for their own system they used an egalitarian terminology. According to him, Israelite spatial perception reflects 'a collective mental map of a tribal, egalitarian and non-hierarchical society' (1999: 72), a further indication of a contrast between how Israel viewed itself and the Philistine–Canaanite system (see also A. Mazar 1985b: 68; see Chapters 15, 16, and 17).

The above has outlined many past studies that supply a wealth of evidence indicating that the Israelite society was one with an egalitarian ethos. Even if all the textual evidence is no more than 'propaganda',[21] its very existence proves that there was an audience for it. Its purpose as a mere justification or an effort to disguise actuality would still indicate that such a cover-up was needed—that people 'demanded' it. This by itself indicates that an egalitarian ethos of a sort existed in ancient Israel. In Egypt, such propaganda was unnecessary, and no one would have bothered to execute it. There the king was divine, and no human councils or assemblies could challenge that (e.g. Humphrey 1978: 182; Lamberg-Karlovsky 1985: 23; Blanton 1998: 160).

Israelite society was intertwined with a democratic/egalitarian ethos in its being part of the ancient Near East, but in contrast with most other Near East societies, in ancient Israel this ethos played a crucial role in the group's self-identification. Part of this difference can be explained by the fact that the

---

21. It should be noted that most studies of ideology in archaeology have defined the term 'ideology' in a negative manner, usually as a means by which a minority legitimizes its domination over the majority (e.g. Hodder 1982b: 152; Shanks and Tilley 1982; Parker Pearson 1982; see also Miller and Tilley 1984; Giddens 1979, 1984). This need not be the case (e.g. Blanton 1998: 163-64; Scarre 1998: 181-83; Stein 1994: 42), and thus the term is not used in such a way here.

formation process of the Israelite state was secondary, and occurred much faster than 'pristine state formation'; the state and the accompanying social stratification also emerged much more rapidly. This stands in contrast to Mesopotamia, where these processes occurred very slowly, so that the former social structure had completely been altered by the time the full-blown state finally emerged. There a huge parity existed between social reality and social ideology; not so in ancient Israel, where the state emerged when the society was not completely altered. Moreover, in ancient Israel the formation of ethnicity occurred in tandem with, and probably even slightly before, the formation of the state. Elements that were chosen as markers in the process of ethnic formation were present during the state formation process, could impact it, and were thus more likely to survive it. These processes will be revisited in Chapters 15, 16, and 17.

A Comment on the Transition from Reverse Hierarchy to Orthodox Hierarchy and the Data from Ancient Israel

An interesting question discussed by Boehm and others (e.g. Boehm 1993: 236-38; Hill 1993: 242) addresses the nature of the transition from reverse hierarchy to orthodox hierarchy, namely, whether it is consensual and gradual, or conflictive, abrupt, and violent; Boehm in the end leaves the issue open (1993: 240). While this discussion exceeds the scope of the present monograph, it should be noted that in our case the process had indeed resulted from conflict, but with another group, so that internally it should be considered consensual (see Chapter 12). This is yet another reason why the ethos is so important—its continuation due to the various reasons mentioned above made the changes that accompanied the formation of the state and the rise of the orthodox hierarchy appear less severe for members of the group. It is precisely this continuation of the ethos that allowed the process to be so non-conflictive.[22]

Summary

It is clear in light of the above that the Israelite society had a strong egalitarian/democratic ethos, resulting from its location among similarly disposed Near Eastern societies, the specific circumstances through which it evolved, and the fact that it emerged through interaction (and hostility) with other

---

22. This is a point not discussed by Boehm. Initially he refers to incipient chiefdoms and states as hierarchical societies with no such ethos (see 1993: 236, 238, 250). Even later, when agreeing that the states could have such an ethos (p. 246), he refers only to the re-emergence of it—not to its continuation. I believe the present case study can supply additional data that might help address this issue.

groups seen by the Israelites as hierarchical. The egalitarian ethos became for the Israelites an important part of their distinct identity *vis-à-vis* other groups (cf. A.P. Cohen 1985: 33-36). It is even likely that in Israel, more than in many other similar societies, the ethos had some impact on social reality (which still remained, nevertheless, hierarchical). It is also clear that this ethos had an impact on many facets of material culture that were discussed earlier, both during the Iron Age I, when the discrepancy between the ethos and social reality was small, and Iron Age II, when the disparity was great.

It should be stressed that the above constitutes only a preliminary discussion of Israel's egalitarian ethos. A full discussion would exceed the scope of this monograph. Moreover, the subject deserves a discussion in its own right, whereas the present chapter discusses it mainly in relation to its importance for Israelite ethnicity.

Part III

ISRAEL'S IDENTITY AND THE PHILISTINES

12

SETTLEMENT PATTERNS
IN THE IRON AGE I–IRON AGE II TRANSITION

In the previous chapters we have seen that many of the Israelites' ethnic traits and behaviors were meaningful, or could have been meaningful, in the context of the Iron Age I. Moreover, while some of the abovementioned traits may be explained also in relation to other groups, some could only have emerged as a result of interaction with the Philistines.

The following chapters attempt to describe the nature of the interaction between the Israelites and Philistines and the importance of the impact of the latter on the former. The present chapter will tackle the historical and social context that has given rise to the developments of the late twelfth and eleventh centuries BCE.

The Iron I Settlement

As mentioned earlier, during the late thirteenth century BCE and onward hundreds of small settlements were established in the highlands of ancient Israel. Small describes the society which inhabited these settlements as a totemic one, composed of small and equal interacting groups that slowly and gradually became more complex (1997; see Finkelstein 1989; see also Chapter 15). Dever applies Marshal Sahlins' model of the 'domestic mode of production' to this society, and discusses a 'society without a sovereign' (Dever 1995a: 207; Sahlins 1972). These are but representative views on the nature of the Iron I society in the highland in light of archaeological evidence (the social reality of the Iron Age I received a great deal of discussion; see Wilson 1977; Hopkins 1985; Lemche 1985; Stager 1985c; Rogerson 1986). Whatever the origin of this population, an issue of heated debate, there is no doubt that as far as settlement patterns and socioeconomic structure are concerned, the discussed population was very much different from everything else in existence during the Late Bronze Age.[1]

---

1. While there seems to be a consensus regarding this fact (see Finkelstein 1988; Dever 1995a: 208), we should be aware that such differences could be, and have been

However, gradual but significant changes occurred during the latter half of the Iron Age I, mainly in the eleventh–early tenth centuries BCE.[2] These changes were connected with the processes that accompanied the formation of the Israelite state and the growing social complexity that emerged during the second phase of the Iron Age I, and are revealed mainly through a re-examination of settlement patterns. As will be shown later, these processes are of great importance to the study of Israelite ethnicity.

Israelite State Formation and Social Complexity[3]

The re-urbanization and state formation processes that took place in ancient Israel in the Iron Age have been discussed intensively in historical and archaeological research. Much research has dealt with the changes that occurred during the transition from Iron I to Iron II and the establishment of the monarchy and numerous urban centers at the time (see, e.g., de Geus 1988; Finkelstein 1989; Fritz 1996; Dever 1994, 1997a, 1997d).

Due to the inherent 'urban bias' in the field (e.g. London 1989), however, most past studies, although paying much attention to the rural sites of Iron I (roughly twelfth–eleventh centuries BCE), have dealt *exclusively* with urban centers, from the beginning of the re-urbanization in the tenth century onward. They have, therefore, overlooked the fate of the Iron Age I villages, precisely at the time of this growing complexity. In contrast, the present chapter will concentrate on the evidence from the rural sector—a sector that has been usually neglected by traditional 'tell-minded' Syro-Palestinian archaeology (Ahlstrom 1982a: 25; see also London 1989). Through an examination of this sector we shall try to portray the Israelite state formation processes in a new light.

(note, e.g., London 1989) explained as socioeconomic differences between dissimilar components within the same ethnic group, i.e., urban vs. rural (see also Kamp and Yoffee 1980: 87-88). Theoretically, it is therefore possible that the inhabitants of these settlements regarded themselves to be and were seen as Canaanites, i.e., were part of a larger ethnic group (though the Merenptah stela should not be forgotten). The initial stage of this settlement will be discussed later in some detail.

2.   Notably, I follow the traditional chronology, which, despite the challenges (e.g. Finkelstein 1996c, 1998, 2002a), is accepted by the majority of scholars (e.g. A. Mazar 1997, 2001; Zarzeki-Peleg 1997; Ben-Tor and Ben-Ami 1998; Dever 2001; Bunimovitz and Faust 2001; Stager 2003). The exact dating for the discussed processes, as important as it is, is of less importance for the present discussion.

3.   Much of the discussion that follows is an updated summary of Faust 1999a and 2003a. Some issues, such as chronology, are discussed in the earlier studies, and so are not summarized here.

The Accepted View of Tenth-Century BCE Urbanization

According to biblical narrative, at the beginning of the tenth century a united monarchy was established in ancient Israel. Archaeological research has discovered many urban centers erected approximately at the same time, and even if the uniformity of their fortification is no longer accepted (contrary to Yadin 1972; E. Stern 1989; see also Holladay 1995; Barkay 1992), extensive urbanization is still evident. Such is the case at Hazor, Megiddo, Tell el-Farah (N), Shiqmona, Beth-Shemesh, Beersheba, and many others. It is obvious that this stands in contrast to the Iron I, when there were no major urban centers in the highlands, or in the Judean lowlands. Many scholars have attributed this urbanization process to the newly established monarchy (see more below);[4] it is also evidenced by the many innovations in public construction of the tenth century—while only minor changes occurred in domestic architecture (Fritz 1996)—and the significant changes in ceramic tradition (Faust 2002, and references).

Most scholars were of the opinion that, aside from the great rise of urban centers, the general settlement pattern did not change much during the tenth century; these conclusions were based primarily on the interpretation of survey data. They assumed that the villages continued to be the most prevalent form, and that most of the population dwelt at such sites (e.g. Herr 1997: 124; see also Na'aman 1996: 23).[5]

Furthermore, some scholars even believe that settlement in the highland had become so dense that the 'highland frontier' was practically closed (e.g. Stager 1985c; see also Holladay 1995). According to this view, when all the land had been occupied and cultivated, it was impossible to divide the inheritances any further, for such a division would have created plots of land too small to support their owners. The establishment of the monarchy and the accompanying urbanization provided a 'safety valve' for the many of the younger generation that could not inherit. The new opportunities for the young people who moved to the new centers would have existed in areas including military and government service, the priesthood, and likely commerce. It can be assumed that many of the young that did not find much success had to become petty wage workers, and thus constituted the lower

4. Although most scholars accept the historicity of the united monarchy (although not in the scale and form described in the Bible; see Dever 1996; Na'aman 1996; Fritz 1996, and bibliography there), its existence has been questioned by other scholars (see Whitelam 1996b; see also Grabbe 1997, and bibliography there). The scenario described below suggests that some important changes did take place at the time.

5. There seems to be a discrepancy between the results of excavations and surveys. The issue exceeds the scope of the present chapter, but I should note that it is clear that there is a problem in the interpretation of the surveys (for more details, see Faust 2001b, 2003b; Faust and Safrai 2005).

Figure 12.1. *A Table of Iron I Villages Destroyed or Abandoned before the Iron II.*[6]

Site	Location	Dates[7]	References	Comments
Sasa	Upper Galilee	eleventh century	Gal 1993b; Golani and Yogev 1996; but see Stepansky, Segal and Carmi 1996	
Kh. Avot	Upper Galilee	Probably eleventh century	Finkelstein 1998: 105; E. Braun 1993; see also Finkelstein 1998: 101	
Tel Harashim	Upper Galilee	Iron I	Gal 1993c	The Iron I site was abandoned during the Iron I. The Iron II site was founded following an occupational gap.
Karmi'el	Near Karmi'el	Iron Age I	Gal and Shalem 1999	
Tel 'Alil/Ras 'Ali	Lower Galilee	Late thirteenth–late eleventh or early tenth century	Gal 1992a: 94-96, see also pp. 20-21	The site was only surveyed.
The 'Bull Site'	Northern Samaria	First half of twelfth century	A. Mazar 1982a	Probably a cultic site (and not a regular settlement).
Mt Ebal	Samaria	Late thirteenth or early twelfth century to late twelfth or early eleventh century	Zertal 1986–87; see also Finkelstein 1988: 82-85	Probably a cultic site (and not a regular settlement).
Shiloh	Southern Samaria	twelfth century to mid-eleventh century	Finkelstein 1993	
'Izbet Sartah	Western Samaria	Late thirteenth or early twelfth century to early tenth century	Finkelstein 1988: 73-80	

6. For further comments and discussion, see Faust 2003a.

7. Admittedly, the dating of the destruction of some sites is historical or circumstantial (Finkelstein 1988: 68). Still, the pattern is quite clear. For a more detailed discussion, see Faust 2003a.

Site	Region	Date	Reference	Comments
Kh. Raddana	Southern Samaria	Late thirteenth century to mid-eleventh century	Finkelstein 1988: 67-69	
Kh. el-Maqatir	Southern Samaria	twelfth–eleventh centuries	Wood 2001	
'Ai	Southern Samaria	1220–1050 BCE	Finkelstein 1988: 69-72, and additional references	
Tell el-Ful	Southern Samaria	twelfth century?	Finkelstein 1988: 56-60, and additional references	The discussion refers only to the village and not the fort. There is a debate over the dating.
Giloh	Northern Judea	twelfth century	A. Mazar 1981, 1990b	
Kh. Umm et-Tala	Northern Judea	Iron I	Ofer 1990: 200, 202; see also Ofer 1994: 96, 120	
Alon Shevut/ Jebel el-Habun	Northern Judea	eleventh century	Amit 2000	
Tel Masos	Beersheba valley	Late thirteenth–early tenth centuries	Finkelstein 1988: 41-46, and references	
Tel Esdar[8]	Beersheba valley	eleventh–(early) tenth centuries	Kochavi 1969: 45	Finkelstein dates it mainly to the second half of the eleventh century (1996b: 118).
Nahal Yatir	Beersheba valley	eleventh–(early) tenth century	Govrin 1990: 22*	Finkelstein connects it with the Tel Masos Phenomenon (1996b: 118).

8. It should be noted that while the village of Stratum III at Tel Esdar was indeed destroyed in the beginning of the tenth century, there was some occupation (probably a farmstead) at the site during the tenth century, perhaps as part of the 'haserim' phenomenon (Kochavi 1969). This phenomenon relates mainly to the southern coastal plain (Gophna 1963, 1964, 1966, 1970), an area that is not discussed here. Sites which are probably dated to this period also existed in the Negev highland (e.g. Haiman 1994, and bibliography there; for this see also Faust 2003a, forthcoming). All these regions are marginal for the processes discussed here, and their situation might have differed to some extent.

stratum of population in the cities. Needless to say, such a process would have contributed greatly to urbanization.[9] Yet this view also exemplifies the widely held assumption that the tenth century BCE was a period in which rural sites were abundant.

The Rural Sector (Villages) at the Iron I–Iron II Transition[10]

Many Iron I sites were abandoned or destroyed at the end of the Iron I or the beginning of the Iron II (A. Mazar 1985b: 64; 1992b: 301; Dever 1994: 218; 1997d: 182). Various explanations have been given for the process, but most only refer to the local level, as, for example, at the settlement in Giloh (A. Mazar 1994: 89-90) and nearby sites (Ofer 1994: 120), Shiloh (Finkelstein 1988: 68, 232), Raddana (Finkelstein 1988: 68), 'Izbet Sartah (Finkelstein 1988: 80), Tel Masos, and several sites in the Beersheba basin (Herzog 1994: 143-45; see Finkelstein 1996b: 103-26). A relatively broader explanation was given in regard to the abandonment of several sites in the Galilee. According to Gal, these sites were abandoned because fortified settlements became the standard settlement type during the Iron Age II and were established in more appropriate locations (1992a: 94-96). Few scholars, however, have identified the overall pattern of the abandonment process. Dever considered the abandonment process of the Iron I sites as an indication of the urbanization process of the tenth century (1997d: 182; see also 1994: 218), and Mazar simply states that 'many settlements were deserted at the end of the eleventh century and beginning of the tenth century B.C.E.', relating it to the concentration of the population in towns during the period of the monarchy (1990a: 338, see also p. 378).

The abandonment, however, seems to be too extensive to be accounted for by these explanations. *None* of the Iron Age I highland villages excavated so far continued to exist as a rural site in Iron II. Figure 12.1 (above) contains a short list of excavated Iron I sites in the highlands and the Beersheba Valley that were abandoned or destroyed at the time. Due to limitations on

---

9.   It is inappropriate to speak of 'closing the frontier' during this period. The highlands reached a much higher settlement peak in the eighth century BCE (without any technological innovations that could have increased the carrying capacity of the area during this period), but it is questionable if even then we can use that term.

10.   The distinction between rural and urban sites has received a great deal of attention (e.g. Roberts 1996: 15-19; Van de Mieroop 1997: 10-12, and bibliography there). The differences lie in social complexity, stratification, specialization, size, density, and monumental construction. In any event, there is a clear difference between the smallest towns, such as Tell Beit-Mirsim, and villages such as those discussed below (for both the Iron I and Iron II). I therefore believe that the distinction is quite clear and there appears to be a general agreement on the nature of rural sites (mainly villages) discussed here, and the differences between them and their contemporary towns and cities (e.g. Herzog 1992).

space, sites in the northern valleys are only mentioned briefly when relevant, and Philistia, the coastal plain, and Transjordan are not discussed at all.[11]

Only relatively few Iron I sites continued to exist during the Iron Age II, and these usually became cities (e.g. Tell en-Nasbeh, Tell el-Farah [N], Gibeon, Beth-Shemesh, Beersheba, Bethel, and Dan). Cities were also built at Hazor and Tell Beit-Mirsim too, but they were established on pits or tents sites rather than on villages (Finkelstein 1988: 54, 98; Herzog 1992: 232). And while it is possible that not all the sites were already urban centers in the tenth century—the stratigraphy is sometimes very complex—it should be stressed that none, as indicated by the excavations, were a village or a farmstead during this period.

In the northern valleys there are several other, mainly single-occupation, sites that ceased to exist during the Iron I or at the beginning of the Iron II,[12] as at Tell el-Wawiyat (Alpert Nakhai *et al.* 1993), Tel 'Ein Zippori (Dessel 1999), 'Afula (M. Dothan 1955, 1993b) and a site near Tel Menorah (Gal 1979), but their exact nature is unclear and they were probably Canaanite (Gal 1979; see also Dessel 1999; Faust 2000a; and more below). In this context the nearby Iron Age I site at 'Ein Hagit should also be considered (Wolff 1998). The situation in the northern valleys, however, is much more complex; another site, Tel Qiri, shows continuity from the Iron I to Iron II (Ben-Tor and Portugali 1987), and another one (Nir David) was probably established only during the tenth century BCE (Edelstein undated; Levy and Edelstein 1972; see more below).

The overall picture, however, is clear. Most excavated Iron I rural settlements throughout the country, and especially in the highlands, were either abandoned or destroyed before the transition to the Iron Age II, or during the first decades of this period. The relatively few excavated Iron I villages that did not cease to exist turned into central settlements, i.e., towns or cities.

Moreover, an examination of Iron Age II rural settlements (villages and farmsteads) in the Land of Israel, and mainly in highlands, reveals that most were established only during the ninth–seventh centuries BCE.[13] This is the

11.   These regions, especially Transjordan, need further study. This, however, is not only beyond the scope of the present chapter—more data from excavated sites is needed.

12.   Har Adir, another Iron Age site, was excavated in the Upper Galilee (Har Adir 1976; the site was founded in late Iron I, i.e., the late eleventh century, and ceased to exist during the ninth century). Although the site is located in the highlands, it was not discussed along with the highland sites because it is usually agreed that it was a Phoenician fort (see Kochavi 1984: 67-68; Frankel 1994: 32-33; Finkelstein 1988: 107-109).

13.   The only excavated exception is, apparently, the Iron Age II site at Rosh Ha'ayin (Avner-Levy and Torge 1997). There the excavators reported that the first phase of settlement was during the tenth–ninth centuries BCE. It is likely that it was founded only during the ninth century, but even a tenth century date, although slightly earlier, is still in accordance with the rest of the data, and does not point to continuity with the Iron Age I.

case with Kh. Jemein (Dar 1986), Beit Aryeh (Riklin 1997), Kh. Malta
(Covello Paran 1998), Kh. Rosh Zayit (Gal 1992b, 1993a [note that I am
referring to the village and *not* to the fort]), Kh. Jarish (Amit 1991), Kh.
Shilhah (Mazar, Amit, and Ilan 1996), Mevasseret Yerushalayim (Edelstein
and Kislev 1981), the farms in the vicinity of Jerusalem (Maitlis 1989; Faust
1997, 2003c; Mai 1999; Weksler-Bdolah 1999), Mt Hebron (Amit 1992) and
on the western slopes of Samaria (Faust 1995b, 2003c, and bibliography
there; note that their connection with the highland is not clear), as well as the
villages which were discovered below the forts at Arad (Goethert and
Amiran 1996), Kh. Abu et-Twein (A. Mazar 1982b), Kh. el Eid (Baruch
1997) and Kh. Uza (Beit-Arieh and Cresson 1991), and others (Faust 1995a,
and bibliography there). The Boqe'a sites were also established only during
the second half of the Iron Age, but since their rural nature is not entirely
secure they will not be discussed here, although they conform to the
situation at other sites (Stager 1976).

Therefore, it seems that almost no rural settlements dating to the tenth
century BCE have been excavated.[14] The previously dominant form of settlement—small villages—simply ceased to exist. Due to the large number of
sites excavated so far, it is unlikely that future discoveries of tenth-century
rural sites will alter the overall picture. The settlement form that characterized the Iron I (at least in the highlands), and comprised the majority of the
settlement during the later Iron II as well (e.g. Broshi and Finkelstein 1992:
56-57), simply *disappeared* in the tenth century, as far as we can tell from
the archaeological evidence. Only one, unique, rural site that existed in the
highland during this period, Kh. ed-Dawwara, has been excavated so far
(Finkelstein 1990a), but even its rural character is questionable (see Faust
2003a, 2006; see more below).

One should also take into account the fact that the site is located on the edge of the
discussed area, at the meeting point between the coastal plain and Samaria's foothills (not
far from 'Izbet Sartah); the coastal plain is not discussed here.

    14. As mentioned above, at least one rural site in the northern valleys existed during
the tenth century, but it was completely different from the sites discussed here, and
existed outside the core of the Israelite state. Other sites, such as 'Izbet Sartah and Nahal
Yatir were in existence during the tenth century but probably only during its first decades.
It is possible that some other sites were actively settled throughout the tenth century
(such as Kh. ed-Dawwara, see below), but such are exceptions. Note that Hizmi (2004)
reports a tenth-century phase at the village of el-Khirbe. The site, however, lacks clear
stratigraphy, and its existence at the time discussed here is simply speculated on the basis
of some pottery forms common in the tenth century, but not limited to it. The pottery
assigned to this period is therefore not a typical excavated assemblage, but consists of
finds 'artificially' assembled together. In this respect it is more similar to finds from
surveys; on the discrepancy between surveys and excavations, see Faust 2003a; Faust and
Safrai 2005).

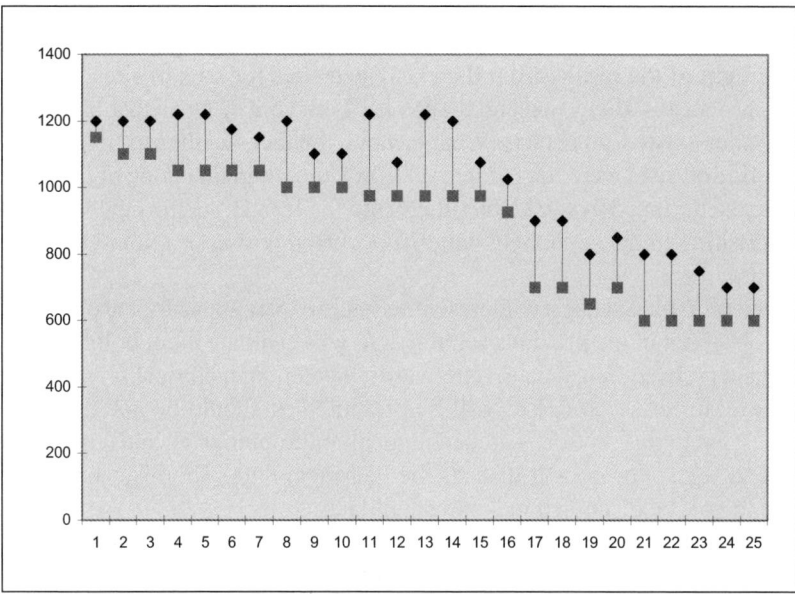

Figure 12.2. *Occupation Period of Selected Rural Iron Age Sites.*
This table represents the occupation period of selected Iron Age rural settlements. Two distinct groups are easily recognized: the first, which includes Iron Age I sites, is concentrated on the left of the table; the second, which includes sites that existed during the ninth–sixth centuries BCE, is concentrated on the right. There is an obvious gap around the tenth century BCE (the unique site of Kh. ed-Dawwara 'fills' some of this gap).

It should be noted that the table is not exhaustive. The represented sites are: 1. The 'Bull Site'; 2. Mt Ebal; 3. Giloh; 4. Kh. Raddana; 5. 'Ai; 6. Shiloh; 7. Tell el-Ful; 8. Kh. Avot; 9. Sasa; 10. Jebel el-Habun; 11. Tel Masos; 12. N. Yatir; 13. Ras 'Ali; 14. 'Izbet Sartah; 15. Tel Esdar; 16. Kh. ed-Dawwara; 17. Kh. Hudash/Beit-Aryeh; 18. Kh. Malta; 19. Kh. Jemein; 20. Kh. Rosh Zayit; 21. Farms at Mt Hebron (at least three sites); 22. Mevasseret Yerushalayim; 23. Farms near Jerusalem (seven sites); 24. Kh. Jarish 25, Kh. Shilhah. As mentioned above, some other Iron I rural sites continued to exist in Iron II as urban settlements; these sites are not represented here, but they seem to correspond with the general picture presented. Other sites, such as Kh. Umm et-Tala, Karmi'el, Kh. el-Maqatir, and Tel Harashim, are also not represented due to imprecise information on the time of their abandonment, but they too correspond to the picture presented above. One rural site in the northern valleys that existed throughout the Iron Age and another that was established at the time (Nir David; see Edelstein, undated; Levy and Edelstein 1972) are the only exceptions in the regions discussed here, and are also not represented. Note that other Iron II sites are grouped together as farms in some regions, and other sites, such as the villages at Arad, Kh. el Eid, Kh. Abu et-Twein, Kh. Uza, the Samaria foothills' farmsteads, and the Boqe'a sites, are not represented.

Possible Explanations

In light of the results from the excavated sites (dozens of sites; villages and farmsteads alike) presented above, I believe it is clear that almost no rural sites existed at the time. What is more, the fact that the vast majority of Iron II rural sites were not located on Iron I sites, and that none of the Iron I villages continued to exist as a village into the Iron II, support the view that major shifts in the settlement patterns occurred during or around the tenth century BCE.

The following section will present possible explanations for the phenomenon observed in the previous section, and will evaluate them in light of the relevant archaeological data. Afterwards, a potential historical scenario that can explain these processes will be presented. It should be noted that the discussion in this section is archaeological-anthropological, and tends not to refer to texts, nor does it discuss the historical data. The historical background will be discussed in some detail later.

Several theoretical explanations can be postulated to a phenomenon in which the rural settlements disappear contemporaneously with the appearance of new urban centers. These include a nomadization of the rural population, immigration to the new urban sites or to areas more attractive due to various incentives, abandonment of the countryside because of security problems, forced settlement, and silting or climatic changes, among others. Methodological problems of the issue will also be considered.

Nomadization

The traditional society in the Near East had the ability to shift from one mode of existence to another rather rapidly in reaction to changing circumstances. It was a dimorphic, or even a polymorphic society, so that factors such as pressure from the authorities or security problems could cause inhabitants to choose a different subsistence strategy. However, while it is theoretically possible that the villagers went through a process of nomadization (for a more general reference to the subject, see Bar-Yosef and Khazanov 1992; see also Lemche 1985: 152-63; Bunimovitz 1994; Finkelstein 1996b: 37-49, and bibliography there), we do not know of any possible reason for such a process in the tenth century BCE. Moreover, such a process would very likely not cause the massive abandonment of villages evident on the archaeological record.

Economic Incentives in Cities or Other Areas

It is also possible that at the beginning of Iron II, following the new state's expansion to the agriculturally and commercially advantageous areas of the lowlands, the inhabitants of the highland villages abandoned their settlements *en masse* and moved to the new areas opened to them (as was suggested for the abandonment of 'Izbet Sartah, for example). However, although such a mechanism could of course operate, it is highly unlikely that nearly *all* the villages were completely abandoned because of the new options in the lowland. The same reason seems to refute any claim that prosperity due to trade or any other economic reason in the new centers attracted the rural population. Regardless, any of these claims, such as the importance of trade in these new centers (cf. Smith-Kipp and Schortman 1989), must be based on convincing evidence, which we do not possess at the moment.

Ecology
Ecological explanations, such as silting, can also be raised (e.g. Demand 1990: 4-5, 171-73, for the Greek world). But even without going into a detailed analysis of the archaeological finds, which it so happens appear not to support explanations such as silting or salting, they could be rejected at the outset for the same reason given above: even if they could explain the abandonment of a given site or even a region, they cannot account for the desertion of so many sites scattered over many regions.

A similar explanation of climatic changes, i.e., less rain, should also be rejected on the same grounds. This is particularly evident when taking into account that some of the new urban centers were probably not located near a good water source, which theoretically could have explained their prosperity. Tell en-Nasbeh, for example, was not located near a major spring (the nearest good water source was half a kilometer away, and perhaps even further if precipitation was lower). Moreover, the results of the archaeological excavation there clearly indicate that the inhabitants depended heavily on *rain* to supply their drinking water, as dozens of cisterns were exposed (see Zorn 1994: 42-43). And, of course, any claim of climatic changes would require evidence (see, e.g., Herzog 1994: 124-26; but see also Finkelstein 1996b: 31-35). Thus, due to the insufficiency of these explanations, an evaluation of the evidence for such a change will not be further developed here.

Methodology
Another possibility is that the explanation has to do with the present state of research. It could be argued that the first phase (tenth century) of rural settlement in the Iron II has not yet been identified because of an unrecognized difference in the nature of finds in the villages as compared to those in the better known contemporary towns. The difference could be connected with the formation processes of rural sites, or with the nature of the finds within them. However, while the poor state of research of the rural sector makes this explanation attractive, it should be remembered that we are not

discussing a 'missing stratum'; since there is no *continuation* between the rural sites of Iron I and II, it is obvious that major changes occurred in the transitional period. Therefore I tend to not accept this explanation.

In this context it could also be argued that the finds reflect a methodology that is selective and biased. That is, because of the great interest of scholars in the Settlement period, the sites that were chosen for excavations were single-occupation sites, in which more extensive exposures of the Iron I horizons could be carried out. Such a selection could easily slant the picture that emerges from excavated sites.

But this explanation is also inadequate. Some Iron I villages were excavated in salvage excavations (such as Karmi'el, Kh. Raddana) and were not hand-picked for excavation. Furthermore, since almost all Iron II sites were dug in salvage excavations, the lack of continuity from Iron I to Iron II villages does indicate that all were established as new settlements on new sites.

Security Problems
Security problems could have motivated villagers to choose a strategy other than nomadization, such as moving into larger centers where they were more secure. A view that emphasized security problems posed by the Philistines as a major factor in the formation of the Israelite state has been popular, but is less fashionable today (e.g. Finkelstein 1989, and bibliography there). However, security problems could, at least theoretically, account for such a process, clarify its extent, and explain why it involved only small sites; in times of instability the smaller sites are much more likely to be affected, while larger settlements had a better chance of survival. Moreover, when populations leave small sites and migrate to larger ones, the latter become better equipped to deal with security issues.

Such has indeed been the explanation for some aspects of the settlement pattern in the Land of Israel in more recent times (e.g. Amiran 1953). In addition, a thorough study by Demand of settlement relocation in the Greek world has demonstrated that no economical or ecological reason can account for the phenomenon, and that only significant external threats lie behind these relocations (1990; see also Marcus and Flannery 1996: 141-43).

As compared to the previous explanations discussed above, this explanation is more convincing. If security problems indeed gradually caused an increased abandonment of the rural sector and led to concentrations of people in larger, semi-urban centers, then they may have also served as another catalyst for urbanization, the formation of the state, and the establishment of the monarchy (see more below). Further, it indicates that the urbanization process started during the late Iron I and continued during the Iron II (the period of the monarchy).

Forced Urbanization or Resettlement

It is also possible that the newly established monarchy employed resettlement or forced settlement. Resettlement has been imposed by central governments throughout history, and all over the world (e.g. Oppenheim 1977: 118; de Montmolin 1987; Patterson 1991: 77-78, 152; Roberts 1996: 112-13; Marcus and Flannery 1996: 139-54; see also Sinopoli 1994: 165; Smith and Montiel 2001: 249). Halpern suggests a similar idea regarding Judah of the eighth century BCE, in what he calls 'Hezekiah's centralized urbanization of the rural population' (1991: 26, 27). Kempinski has made a similar suggestion concerning the Early Bronze Age (1978: 15-16), and more recently Bunimovitz has offered the same suggestion regarding the Philistines in Iron I (Bunimovitz 1998). It should be clear that unlike the previous explanation, which sees the abandonment of sites as a response of local communities to outside threats, the present explanation concerns a coercive act forced upon a rural population (see Demand 1990: 6-7).

Several scholars have tried to explain why various rulers chose forced urbanization for their subjects (de Montmolin 1987: 232-48; Roberts 1996: 112; Smith and Montiel 2001: 249). Some have stressed economic and administrative considerations in noting that forced urbanization lowers costs (de Montmolin 1987: 232-33). Others have emphasized political considerations and observed that a concentrated population helps rulers control their subordinates, and minimizes the efforts involved in delivering sanctions—be it normative, remunerative, or coercive—while maximizing its effectiveness (de Montmolin 1987: 233, 235-36; Smith and Montiel 2001: 249).

Resettlement, which could include the transfer of hostile groups for punitive or security purposes (sometimes over large distances), was also widely practiced (see, e.g., Oded 1979; Patterson 1991: 77-78, 152-53; Small 1997: 279; the issue will be developed below).[15] Resettlement and forced urbanization are both possible explanations for the discussed phenomenon; this is to say that in tandem with the formation of the new state and in order to populate the newly established centers, the state conducted at least a partial forced urbanization or resettlement of parts of the population.

A Possible Scenario

The last two options seem most probable, as they can explain the phenomenon; perhaps a combination of the two is even more accurate. It is possible that security problems resulting from conflicts with other groups instigated a gradual concentration of the population in regional (semi-urban?) centers. As a result, some larger villages were transformed into towns; Tell en-Nasbeh,

---

15. Note that in some cases transferring loyal groups to more secure or more economically sound regions can be seen as a reward.

for example, probably became a center during the eleventh century BCE
(Ahlstrom 1982b: 134), and it seems as if Tell el-Farah (N) went through a
similar process at the same time (Chambon 1993: 439). These developments
may have escalated the process that led to the formation of the state and the
establishment of the monarchy in ancient Israel. Once the monarchy was
established, the process was continued by force.

A diachronic examination of the abandonment process (see Fig. 12.2) on
a regional basis can confirm and even strengthen this scenario (Fig. 12.3). It
appears as if all the sites in the core of the highland were abandoned during
the last decades of the twelfth century (e.g. Giloh, and perhaps also the 'Bull
Site', and Mt Ebal), or, mainly, around the middle of the eleventh century
BCE (e.g. Kh. Raddana, 'Ai, Shiloh, and perhaps Tell el-Ful). Most of the
excavated sites in other areas seem to have been abandoned only later,
during the second half of the eleventh century or even around the year 1000
BCE and slightly afterward (e.g. 'Izbet Sartah, Tel Masos, and nearby sites,
Ras 'Ali, and perhaps Kh. Avot and Tel Harashim).[16]

This spatial division corresponds with the picture presented above.
External pressure on the highland area pushed its inhabitants to leave most
of their settlements and gather in several centers; Tell en-Nasbeh, Tell el
Farah (N), and perhaps Bethel are examples of such centers, although the
evidence in some of the more urban sites is very problematic (see, e.g.,
Finkelstein 1988: 72-73). The concentration of a large population in one place
in resistance to a threat probably caused a sharp increase in the leadership's

    16. As already noted, the situation in the northern valleys is complex. The last Iron I
stratum at Tell el-Wawiyat existed during the eleventh century (Alpert Nakhai *et al.*
1993). It is not clear exactly when the site was abandoned, but it is reasonable to assume
that it happened during the latter part of the century. 'Afula was abandoned, according to
the excavators, around 1025 BCE, perhaps because of Saul's activities (M. Dothan 1955;
note that this dating is dubious). Tel Qiri continued to exist throughout the Iron Age
(Ben-Tor and Portugali 1987). Tel Menorah, on the other hand, was abandoned during
the twelfth century (Gal 1979). Another site, Nir David, was probably founded only
during the tenth century (Edelstein, undated; Levy and Edelstein 1972). This complex
reality indicates that the situation in the valleys was somewhat different. It is possible that
some of the sites were abandoned during the Iron I due to lack of security (perhaps at Tel
Menorah). Other sites, such as Tell el-Wawiyat and 'Afula, were abandoned around or
after 1000 BCE, probably as part of the events and processes that accompanied the incorporation of the area into the Israelite state, as seen at 'Izbet Sartah. The settlement at Tel
Qiri probably reflects some continuity of the local population. The site at Nir David was
likely established due to the relocation of the urban population from sites like Megiddo
(cf. Halpern 2000: 557-61). It seems as if the complex reality in this area should be
attributed to ethnic differences within the area's inhabitants, and between them and the
inhabitants of other regions (Faust 2000a; see more below). It should be noted that the
situation in other regions is not discussed here, but generally seems to correspond with
the presented scenario.

Figure 12.3. *Schematic Map Showing the Two Phases
of Iron I Sites' Abandonment.*

power and a gradual growth in organization and the administration, which eventually led to the formation of a state in the highlands. During this time the inhabitants of the villages in the marginal areas did not abandon their settlements, perhaps because they were farther away from the source of threat, or because they surrendered to it; this is exactly why they were left on the margins of the new state. Only after the state emerged at the beginning of the tenth century BCE and after its subsequent expansion to these regions were these sites abandoned as well. This possibly occurred in part because better areas were open to their inhabitants in the adjacent lowland (e.g. perhaps in the case of 'Izbet Sartah), and also, if not mainly, because of forced settlement into the new cities or other regions (probably at Ras 'Ali and Tel Masos; see also Faust forthcoming). Other sites were perhaps destroyed in the events that accompanied the expansion of the state.

If the suggested scenario is correct, then it is necessary to re-examine the weight of each of the factors which influenced the establishment of the monarchy and the formation of the Israelite state (e.g. Finkelstein 1989), with perhaps a little more importance attached to the issue of conflict with other groups. It is not necessary, of course, to claim that all the sites were destroyed or abandoned as part of this scenario; some, particularly the earlier ones, could have ceased to exist because of local events or other causes, as discussed above. The general picture, however, supports this reconstruction, and we shall develop it later.

Summary of Archaeological Evidence

Several conclusions can be drawn on the basis of the archaeological evidence presented. One, during the eleventh and beginning of the tenth centuries BCE a major change in the settlement pattern occurred. Almost all the excavated rural sites so characteristic of the Iron I ceased to exist during this time period. Two, this process occurred in two stages, lasting about 100 years. The first took place mainly during the first half of the eleventh century BCE, and the second during the first decades of the tenth century BCE (see Fig. 12.2). Three, the two stages took place in different areas (Fig. 12.3). The first phase of the abandonment process occurred in the core of the highland, namely Benjamin, Samaria, and perhaps northern Judea, while the second phase took place in the remainder of the country, namely the Negev, the Galilee, and even the western slopes of Samaria. And four, during the tenth century BCE a major process of urbanization occurred in ancient Israel, which began mainly simultaneously with the second phase of the countryside abandonment.

Based on this evidence, I believe the abovementioned first phase—during which most of the central highlands sites were abandoned and the population started to concentrate in urban centers—constitutes a state formation process (see more discussion below). This process lasted through much of the eleventh century BCE, mainly unfolding in its second half. The second phase, which took place during the first decades of the tenth century BCE, was accompanied by significant urbanization, which can partially be seen as 'forced settlement' carried out by the newly established state (see more below).

The Formation of the Israelite State

On the basis of the data presented above, I have outlined a scenario that could explain the observed phenomenon. The present section aims to develop this scenario in light of the archaeological record, the anthropological literature and, to some extent, the historical data.

A full discussion of secondary state formation is beyond the scope of the present chapter (see, e.g., Carneiro 1970; Renfrew 1972; Cohen and Service 1978; Claessen and Skalnik 1978; Marcus and Flannery 1996; and Flannery 1999). It should be noted, however, that in secondary state formation there is always much involvement of outside factors. According to Price, a secondary state is created when 'an existing state, pristine or secondary, expands into areas inhabited by populations not heretofore state-organized'.[17] She continues:

> Two sub-types, which are more correctly regarded as poles of a continuum, may be distinguished: one involved direct pressure in the form of political incorporation of a massive economic takeover and control—a relatively overt colonialism. The other involves more indirect modification by irrevocable alteration of the socioeconomic environment, thereby creating conditions for the transformation of the infrastructure and institutional arrangement of the target area. (1978: 161)

Two approaches, integration vs. conflict, have dominated the research, but today it is clear to most scholars that each 'has some validity' (R. Cohen 1978b: 7; see, for early Israel, Finkelstein 1989; Dever 1994: 219).

The processes that preceded and accompanied the establishment of the Israelite state have been discussed intensively in biblical, historical, and archaeological research (e.g. Frick 1985; Hauer 1986; Whitelam 1986; Dever 1994; Finkelstein 1989, and bibliography there; see also below). In the past, following the description in the Bible, most scholars were of the opinion that

---

17. According to Price, the term 'secondary state formation' might also imply a situation when a state is formed 'via historical succession from a preexisting state' (1978: 161). For my purposes, however, this is irrelevant.

the monarchy, i.e., statehood, developed as a response to the Philistine threat (see the summary in Finkelstein 1989). This view was modified lately, mainly during the 1980s, by many scholars who considered the biblical narrative to be too simplistic, and, of course, problematic as a historical source. They considered various other explanations in light of anthropological literature, and tended to stress internal rather than external causes, or to combine the two (see, e.g., Gottwald 1979; Chaney 1986; Hauer 1986; Whitelam 1986; for a summary of the various opinions, see Finkelstein 1989; Dever 1994: 220-21; Faust 2003a). The evidence presented above on the countryside abandonment during the second half of the Iron I indicates, however, that the weight of the various factors should be re-evaluated.

In her study of similar settlement processes in the ancient Greek world, Demand stresses that such processes never occur because of environmental, agricultural, or economical reasons (1990). For her, the cause for the concentrating of populations into large settlements and complete abandonment of previous sites (or the countryside, as in the present case) is always a strong external threat (Demand 1990: 166-67; see also Marcus and Flannery 1996: 141, who discuss a similar situation). Even if an external threat may not be the only explanation for such processes, Demand's study establishes that it is likely an important one.

Since the archaeological evidence indicates that the process of abandonment of small sites and concentration into larger ones started sometime before the establishment of the monarchy, perhaps at around 1100–1050 BCE if we consider the various evidence,[18] then we must acknowledge that the external threat was an important factor in the processes that preceded the formation of the state. It seems that, while the existence of a minimal level of complexity of the economic and social structure was necessary for this process to begin (otherwise the area under discussion would simply have been colonized; see Carneiro 1970), the external threat played a crucial role. From the middle of the Iron I, the conflict between various groups—probably beyond that of the Israelites and Philistines and including perhaps Canaanites, Ammonites, and others (some of whom probably went through the same process at about the same time), led to a gradual concentration of populations in the highland centers, and to the creation of a stronger leadership; this was probably followed by a more sophisticated and advanced administration. In this respect it is important to note that urban relocation is likely to create an environment in which intellectual life flourishes (Demand 1990: 3; Marcus and Flannery 1996: 158). Economic growth and prosperity were to a large extent a result of the process, and not its catalyst (Demand 1990: 169).

18.   The dating is, in many cases, problematic, but the overall picture is quite clear (see, e.g., Faust 2003a: 153).

Yet this is not to suggest that an external threat was the only reason for state formation. As already mentioned, a certain degree of social organization was necessary to respond to the threat, and the processes that subsequently formed the state were to a large extent internal. However, the archaeological evidence indicates that the formation of the state was accompanied by clear changes in the settlement pattern (for the importance of this class of data, see Price 1978: 165; Finkelstein 1989), which could probably result *only* from an external threat. Therefore it played a crucial, though not exclusive, role in the process.[19]

The Land of Benjamin: Architecture and Resistance

The core of the abovementioned process seems to have taken place in southern Samaria, just north of Jerusalem (in the biblical 'land of Benjamin'). This is attested not only by the concentration of large sites in this region, but also from the fact that the first Iron Age fortifications in the highlands were found there. Both these and the finds in some of the sites mentioned above can indicate the importance of the region for this process (for a more detailed discussion, see Faust 2006).

Kh. ed-Dawwara

The massive fortifications erected at the site during the late Iron I have received a great deal of scholarly attention. In analyzing the architecture of the site, Finkelstein wrote, 'this makes the Khirbet ed-Dawwara fortifications the earliest example of a developed Iron Age defense system in the hill country, and therefore the earliest full-scale Israelite fortification' (1990a: 196-97). Moreover, according to Finkelstein, 'Khirbet ed-Dawwara provides the only solid evidence for public building activity in the early monarchic period' (1990a: 197). Fritz too, when discussing the forms of settlements and the urbanization processes of the Iron Age, mentioned the site after his discussion of the Iron Age I and just before the discussion of 'the first cities during Iron Age II'. According to him,

> toward the end of the eleventh century, encircling walls which provide protection...are met for the first time in Khirbet ed-Dawwara... But these enclosures were by no means city walls: although built for protection they lack the strength of a real fortification. They certainly mark a step in the direction of the fortified city even though they are only enclosed settlements that lack all other characteristics of urban culture. (1994: 235)

Thus there should be no doubt that this is an important site.

19. As proposed above, the newly established state continued the process through forced settlement. This phase, however, does not concern us here (see Faust 2003a; forthcoming).

But why was such a small and isolated site the first to develop fortifications? Finkelstein, who excavated the site and identified its significance, suggested possible explanations for its importance (1990a: 201-205). He claimed that three factors make the site important for analysis: 'its architectural uniqueness, its location and its date' (p. 201). Its architectural uniqueness is clear, its location on the desert fringe is indeed puzzling, and its date —the eleventh–tenth centuries—is very important: Finkelstein connected it with the biblical texts regarding the late eleventh-century BCE events as described in (parts of) 1 Samuel 7–13. I would also like to stress an additional aspect which should be noted regarding the site's date: it prospers precisely when all small and rural sites were destroyed or abandoned. This, along with the lack of silos, sickle blades, etc. (pp. 196, 202) is indeed unique, and Finkelstein correctly questioned the rural nature of the site (p. 202). He raised several possible explanations, but concluded that the only plausible (though problematic) one is that the site was established as an Israelite center during the struggle with the Philistines, which, according to him, 'would explain the location of the site in this isolated place, and the need for such massive fortification' (p. 202). It also explains the site's date (p. 203) and the nature of the finds, specifically the lack of significant evidence for agriculture, which stands in contrast to all nearby sites, such as Raddanah (Cooley 1997: 402) and 'Ai (Callaway 1993: 45). Finkelstein even raised the possibility that the site should be identified with the Gilgal, though he left a question mark on the issue of identification (1990a: 203-205).

Whether the site is connected with biblical traditions or not, it is emphasized that the first massively fortified settlement in the highland (of the late eleventh century BCE) was built in the land of Benjamin on a site that was probably not agricultural.

Tell el-Ful

Whatever the exact date of the village excavated at the site (see above, Fig. 12.1), there is a near consensus regarding the existence of a fort (or a monumental building) of some nature at Tell el-Ful during the late eleventh century BCE (Finkelstein [1988: 60] being a notable exception). Forts do not seem to be abundant in the Iron Age I, and the fact that likely the only one of this kind is found here might indicate the importance of the region, even without going into its historical reconstructions, which are abundant in the research literature on this fort (see, e.g., Finkelstein 1988: 57; Graham 1981a, 1981b). It is, in any event, one of the earliest 'true' fortifications in the central highland—perhaps the earliest that is squared in form.

Gibeon

The situation here is somewhat problematic, but it is likely that here too there were some major public structures during the Iron I. Pritchard writes, 'during the early part of the Iron Age, a massive city wall was built…and the great pool was cut into the rock' (1993: 513).[20] Without going into the question of whether the site was Israelite or Gibeonite (the latter of which requires giving much weight to the biblical evidence), and while remembering that precise dating is problematic,[21] the mere existence of such structures is an indication for the importance of the site during the Iron Age I, and to the relatively complex society which inhabited it at such an early stage.

Discussion

While reconstructions regarding the specific historical background behind any of the above are important, they do not concern us here. Essential to our discussion is the overall archaeological picture. All of the above findings indicate that the land of Benjamin appears to have had the most elaborate and complex social structure in the highland during the eleventh century BCE, particularly its latter part.[22] This is matched by the existence of quite a few central sites in this small region—to the above-listed sites are joined Tell en-Nasbeh and Bethel. This density of sites is another indication of the centrality and importance of this area for the state formation process

20. In the report, Pritchard usually attributes the wall to the twelfth century, but mentions 'a possible overlap into the 11th century' (1964: 39, see also p. 35). It is likely, however, that an exact dating within the Iron I is impossible.

21. The report received severe criticism (e.g. Parr 1966; P.W. Lapp 1968). While much of the criticism appears to be founded, it is important to note that the dating of the Iron I wall seems to be one of the elements which is less dubious (e.g. Lapp 1968: 393). For a critical view of this dating, see, e.g., Albright 1966: 33. Note, however, that ironically, Albright's critique is based only on historical assumptions and not on archaeological reasoning. Since Albright is frequently quoted by later scholars in this regard, it should be noted that his doubts are based on the fact that the period of the Judges is not suitable for such fortifications, while Pritchard's dating is based on pottery (1993: 513). It seems, therefore, that the original dating cannot be so easily overruled. It has been accepted by various scholars, including A. Mazar (1981: 16-17) and B. Mazar (1981: 76); see also Finkelstein 1988: 61, 261, where he basically accepts the data, and his reservations are based only on the limited scope of excavations. The issue deserves further discussion that is beyond the scope of the present monograph.

22. While the history of Jerusalem per se is irrelevant for the present discussion, due to Jerusalem's proximity to the area of Benjamin, a word on the archaeological finds there is in order. Although there is a fierce debate about the nature of the finds in Jerusalem and its dating, there seems to be a consensus regarding the existence at the time of a structure of monumental character—the so-called 'stepped stone structure'. According to some the entire structure existed at the time (Cahill 1998, 2003), while others (e.g. Steiner 1998) date only the unique terraces (the lower part of the monumental structure) to this period. Recently, E. Mazar evacuated a monumental structure in in the City of David, which she dates to the tenth century (E. Mazar 2006), but which was, in my view, erected during the Iron Age I. In any event, it is clear that monumental construction existed at Jerusalem at the time, and this data seems to correspond with that of nearby Benjamin.

(discussed above; note that it is unlikely that this is only a result of biased research).

All of this might indicate that the society in this region was more complex (compare, e.g., the process decribed in Finkelstein 1989), and in view of the mechanism discussed above, it is likely that the state formation process was also more advanced here, or in other words, that this area was the 'core' of the process.[23]

The central position of this region should come as no surprise. Quite clearly, it is a result of a combination of social and geographic factors. The Philistines were the major entity in the region at that time (e.g. Hauer 1986: 9; see also Stager 1995; the issue will be discussed in detail in Chapter 14), and were probably the external threat mentioned above. While the Judean hill country is much closer to Philistia than that of Benjamin, it is clear that it was not densely settled then (Finkelstein 1994, 1996d: 236; Ofer 1994: 107). Moreover, its dispersed and limited population, whose social structure was much less complex than nearby regions, could not have resisted the Philistine threat, and the region was probably 'colonized', i.e., absorbed into the Philistine (economic?) realm.[24] Therefore, the Land of Benjamin was the nearest, significantly populated part of the hill country to Philistia; it also had better ecological conditions. The Philistine impact was thus felt most strongly here, which in turn had an impact on the centralization process.[25] This is precisely the region where 'resistance' is expected.

23. Although the question of the relationship of the biblical traditions with the archaeological finds is not of direct importance to the present study, a few words on the subject are in order. It should be noted that the nature of the processes discussed here does not allow them to be closely related to the events described in 1–2 Samuel and 1 Kings. Moreover, it is possible that even the nature of the texts themselves does not permit using them to reconstruct the events that preceded the establishment of the monarchy (e.g. Edelman 1997). Rather, only general processes described in the Bible can be examined against the archaeological finds. In the Bible, the state formation processes are described as taking place during the second half of the eleventh century BCE in the central highland. This temporal and spatial description is supported by the abandonment process of the small villages and hamlets and the concentration of population in larger sites as described above. This was to a large extent a result of conflict with other groups, and this information too, correlates with the biblical traditions regarding the confrontations with the Philistines. The formation of the state was accompanied by its expansion to other regions of the country, as can be seen by the expansion of the abandonment process. Therefore, the biblical description concerning the time, place, and to a certain degree, even the motives for the processes discussed seems to be, to some extent, matched by the archaeological finds.

24. Cf. Judah's position on the Philistines in the Samson stories (e.g. Judg. 15.9-13).

25. As we shall see below (Chapter 19), hardly any Philistine pottery was found in the highlands. It is interesting, therefore, that the majority of the Philistine pottery found was discovered in the Benjamin region. This seems to indicate that the 'main' interaction with the Philistines took place here.

The Philistine Threat

Let us now summarize the several lines of evidence, some circumstantial and some direct, that indicate that the Philistine were responsible for all the above. First, the Philistines were the major power in the region at the time, and they are the only real power that could have initiated the process (Hauer 1986; Stager 1995, 1998; see more below, Chapter 14). Second, the fact that it is in Benjamin that the process was most advanced strengthens the Philistine connection, as this is the populated region of the highland nearest to Philistia. If the threat was posed by a force in the northern valleys, for example, then we would have expected the process to have been manifested in northern Samaria. And third, the biblical narratives, whose core description regarding the processes leading to the formation of the state seems to be substantiated by this scenario, pinpoint the Philistines. Since the 'grand narrative' seems to reflect historical memory, it is likely that this detail is correct too.[26] Furthermore, it should be emphasized that all of these are in accordance with the importance of the Philistines regarding many of the traits discussed in Chapters 4–11; that all of these distinct lines of enquiry point in the same direction strengthens the overall argument that the Philistines were the external threat responsible for the processes of abandonment and state formation.

Summary

During the tenth century BCE there appears to have been a gap in rural settlement in the highlands of Israel.[27] Iron I villages were already deserted when the first Iron II villages came to be established, usually on other sites. While some tenth-century rural sites may be discovered in the future, it is extremely unlikely, in light of the large number of sites excavated so far, that such finds will alter this picture. Several possible explanations have been proposed for the phenomenon, but only two seem to be probable: the existence of security problems which caused abandonment and destruction of many villages during the latter half of Iron I, or forced settlement by the newly established monarchy.

26.   See above for the 'grand narrative' of the formation of the monarchy; see also Chapter 10 on the likelihood of a historical basis to some of the stories referring to the Iron Age I. In any event, while the presented scenario can be supported by the texts, it is not dependent upon them.

27.   It is interesting and important to note that while on the one hand there is no continuation between Iron I and Iron II villages on the site level, on the other there seem to be large similarities between the forms of the villages. This fact indicates strong cultural continuities, and that both groups of villages belonged to the same society.

A combination of the two factors is most likely. A lack of security, probably as a result of Philistine activity, would have caused a gradual concentration of the rural population in regional centers in the highlands, and eventually would have led to the establishment of cities. This process probably played an important role in the formation of the Israelite state that occurred at the same time in the highlands, and might demonstrate the importance of security problems in state formation processes. After its establishment, the monarchy (the 'state') continued the process of population concentration by force.

This is the background for the processes that took place during the eleventh–early tenth century (possibly beginning as early as the late twelfth century). The importance of these processes and particularly Israelite–Philistine relations for the study of ethnicity will be discussed in the following chapters.

13

ETHNICITY AND STATEHOOD IN ANCIENT ISRAEL

In the previous chapter I analyzed the processes that preceded and accompanied the formation of the Israelite state. These processes also form part of the socio-historical background for the emergence and formation of Israelite ethnicity, the theme of this section of the book. This is the place, therefore, for a brief discussion on the relations between ethnicity and state. This discussion will explain how the data from the previous chapter can fit into a systematic study of Israelite ethnicity even though it did not touch upon it, thus putting it in its relevant context. It should be stressed that the discussion here is partial, and relates only to the impact of states on ethnicity. The reality prior to this impact, and how the changes occurred, will be discussed only in Chapter 15.

Ethnicity and States

Many scholars have stressed that ethnicity is closely related to statehood, as was touched upon earlier (Chapter 2). Emberling claims that 'ethnic groups are not states but exist in some relationship with them' (1997: 304) and he mentions the connection between processes of ethnogenesis and state formation and control (1997: 308; see also Patterson 1991: 31). For example, ethnic identity can develop when an area inhabited by an independent group or groups is incorporated into or conquered by a state. Shennan also refers to these relations, and believes that 'several arguments can be advanced in favour of the view that it [ethnicity] is indeed a product of the appearance of states' (1989: 15). Further, in summarizing his discussion of 'ethnicity and archaeology', he writes: 'in other words...ethnicity as defined above... does not exist outside the orbit of early states' (1989: 16-17).

While there seems to be a near consensus regarding the close relationship of ethnicity and statehood, the relations can take one of two forms: ethnicity as a form of resistance, and ethnicity as a direct product of state activity.[1]

---

1. The issue of ethnicity in pristine states is interesting, but irrelevant for the present discussion, since, as we have seen, Iron Age Israel involved only secondary state formation. Forms of pre-ethnic identities will be discussed later in the book.

Ethnicity as a Form of Resistance

Emberling mentions that ethnic identity often develops when independent groups are encompassed by a state; the emergence of ethnicity can therefore be seen 'as a form of resistance' (1997: 308). Wiessner, too, believes that circumstances that might activate group identity include fear, competition or aggression among groups, need for cooperation, and imposed political control that necessitates 'group action' (1990: 109). Most of these, particularly the latter, can be seen as a form of group resistance from outside control. According to A.S. Smith, 'ethnicism is fundamentally defensive. It is a response to outside threats and divisions within' (1986: 55; see also pp. 38-39, 54-57). Defining oneself in resistance of pressure from the outside is therefore clearly a major mechanism of ethnogenesis.

Ethnicity as a Direct Product of State Activity

It is also true that states can actively encourage and develop the formation of ethnic groups. We have seen in Chapter 2 that ethnicity equals, in many instances, hierarchy or asymmetrical relations. It should be noted, therefore, that in some cases 'the ascription of ethnic identity to a particular group of people...has, in itself, been a major mechanism of political control' used by the state (Ucko 1988: xi). In the Inca state,

> the state crystallized ethnicity and formed new collective identities that reified and distorted old cultural patterns to provide the illusion of continuity of old institutions and practices in new contexts. The ethnic groups were territorially based and organized. Their vertical integration emphasized shared cultural features and the linkages between them and the emerging class structure of the imperial state. (Patterson 1991: 79)

And Comaroff and Comaroff concluded that for a subordinate group, ethnic association could have originated by an ascription of collective identity by others.[2] The following quotation is also revealing:

> Betsileo have not always shared...consciousness of themselves as a distinct ethnic unit. Prior to their conquest by the Merina, there appear to have been no Betsileo. Rather, there were several statelets and chiefdoms located in different parts of what is now the Betsileo homeland. Their conquerors... created the Betsileo province of the Merina state...and in so doing, provided the basis for Betsileo consciousness to develop through the present. (Kottak 1980: 4-5, quoted by Comaroff and Comaroff 1992: 57)

---

2.   It should be noted that while colonialism had indeed shaped the identity of many groups, ethnic identity is not a product of the modern world and of colonialism. This can clearly be seen by the following examples by Comaroff and Comaroff (e.g. 1992: 57) as well as by Smith (1986: 41), and many others.

Comaroff and Comaroff therefore summarized: 'ethnic consciousness, it seems, has increased throughout Malagasy as a function of political consolidation' (1992: 57). Thus it is clear that the attribution of ethnic affiliation on behalf of others (a state or a dominant group) is also a major mechanism of self-definition. (This can be seen in the creation of most modern states in Africa; see Comaroff and Comaroff 1992.)

The two mechanisms of resistance and state activity are by no means contradictory and can very well operate together, as can clearly be seen from the above quotation referring to the situation in Malagasy. A similar situation was also observed by Patterson: 'at one level this cultural transformation may involve hybridization, fusion, or even replacement by state-imposed forms; at another, it may manifest itself in resistance or attempts to assert or invert tradition' (1991: 31). The activity of a central government can both 'impose' an identity on a group of people, even if they did not have this identity before, and also promote the emergence of an identity as a form of resistance to its activities; these could very well be the 'same' identity. The two processes can at times be one.

We are left to conclude that ethnicity results, one way or the other, from statehood. This is not to say that a certain group must live within the physical boundaries of a state in order to have ethnic identity. It must, however, exist within the orbit of a state.

Ethnicity and Statehood in Ancient Israel

The abovementioned types of relations between states and ethnicity accord well with the processes described in the previous chapter. Though states existed earlier, at the time discussed here the Israelites were under strong pressure from the Philistine state or states, and were therefore inside 'the orbit of early states' (Shennan 1989: 17). It is very likely, in light of the above, that such an interaction would result in ethnic consciousness. Moreover, the entire process of village abandonment and population concentration in larger settlements was in fact the formation process of the Israelite state itself (see above; see also Faust 1999a, 2003a).

It is for this reason that any claim that the Israelite ethnicity could not have been established prior to the Iron II should be rejected. Small, in his most insightful study, 'Group Identification and Ethnicity in the Construction of the Early State of Israel—from the Outside Looking In', has indeed claimed that ethnicity requires asymmetrical relations, but that such relations did not exist prior to the establishment of the monarchy (1997: 272). This issue will be discussed in detail in Chapter 15, but it should be stressed here that while it is likely that Small is correct regarding the importance of asymmetrical relations, it seems that such relations *did* exist prior to the Iron II, and the abovementioned process of abandonment exemplifies it quite clearly.

The late twelfth- and mainly the eleventh-century timespan appears to be a suitable background for the appearance of the Israelites as an ethnic group, as we know them in the Iron Age II. Moreover, as discussed above, the relocation processes created, in many cases, 'environments in which intellectual life flourished' (Demand 1990: 3; see also Marcus and Flannery 1996: 158). This process inevitably led to a clarification or at least a creation of self-identification. No more were there small isolated villages with little connection and self-awareness within the larger group, but rather there existed a large group of villages or towns facing an external threat from what would be, at least from now on, another group.

When there is interaction and/or competition between groups, each will find ways to demarcate its boundaries more clearly. Whether the villagers discussed here had an ethnic consciousness earlier or not, they *must* have developed one when facing another group on such terms.[3] The external threat created a dichotomy of 'we' as opposed to 'them', therefore defining the sense of togetherness ('we-ness'), so necessary for the formation and existence of ethnic groups. The inhabitants of the settlements discussed here had to develop some sort of common ground that united them against those who threatened them.

It is recalled that ethnic identity is also manifested archaeologically, either by ethnic markers or through the pattern created by ethnically specific behavior. The development of the traits described above—dietary customs, a limited ceramic repertoire, a lack of decoration and imports, architecture, and the egalitarian ethos (the latter responsible for many of the former)—should therefore be seen in light of this process. We have seen that these traits have resulted, or at least could have resulted, from an interaction with the Philistines, who, as we have seen, appear to have been the outside pressure that caused the Israelite to resist and to form an ethnic identity. It is therefore appropriate at this point to have a closer look at the Philistines.

3.   Or, as sometimes happens, became part of the dominant 'ethnos'.

14

THE PHILISTINES IN THE IRON AGE I

The previous chapters discussed the formation of the Israelite state (Chapter 12), and the relationship between states and ethnicity (Chapter 13). We have seen that the Israelite state was formed to a large extent as a result of a threat from the Philistines, a very dominant group whose pressure forced the population of the highland to develop a larger and eventually more sophisticated socio-political organization, in order to cope with the threat. One of the inevitable outcomes of such resistance was the development of a sense of togetherness, in opposition to the enemy, the 'other'. The present chapter aims to give a short background on this group, the Philistines.

Background

The Philistines arrived at Israel's southern coastal plain during the twelfth century BCE, most probably during its first half (e.g. Dothan 1982; Dothan and Dothan 1992; Stager 1995; 1998: 152-71; Yasur-Landau 2003; note that the exact date is currently debated; see Finkelstein 1995a, 2000; and then A. Mazar 1997; Bunimovitz and Faust 2001). It is also clear, based on both archaeological and textual evidence, that the Philistines arrived from somewhere around the Aegean world (though the exact place of origin is debated; see T. Dothan 1982; Stager 1995, 1998; Singer 1988b, and references).[1]

It seems as if soon after their arrival, the Philistines expanded their territory, and were the dominant group in the southern coastal plain (see Fig. 14.1 [next page]). They occupied very large cities, which seem to exhibit a high level of urbanism, as well as social complexity and hierarchy (e.g. Stager 1995; 1998: 166-68; Bunimovitz 1990). The high level of socio-political complexity of these newcomers can be seen through various lines of evidence, both the archaeological record and written sources, and there seems

---

1. Note that a small minority of scholars view the Philistines as a social phenomenon connected with trade, rather than a group of immigrants (e.g. Sherratt 1998; Bauer 1998). This view, however, is disregarded by the vast majority of scholars (see recently Barako 2000), and need not be addressed here.

Figure 14.1. *Schematic Map of Philistia in the Iron Age I.*
Phase 1 corresponds with the initial phase of the Philistine Settlement in Canaan
(the 'monochrome phase'), while Phase 2 corresponds to their expansion in the
later phases of the Iron Age I (the 'bichrome phase').

to be a consensus that the Philistines were probably the most complex society during the Iron Age I (e.g. Hauer 1986: 9; Singer 1994: 299; Finkelstein 1996d: 236; Stager 1998: 168; see more below).

The Archaeological Evidence

This is not the place to go into a detailed or stratigraphical discussion of the finds from the various sites; a short summary will suffice, as the archaeological evidence regarding Philistine society's complexity seems quite straightforward.

The Iron Age I is usually regarded as a period of urban decline, and this for most parts of the region. The highlands, for example, were practically devoid of any genuine large-scale settlement, or any indication of true social or economic hierarchy (see above; note that this stands in contrast to earlier periods; see, e.g., the Early Bronze or Middle Bronze Ages in the same region).[2] Urban decline occurred also in the northern valleys, which in earlier periods were the most urbanized part of ancient Israel (on these fluctuations, see, e.g., A. Mazar 1992b: 296-97; Finkelstein 1999). While Egyptian hegemony and presence did continue into the beginning of the Iron Age I, it disappeared in the later parts of this period, and the archaeological evidence indicates partial decline in urbanism and social complexity.

The circumstances on the southern coastal plain, however, were radically different. Here we see a significant concentration of populations in urban centers. The major cities that are known archaeologically are Miqne (biblical Ekron), Ashkelon, and Ashdod, and to a lesser extent also Tel Zafit (Tell es-Safi, biblical Gath).[3] These were accompanied by several smaller sites, such as Tel Qasile. The findings from some of these sites can demonstrate their importance.

Urbanization
The Philistine cities were large and prosperous during the Iron Age I. According to Stager, Ashkelon in the late twelfth century BCE had expanded

---

2. The only exception to such seems to be Gibeon (Pritchard 1964; see the discussion in Chapter 12). Even if this site, however, did show a certain degree of urbanism, it is not comparable by any means to that of the southern coastal plain (the other two sites discussed in Chapter 12 are both extremely small and cannot be regarded as urban centers, and they also date only to the end of the Iron Age I, the late eleventh century BCE).

3. The excavations at Tel Zafit are only in their early stages. It should be noted that the discovery of *in situ* Iron Age I finds in the lower tel (Maeir 2001: 113) seems to indicate that the Iron I settlement was extremely large (more below). The situation at the last of the 'pentapolis' cities, Gaza, is less clear; it is, and probably will continue to be, a mystery from an archaeological perspective.

to urban proportions, with finds including fortifications such as a mud-brick tower protected by a glacis. Stager adds, 'The fortification continued in use throughout the Iron Age II, and protected a Philistine seaport, not of 15 a. as Garstang suggested, but of 150 a. [app. 600 dunams]' (1993: 107). Dothan and Gitin had a similar view of Ekron; according to them, the Iron Age I city covered the entire site, reaching approximately 200 dunams (1993: 1054). Stager also believes that from its establishment as a Philistine city, Ekron was a large and planned city, which had a line of fortification, an industrial zone, private dwellings and, in the center, a public building including a temple-palace complex (1998: 166). As for biblical Gath, the new expedition to Tel Zafit, combining excavations and a sophisticated, detailed survey concluded that the Iron Age I site was 230 dunams large (Uziel 2003: 42, 62). Signs of advanced town-planning and complexity were also found at other sites, such as Tel Qasile (A. Mazar 1980, 1985a).

The Philistine urban centers were therefore the largest in the region at the time. Stager summarizes: 'Ashkelon, like Miqne/Ekron and Ashdod, was a large heavily fortified Philistine city' (1993: 107). The large size of these sites, their public structures and fortifications, clearly indicate social complexity, particularly in comparison to other parts of the country, mainly the highlands, where, as we have seen, small sites of only a few dunams were the norm.

Settlement Hierarchy
This complexity can also be evidenced by the existence of a developed settlement hierarchy (Finkelstein 1996d). The large urban centers mentioned above were accompanied by a number of smaller ones, as had been demonstrated by Finkelstein's (1996d) study of the Philistine countryside. It should be noted that the number of small sites is relatively small, but there is a marked contrast between them and the large urban centers on which they were probably dependent (for an implication of this 'hierarchy' on other realms of life, see Chapter 11).

Demography
Finally, one must remember that Philistia was much more densely populated than the highlands (Finkelstein 1996d: 236; Stager 1998: 163; especially in comparison with Judah). While we do not believe we are (yet?) in a position of being able to count an ancient population, the following figures are very instructive at least on a comparative level. Stager estimated the total occupied area of the Philistine pentapolis to be at least 1000 dunams, with the total population as approximately 25,000 (1998: 163). Finkelstein reached a slightly different figure of c. 30,000 people in the Iron Age I (1996d: 235-36), then went on to compare this figure with his estimation of the

situation in the Judean hills. Even with all the possible reservations regarding demographic studies, the comparison is striking.[4] According to Finkelstein, the built-up area in the Judean hills was only about 110 dunams, and he estimated the population to be some 2200 people (1996d: 236).

All in all, the archaeological record clearly indicates that the Philistines were the most dominant power in the Iron Age I, as suggested by so many scholars.

The Textual Description

This is not the place to go into a detailed discussion of the textual evidence regarding the structure of Philistine society; such an exercise has been done many times in the past and there is nothing new we can add to it, and in any event, these texts are not our main source of information.[5] Moreover, the archaeological evidence described above seems sufficient to establish the Philistine dominance. The following is, therefore, an extremely short summary of previous historical research on Philistine society.

The Philistines are known from several Egyptian sources, but their value for the present discussion is limited (see, e.g., T. Dothan 1982: 1-13). We know that they arrived as immigrants by way of the sea and land (T. Dothan 1982; Stager 1995, 1998; see also Yasur-Landau 2003; Barako 2003; Sweeney and Yasur-Landau 1999). Their description in the Bible is much more detailed (e.g. T. Dothan 1982: 13-23; Machinist 2000), and includes a mention of their foreign origin (e.g. Amos 9.7; Jer. 47.4). Their political organization was composed of several major cities (the abovementioned pentapolis), ruled by *seranim* (T. Dothan 1982: 17-19; Machinist 2000: 57-59), and they are described as dominating the Iron Age I scene for several generations (e.g. T. Dothan 1982: 15).

Their overall superiority over the Israelites, in light of the Bible, is summarized by Machinist:

> overall, the Bible leaves an unmistakable impression of the military prowess the Philistines were able to exercise. Especially in 1 Sam, we watch them moving inexorably over the Palestinian landscape, with only occasional setbacks (1 Sam 7, 14, 17). This movement is framed symmetrically between two great peaks of victory over the Israelite forces, in 1 Sam 4 and 29/31... In the biblical view...only with David and his assumption of Kingship was this movement decisively stopped and turned back (2 Sam 5:17-25; 8:1, 11-12/1 Chr

---

4. This is not the place to discuss the figures and the methods by which they were reached. My aim in mentioning this material is to give some sort of comparison between Philistia and the highlands.

5. Note, however, that it is likely that some of the stories are quite old, as we have seen in Chapter 10.

18:1, 11; 2 Sam 19:10). David's willingness, in turn, to incorporate visible
units of these Philistines…into his own army…was both a mark of his decisive
defeat of them and yet also his testimony to their prowess… (2000: 59)[6]

The Philistines as the Major Force in Iron Age I Israel

While not identical, the archaeological evidence seems to be matched by the
basic relevant statements of the biblical narrative, which indicate that the
Philistines were the most advanced and well-organized group in Canaan at
the time.

Although much of the Philistines' socio-economic reality and political
organization during both the Iron I and II has yet to be studied, we have seen
some clear archaeological indications for the advanced and complex level of
organization of the Philistine cities during the Iron Age I. The above archaeological as well as textual data indicate quite plainly that the Philistines were
the major power in the region during the Iron Age I; this has been echoed in
the words of practically every scholar who has studied the archaeological
finds of the Iron Age I.

Finkelstein, for example, wrote the following: 'archaeology indicates,
therefore, that the Philistines, as an urban society, had both the technological
and demographic edge over the people of the highlands' (1996d: 236). The
same idea is expressed in Singer's words: 'the cities of the Philistine rulers
were the largest and richest in Palestine during the Iron Age. Merely comparing them to the small, poor Israelite settlements of the early Iron Age will
give an accurate picture of the balance of forces in the country during the
period under discussion' (1994: 299).[7] Stager's words express a similar sen-
timent: 'one need only compare the large, cosmopolitan cities of the plain
and their rich, fertile countryside to the impoverished villages of the hills
and their tiny tract of arable land to appreciate the advantages in wealth and
power that the Philistines had over the Israelites' (1998: 168).

Various ideas were raised as to the reason for the Philistines' interest in
the highlands, such as economic prosperity and the agricultural surpluses
there (Chaney 1986; Finkelstein 1989, and additional references). The exact
reasons, however, are not important; rather significant here is that the
Philistines are seen as the main element of the 'external threat' mentioned in
Chapter 12.

---

6.   Some additional elements will be discussed in the next chapter. Also, note that
according to some scholars, the Philistines had a monopoly over iron production, which
added to their superiority (e.g. T. Dothan 1982: 20); this view, however, is not usually
accepted today.

7.   Singer rightly points out that the only cities during the Iron Age that were even
larger were Jerusalem and Samaria. These, however, reached their large size hundreds of
years later.

Philistine Relations with their Neighbors

From their arrival, the Philistines appear to have been involved in hostile relations with their neighbors. This can be seen from the time of their initial settlement in Canaan, in their relations with the Egyptians and Canaanites, and in the absence of Philistine Myc. IIIC1 (henceforth monochrome) pottery at Egyptian–Canaanite centers of the twelfth century BCE. This last piece of evidence has been used by some as an indication of chronological separation (e.g. Finkelstein 1995a, 2000), i.e., that the sites where no monochrome was found ceased to exist prior to the use of this pottery; but this idea is very problematic. It is sufficient to say here that such an hypothesis would require us to accept that the entire northern Shephelah was abandoned precisely during the monochrome phase, as no such pottery was found not only at Lachish, but also at Beth-Shemesh, Gezer, and Tel Batash; however, this abandonment has not left a trace, as no one has identified it in the archaeological record (including Finkelstein himself; see Finkelstein 1996d: 233; 2000: 171).

Elsewhere Bunimovitz and I have attempted to explain the absence of monochrome as resulting from the nature of the relations between the Philistines and the Egyptians and Canaanites (2001); the tension and competition that characterized this relationship resulted in a pattern in which members of both groups exhibited their group affiliation by avoiding symbols of the 'other', and hence the absence of monochrome Philistine pottery in many sites. The issue will be discussed in more detail in Chapter 19; here it can be said that it seems that a somewhat similar, even if not identical, pattern continued throughout the Iron Age I, including the use of the later Philistine bichrome pottery, which is practically absent in the highland (and even from one quarter of Tel Qasile; for a fuller discussion see Bunimovitz and Faust 2001, In prep.; Finkelstein 2002a; see also Chapter 19).

Given that background, it is quite clear that the Philistines' hostility was directed not only at Egyptian–Canaanite centers; their relations with the highlanders, although established only later, were also on similar terms. Some archaeological aspects of the relations between Israelites and Philistines have been discussed; here I would like to supply additional textual data that support the view that the relationship was basically hostile.

The texts clearly portray the Philistines as the primary group with which the Israelites dealt. According to Gitin, 'the Philistines were portrayed in the Iron Age I and for much of the Iron Age II as the Israelites' principal "other" or main antagonist, both in military and cultic terms' (1998: 162; see also Dothan and Cohn 1994; Machinist 2000: 67-69). Gitin states that out of 919 biblical references to Israel's foes, 423 (46%) refer to the Philistines, 273 (30%) to Egypt, 164 (18%) to the Trans-Jordanian peoples of Ammon,

Moab, and Edom, along with 'Amalek, and 59 (6%) to the Phoenician cities of Tyre and Sidon. 'In the Bible', says Gitin, 'Philistia is clearly considered ancient Israel's most significant enemy' (1998: 163 n. 4). It is interesting that 76% (320) of the references to the Philistines, Philistia, and its cities are related to the Iron Age I, while only 24% (103) to the Iron II, mainly during the Neo-Assyrian period (Gitin 1998: 162 n. 2), therefore indicating the importance of the Philistines as Israel's main enemy at the time.[8]

A Note on the Philistines in the Iron Age II

The present chapter deals with the Iron Age I only, but a few words regarding the Philistines in the Iron Age II are in order. As we have already seen, the Philistine culture went through drastic changes during the Iron Age II, to such an extent that in the past most scholars spoke of their assimilation, as mentioned above (e.g. T. Dothan 1982: 296; A. Mazar 1986; Bunimovitz 1990; Dothan and Dothan 1992: 85-86). However, as is becoming clearer and clearer, the Philistines kept their identity throughout the period (Kempinsky 1986, 1987; Eph'al 1997). The process by which they ceased to produce bichrome pottery (and probably started to circumcise, among other customs) should be therefore viewed as acculturation, rather than assimilation (following B.J. Stone 1995; see also Maeir forthcoming, who preferred the term 'creolization').

Summary

The archaeological evidence, in accordance with the written sources, seems to indicate that the Philistines were the most complex society during the Iron Age I. Both archaeological finds and texts also give a clear impression that they were the Israelites' main enemy. Thus it is quite clear that the Philistines were the 'external threat' discussed in Chapter 12, and a force in relation to which the Israelites defined themselves. This accords well with the fact that at least some of the traits discussed in Chapters 4–11 could have developed only as part of the interaction with the Philistines. It is time to examine in detail the latter's impact on Israel's identity.

---

8.   And this division tends to give the texts more credibility (cf. Chapter 10).

15

TOTEMISM TO ETHNICITY:
THE PHILISTINES AND ISRAEL'S SELF-IDENTIFICATION

The Philistine Impact on Israelite Identity: A Review

As we have seen in previous chapters, the Philistines were socially, politically, and economically the most advanced group in the Iron I. Interaction and competition with them forced the Israelites to define (or redefine) themselves in an effort at maintaining a clear ethnic boundary between them. Their efforts were materialized on a number of fronts.

The avoidance of pork can be seen as resulting directly from this interaction, and, for reasons given above, could be dated only to the Iron I. Though pigs are also absent from twelfth-century contexts (e.g. at Mt Ebal), it is probable that this pre-existing behavior was canonized due to the interaction with the Philistines.

Circumcision too was most probably practiced by the highland population, as well as by other ancient Near Eastern groups, prior to their contact with the Philistines. It is quite clear, however, that this behavior was canonized as an ethnic marker only in relation to the Philistines, and only in the Iron Age I (the late twelfth or eleventh centuries seems most appropriate for it).

Since the Philistines used elaborately decorated pottery, which, based on other considerations, was indeed ethnically and symbolically meaningful, both in the eyes of the Philistines and of the Canaanites and Egyptians (Bunimovitz and Faust 2001; see also Chapter 19), the Israelites not only avoided their pottery, but also set themselves apart by not decorating pottery at all.[1] It is likely that this phenomenon of lack of decoration existed already earlier, perhaps due to functional/technical reasons (but see below). But from this point forward it became canonized and was strictly obeyed.

---

1. The absence of Philistine pottery in many highland settlement villages is usually regarded as a result of lack of interaction (e.g. Finkelstein 1988: 59-60, 322-23; Bunimovitz and Finkelstein 1993: 162, where it is also discussed as a chronological indicator). It is more likely that its absence was part of boundary maintenance (see Chapter 19).

The four-room house is, seemingly, a result of Israelite behavior. Though the house can be found in earlier contexts, it was finally crystallized only during the late twelfth and, mainly, the eleventh centuries BCE (the process continuing into the Iron II), probably as a result of the formation of Israelite ethnicity at this time. This specific trait cannot be *directly* connected with the Philistines, but its dating to the Iron I strengthens the idea that Israel's ethnogenesis occurred then. The exact reasons behind the four-room house are of less importance for the present discussion (see above), but it seems as if, at least partially, it is a result of egalitarian ideology.

The same ideology is probably also responsible for the limited ceramic repertoire of the Israelites, and its roots seem to lie at the earlier stages of Iron I. As for the absence of imported pottery, it also could have resulted from the Israelite ethnic definition formed at the same time. It can be suggested that the Israelites avoided Philistine pottery, and as part of their self-definition decided to avoid all kinds of foreign pottery as well. This, however, was incorporated into, and justified by, a larger worldview.[2]

It is quite clear then that the Philistines are directly responsible for at least some of the Israelites' ethnic markers and behaviors, such as the avoidance of pork and the practice of circumcision, and that they were canonized as part of the interaction that took place in the late twelfth–eleventh centuries BCE. Moreover, it is more than probable that the Philistines had an impact on the configuration of additional markers or elements of behaviors, e.g., the lack of decoration and the avoidance of imported pottery, although the latter might have a more complex history (see Chapter 16). With this we have arrived at a partial answer for one of the main questions of this monograph, namely, when Israel emerged. But I would like to stress the fact that some of these traits/behaviors were practiced prior to the arrival of the Philistines, the interaction with whom, in many instances, caused only the canonization of existing practices.

It appears, in light of the above, that the interaction with the Philistines— a process that was finalized in the late eleventh century—was responsible for many facets of Israel's emerging identity. The Philistines seem to have been the anvil on which Israel's identity was forged.

There remain two additional questions: What was the reality in the highland prior to the settlers' interaction there with the Philistines? And what were the processes by which certain existing traits were chosen and invested with additional meaning?

---

2.   As we shall see below, however, although it is possible that the interaction with the Philistines strengthened the significance of this trait, it is more likely that it was meaningful even earlier, as a result of interaction with a Late Bronze Age culture or cultures.

Symmetrical Relations and Totemism:
The Highland Society Prior to the Interaction with the Philistines

While the importance and interrelation of statehood and ethnicity are well known and have received attention here, we have seen that not much is known on the situation that preceded the emergence of ethnic conscience. Emberling, after evaluating various evidence for the emergence of ethnicity in tandem with or prior to that of states, writes: 'to some extent, however, this is an empiric question: the nature of prestate social boundaries is not well understood' (1997: 308). And, in the words of A. Smith: 'the origins of ethnic differentiation itself are shrouded in obscurity…' (1986: 41). I believe that the Iron I case study is sufficiently detailed, and can therefore contribute to these neglected aspects of research into the question of identity. Thus we may set out in attempting to define the identity of the inhabitants of the tiny highland villages of the Iron I before they were transformed into an ethnic entity.

It seems that part of the analysis of ethnicity by Comaroff and Comaroff (1992), and especially the distinction there between ethnicity and totemism, can shed more light on this process. They claim that, while past groups had some kind of self-identification, this is not always the same as an ethnic identity (p. 51). They differentiate between totemic conscience and ethnic conscience (e.g. pp. 51-52). Totemism, according to them, 'emerges with the establishment of symmetrical relations between structurally similar social groupings—groupings which may or may not come to be integrated into one political community' (p. 54). Ethnicity, in contrast, 'has its origins in the asymmetric incorporation of structurally dissimilar grouping into a single political economy'. They continue,

> more specifically, totemic consciousness arises with the interaction of social units that retain—or appear from within to retain—control over the means of their own production and reproduction. It is, in short, a function of processes in which autonomous groupings enter into relations of equivalence or complementary interdependence and, in so doing, fashion their collective identities by contrast to one another. (pp. 54-55)

According to Comaroff and Comaroff, ethnicity has two main qualities: (1) a subjective classification of the world into social entities; and (2) a stereotypical attribution of these groupings, usually in a hierarchical way, into niches in the social division of labor (p. 52). Neither of these qualities is unique to ethnic conscience. The first exists in totemism, while the latter in class. It is, however, the combination of the two where the uniqueness of ethnicity lies. They add that for the subordinate group, ethnic affiliation may be ascribed to them by others (p. 53). At times, the creation of such identities has no foundation in pre-existing sociological reality, but even when a

social identity had been assigned to them, subordinate groups usually clas-
sify their 'new' identity as a symbol of common predicament and interest,
and they 'may begin to assert a shared commitment to an order of symbols
and meanings and, sometimes, a moral code' (p. 53). They also note that
in many cases the different parties tend to negate the humanity of the other
group, and summarize the point with the claim that ethnic identity leads to
both the assertion of the 'collective self' and the denial of the 'collective
other' (p. 53).

It should be stressed that the difference between totemic conscience and
ethnic conscience is not a chronological or an evolutionary one. There were
ethnic groups in pre-colonial Africa, and totemism exists in the modern
world. The difference lies in the context; in other words, the division of 'we'
vs. 'them' is primordial—and only the form of the division depends on the
historical context (Comaroff and Comaroff 1992: 54). According to Comaroff and Comaroff, 'contrary to the tendency, in the Weberian tradition, to
view it as a function of primordial ties, ethnicity always has its genesis in
specific historical forces, forces which are simultaneously structural and
cultural' (p. 50). It exists when there is inequality between groups (pp. 52-
55).

Despite the differences, however, ethnicity and totemism share many qualities. Both are, in the words of Comaroff and Comaroff, 'modes of social
classifications and social consciousness, markers of identity and collective
relations' (p. 53). We should therefore stress that the dichotomy between
totemism and ethnicity, as important an analytical tool as it is, is somewhat
misleading. After all, we are dealing with a continuum, and there might be
cases when it will be difficult to ascribe such a title to a certain group.
Moreover, it is likely that the development process from one to another is
not linear, i.e., not a one-directional evolutionary process (this issue will be
developed further in Chapter 17).

From Totemism to Ethnicity

And how does this information contribute to our understanding of Israel's
ethnicity? It is likely that the inhabitants of twelfth-century villages were not
all members of a single group, but had more then one identity.[3] This is based
on both the lack of hierarchical relations between these villages (Small 1997;
see more below) and the impression one receives from the, albeit problematic, written sources. Most, if not all, of these identities should probably
be regarded more as totemic identities than as ethnic ones, or at least nearer

---

3. Note that this is a near consensus; see also Chapter 3, and a more detailed discussion in Chapter 22.

to the totemic pole of the continuum, as quite obvious from the nature of the small and isolated villages themselves, a topic discussed in detail above. Their inter-village relations seem to have been symmetrical, and it is unlikely that the villages where at the time under strong pressure, politically or economically, from any other 'more complex' group, which could have been reason for them to develop an ethnic identity. The Canaanite city-states were vanishing; the Egyptians, though still in control of parts of the lowland, were not in a position to make incursions into the highlands, something which they did not often do even in the Late Bronze Age; and the Philistines, who had indeed arrived already in the first half of the twelfth century, took some time to sever the '*cordon sanitaire*' and begin their expansion (Stager 1995: 344). All of the above gives good indication that the identity of the inhabitants of these villages was relatively a totemic one. It is clear that one of the highland groups was called 'Israel', as can be seen by an independent contemporary source, the Merenptah stele, which will be discussed in detail later.

Slowly, with the advent of the Iron Age I, two related processes occurred. The highland economy developed. Surpluses were traded between different villages and regions, perhaps even outside of the highland (Finkelstein 1989). This allowed the inhabitants of different villages to get to know each other, something that, in the end, made it possible for them to develop a shared identity. At the same time, the Philistines had consolidated their power, and began their incursions into the highlands. It is most likely that these incursions were spurred by economic incentives, namely, the above-mentioned surpluses (e.g. Chaney 1986; Finkelstein 1989). These, and the incorporation of the local economy into a larger network including the lowland, gradually changed the nature of the relations the highlanders experienced from symmetrical relations (among themselves) to assymetrical relations (with the Philistines).

It is likely that the Philistines' treatment towards the highlanders spurred the latter to amalgamate into one group. It is common for a dominant group to relate to all 'others' as one, usually in a denigrating way. Roosens, for example, observed that the groups he studied 'disappeared' in a city environment. The local urban population treated all of them, undifferentiated, as primitives: 'anyone from Central Kwaango who moved into Kinshasa in the 1960s was classified by the city dwellers as a Muyaka. In Kinshasa, the term "Muyaka" sounded like an insult: it carried the connotation of being under-developed, being a peasant, a rural primitive, and so on... The urban population did not make the subtle distinction between Luunda and non-Luunda.' This had an impact on people's behavior. According to Roosens, in the city members of the weaker group tended to behave in a way that made them 'ethnically invisible', and, when outside their familiar surroundings, they preferred to speak a version of the local language even among themselves (1995: 123; see also Comaroff and Comaroff 1992: 53, 57).

While the situation in the Iron I was by no means identical to this, it can be supposed that the Philistines treated all of highlanders in the same disparaging manner, viewing them as backwards, paltry, or primitive, with no care taken to notice their internal distinctions. The actual cultural differences between the Philistines and all highlanders, reflections of which are seen in customs such as circumcision and pork avoidance, made the above distinction between them and the Philistines all the more apparent. This, as we have already seen in Chapters 2 and 13, is precisely the context for the development of ethnic identity as resistance. As Wiessner claims, 'situations that switch on group identity include fear, inter-group competition and aggression, need for cooperation to reach certain goals, and imposed political control, requiring group action' (1990: 109). Small, too, mentions the impact of the state (1997: 279-81), and claims that, in many instances, states created ethnicities.

This is where we close the circle opened in Chapter 13. The totemic groups of the twelfth century have achieved an ethnic identity, the most appropriate time for which seems to be the eleventh century BCE. This is precisely the 'historical context' mentioned by Comaroff and Comaroff (1992).[4] Now we shall examine some of the details of this process, in order to see how the traits identified as ethnic markers or behaviors were chosen to be such.

The Choosing of Traits: Habitus *and Ethnicity*

In our attempt to establish how the 'Israelite' traits and behaviors were chosen by the highland population, we are reminded that most were chosen because they contrasted the behavior of other groups, particularly the Philistines. We have seen that some of these traits (e.g. pork avoidance, circumcision) were likely practiced by the highland totemic groups prior to interaction with the Philistines, but in their contrasting the Philistines' behavior they were given additional importance at the time when the highlanders defined their identity in relation to them.

In the present section of the chapter, the mechanisms by which such traits were chosen and transformed will be discussed. This is a complex issue, which has not received a great deal of attention in past studies. The key concept for the present analysis is Bourdieu's *habitus* (1977) and its application to archaeology of ethnicity (e.g. Jones 1997). According to Bourdieu,

---

4.   Note that this section has discussed only the processes in the late twelfth–eleventh centuries BCE; the thirteenth–late twelfth-century context will be dealt with in Chapters 16 and 17.

> The structures constitutive of a particular type of environment (e.g. the mate-
> rial conditions of existence characteristic of a class condition) produce *habitus*,
> systems of durable, transposable *dispositions*, structured structures predisposed
> to function as structuring structures, that is, as principles of the generation and
> structuring of practices and representations which can be objectively 'regu-
> lated' and 'regular' without in any way being the product of obedience to
> rules. (1977: 72)

According to Jary and Jary, the *habitus* is made of a set of 'classificatory
schemes' and 'ultimate values'. These are the means by which groups man-
age, or fail, to impose on their members perspectives that are advantageous
to them (1995: 275). According to Shenan, the *habitus* is, unconsciously,
what individuals learn to do and think from birth onwards, merely by virtue
of their having been brought up in one place rather than another (1989: 20).

Jones understands Bourdieu's *habitus* to be made up of 'durable dispositions toward certain perceptions and practices, which becomes part of an
individual's sense of self at an early age, and which can be transposed from
one context to another...the *habitus* involves a process of socialization
whereby new experiences are structured in accordance with the structures
produced by past experiences...' (1997: 88).

The *habitus* generates response and action. It is not static. It is dependant
on the practices of human agents, who reproduce and transform the condi-
tion which constitutes it, and thus it entails social changes through continued
alterations in its structured dispositions (Jones 1997: 89; cf. Giddens's
'structuration theory' (1984); see also Jary and Jary 1995: 662-64).

Jones builds on Bourdieu's *habitus*. According to her,

> sensations of ethnic affinity are based on the recognition...of similar habitual
> dispositions which are embodied in the cultural practices and social relations
> in which people are engaged. Such structural dispositions provide the basis
> for the perceptions of ethnic similarity and difference when people from
> diverse cultural traditions come into interaction with one another, leading to
> forms of self-reflexive cultural comparison. It is in such contexts that particu-
> lar cultural practices and beliefs, which to some extent embody the underly-
> ing structures of the *habitus*, becomes objectified and rationalized in the
> representation of ethnic difference. Ethnicity is not a direct reflection of
> *habitus*, or of culture. The construction of ethnicity...is a product of the inter-
> section of people's habitual dispositions with the concrete social conditions
> characterizing any given historical situation. (1997: 120)

According to Shenan (1989: 20; see also Jones 1997: 122), the *habitus* provides the resources for ethnic identity and for the 'emblemic' and 'assertive'
usage of style. That is, the *habitus* is not synonymous with ethnicity, but is,
in a sense, the tool-kit from which ethnicity chooses its traits.

Similarly, Jones accepts that some traits of material culture may be chosen to transmit ethnicity, while others will cross-cut ethnic boundaries (see Chapter 2). However, she claims that the traits which are chosen are *not* chosen arbitrarily, but are linked to the *habitus,* and in many cases to cultural practices and differentiation within the group (1997: 120-21, and references). In referring to style, she claims that

> the way in which particular styles of material culture are meaningfully involved in the articulation of ethnicity may be arbitrary across cultures, but it is not random within a particular socio-historical context. Ethnic symbolism is generated…from the existing cultural practices…characterizing various social domains, such as gender and status differentiation, or the organization of space within households. (p. 125)

According to her, ethnicity results from the intersection of similarities and differences in peoples' *habitus* within any given historical context (p. 126). After stressing the importance of an historical approach and a broad study of social organization (see also Chapter 1), she claims that an examination of diachronic processes within a particular historical context will enable researchers to identify the changes of habitual aspects into active and conscious ethnic symbolism (p. 126).

Yet, one must remember that the *habitus* cannot be the only source for ethnic symbols. These may be forced upon a group, and thus could not have been necessarily connected to the *habitus* (although their development later requires more attention). Symbols may also be chosen merely in contrast to those of other groups. These may come from within the group, and could therefore be connected to the *habitus*, but it is likely that such is not always the case. In any event, the *habitus* is quite probably the *major* channel for the developing of ethnic traits and behaviors.

In this light, we can see not only why the abovementioned symbols or behavior were chosen—namely, for their being in contrast to those of the Philistines—but also *how*. It is very likely, as already ascertained above, that pork avoidance was well established prior to the Iron Age among certain groups. It is also likely that the population from which the Israelites evolved (and most probably those mentioned in the Merenptah stele) practiced circumcision prior to the arrival of the Philistines, or that this society was quite egalitarian, and so on. The traits which would later come to demarcate the ethnic boundaries with the Philistines, should be understood as having been selected from the pre-existing *habitus* of the highlanders.

It was the contact with the Philistine 'state' (or 'states') that promoted the emergence of ethnicity, and made certain traits more relevant than others. Various elements that were part and parcel of the highlanders' *habitus* and daily life stood now in sharp contrast to the Philistines' way of life, and were therefore redefined and invested with additional meaning. While the pig taboo and circumcision are clear examples, it is also likely that the absence of pottery decoration, the avoidance of imported pottery, and the limited ceramic repertoire also came to have new meaning and were redefined at the time the highland population faced the Philistines, for whom all of these traits had in some way an important place in their social and symbolic life.

Summary

It is likely that the early Iron Age villagers, on the eve of the Philistine's expansion into the highlands during the late twelfth and the eleventh centuries BCE, did not have direct contact with a complex polity, and exhibited symmetrical relations (among themselves). Consequently, we can assume the highlanders possessed a kind of totemic conscience. 'Israel' was probably the name of one or several of these groups, as is witnessed by the Merenptah stele (but see below). Gradually, these groups developed the highland economy, produced surpluses, and traded with each other and perhaps also with groups outside of the highland. One of the results was that they became more familiar with each other, perhaps even sharing a growing sense of identity. Another was the growing interest of a nearby state (or states) in these surpluses. This led to the eventual inclusion of the highland into the 'orbit' of the early Philistine state(s) of the southern coastal plain, and into its political economy.

The Philistines likely did not care about the local distinctions between the various groups in the highland, but treated them all as one, probably using a common pejorative (Hebrews? Israel?) in referring to them. The emerging asymmetrical relations, including economic pressure and military threat, led the highlanders to redefine themselves in contrast to the Philistines, and resulted in the emergence of their ethnic identity. Their redefinition involved a choosing of traits—most of which at least were already practiced—that contrasted those of the 'other', and vesting them with new meaning. The name 'Israel' appears to have been chosen for the entire new group,[5] perhaps because the name referred to a group of special importance in the process.

On the face of it, with this one might say we have reached the end of our endeavor. That is, we have understood the processes by which the totemic groups of the highland came to be unified into a single ethnic group, as well as the process by which they chose their ethnic markers and behaviors. Merenptah's Israel could, in this light, be seen as one important faction

---

5. It is impossible to estimate the group's percentage out of the total highland population; it could have been great or very little. Note, however, that the process of redefinition was a long one, and internal relations were probably quite dynamic (even before the process). For the speed by which one group can absorb many new members, see the example of the Zulu state, discussed below (L. Thompson 1969: 342-45).

among these totemic groups, one that probably gave its name, and perhaps some of its history, to the new ethnic group that evolved. Indeed, this is approximately the script I had in mind when I began writing this book.

There are, however, several compelling features which indicate that we have revealed only part of the picture, and that while all of the above is a good description of the processes that took place in the highland during the late twelfth to eleventh centuries, the situation in the late thirteenth and much of the twelfth centuries requires more study.

It seems that some of Israel's ethnic traits, i.e., the avoidance of imported pottery, the absence of decoration, the limited ceramic repertoire, and even the egalitarian ethos—while they were later used and further transformed in the interaction with the Philistines—can *better* be explained as resulting from an earlier interaction with other groups, and as contrasting the Late Bronze Age culture. This logically follows what we have seen regarding the pre-existence of these traits before Israel's interaction with the Philistines. Another issue that one needs to bear in mind is the existence of the Merenptah stele, which specifically mentions Israel as an ethnic group, or better, an 'identity group', in the late thirteenth century.

The fourth part of the book is therefore devoted to this period.

Part IV

MERENPTAH'S ISRAEL: THE BEGINNINGS

16

MERENPTAH'S ISRAEL:
ISRAEL IN THE LATE THIRTEENTH CENTURY BCE

We have seen that many traits crucial to Israel's self-definition existed prior to their (re)development *vis-à-vis* the Philistines, beginning by the late twelfth century BCE. While the interaction with the Philistines reshaped these traits, it is possible and even likely that they were meaningful earlier, particularly in relation to the Late Bronze Age society of the thirteenth century. Note that the lack of both decorated and imported pottery, for example, stands in much greater contrast in this context than in any other. Israel is also explicitly mentioned as a people in the late thirteenth century, an important datum not properly addressed until now in the present work, but one that cannot be ignored.

The present chapter aims, therefore, to examine the reality of the thirteenth and twelfth centuries *before* the impact of the Philistines was felt, and to see what can be said about Israel at this time. This will be done by an examination of settlement patterns and a new analysis of the formation of the period's material culture, all in light of the Merenptah stela.

The Beginning of the Settlement Process

As we have already seen in previous chapters, much has been written on the process of the Iron Age I settlement in the highlands. It appears to have been a gradual one, one which lasted probably until the eleventh century, and in some regions perhaps even later (e.g. Finkelstein 1988: 352-53). The question of when it started was once hotly debated, with opinions ranging from the fourteenth to thirteenth centuries (for a summary, see Finkelstein 1988: 315-21). Recently, however, the earlier dates have been abandoned, and the consensus seems to concentrate around the late thirteenth to early twelfth centuries (1988: especially pp. 320-21).

Most of the local 'highland' pottery of the Iron I is in the Late Bronze Age tradition (above), and therefore chronological distinctions are practically impossible on this basis (Wengrow 1997: 311-12). Imports, a feature so typical of Late Bronze Age society, are absent in the highland sites; this has usually caused scholars to lower the date of those sites, so that most sites in which no imports were found have been regarded as being occupied no earlier than the twelfth century, after the cessation of the international trade (Finkelstein 1988: 319-20). But as we shall see below (see also Chapter 7), the lack of imports might be a result of reasons other than a 'chronological separation'. This means that archaeologically, chronological distinctions are nearly impossible to make at these sites, since local pottery is relatively similar throughout the thirteenth to eleventh centuries (and perhaps even earlier). Finkelstein has observed, however, that there are some clear indications that some sites were established in the thirteenth century, for example the presence of a collared-rim jar in Canaanite Aphek (1988: 320-21). His findings were recently supplemented by data from other sites, particularly collared-rim jars found in secure thirteenth-century contexts, for example, at Tel Nami (Artzy 1993: 1097; 1994), and perhaps also at Manahat (e.g. Edelstein and Milevski 1994: 19-20; but see Maeir 2000: 64). The core of collered-rim jar manufacture was in the highlands, where they cannot be dated with any precision. The few that reached thirteenth-century sites in the lowland allow us also to date the beginning of the phenomenon in highland sites.[1] Together the evidence establishes that the settlement process started during the thirteenth century (see also Wengrow 1997: 311-12; Tubb 1998b: 168), and probably continued for quite some time until the eleventh century BCE.

Late Bronze Age Canaan:
An Anthropological Context for the Emergence of Traits

We now turn to the Egyptio-Canaanite world of the closing years of the Late Bronze Age,[2] in which some of the ethnic traits discussed here are likely to have become meaningful. While a lengthy discussion of Late Bronze Age society is beyond the scope of this work (see, e.g., Bunimovitz 1989, 1995), some issues are worth commenting on here. Canaan was at the time an Egyptian province, ruled mainly by local princes who paid tribute to Egypt, or in some cases directly by the Egyptians. The society was composed of many classes, and was probably highly stratified, as can be seen quite clearly in many of the period's historical sources (e.g. Aharoni 1979: 168-69; see

---

1. Note that the idea raised by some scholars that these jars first appear in the lowland is unfounded (for this, and for a more detailed discussion of the collared-rim jar, see below, Chapter 19).

2. Some scholars have already commented on the importance of this 'Egypt' for the emergence of Israel (e.g. Wengrow 1996; Tubb 1998b). This is an issue of great importance, but it exceeds the scope of the present work.

also Rainey 2003: 172-76), as well as its material culture, which exhibits various types of palaces, temples, residences (both Egyptian and Canaanite), and tombs.

It is the most 'international' period in the history of the region (e.g. Nicolaou 1982; Killebrew 1998; Caubet 1998; Sherratt and Sherratt 1991; see also Killebrew 2005). Imported pottery from various sources is found in abundance at practically every site, and, even if not expensive, likely played an important role in the period's symbolism, and helped to create and maintain the class distinctions that are so manifest in this period (e.g. Van Wijngaarden 1999; see also Sherratt and Sherratt 1998). Without attempting to decipher its full meaning, it is quite likely that this imported and highly decorated pottery (along with more expensive commodities of course) was used as part of a large assemblage of vessels in various social contexts, and was of immense importance in reinforcing social identities. Thus, any individual or group that rejected this social system would have salient symbols on which they could give comment. The following briefly summarizes the possible relations between the Late Bronze Age features and some of Israel's ethnic traits discussed above:

Imports
Due to the importance of imported pottery in establishing and maintaining social positions and relations in the Late Bronze Age, it is likely that any refutation of this social world and its symbols would entail the avoidance of imported pottery and its complex messages.

Decoration
Similar to imported pottery, it is clear that decoration on local pottery of the Late Bronze Age carried social meaning (see Chapter 6). Abandoning this tradition altogether can easily be interpreted as a form of boundary creation, or even resistance (below).

Repertoire
Again, the large Late Bronze Age repertoire of both local and imported pottery was used in a sophisticated manner to carry social meanings, probably in the form of elaborate feasts and meals. Rejection of the social system entailed the rejection of all of its manifestations, including the extravagant repertoire (see also Chapter 8, particularly the reference to Goody 1982).

Elaborate Burials
One of the main characteristics of the Late Bronze Age is the large number of tombs that have been found, especially remarkable in proportion to the number of excavated sites, and their great variety (Gonen 1992a). These tombs must have been used to convey social messages pertaining to status,

religious beliefs, and probably even group affiliation. The almost complete absence of burials that can be associated with the Israelites from before the ninth and eighth centuries BCE cannot be a mere chance. It is likely that the Israelites rejected all of the social connotations of these burials and buried their dead in simple inhumations (Faust 2004a).

Notably, this trait is of particular importance in establishing the significance of contact with the Egyptio-Canaanite system. Philistine burials were seemingly not very impressive and numerous and, contrary to all other traits, it cannot be postulated that contact with the Philistines shaped this trait.

Temples
Although the period's sites have been excavated to a small extent only, a surprising number of more than 20 temples have been found, with one or more at practically every site (e.g. A. Mazar 1992a; Gonen 1992b). Such permanent temples, by definition, indicate that the society was stratified, with those (i.e. priests) who benefited from economic surpluses. And yet, despite the fact that Israelite sites have been extensively excavated, especially so for those dating to the Iron Age II, virtually no Israelite temples have been found; the exceptions, such as at Arad, only testify to the rule. Again, due to the disproportionate number of Late Bronze temples, their absence in Israelite society is likely to have been a reaction to what they symbolized in the Egyptio-Canaanite world of the Late Bronze Age.

Discussion
All of the above were used in the Late Bronze Age as a means to enhance social status, and probably for social exclusion and inclusion. Their part in a very stratified society implies that the new highland settlers rejected such a social order and its symbolism in advancing a more egalitarian worldview. The egalitarian ideology itself should therefore be viewed as a comment on the Late Bronze Age society of the thirteenth century. All of these traits, probably with the exception of burials, have been understood as part of ethnic negotiation with the Philistines and join other traits whose Philistine connection is unquestioned; but the present context seems much more suitable for their emergence. It is therefore likely that, as far as those traits were concerned, the interaction with the Philistines only *modified* existing traits and behaviors.

This rejection of existing symbols and markers is a well-known phenomenon, which can occur in the process of boundary maintenance or resistance (e.g. Ferguson 1991; J. Levy 1998; Shackel 2000; Bunimovitz and Faust 2001, and references). Various examples of cultural avoidance were presented above (see especially Chapter 7), and it is likely that all of those were behind the Israelite ethos, which overtly rejected the Late Bronze Age social ideological systems. As Rayner noted, 'indeed, many egalitarian societies…

exist as a consequence of withdrawal from contact with or participation in hierarchical systems' (1993: 245; see also Hodder 1982c: 208).[3]

Israel in the Merenptah Stela

The reference to Israel in the famous Merenptah's stela of the thirteenth century is another important piece of evidence indicating that Israel had earlier roots. It has attracted much attention in research over the last hundred years or so (e.g. Stager 1985a; Bimson 1991; Hasel 1994, 2003, 2004; Rainey 1991, 2001; Yurco 1991). Nearly all scholars who read the inscription see 'Israel' as describing a 'people', in contrast to cities also mentioned in the inscription. While this has been a subject of heated debate in the past, namely, when a few scholars attempted to challenge this view (Ahlstrom and Edleman 1985; see now also Hjelm and Thompson 2002), it seems as if today this skepticism deserves no more then a passing remark in summarizing past research, as the detailed studies conducted recently all seem to approve the accepted view of Israel as an ethnic (identity) group (e.g. Stager 1985a; Hasel 1994, 2003, 2004; Rainey 2001; Yurco 1991; Kitchen 2004; see also Redford 1992; Na'aman 1994b: 247).

Not only does the stela indicate that Israel was a group in the late thirteenth-century BCE Canaan, it also implies that it was of some importance as far as the Egyptians were concerned (e.g. Stager 1985a: 61; Yurco 1991: 61; Bimson 1991: 22-23; Hasel 1994: 54; Dever 1995a: 208; see also Chapter 18) in their mentioning it and taking pride in claiming to have defeated it,[4]

3.   This is reminiscent of Gottwald's ideas, and a short comment is in order. As we have seen, Gottwald gave extensive treatment to Israel's egalitarian ethos, and while he was not the first to identify it, he was no doubt the first, following Mendenhall (1962), to deal with the topic so thoroughly (and, in my opinion, find its appropriate place in Israel's social world). Gottwald's ideas were extremely influential but drew a lot of criticism (some of which has been discussed in Chapter 11, and will receive more discussion also in Chapter 18). Despite the criticism, it is clear that his idea was both brilliant and insightful, and as we have seen, there are many traits with which Gottwald was not familiar that support this part of his reconstruction.

There are, of course, many problems with his theory. For example, if the Israelites were Canaanite peasants who rebelled against the oppressing Canaanite system, we would expect to find them in other places (on this, as well as other problems, see Finkelstein 1988: 306-14; in this regard, not much has changed since this book was published; see also Redford 1992: 267-69; Chapter 11 above, and Chapter 18 below; note that the question of the population source or sources is irrelevant to the main question discussed here). While much, or even most, of this criticism is justified, it does not deprive his observation regarding the egalitarian ethos of its validity (see Chapter 11).

4.   Whether the campaign occurred or not, and whatever its scale (e.g. Redford 1986: 196-99), the very mention of this group by the Egyptians is an indication of its importance (e.g. Bimson 1991: 23-24).

along with several major cities. In Hasel's words, 'our study...has given additional support to the understanding that *Israel* functioned as an agri-culturally-based/sedentary socioethnic entity in the late thirteenth century B.C., one that is significant enough to be included in the military campaign against political powers in Canaan' (1994: 54). More will be said on the matter later.

Locating and Identifying Merenptah's Israel

Where was Merenptah's Israel located? Placing it in the central highland, particularly Samaria, has for obvious reasons been a popular idea. We know this is where biblical Israel emerged, and the hundreds of villages that were established there at the time have typically been identified with that Israel.

However, there are some problems with this idea. Na'aman, for example, claims that the fact that in the stela there was probably no 'sequential order of listing...opens the way for identifying Israel according to each scholar's historical reconstruction, but makes conjectured location highly speculative' (1994b: 248, 249). He calls the locating of Israel in the region of Shechem 'guesswork'. Moreover, Na'aman draws attention to the gap between the mention of Israel in Merenptah's stela and the next occurrence of the name, and argues that 'the maintenance of a name of a social organization does not necessarily imply any other sort of cultural continuity'. It is clear that Na'aman's caution is in order, and that specifically his last observation is correct (after all, it relates to a theme that repeats itself throughout this book). However, I believe there are several factors that enable us to locate Merenptah's Israel in the central highland.

First, the appearance of a new socioethnic group in the inscription together with the phenomenon of the highland settlements (the sites that already were in existence at the time) is not likely to be a coincidence (Dever 1995a: 208; see also 2003: 200-201).

Second, this notion is strengthened when one examines the determinative that is used for Israel. It clearly relates either to pastoralists or to 'a popula-tion grouped in small, unfortified settlements without a city-state capital' (Yurco 1991; for a similar assessment with a slightly different emphasis, see also Rainey 2001: 65-66, but see Hasel 1994, 2003; for the settled/pastoral-ist debate see below, and there additional references). Since the highlands as reflected in the archaeological record are more likely than any other region to have inhabited such a social system, this correspondence is rein-forced.

Third, we know from inscriptions (and also from the Bible, of course) that the Israel of the Iron II was located there (and probably in parts of Transjordan [see Chapter 20]), and the chances are quite low that the Israel of the Iron I was located in another region from that of the Iron II, or that there is no relation between the two; we can also show archaeological continuity from the Iron Age II to the Iron Age I in ethnically meaningful traits. It is clear, as mentioned above, that some of the ethnic traits that can be attributed to the later Israel of the Iron Age II became meaningful precisely in the timeframe discussed here, and that they can be found at these early Iron I sites. Indeed, the Israel of the Iron II appears to be the development of the Iron Age I in the highland. Therefore, the Israel of the thirteenth century should likely be sought where the Israel of the Iron II had its roots. Any attempt to locate Merenptah's Israel elsewhere carries the burden of proof, and in the absence of such evidence we are left to place it in the central highlands (and perhaps Transjordan).[5]

It should be noted that the early Iron I settlements, i.e., those that can be dated to the time of the stela, are relatively very few in number. Examples may include the sites at Giloh and Ebal among several others, which are distributed geographically from Jerusalem (Giloh probably being the southernmost excavated site) to central/northern Samaria. This is a very limited region, and while it is not impossible that the thirteenth-century settlers were regarded as forming more then one group in identity, there is neither evidence for that, nor need, as the number would have been very small, making more than one identity group unnecessary (the 'other' group could have been outside the highlands, see below).

This limited distribution of settlements and their identification with the Israel of Merenptah's stele is in support of previous views, such as the one advanced, for example, by Redford (though for different reasons). According to him, 'reasonably certain would appear the postulate that in the "Israel" of Merenptah's stela we should construe what the Bible calls the "House of Joseph" ensconced on Mount Ephraim around Shechem' (1992: 295).

Although Redford's suggestion is based mainly on the analysis of texts, such a proposal is very much in line with the archaeological evidence presented so far. Israel of the thirteenth century is indeed to be located in Samaria, mainly from the region north of Jerusalem to central or northern Samaria.[6]

---

5. Lemche's assertion regarding the question at hand that 'any endeavor to choose between these options…is nothing except free speculation' is simply wishful thinking on his behalf (1998b: 42). It is clear that even the data presented by Lemche are sufficient to claim that one scenario is much more probable. The chances that 'a traditional name that was remembered in northern Palestine' (p. 42) was chosen as the name of a state established hundreds of years later for *no* apparent reason seem to be extremely low!

6. Transjordan, or parts of it, were probably also involved in the discussed process, but due to both the relative rarity of information from these regions and the fact that they are usually discussed separately from Cisjordan (as problematic as it is), the issue will be discussed in a chapter of its own (Chapter 20).

But we are confronted now with an apparent contradiction. If we identify the Israel of the late thirteenth century BCE as an ethnic group, how could it have been claimed that the late twelfth-century villages had a totemic identity? This question will be examined in the next chapter.

17

ISRAEL'S EMERGENCE: THE BEGINNINGS

In the thirteenth century various settlements were established in the high-lands, most concentrated in a region stretching over a rather limited area from Jerusalem in the south to northern Samaria in the north. The origins of the population that settled here are highly debated, whether they be seden-tary Canaanites, pastoralist Shasu, etc., but it is recalled that the question of origin is not necessarily connected with identity (see more Chapter 18). Here we are interested in the question of when we can begin to call this popula-tion 'Israel'.

The Thirteenth Century BCE: The Context

During the thirteenth century the Egyptians had strengthened their control over Canaan (e.g. Bunimovitz 1994; Oren 1984; Singer 1988a), perhaps even minimizing contact and interaction between the Canaanite city-states and other (para-social, semi-nomadic,[1] etc.) groups, of whatever origin. Bun-imovitz, who has adopted the concept of the shifting frontier to describe the reality in Canaan during the Late Bronze and Early Iron Ages (1994: 196-202), suggests that during the fifteenth–fourteenth centuries, the 'frontier spilled over from the central hill country to the lowland' (p. 200), meaning that the para-social and/or semi-nomadic groups that inhabited the 'frontier' were now interacting with the cities of the lowland. Later, however, during the time of the Nineteenth and Twentieth dynasties, a new situation emerged, as Bunimovitz explains:

> ...the Egyptians had revolutionized both the nature and extent of their involve-ment in Palestine. Gradually strengthening their hold on the lowlands, and finally instituted their *de facto* annexation of Canaan to Egypt. The deepening Egyptian involvement and increased administrative and military presence in these regions presented the non-sedentary population with a new situation: the broad frontier that characterized Palestine in the fifteenth–thirteenth centuries BCE quickly shrank and receded to the hill country and the steppe. (1994: 200)

1. I usually used terms such as 'semi-nomads' or 'pastoral nomads'. Notably, when the term 'nomads' was used it also refers, of course, to semi-nomads.

The new policy closed the lower regions to the various groups, and drove them to the empty areas, including the highlands where they now settled down and began to grow cereals, which could no longer be traded (cf. Finkelstein 1988, 1999; Bunimovitz 1994, and others; note that while Bunimovitz explicitly refers to a non-sedentary population, it is clear that the same could have accounted for other 'outcasts'; see Chapter 18). The new settlers in the highland therefore faced a reality in which they were 'marked' by the Egyptio-Canaanite system. A way of life that contrasted the Canaanite–Egyptian world is expected, and to some extent perhaps even inevitable.

The Nature of Merenptah's Israel

As we have seen above, it is likely that Merenptah's Israel should be identified with some or even all of the new villagers that settled in the highland during the late thirteenth century BCE, and that many of the traits that were used by Israelites in later periods became meaningful at the time, due to the interaction with the Late Bronze Egyptio-Canaanite system.

But how should we define this 'Israel'? Was it in actuality an ethnic group at such an early stage? After all, I have claimed earlier that the twelfth-century settlers had a totemic conscience that evolved into an ethnic one only during the eleventh century. First, in resolving this issue, one should remember that our modern Western definitions of groups do not necessarily apply to other cultures. It is clear that Israel was in existence, and that it had an identity, or was something like a 'people' as defined by the stela. Second, we should bear in mind that the totemic/ethnic distinction is an artificial one, and that in reality we are dealing with a continuum; Israel's dealings with the Canaanite–Egyptian system in the thirteenth century made the relations between the two asymmetrical, and it is therefore likely that Merenptah's Israel was quite far from the totemic end of the spectrum. The nature of the relations between the first settlers in the thirteenth century and the lowland political entity therefore drove the former to form a type of identity that can only be identified at the 'ethnic half' of the totemic–ethnic continuum. A final comment is one I have stressed above: the number of sites at this time was relatively small, and they were concentrated in a relatively small area; their population could easily have been accommodated within one identity group, especially when confronting such a dominant 'other'.

The Reality in the Twelfth Century: From Ethnicity to Totemism

If the Israel of the late thirteenth century was an ethnic group, how could we view the twelfth-century highlanders as comprising totemic groups? An ethnic group, after all, is expected to be a 'more advanced' form of identification.[2] In answering this we must look at several processes that operated in the highlands in the late thirteenth and twelfth centuries BCE and influenced the self-identification of the settlers. These were segregation, growth, and internal division.

Segregation

The segregation of the highlanders from the lowlanders caused them to become self-sufficient. A few developments contributed to this separation. Initially it resulted from the abovementioned Egyptian policy that drove the para-social elements away from what used to be the settled land. Later, however, the segregation resulted from the complete disappearance of the Egyptian hegemony and the collapse of this centralized system altogether. The absence of any real connection or intensive interaction with the lowland in lieu of the abovementioned policy, and the absence of the control of the lowland system following its collapse, gradually eliminated the asymmetrical relations that had given rise to the highlanders' identity.

Growth and Internal Division

A continuing settlement process also took place at the time. By this we mean the process in which more and more settlements were established throughout the late thirteenth–late eleventh centuries BCE, probably as a result of both natural growth and the settlement of additional peoples (whether new to the area or not). The increasing number of highlanders made internal divisions and factions much more likely. In the absence of a powerful outside force, however, the main element in the relations between the factions became symmetrical, and in terms of their identity these groups tended more toward the totemic end of the spectrum (as was discussed in Chapter 15). Later, the emergence of the Philistines and the threat they posed consolidated these groups into one full-fledged ethnic group, as we have seen above.

The question of how the ethnic traits that defined Merenptah's Israel were chosen will be discussed only at the end of the following chapter, as it seems to be of importance also for the study of origins, the main subject of that chapter.

2. Notably, we must beware of understanding this process in unilineal evolutionary terms, and as we shall see below, ethnic groups can, if circumstances change, 'retreat' to forms of totemic conscience.

18

ORIGINS RECONSIDERED

The question of Israel's origins has received a great deal of scholarly discussion. Did the Israelites come from Egypt via Sinai and conquer Canaan in a military campaign, or did they enter Canaan from Transjordan in a slow and relatively peaceful process? Did some of the Israelites come from Mesopotamia, as is indicated by the Patriarchal narratives? Could the Israelites simply be Canaanite peasants/serfs who rebelled against their landlords and the corrupted system that exploited them? Or were they merely the local, semi-nomadic population of the central highland that resettled in the thirteenth–eleventh centuries BCE, as part of a long and cyclic process? Were they local Canaanite outcasts or newcomers from afar? All of the above scenarios, and various combinations of them, have been suggested as possible origins of the Iron Age Israelites. It is one of the most hotly debated questions in biblical and archaeological research of ancient Israel, and indeed a very interesting one.

The issue of origins is usually discussed together with that of Israel's identity and ethnicity. Their presumed interdependence can be seen in most studies of ancient Israelite ethnicity, and is reflected in many cases even in the title of such studies (e.g. Dever 1993b, 1995a, 2003; Finkelstein 1996a; Ahituv and Oren 1998). The two are indeed related, but it must be underscored that they remain two distinct issues.

Identity and Origin

As we have seen in Chapter 2, a people's identity is not necessarily connected with their origins. People can change their identity and, if necessary, 'reinvent' their origins. (Canaanites could become Israelites.) While this truism may be accepted by all who participate in the current discussion, the majority of works still connect the issue of identity with origins, sometimes in a non-productive way.

Yet not all have fallen into the trap of confusing the two. Stager, for example, has explicitly called for their separation:

as for the elusive problem of Israelite 'origins' before the twelfth century BCE, I prefer for the time being to adopt the stance of the French sociologist Francois Simiand, who nearly a century ago chided the historians for bowing down before the 'idol of origin', that is, showing an obsessive concern for when a phenomenon first began to appear rather than when it became important. (1985b: 86)

Admittedly, while such explicit statements are rare, many participants of the discussion know in practice to differentiate between the two issues, even though they discussed them as one.[1] This can be seen by the following comment by Dever:

the pottery may continue Late Bronze traditions generally; but the aesthetic and religious values of the 'Canaanite' culture, as expressed in the frequent imports and luxury wares and in numerous cult vessels of the Late Bronze Age, are now either forgotten or are irrelevant in a frontier society and substitute economy. The 'utilitarian' character of the pottery would seem to reflect a similarly utilitarian society. (1995a: 205; see also 1993b: 30*, regarding internal changes)

Still, many have fallen into the trap of interconnecting the two questions (e.g. Skjeggestand 1992: 171; Wengrow 1997: 307-308; Coote and Whitelam 1987: 125-27). These works usually trace the origin of an artifact or a feature (see below) in order to learn about the origins of the people to which they are associated.

While the problem of a people's origins is clear to everyone, since the changing nature of ethnic identity is well known, the origins of artifacts actually pose an even greater problem. The origin of an object can be completely insignificant when trying to decipher its meaning in a given context.[2] Artifacts can be manufactured for one purpose, and have another meaning invested in them later. As Abner Cohen describes, 'the history of a cultural trait will tell us very little about its social significance within the situation in which it is found at present' (1974a: 3). After all, 'objects are not what they were made to be but what they have become' (N. Thomas 1991: 4).[3]

The implications of this for the present study are clear, since the presumed Canaanite origin of various Israelite traits has been used as evidence that the Israelites originated from the Canaanites (regarding the four-room

---

1. Nevertheless, even when scholars did differentiate in practice, I believe it would have been better methodologically to keep the two apart, at least during the first stage of analysis.

2. An artifact's origin may be an important factor in establishing its meaning, but such need not be the case. One must study the meaning of the artifact, and should not assume that its origins are important, especially when dealing with an object not particularly distinguishable.

3. This is similar to the abovementioned example of the Hassidic *schtreimel*.

house, see, e.g., Givon 1999).[4] While the data on which some of these assertions are based are dubious (e.g. regarding the Late Bronze Age 'origins' of
the four-room house), it is emphasized that they have nothing to do with the
identity or the origins of those who chose to use them later. Or, to state it
boldly, while it is quite clear today that many of the Iron II Israelites were
descendents of Canaanites (see below), this cannot simply be learned from
the fact that they used pottery that continues Bronze Age forms. Although
the degree of continuity should be considered, only a contextual study will
enable us to learn which traits are important, and what is a consequence of
what.

Origins Reconsidered: In Focus

Who Were the Israelites' Ancestors?

While the question of Israel's origin has not, for reasons given above, been
dealt with in any detail so far in this work, it remains an important issue
related to the main theme of the present monograph. This is a good place to
address it briefly.

Israel's origin or emergence was an intensively discussed issue for many
years, with the two dominant schools espousing either the conquest or the
peaceful infiltration model (for a summary and references, see Finkelstein
1988: 295-306). The conquest theory was led by dominant figures such as
Albright and Yadin, who claimed, following the narratives of the Exodus
and conquest, that the Israelites entered Canaan as a unified group and conquered it. The peaceful infiltration model, supported by Alt, Noth, and
Aharoni, assumed that the Israelites were semi-nomads who entered Canaan
from Transjordan as part of a long process of migration. They settled mainly
in the regions lacking dense Canaanite settlement.

Following Mendenhall's (1962) paper on the 'Hebrew Conquest of Palestine', and mainly resulting from Gottwald's monumental work (1979), a
third school was established, which advocated an idea known by the name of
'the social revolution' (or 'the peasant revolution'). Their basic idea was that
the Israelites were Canaanite peasants who rebelled against the exploiting
Canaanite elite, left their houses and went to the highlands. There they met a
small group who fled Egypt and brought with them a God of liberation.
These rebels were or became the Israelites.

Finkelstein (1988, 1994) and Bunimovitz (1994), though they differ on
many details, have used a meticulous study of the archaeological remains
and brought to the front another theory. Influenced by the *annales* school,

---

4.   Note that A. Mazar was more careful, and only suggested that it 'is possible that
the pillared buildings of the Iron Age I were inspired by a Canaanite architectural
tradition' (1985b: 68).

they examined the Iron I settlement wave as part of long-term cyclic processes in the highland of Cisjordan. According to them, the Israelites were local pastoralists who became sedentary at the beginning of the Iron I. They had originated from sedentary Canaanites who became semi-nomads following the destruction of the urban system of Canaan in the sixteenth century BCE, and resettled after some 400 years.

A final school mentioned here is one that, similar to the view of Mendenhall and Gottwald, sees the Israelites as local Canaanites who due to various reasons settled down in the highlands, only not after a rebellion. There are many variations among the supporters of this view (called 'evolutionary', 'symbiotic', etc.), and it should be noted that it is held by various scholars who disagree on many if not most of the details (e.g. Lemche 1985; Dever 1995a; and many others).

The consensus today is that all previous suggestions have some truth regarding the origins of the ancient Israelites (Dever 1995a: 210-11; 2003; Finkelstein 1991: 57; Finkelstein and Na'aman 1994: 13; Kempinski 1995; Miller and Hayes 1986: 85; Gottwald 1983: 6; 1992: 72; see also Rainey 2001: 75). In Finkelstein's words on Israel, 'the people who formed this entity came from diverse backgrounds—groups of sedentarizing nomads, withdrawing urban elements, northern people, groups from the southern steppe, etc.', adding that a point of dispute is 'the ratios of the various groups in the Iron I population...' (1991: 57). That is, while all may agree that there is some truth to all of the above, the percentage and weight given to each process varies. Most scholars that accept the core historicity of an Exodus (see below), agree that it is likely that it was a very small group, but one that probably gave much of its history to the new group that emerged.[5] Some other elements could be traced to other groups, whose 'totemic/clan' name might always be a mystery to us (see also Dever 2003).

How Did They Merge?
We know that there was an ethnic (or 'identity') group by the name 'Israel' already at the beginning of the Iron I, and it seems reasonable to assume that that group was extremely dominant in the formation process of the 'full' Israel. When the processes described in the previous chapters took place, through which the Israelite ethnicity as it was to be known later was consolidated, the 'Israel' group was the most dominant. It, therefore, gave its name to the new ethnic group which was formed, and the other groups incorporated into it throughout the Iron Age I became part of this Israel. They also perhaps received some or much of the 'history' of this group, though it is likely that their own history and myths were included as well (see, e.g.,

---

5. It is not necessary that the history (e.g. the Exodus story) and the name were taken from the same group.

Dever 1995a: 210; see also Na'aman 1994b: 231-47; Tubb 1998b: 168-69).
While there may be a consensus among scholars that the exodus did not take
place in the manner described in the Bible, surprisingly most agree that the
narrative has a historical core, and that some of the highland settlers came
from outside Canaan (for a partial list of the various views, see, e.g., Bietak
2003; Gottwald 1979; Herrman 1985: 48; A. Mazar 2001: 76; Na'aman
1994b: 245; Stiebing 1989: 197-99; Halpern 1992: 104, 107; 2003; Dever
1993b: 31*; 1995a: 211; Tubb 1998b: 169; Williamson 1998: 149-50;
Hoffmeier 1997; Weisman 1984a: 15-16; Malamat 1997; Yurco 1997: 44-
51; Machinist 1991: 210; 1994; Hendel 2001, 2002; see also Levy and Holl
2002).[6] It is most likely that in the process of ethnogenesis this story became
part of the common history of all the Israelites.

The process by which all these groups came to share the same history is
best explained by Dever:

> The 'Exodus–Conquest' story is perhaps really about a small group... If one
> asks how the story of the 'house of Joseph' became in time the story of 'all
> Israel' the answer may be deceptively simple. It was they who in the end *told*
> the story; and quite naturally, they included all those who later reckoned
> themselves part of biblical Israel. In time most people no doubt believed that
> they had been in Egypt. A simple analogy may help us to understand this
> phenomenon. In mainstream American tradition, we all celebrate Thanksgiv-
> ing as though we ourselves had come to these shores on the Mayflower. That is
> the myth; yet in fact, most of us got here some other way. My ancestors came
> from the County Donegal in the potato famine 150 years ago. Yours may have
> come as slaves from Africa, or from the ghettos of Europe, or as farm workers
> from Mexico. But spiritually (yes!), we are all pilgrims: this is what makes us
> 'Americans'. So are the myths of Israel's origins, or ours, *true*? Of course they
> are—in the deepest sense. That we can put off our religious or cultural hat, and
> temporarily don the hat of the modern skeptical historian or archaeologist,
> does not necessarily alter or diminish the value of tradition. We are what we
> believe we are, just as ancient Israel was. (1995a: 211; see also Halpern 1992:
> 107; Dever 2003)

While Dever's words seem to give a general idea on how an important story
of one group can become that of a much larger one, I believe Machinist
(1991, particularly pp. 210-11) can be used to explain why this idea was so
important for the emerging group. After all, such a story is somewhat
strange given the background of other ancient Near Eastern societies, and if
it was the story of one small group it could have been easily discarded.
Machinist writes:

---

6.   Though the size of this group is debated, most scholars agree that it is in the range
of only thousands, or even hundreds (note that some, however, give it more weight; see,
e.g., Hoffmeier 1997).

paradoxically, it is the very status as newcomer and marginal, which at first
sight looks so negative and culturally unstable, that is taken by our Biblical
passages as a basis for a positive picture. In other words, if newcomers and
marginal had meant, say, for the Egyptians, barbarians, immoral, and chaotic,
in the Bible they become proof of the choice of the 'almighty God'—of new
freedom, purity, and power. (1991: 211; see also 1994: 51)

This idea seems especially reasonable in light of the previous discussion
regarding the nature of ethnicity. We have seen that a group's characteristics, particularly negative ones, are often given to them by others; this might
be the case here with this small group of newcomers, only here they made
something positive out of it; this, indeed, is not surprising.[7]

How Many Israelites Were There Initially?

We do not know the size of Merenptah's Israel. Since an ethnic group is not
necessarily a kin group, despite what ethnic groups usually claim to be, it
can absorb new members rather quickly; the Zulu can serve as a good
example. The Zulu had some 2000 members at the time of Dingiswayo in
the early nineteenth century; he died in 1818 (L. Thompson 1969: 342). But
after a few years, following his rise and quick expansion, the new Zulu leader
Sahka had an army of tens of thousands of men (p. 344), all of whom were
now Zulu. This was achieved because, along with his quick expansion and
conquering of other groups, Thompson states that 'tradition of the Zulu royal
lineage became tradition of the nation; the Zulu dialect became the language
of the nation; and every inhabitant, whatever his origins, became a Zulu,
owing allegiance to Shaka... In these ways an area previously occupied by
many autonomous chiefdoms became transformed into a single kingdom;
and many tribes became moulded in a single nation' (p. 345). This example
is unique, and there are many clear differences between the two cases, but it
exemplifies how an ethnic group can easily absorb many new members.

It is likely that in this case too some of the new members joined only
under the monarchy (Iron Age II), while many likely joined in a slow process throughout the Iron Age I. Israel's demographic growth was probably a
result of both these newcomers and natural growth.

Origins After All: The Origins of Merenptah's Israel

So far we have attempted to reconstruct the way in which Merenptah's Israel
grew to include peoples of various origins, explaining how all theories have
some validity. But what was the origin of Merenptah's Israel itself? Where
did the original group that settled in the highland in the late thirteenth century
or their ancestors specifically come from? And what was their identity?

---

7. Seen in this light, the mere existence of this story seems to give it some credibility.

'Dead' Theories

Two views that seem to have been discredited by the vast majority of scholars are the military conquest and the social revolution theories. The former is
not supported by evidence and consequently by practically no archaeologist
or historian (see, e.g., Weinstein 1997: 87-88). There is no need therefore to
discuss it here. Regarding the social revolution theory, although it was very
influential in establishing some of the other schools, the entirety of evidence
appears to be against it, and it has been disproved on various grounds (see,
e.g., Weinstein 1997: 87-88; Finkelstein 1988: 306-14). Finkelstein has
meticulously shown that this theory is divorced from both the ecology and
topography of ancient Israel, and the archaeological remains (e.g. 1988: 306-
14). There is no need to repeat his arguments in detail, but they seem to
prove that this theory has nothing to do with ancient Israel (see, most
recently, Levy and Holl 2002: 89). I should add a few points, directed more
to the issue at hand.

It is interesting that Gottwald's impressive work (1979) did not tackle the
issue of ethnicity at all (Fredric Barth does not even appear in his index), nor
does it attempt to show how the rebels became a distinct ethnic group (and I
believe this would be a very difficult task). Moreover, while peasants'
revolutions do occur (Gottwald 1979: 585-86), they usually do not produce a
new ethnicity; they do, at times, replace the 'government'. Gottwald suggested a revolution that is contrary to what we know of such incidents: one
that did not overthrow the 'government'/elite, but did produce a new ethnicity. This alone is very unlikely, not to mention in combination with the other
lines of evidence suggested above.

The Present Debate

Today, the main debate can be divided into two questions: (1) whether the
first Israelites were semi-nomads or a sedentary group, and (2) whether they
came from outside Cisjordan or not. Obviously, those who believe that the
Israelites were sedentary also claim that they were indigenous to Cisjordan
(as the debate usually refers to this region; see Chapter 20 below); those who
claim that they were semi-nomads are divided into those who believe they
came from the outside or were local.[8]

The first group of scholars to be discussed here are the supporters of
'foreign' origin, i.e., those that see Israel as having originated from semi-
nomads who came from Transjordan. This is basically the original 'Peaceful
Infiltration school', although in a much more sophisticated manner. Following the Egyptian records, these semi-nomads are now identified mainly with

---

8. It should be noted that we are referring, of course, to Merenptah's Israel of the late
thirteenth century, as all scholars agree that in the end (i.e. Israel of the late Iron I and
Iron II) all of these views have some validity (see above).

the Shasu (e.g. M. Weippert 1979: 32-34). This view is supported today by
Rainey (1991, 2001), Redford (1992), Van der Steen (e.g. 1999), Levy and
Holl (2002) and others. It should be noted, however, that these scholars do
not claim that all Shasu were Israelites, but that Israel was one Shasu group
(e.g. Rainey 2001; Levy and Holl 2002).

The local nomads school views the settlers as semi-nomads who lived in
this area for several hundreds of years, until—as a result of certain circumstances on which Finkelstein (1990b, 1994) and Bunimovitz (1994) differ—
they were forced to settle. This school views it as part of a cyclic process of
sedentarization and nomadization in the highlands; it is represented mainly
by Finkelstein (e.g. 1988, 1990b, 1994) and Bunimovitz (1994).

The Canaanite origins school, while clearly not homogeneous, rejects all
evidence for nomadic (or semi-nomadic) origins for the highland settlers. As
an alterative, they propose that the settlers came from within Canaanite
society. This is a very wide school of thought, and includes scholars such as
Lemche (1985) and Dever (e.g. 1993b). Its view can be exemplified by the
following comment by Dever:

> the early Israelites are best seen as homesteaders—pioneer farmers settling
> the hill-country frontier of central Palestine, which had been sparsely
> inhabited before Iron I. They were not pastoral nomads who had originally
> migrated all the way from Mesopotamia… Nor were the early Israelites like
> the modern Bedouin… For the most part, the early Israelites were agricul-
> turalists from the fringes of Canaanite society. (1992a: 52-53)

It should be noted that Dever agrees that the group perhaps also included
some pastoral nomads, and maybe even a small group from Egypt, but in the
end asserts that they were mostly 'indigenous Canaanites' (p. 54; see also
1993b: 31*).

Evaluating the Local Nomads School

The idea that all the nomads were local is unlikely. First, the end of the Late
Bronze Age was a period of decisive population movements (e.g. Kuhrt
1995: 385-87; Na'aman 1994b: 239), which seem to have impacted the
entire region. Na'aman writes accordingly, 'the claim that there was a
limited reservoir of manpower in the peripheral areas of Canaan and that the
settlement was necessarily an inter-Palestinian process, ignores the historical
moment in which the settlement was taking place' (1994b: 239). It is, therefore, extremely unlikely that only the highland west of the Jordan was left
untouched by the social upheavals and migration of the time.

Moreover, the settlements east of the Jordan River need to be addressed.
The Iron Age I settlement process, after all, is not unique to Cisjordan (see
also Rainey 2001: 67). Transjordan is part of the same geographic unit, so

there should be no reason to limit the settlement process of nomads to one side of the Jordan River (cf. Rainey 2001; Van der Steen 1995). This argument is strengthened by the similarity of the processes that took place in the highlands on both sides of the Jordan (below). Thus, even those who do not accept 'foreign intrusion' should not exclude Transjordan. This means that a 'local nomads' theory, which limits the potential origin of the settlers to Cisjordan, is a near impossibility; it practically contradicts the historical and geographical contexts.

This leaves us with two possible theories: sedentary Canaanites and the peaceful infiltration model, i.e., semi-nomads from Transjordan (and perhaps also a theory that will combine settlement of semi-nomads on both sides of the Jordan River; see below).

Evaluating the Canaanite Origins School[9]

The Canaanite origins school is founded on two main arguments. The first is the rejection of all other schools, particularly that which attributes Israel's origins to semi-nomadic groups (whether Cisjordanian semi-nomads or the Shasu). The second is the positive evidence for local Canaanite origins.

Regarding the first argument, the claim is that the peaceful infiltration idea is based on nothing more than a romantic perception of Bedouin life (Dever 1992a: 30). While such 'romantic' views no doubt influenced modern scholarship, it seems that in the present case there is a wealth of modern ethnographic and ethnoarchaeological evidence that can support this notion (e.g. Van der Steen 1999; Levy and Holl 2002). Modern analogies by no means prove a semi-nomadic origin for the settlers, but they show that it is possible. This idea cannot be so easily discredited.

Another reason for discrediting the semi-nomadic origins theory is that the Iron I settlement seems to reflect a developed agriculture (e.g. Ahlstrom 1986: 36; Lederman 1992, 1993; Dever 2003). This line of argument is very problematic, even if one accepts the unlikelihood that semi-nomads had a good knowledge of agriculture. In most sites we cannot differentiate between the initial phase of Iron Age I settlement and the last phase, as exposed in the excavations. It could be that all of the so-called advanced agricultural techniques belong to the last phase of Iron Age I settlement, or, in the least, do not belong to the first. The evidence of terraces and other indicators,

---

9.   Notably, I will not directly discuss the minimalist views, which are also based on this theory. The minimalists do not usually offer a real theory that enables discussion and can be either supported or refuted. In most of their writing since the early 1990s they usually avoid detailed discussion of data, and simply base their writing on assertions. At any event, the criticism below is relevant for their ideas as well, as they are based on this school.

therefore, even if dated to the Iron Age I (for other opinions see de Groot 2000; Gibson 2001; Faust 2005c, and references), cannot prove the origin of the settlers, since we do not and cannot know from which phase of the settlement they came. It is possible that it took the settlers 50 years—more than two generations—before they were built, thus rendering their existence meaningless to the present debate. Moreover, one cannot find such evidence in the Late Bronze Age Canaanite society either, as Dever himself has demonstrated (1993b: 24*). After all, the Late Bronze Age settlements are where the Iron I settlers were supposed to have originated according to this view, but these sites also lack evidence for large-scale advanced agriculture (Faust 2005c). It is clear, then, that the semi-nomadic origins cannot be disproved in this manner.

The other line of argument of the Canaanite origins school is based on material evidence of continuity. If this continuity in material traits would be complete and uninterrupted, then there would be no real doubt that we are discussing the same group. But it is clear that such is not the case. There are some marked differences between the Late Bronze Age material culture and that of the Iron I highlands, which generations of archaeologists have accepted in full. The differences are expressed in almost every aspect, and it is clear that one cannot speak of straightforward and complete continuity. (Compare the patterns of continuity and change during the Late Bronze to Early Iron Age transition with those of the Middle Bronze to Late Bronze transition.[10]) Continuity is therefore identified in certain traits only, which is a problematic procedure, as we have seen, unless the importance of these traits is established. Dever has attempted to examine the overall continuity between the two periods (1993b). While revitalizing at the time, this is a problematic approach, both because of the difficulties to quantify, and the near impossibility of interpreting such 'figures'. But let us take a closer look at Dever's analysis.

10.   One could, of course, claim that personal faith or preconceptions of scholars has been a significant factor in accepting this dichotomy, i.e., artificially differentiating between the 'cultures' of the Late Bronze Age and the Iron Age I. While this is true to some extent, it clearly cannot be used exclusively to explain this widely held view, for several reasons: (1) it is clear that such strong allegations cannot be attributed to all scholars, who come from various backgrounds, and many of whom were secular; (2) moreover, biblical tradition dates the Exodus and Conquest to the fifteenth century BCE. Archaeologists choose a date some 250 years later, not because of the biblical date, but because this is when they can distinguish a suitable change in the material culture; (3) and in any case, these differences in the material culture are acknowledged today even by scholars who reject the Israelite identity of the Iron Age I settlers. They are explained by factors such as ecology, setting (urban vs. rural), etc. While these explanations were refuted earlier, they indicate that the sharp differences are acknowledged by scholars from all schools and backgrounds.

After examining the degree of continuity or discontinuity of various traits (and rating them on a scale of 0 to 5 points), including settlement type and pattern, subsistence, technology (divided into architecture, ceramics, metallurgy, and 'other', i.e., terraces and cisterns), demography, social structure, political organization, art, ideology (language, burials, and religion), and international relations, Dever concluded that there are 23 points on the side of continuity, and 47 for discontinuity (1993b: 23*). Contrary to his conclusions at the time, this seems to indicate marked discontinuity, even more so considering that many of the elements of continuity are irrelevant. Dever found continuity (5 points) in language, for example, but unless one claims that the Israelites have originated somewhere outside of Western Asia, all will agree that there should be full 'continuity' in this matter, even if we are dealing with two different groups; accordingly this criterion should be discarded. For religion, he assigned 4 points for continuity and only 1 for discontinuity; as the abovementioned absence of temples clearly shows, however, Iron I religion in the highland was very much different from that of the Late Bronze Age, a fact acknowledged in his later, more sophisticated, works (e.g. Dever 1995a: 205; see also Dever 2003).[11] Other aspects of discontinuity discussed here are missing, e.g., the ideology of egalitarianism. Lastly, Dever did not grade burials (this rubric was left with question marks). Clearly this is because we do not know much about Iron Age I highland burials, but such is a case in point, because as has been discussed we cannot find them for a reason. Burial should have received 5 points for discontinuity. Also missing is pottery repertoire, and other traits which, too, indicate a chage, hence not supporting the continuity theory.[12]

11. It is probable that Dever himself views things differently today. In addition to the issue of religion noted above, compare his treatment of 'ideology' (i.e. both language and religion) in his 1993(b) paper, where it gets 9 points for continuity and 1 point for discontinuity, with his much more sophisticated treatment of ideology in his 1995(a) paper (p. 205; quoted earlier in this chapter; see also Dever 2003).

12. The main archaeological trait in Dever's list that clearly shows continuity with the Late Bronze Age is part of his 'ceramics'; Dever labeled pottery as one category, and did not differentiate between pottery form and repertoire, but it appears that he agrees today that there were clear differences in the repertoire of the two periods. Pottery forms, on the other hand, do display continuity, perhaps with the exception of the collared-rim jar that appears in the Iron Age I; see below. The 'Canaanite' pottery forms, however, prove nothing. If the settlers were Shasu, what kind of pottery do we expect them to have produced: Egyptian? Mesopotamian? They were in contact with the Canaanite society throughout the Late Bronze Age, and these are probably the forms they were familiar with. If these simple forms were not seen as meaningful, and they probably were not, there would have been no problem in using them. Moreover, they were probably the only forms the new settlers knew, and they had to use something.

In summary, a very low level of continuity is indicated here. The first Israelites may have been 'local' in a loose meaning of the term, but they were most likely *not* settled Canaanites.

Additional Problems with the Canaanite Origins School

Moreover, there appear to be problems with the process by which these Canaanites allegedly became something else. Dever has suggested that 'the early Israelites were a motley lot—urban refugees, people from the country-side, what we might call "social bandits, brigands of various kinds, malcontents, dropouts from society"' (1992a: 54; see now also Killebrew 2005). In another place he refers to 'former urbanites, and 'Apiru-like people from the countryside, but also many farmers and stockbreeders from rural areas who were long familiar with the poor soils, fractured terrain, and the unreliable rains of Palestine—in short, experienced agriculturalists' (Dever 1993b: 31*; see also 1995a: 211; 2003; note that, as mentioned above, he gives credit to the idea that some have other origins).

But what is missing from the various descriptions is an explanation of *how* they became a different ethnic group. In what manner did these people come to view themselves as Israelites, and separate from the Canaanite society of which they were part? What was the process of ethnogenesis? I am not familiar with any satisfactory explanation suggested by supporters of this school. While Gottwald in his theory also did not explain how the 'rebels' became a new ethnic group, he did suggest an explanation as to why (against whom). The evolution model does not suggest even that.

Moreover, according to this theory, from where did the settlers in Transjordan arrive?[13] It is well known that a process similar to the one in the highland took place at the same time in Transjordan (see Chapter 20), but if the source of the settlers was not the Shasu or something similar (below), where did they come from? Surely not from the coastal plain? And why did they settle in these remote areas? The currently available explanations of this school are not sufficient. Identifying the settlers as the Shasu is, as we shall see, more comprehensible.[14]

---

13. As we shall see below, there is some Late Bronze–Iron Age continuity in settlements in some parts of Transjordan. The Late Bronze Age settlements, however, were not sufficient to provide for all the Iron I settlers.

14. It is likely that the processes on both sides of the Jordan River were not entirely identical, and that in Cisjordan there were also other groups of para-social elements that were involved in the process (and they amalgamated with the Shasu into Israel, perhaps even Merenptah's Israel discussed here). Still, it seems as if, on the whole, the settlement was one process. Furthermore, it is not clear whether Israel of Merenptah encompassed Transjordan. Clearly, there are many issues that need a more elaborate discussion than this one chapter enables.

Finally, the problem becomes even clearer when one examines the issue of burials. If the first Israelites were Canaanites, why did they not bury their dead like their ancestors? After all, burials seem to have been an important facet of life in Middle and Late Bronze Age Canaan, *including* in the highlands. If the Israelites were Canaanites they must have consciously chosen to cease this habit; otherwise they would have continued to bury their dead exactly as in preceding centuries. This issue exemplifies the problem of the lack of any clear explanation for the process by which Canaanites became Israelites.

I hold that the Canaanite origins theory is insufficient. The evidence it brings in support is far from sufficient and leaves many holes, while its criticism of the other schools is lacking and fails to disprove them. As such, the old peaceful infiltration model needs to be re-examined (and somewhat modified).

Additional Data in Favor of Semi-Nomadic Origin

There are several additional lines of evidence that support a semi-nomadic origin for the settlers, or at least show that such cannot be easily disproved. The first is the form of the earliest settlement sites, which appear to be 'Izbet Sartah III, Giloh, and Mt Ebal. The form of the first two—an oval courtyard or a large fenced yard—might indicate that herding was an important aspect of the economy (e.g. Finkelstein 1988; Levy and Holl 2002: 91-93).[15] The third is not a typical settlement site, but the faunal assemblage in it, as well as at the other sites, still indicates that herding (and perhaps hunting) was of importance. I agree that evidence of sheep/goat husbandry as reflected in the faunal assemblage does not prove nomadic origins, but it clearly does not disprove it (very few sites yield a large number of cow bones, for example, but even this does not disprove a semi-nomadic background, see, e.g., the reality in East Africa, when most pastoral groups use cattle).

Levy and Holl's recent analysis (2002), particularly of the archaeological finds in regards to the oval courtyards, adds ethnographic data that seems to support the view that a semi-nomadic beginning for Israel is likely, or at least possible.[16] They also add an interesting new direction in their innovative linguistic analysis of biblical terms that also can support semi-nomadic origin. They show that the Hebrew words for 'tent', 'small cattle', and 'large cattle' appear in substantially larger numbers in the Pentateuch than in

15. While the plan of Izbet Sartah is reconstructed, it is quite clear that the site had at least a large courtyard.

16. While their analysis of the archaeological material seems sound, we should state that the 'nomadic' origin of the four-room house is not usually accepted in scholarship, and seems unlikely.

Joshua and 2 Kings narratives (2002: 94). While not free of criticism, as might be warranted in their examination of the Pentateuch as one unit, the new approach seems promising, and does seem to support the pastoral origins of the Israelites and is worth mentioning here.

Furthermore, Stager's (1988) analysis of the Song of Deborah in light of the archaeological finds clearly indicates that in the late Iron Age I Israel had a semi-nomadic component (though it proves nothing regarding Merenptah's Israel).[17] In addition, while the traditions regarding Reuben's seniority will receive a brief treatment below (e.g. Cross 1988), one should remember that the tribe of Reuben was pastoralist.[18] Does this show that pastoralists were the first Israelites? This is hard to tell of course, but it is an additional piece of information that should be remembered in this wide and complex context, and one that might give additional support to pastoralist origins.

Altogether, the above discussion shows that Merenptah's Israel is unlikely to have developed from sedentary Canaanites. It is likely that we should not artificially differentiate between Cisjordan and Transjordan. The majority of the settlers in the hill country in the thirteenth century were most likely semi-nomads on both sides of the Jordan River. It seems as if a modified peaceful infiltration model is very likely to have been a major mechanism in the process and that at least many of those who constituted what the Merenptah's stela called Israel had their origins with the Shasu and similar groups on both sides of the Jordan (Ward 1992: 1166-67). This is even strengthened by an examination of the process by which Israel's traits were chosen.

In the following section, therefore, I would like to add an additional line of evidence, and to show how the main discussion of this book can contribute also to the separate question of Israel origins. This will require us to look again at the ethnic traits, and try to understand how they developed.

The Choosing of Traits and Israel's Origins: A Final Comment

As we have seen, the *habitus* seems to be a source from which meaningful traits were chosen or developed. Here, perhaps, we can use the above arguments and try to learn something about the background, or origins, of the first settlers.

17. I do not wish to discuss the text and its dating, which is beyond the scope of the present work. See also Sparks 1998 and references.

18. Note the claim that this seniority is connected with the first settlements in Transjordan, some of which are even a continuation of Late Bronze Age sites (below). This might indicate a sedentary background for this tribe. It is likely, however, that like many others, this was basically a pastoralist group with a 'more sedentary segment'. They had some connection with the Late Bronze Age sites in the nearby region, and some probably lived in these sites. The situation in Transjordan will be discussed briefly later, but a full discussion is beyond the scope of the present work.

If the observation regarding the importance of the *habitus* is correct, namely, that the relevant traits are usually chosen from it, then it is likely that the early settlers did not originate directly from Canaanite, or at least, mainstream settled Canaanite society; they more likely came from groups who were not fully sedentary, did not use imported and decorated pottery, had a limited ceramic repertoire, used simple inhumations, and embraced a relatively egalitarian ethos. While it may be possible that all of these qualities were only developed later in contrast to the group's 'other'—such that Gottwald's idea cannot be entirely ruled out—it is much more likely that not *all* of these were developed anew, but that some were indeed 'chosen' from the settlers' *habitus*.

Burial practices, whose importance was stressed above, can serve as an example. Why did the highland settlers use simple inhumations? After all, given the egalitarian ethos and in contrast with the Late Bronze Age ideological system, they could still have used multiple burials in natural caves, as was common in the second millennium BCE. Their practice of another custom implies that it came from a different 'source'.[19] While we do not know much about the Shasu, it is likely that they did not bury their dead in a monumental way, but used simple inhumations. Indeed, the current lack of archaeological indications for this group (Finkelstein 1996b; but see Levy, Adams, and Muniz 2004) might support the notion that such is the case. Furthermore, Levy, Adams, and Muniz have recently published a cemetery which they attribute to the Shasu population. It is therefore worth noting that the burials were relatively simple, and the authors explicitly wrote that 'we assume some kind of "egalitarian" principle was at work in the burial tradition' (2004: 83). But since not much is known archaeologically about the Shasu, more studies must be carried out before we can identify them as the source for the Israelite's burial customs.

What follows is that the first settlers were, to a very large extent at least, semi-nomads, as *all* of the above qualities are expected to be found among semi-nomads and were not present, as far as we know, among any known Late Bronze Age sedentary Canaanite group. These semi-nomads came, most probably, from among the Shasu groups (perhaps including a small group of 'local' 'Apiru, or outcast Canaanites).[20] Gradually, they absorbed

---

19. Regarding this specific trait, one could raise the possibility that the settlers came from a certain group within the Late Bronze Age Canaanite society which might have practiced such burials. While it is possible that some segments of the Late Bronze Age population practiced simple inhumations, such a reconstruction seems unlikely, and cannot withstand the overall evidence that supports a semi-nomadic origin.

20. Note that while 'Apiru is not an 'ethic' term, names can attain a new meaning, hence the term could, in some later contexts, be used (or adapted) to refer to highland settlers' identity (the same is true regarding the Shasu; cf. Ward 1992).

more people; their main growth occurred during the eleventh century, when they merged with many other totemic groups, all of whom came to be identified as Israel (see also Chapter 15; Stager 1988).

Israel in Merenptah's Stela and Reliefs

All of the above is closely dependent on our understanding of Israel in Merenptah's stela and Karnak reliefs—an issue of heated debate recently. We have seen that while there is a consensus that on the stela Israel refers to a people, or an ethnic group (see above), recently there is less agreement regarding the nature of this group. Many claim now, in accordance with the recent views regarding the origin of ancient Israel, that this Israel refers to a sedentary population. Since the inscription does not say much about Israel, such is deduced from the use of *prt* (Hasel 1994; see also 2003). This claim was refuted in a very detailed discussion by Rainey (2001: 57-66), who summarized that Israel 'is defined by the determinative for a socio-ethnic group. The group thus designated might be living on the level of village culture, or could be pastoralist still in the nomadic stage' (pp. 65-66).

While it is likely that this is not the final word on the debate, it should be stressed that even if the stela does refer to a sedentary group, such would be meaningless for the debate of origins. Nobody would argue that the settlers in Giloh were not sedentary; the question is not what they were in the late thirteenth century, when the stela was inscribed, but what they were several dozens of years earlier. Therefore, regardless of who is right in the debate regarding the wording of the text, it cannot be used to disprove a semi-nomadic background.

Hasel (2003) has recently made several claims that seem to disprove the association of Shasu with Israel; he has shown that, in other places, the determinative used for Israel was not used in reference to the Shasu. But again, this relates to how the Egyptian viewed Israel in the late thirteenth century, not to whom their ancestors were a generation to two earlier.

The Karnak wall reliefs, previously attributed to Raamses II, were identified by Yurco almost 20 years ago as dating to the time of Merenptah. Yurco also showed that they describe the same events mentioned in the stela. His view is generally accepted (Yurco 1990, 1991; Stager 1985a; Rainey 1991, 2001; although not by all: see, e.g., Redford 1986; 1992: 275 n. 85), and led to a heated debate on the manner and the place where the Israelites are depicted. Yurco (e.g. 1990, 1991), followed by others (e.g. Stager 1985a), claimed that the Israelites are depicted as Canaanites. If this is correct it could pose a problem for the semi-nomadic origin school, as it would indicate that the Egyptians viewed this 'Israel' as being made up of Canaanites. There are several problems, however, before such a conclusion can be reached. For example, Rainey (2001), who strongly opposes this interpretation, views the Israelites as being depicted as Shasu (of which he thinks Israel was one group) captives. He claims that the Israelites did not have chariots, while the Canaanites with which Yurco identifies Israel are depicted with them. Yurco basically agrees (1991), but suggests several scenarios by which the Israelites could have acquired them, which Rainy does not accept.[21]

Presently, the reliefs do pose a bit of a problem for the identification of Israel with the Shasu, although this evidence also is problematic, and I believe that as a whole the arguments presented above in favor of the semi-nomadic explanation are more sound. Moreover, one should note that there is even a debate regarding the true extent of Merenptah's campaign (above). If it had been very limited in scope, it is possible that the Egyptians had only heard of the Israelites and chose to depict them, while not really knowing exactly what they were. And finally, they depicted the Israel of the late thirteenth century, not that of a generation earlier or their ancestors.

Summary

The issue of Israel's origins is hotly debated. Although it is of interest, and is closely related to the question of identity, I have tried to show that the two issues should be dealt with separately, since they are different questions. The origins of either a people or a trait will not necessarily tell us much about the people's identity or the trait's meaning at any given moment. While I have attempted to demonstrate that the issues of identity and origin might be related through the process by which some meaningful traits are developed to serve as ethnic markers/behaviors from the *habitus*, I would like to stress that discussing the two together at any other point than an advanced stage of analysis may cause more confusion than it can resolve.

And as for Israel's actual origins, it seems as if ancient Israel was composed of peoples who came from various backgrounds: a semi-nomadic population who lived on the fringe of settlement, settled Canaanites who for various reasons changed their identity, tribes from Transjordan, and probably even a group who fled Egypt. In the end it is likely that many, if not most, Israelites had Canaanite origins. This was clearly the case in the period of the monarchy, in which many Canaanites in the lowland became Israelites. The intake of people of various backgrounds was at times the main source of Israel's population increase, in addition to natural growth; they were

---

21. While Yurco claims that the Israelites are not to be identified with the Shasu, he agrees that some of the Israelites came from a pastoralist background (which, in turn, could be Shasu) (Yurco 1997: 41-42).

all integrated and assimilated into the main group Israel. The original group —those who came on the 'Mayflower' to use Dever's metaphor—likely included many Shasu along with (given their importance in Late Bronze Egyptian sources on Cisjordan) some non-sedentary 'outcast' population.[22]

22. It is not clear when the 'exodus group' made its appearance.

Part V

ASPECTS OF DISTRIBUTION

19

POTS AND PEOPLES REVISITED:
ISRAELITES, PHILISTINES, AND CANAANITES

The previous chapters have discussed various aspects of Canaanite, Philistine, and Israelite interaction, and have examined the impact of the two former groups on the Israelites' emerging ethnicity. A re-examination of some material traits, particularly certain aspects of the ceramic repertoire of the time, can shed more light on the complex relationship between the various ethnic groups in existence during the Iron Age I, specifically the differences between the relationship the Israelites (or proto-Israelites, denoting the Israelites and other totemic groups in the highlands then) had with the Philistines as compared to that with the Canaanites.

The first material item to be discussed is the collared-rim jar, and it, too, can exemplify both the importance of the Philistines for Israel's ethnogenesis and the complex nature of ethnic negotiation.

The Collared-Rim Jar Revisited: Summary of Previous Research

The collared-rim jar (CRJ) cannot be discussed here in full detail, but a short summary of previous research and a quick look at its distribution are very instructive.

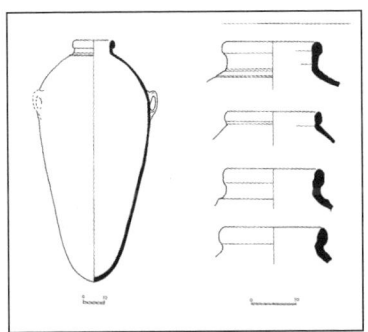

Figure 19.1. *Collared-Rim Jars*
(based on Bunimovitz and Finkelstein 1993: Figs. 6.51\4, 6.57\3,5,7,9).

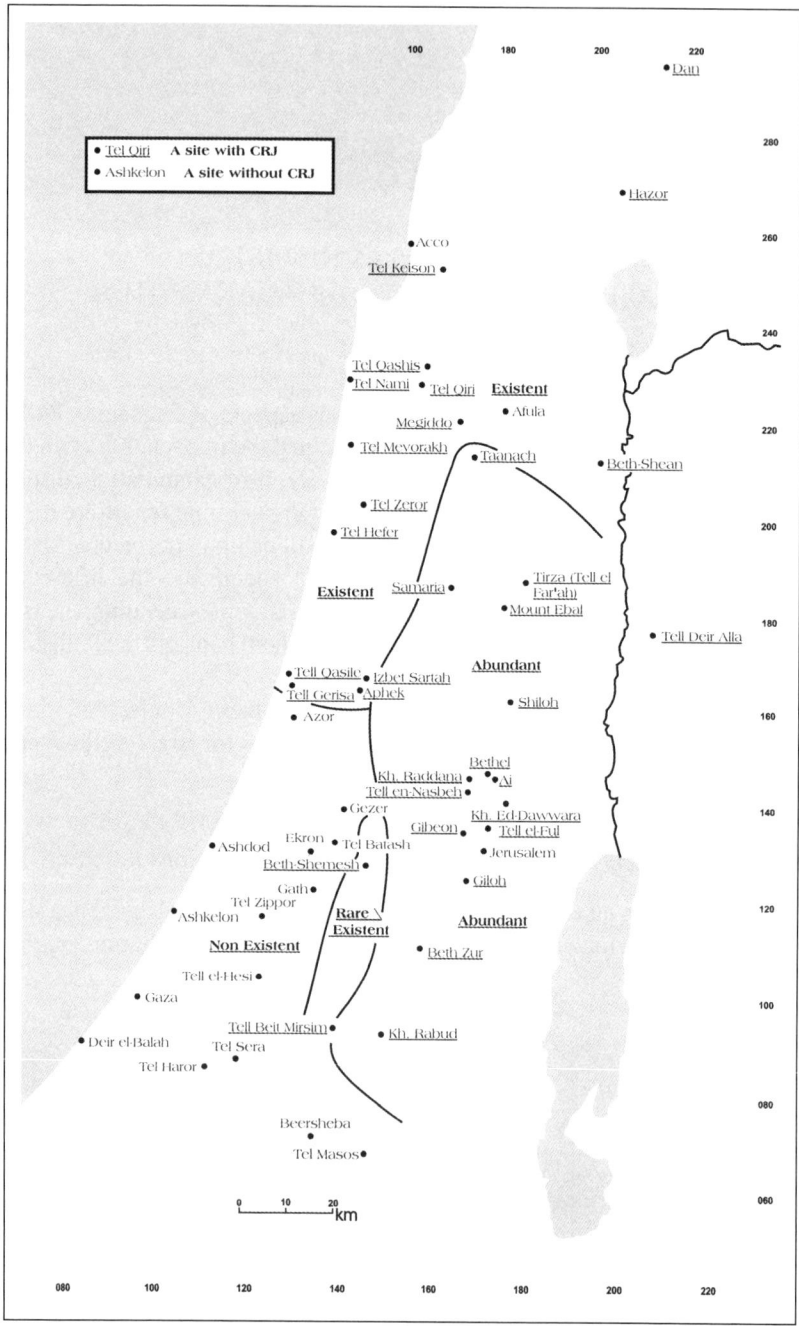

Figure 19.2. *Distribution Map of Collared-Rim Jars.*

The CRJ, initially identified during the 1920s, is a large pithos (Fig. 19.1), typical of the Iron Age I (for a summary of the history of research up to the 1980s, see Esse 1991: 99-105). As research progressed during the early 1930s, it came to be viewed as 'characteristic' of the early Iron Age (Esse 1991: 100). Because the 'archaeological culture' of the Iron I highland seems to have had similar boundaries to those the Israelites had, on the basis of the biblical description, that culture—and the CRJ in particular—became synonymous with the Israelites (Albright 1937: 25), in accord with the prevailing cultural history tradition, and together with the identification of the material culture of other ethnic groups in the ancient Near East (Esse 1991: 102; cf. Chapters 2–3). This identification, soon to become mainstream, was led by Albright (the most notable example of this association was by Aharoni 1970; see also Chapter 3. Note that this view was not without objections, even as early as Engberg 1940).

The presence of CRJ in areas or sites that were not thought of as 'Israelite' was observed already during the 1950s and 1960s, therefore casting some doubt on the justification of equating the two (Esse 1991: 103-104). Archaeological work in the 1970s and 1980s added numerous such jars to our database, and while most of these were in accordance with the above ('Israelite') distribution, more and more were discovered in other regions (Fig. 19.2[1]).

Most notable are those CRJs excavated in Transjordan, especially at Sahab (Ibrahim 1978; 1997: 451). These exceptions discredited the ethnic identification, and along with the more functional approaches that seem to have stemmed (indirectly) from the New Archaeology, scholars tended to explain the CRJ distribution as a result of its functionality (see also, from a different perspective, Zertal 1988). The following statement by A. Mazar is representative:

> The Collared Rim Pithos…became one of the most common vessels in the hill country sites. This is probably due to its suitability to the local environment and economic conditions, especially the need for storing water at hilly sites usually located far from permanent water sources. While the Collared Rim Pithos is not unique to the Israelite settlements, and is found in Canaanite and Philistine sites such as Megiddo and Tel Qasile as well as at Ammonite

1.   Figure 19.2 is a schematic map that is intended to show the main distribution of the collared-rim jar, and is not intended to locate every single jar. Note that in order to overcome some of the shortcomings of distribution maps, this map attempts to show both the presence and absence of this type of jar. I have also commented on the frequency of the collared-rim jar in the various sites and regions. In some of the regions, designated as 'existent', the CRJ can be found at some sites (or neighborhoods), but not in others. Furthermore, at times there were changes regarding the presence or absence of the CRJ over time within a site. Notably, due to the many subtleties involved, the map should not be used without a close reading of the text

> sites such as Sahab and Tell el-'Umeiri, it is dominant in the Iron Age I sites
> of the central hill country. Therefore, it should not be viewed as a vessel
> reflecting ethnicity, but rather as a vessel type chosen by the hill country
> settlers as especially suited to their daily needs. (A. Mazar 1994: 88)

Such 'functional' views have become mainstream, and have lead to the more sophisticated claim that these jars are characteristic of rural sites, and that scholars had erroneously compared the finds from rural sites in the highlands to urban sites in the lowland (London 1989). According to London, the differences reflect different lifestyles and not ethnicity.

The identification of CRJs at various sites in Transjordan and in the coastal plain and northern valleys (Esse 1991: 104-105, and references) seems to undermine much of the logic behind the view that associated the CRJ with the Israelites. In Esse's words, 'from the foregoing evidence it is apparent that the geographic distribution of the collared jar is much greater than Albright ever imagined. Although it remains dominant at sites in the central hill country of Cisjordan, its appearance in central Transjordan in significant quantities and at an increasing number of sites in the Sharon Plain forces a reappraisal of its value as a 'type fossil' to trace the Israelite settlement process' (1991: 105).

Esse's summary seems to echo the prevalent view today. According to Finkelstein, for example, the prevalence of the CRJ in lowland sites and in Iron I sites on the Transjordanian plateau implies that it was dominant in hill country sites for 'economic, environmental, and social factors, such as horticulture-based subsistence and distance of the Iron I communities from stable water sources', rather than because of the ethnic background of the population (1996a: 204). Mazar similarly sees the vessel as a 'common feature in the central part of Palestine on either side of the Jordan' and explains its widespread use as a factor of its 'specific suitability' to the needs of the Israelite settlers there (1985b: 69; for negative assessments on the connection between the CRJ and the Israelites, see also Bloch-Smith 2003: 408-409; R.D. Miller 2004: 57).

A Re-examination of the CRJ Distribution

Can Functionality Explain the Distribution?
The new consensus is very problematic in the face of the evidence. Not only is the symbolism–function dichotomy unwarranted in many cases, but the claims raised by these scholars are contradictory. The above quotations show that the discrepancy between the presumed boundaries of the Israelites and the distribution of the CRJ (e.g. its presence in the northern valleys) was sufficient to disassociate them. At the same time, however, the same scholars claimed that the appearance of the CRJ in the highlands is a result of its

functional suitability to the needs of the highlands population. If the CRJ was used in the highlands due to its economic advantages, why is it found, for example, at Megiddo in such large quantities? The same logic used to disprove the ethnic explanation should have been employed for the functional one.

Of course, it could be claimed that the CRJ is still expected to be found in some quantity outside of its core region in the highlands, whatever the reason may be for its concentration there. Specifically, one would expect to find a gradient of some sort from the highland to the periphery in the lowland. But this is categorically *not* the case. Despite the large quantity of the CRJ discovered at Megiddo (used by many to undermine its association with the highlanders), at nearby 'Afula hundreds of Iron Age I storage jars were found in Stratum III, only one of which is of the CRJ type (N. Dothan 1955: 36). This discrepancy does not reflect the expected gradient, and it also disproves London's (1989) suggestion that the CRJ reflects rural society,[2] as in this case the pattern is just the opposite. (The finds from Megiddo and 'Afula will be discussed in greater detail below.) This, as well as some other problems mentioned below, cast a dark shadow over the functional explanation and are cause for a new examination. Let us first have a closer look at the distribution map.

Distribution
The CRJ is indeed found in various regions (Fig. 19.2). Generally speaking, its provenance extends from the northern valleys/Lower Galilee (Dan being an exceptional, northernmost site) in the north to the southern Hebron hill country in the south, from the Transjordanian highlands in the east to the Sharon Plain in the west. It should be noted, however, that at least in some of the sites in these regions the CRJ is found in extremely small quantities,[3] as in some sites in the northern valleys, for example (Esse 1991: 106-107). Its primary distribution is in the central highlands; it is also very common in Transjordan,[4] and is found in the western Jezreel valley, with an extension into the Akko Plain, and further south along the coast on the Sharon Plain (Esse 1991: 107; also Raban 1991; S. Wolff 1998: 453). But it is hardly found, as Esse notes, in 'Philistia, the Northern Negev, and the Jordan valley up to Beth Shan, the eastern Jezreel valley and upper Galilee' (1991: 107).

2. Even if the pattern was as London claimed, it would not necessarily have supported her hypothesis (Dever 1995a: 204). Since, however, the pattern she suggested is incorrect, there is no need to go into a detailed discussion on the logic of her assumption.

3. As we have seen in Chapter 7, distribution maps are problematic. They do not usually show figures/frequencies/density, nor do they usually show the absence of finds, which can be even more significant.

4. Note that according to Ji (1997a: 409, 410) they are not present in all parts of this region. Transjordan will be discussed in more detail in the next chapter.

Esse suggested that research should concentrate on economic aspects of the CRJ's production and distribution, and believed that these vessels were locally manufactured and not transported far from their centers of production (1991: 107; see below). He also proposed that the CRJ were manufactured by 'itinerant potters, probably kin-based', who were 'either 'Israelites' or at least that the Israelites were their best customers' (p. 108). In this case, the abovementioned distribution can serve as an indication that, in Esse's words,

> commerce between these areas, which by most formulations were either Israelite (highlands) or Canaanite (lowlands), was relatively free and open... This is not to say that ethnicity did not play a role in restricting the distribution of material culture traits. This is convincingly demonstrated by the insignificant presence of the standard hill country repertoire at sites in Philistia... What is blurred, however, is the distinction between areas traditionally associated with Canaanites...and Israelites. (1991: 108)

The distribution map is indeed quite strange if it is to reflect economic factors (see also Small 1997). As we shall see below, the general patterns observed by Esse are valid and of crucial importance.[5]

Before moving on, I would like to mention another indication that function was not the main reason for the CRJ's distribution. There were farmers and farmsteads in the highlands during the Iron Age II, but no such jars were found in that context! These farmers lived without them (for possible reasons, and for the situation in Transjordan, see below).

'Associations' between Artifacts and Peoples
For now it can be stated that, in accordance with Esse's conclusions and the abovementioned distribution maps, it is quite clear that the *main* users and producers of the CRJ were the Israelites (or 'proto-Israelites'), whether the jar was ethnically meaningful or not. This general correspondence cannot be disputed, and may lead to the supposition that the vessel was associated with the Israelites, which in turn can explain the awkward distribution mentioned above. But let me first explain what I mean by saying that they were associated with the Israelites (or the relevant highland groups as discussed above): these jars were not an ethnic marker per se, and were not used to transmit messages concerning ethnicity directly. In other words, no one used them specifically so people would see and know they were Israelite. Their use by the Israelites for various other reasons, the transmission of internal messages being one (see below), was grounds for them to be identified with the Israelites in a very general sense.

---

5. However, one should not ignore the problems that exist even at a lower level, as we have seen in the case of Megiddo and 'Afula. Such a pattern is not a simple result of trade or any other economic activity. The explanation must have been more complex.

This is similar, for example, to what Hodder observed in Kenya regarding the distribution of the Njemps stool type. These stools were an integral part of the Njemps cultural world, so that the neighboring Tugen usually refrained from obtaining these stools simply because, as it may be said, 'they are Njemps stools'. In this way, these objects came to express the difference between the Njemps and others (Hodder 1982a: 48-54). An additional example can be seen in the distribution of spoons among Lozi and Mbunda villages in another part of Africa. In an analysis of the material culture of the modern Lozi, Hodder noted some differences between the Lozi and the Mbunda in certain artifact types, such as baskets and spoons; he noted a rarity of spoons in the Mbunda villages (1982a: 111-17). In Hodder's words, 'such differences are not a result of a lack of awareness of each other's items. The symbiotic relationship results in intense interaction between Mbunda and Lozi. While Mbunda know of Lozi spoons, can describe them and could easily make them, "they are Lozi objects and we do not have them"' (Hodder 1982a: 115).

As these examples show, objects used by a group for whatever reason can become associated with that group, and as a result, be used in boundary negotiations in certain contexts. It is likely that the CRJ should be viewed in a similar way. We shall now see how accepting this 'Israelite association' for the CRJ can explain its distribution.[6]

The CRJ's 'Association' and its Distribution

The somewhat awkward distribution of the CRJ can be discussed on two levels. On the macro level, one should remember Esse's observation that the CRJ was hardly found in the Shephaleh and in the southern coastal plain, while it is abundant in the nearby highlands and is present, although usually in relatively smaller quantities, in most sites in the northern valleys. A conclusion that can be drawn from this is that boundaries were not kept between the Israelites of the highland (or other settlers in this region) and the Canaanites of the northern valleys in the same manner they were kept between the highlanders and the Philistines of the southern coastal plain.[7]

It is clear that boundaries were maintained in both cases, but the degree differed greatly. Again, this corresponds with ethnographic observations on other peoples, as by Hodder (1979b, 1982a; see also Bunimovitz and Faust 2001), who identified that at the northwestern edge of the Baringo Lake, the border between the Pokot and the Tugen is not clear cut, and people can be seen wearing symbols of both groups simultaneously. Some material traits,

---

6. Viewed in this way one could say that the use of CRJ is similar to what was defined earlier as 'resulting from ethnic behavior'.

7. Their absence from the eastern Jezreel valley is worth noting; the situation in Transjordan will be discussed in more detail below.

such as wooden milk jugs, spread from the Pokot well into the Tugen area—
a blurring of symbols that has also been identified between the Pokot and the
Njemps on the northeastern side of the lake and was explained by a low
level of economic competition and pressure. Moving eastward away from
the lake the Pokot and Njemps still have a common border, but identities
expressed in terms of dress and other traits of material culture are more
rigidly kept. There no one was found wearing items of both Njemps and
Pokot dress, despite the fact that Njemps and Pokot compounds were inter-
mingled. Hodder explained the stricter boundary maintenance as resulting
from an atmosphere of greater economic pressure and tension between the
two groups because of competition caused by the scarcity of grazing land
(Hodder 1982a: 27-31).

   Hodder's observations are quite revealing for our case. The boundaries
between Israelites and Philistines were maintained much more strictly,
probably because of the competition and tension between the groups, which
exceeded that of the Israelites and the Canaanites. This is another
demonstration of the extent to which the Philistines were the major factor in
confrontation with the Israelites at this time.

   On the micro level, one should consider the situation in the northern
valleys. The CRJ may have generally been found in this region, but it was
not present at all sites. The differential distribution of CRJ in these sites
seems significant when comparing 'Afula, where hundreds of *other* storage
jars were found, with sites such as Megiddo, where 62 examples of the CRJ
were found in Area CC, and where it composed some 10 per cent of the
area's entire assemblage (Esse 1992: 93; see now also Harrison 2004: 31-32,
with slightly updated figures). Moreover, it is likely that there is a difference
in the distribution of the CRJ even within sites, an issue to be discussed in
greater detail later in the chapter. I believe this distribution should be
regarded as a result of symbolic behavior, and not of trade or any other
economic explanation (see below).

The CRJ and Trade
It will be worthwhile to examine the use of the CRJ in trade, or, in other
words, to try to get a sense of its 'mobility'. Scholars have previously
assumed that the CRJ did not travel, considering the jar's weight and size.
According to Esse, 'the weight of a nearly complete jar in the Oriental
Institute Museum from Megiddo was over 32 kilograms' (1992: 96 n. 72).[8]
This finding is supported by other examples (Wengrow 1997: 307, and additional references). Given that an empty jar weighs more than 30 kg, and that
its volume is 150–200 liters, then a jar full of wine would have weighed

---

   8. Indeed, this assumption stands at the heart of one of Esse's arguments (1991: 107-
108).

some 180–230 kg (based on Wengrow 1997: 307), though, according to Raban, the CRJ contained only 110–20 liters, and weighed 'well over 150 kg' (2001: 495, 503; for lower weight calculations, see Artzy 1994: 137). Esse maintained that when full with liquid, the jar would have been too heavy for a donkey to carry, and dry goods would have been much easier to carry in sacks (1992: 96 n. 72). According to Raban, such jars when full could not have been lifted even by two individuals and could not have been raised to an animal's back; he also agrees that a donkey could not have carried such a weight (2000: 5; 2001; Esse 1992: 96 n. 72).[9] Esse claims it is possible that a few jars were transported on the back of a donkey, when empty, but this was probably not a common procedure (Esse 1992: 96; this will be further developed below).

So, what was responsible for the distribution of the CRJ in the northern valleys? In his second article, Esse attempted to explain the CRJ distribution beyond the central hill country as resulting from marriage patterns, namely, that the item was manufactured by women who 'married out' and brought their craft with them (1992: 97-101; see also Halpern 2001: 155). His idea has not been accepted by most scholars who have dealt with the issue. Small, for example, claimed that such large vessels *were* transported in some cultures, despite their size and weight (1997: 275; see also Killebrew 2001: 390[10]); he also claimed that the production of the CRJ required much knowledge, and was probably carried out by groups of men, members of large families (Small 1997: 276).

While I find Esse's approach to be convincing, it does, nevertheless, suffer from a major problem: various petrographical and archaeometrical studies (e.g. Yellin and Gunneweg 1989; Glass *et al.* 1993; Killebrew 2001; Cohen-Weinberger and Wolff 2001) have indicated that some of the jars found in various sites *were* transported over relatively long distances. The movement of potters, women or not, cannot explain this fact.[11] Nevertheless, we will return to this theory.

Some have concluded from this that the jars were used in trade or at least to transport products. Artzy (1994) has claimed that the examples of the CRJ found at Tel Nami were part of the incense trade, and were probably carried on camels; but the absence of these jars in the Negev seems to refute her idea. And, even if the trade routes did not go through the Negev but were located in the northern valleys as she suggested (1994: 132, Fig. 11), then

9. Note that, according to Hassig (1985: 216), a mule can carry some 105 kg. This is very far from the weight of a full CRJ, not to speak of the difficulties of transporting a jar due to its shape, breakability, etc.

10. Note that her 'ethnographic' example relates to sea transport and to the vessels themselves, and not to their contents; in this way her example is irrelevant for the context discussed here.

11. Unless, of course, one assumes that clay for pottery was imported.

we would expect to find these jars at Lachish and other sites in the southern coastal plain, an area prominent on her map.[12] In addition, the lack of camel bones in most sites (see below) causes a problem for her interpretation. Finally, her reconstruction of the trade routes relies on the assumption that all examples of the CRJ found in Transjordan should be dated to the Iron I (following Finkelstein), but it is quite clear today that at least some of the CRJ in Edom should be dated to the Iron Age II (see most recently Herr 2001; and more below). All in all, therefore, there seems to be nothing that can give real support to Artzy's interpretation.

Nevertheless, Wengrow also suggested that the CRJ was used for transporting products, and went even further to say that the Iron I highland settlements were part of an Egyptian economic system (1996). This suggestion does not match any evidence known so far from the archaeological or historical records, in terms of both distribution and date. Following Artzy, Wengrow tried to overcome the problem of the difficulty of transport of the CRJ by suggesting that the beast of burden was a camel (1997: 308,322-24).

This suggestion, however, is not supported by faunal remains from Iron I sites, where camel bones are practically absent. According to Hellwing *et al.* (1993: 348, table 15.50), camel bones were found only at 'Izbet Sartah (8.4%) and Heshbon (3%). They appear to be absent from Shiloh, Beersheba, Tel Masos, Arad, Mt Ebal, and Miqne. Furthermore, the weight of the jars themselves and their form would have made them quite uncomfortable on the back of a camel, as opposed to containers of skin or another material, therefore limiting the carrying capacity even further. Pottery is also breakable. Together, we must conclude that it is extremely unlikely that the CRJ was used for land transport in this way.

Even more problematic for Wengrow's hypothesis, however, is the attempt to connect the jar to an Egyptian economic system. After all, these jars were found mainly in the highland, and in domestic contexts, with relatively few found in the coastal plain, and none, to the best of my knowledge, in Egypt. Moreover, there is nothing in the highland villages to suggest either any real connections there with Egypt or their participation in an advanced economic system prior to the late eleventh century BCE (and the economic system of the eleventh century should be viewed in a different light; see, e.g., Finkelstein 1989). The absence of the CRJ in 'Afula and in the Shephelah also contradicts Wengrow's suggestion.

---

12. One should also remember that her attempt to claim that the CRJ in Nami is earlier to those in the highland is problematic, as highland sites are usually dated late because of the absence of imports (see above). The finds at Tel Nami and additional sites seems to indicate that the CRJ phenomenon (as part of the 'settlement' phenomenon) is earlier and should be dated to the thirteenth century. This is similar to the manner in which Finkelstein correctly interpreted the presence of the CRJ at Aphek (1988: 320).

Another idea was raised by Raban (2001). Since the jars could not have been moved when full, but we know that they *were* transferred, he came to the simple and astute realization that they were moved empty. But his further claim that the jars were used as 'standard measured containers for portions allocated by a hiring entity to its employees' has many problems (2001: 507). First, he attributes the jars to mercenaries, for example, and therefore assumes that the settlement sites of the Iron I were not villages but forts (including 'Izbet Sartah, Giloh, etc.). This contradicts every piece of evidence we currently possess, which declare unambiguously that these sites were villages. Second, Raban disregards the quantities of finds (a typical problem of distribution maps, discussed above in Chapter 7) that indicate that the highland is the core of the CRJ distribution and the lowland is the periphery.[13] Third, the absence of the CRJ in Philistia, where the mercenaries on which he bases his model are supposed to be found, is acknowledged by him (pp. 500, 503), but seems to refute his model altogether.[14] This final piece of evidence can also show that the distribution of the jar *is* connected with ethnicity (below).

A last theory to mention is that of Cohen-Weinberger and Wolff (2001). They also agree that the jars could only have been transferred when empty, and suggest that they were a desired commodity. Their explanation for the illogical distribution of the jars is that consumers looked for the best quality pot at the best price, and therefore bought from different sellers when circumstances changed (p. 654).[15] This explanation is problematic when

13.   The chronological division that he makes, like others, is unfounded, as the dating of the highland sites is insecure (see above). It is much more likely that the jar appeared in the thirteenth century in all regions. His disregard for quantity found at each site led him to conclude that the CRJ is abundant in Egyptian centers. Indeed only one(!) was found in Aphek, as opposed to dozens found in many highland villages. The CRJ is found in all lowland centers in quite minimal numbers, with none found in some sites. Even in Megiddo VIA, where relatively many examples of the CRJ were uncovered, their percentage is much smaller then in the highlands; and, in any case, Megiddo VIA was not an Egyptian center.

14.   Note also that his assumption that the jars could have been manufactured only by 'professional potters in order to meet very specific and highly standardized administrative demands' (Raban 2001: 506) is problematic. There are many examples of such jars manufactured by local or itinerant potters (e.g. London 1989; Killebrew 2001: 388-89, and additional references). Moreover, concentrating on the archaeological finds, we know that some of the jars were manufactured in Samaria near Shechem, and we do not know of a large administrative center in this region at the time, but only of relatively small villages. In addition, despite Raban's attempt to show that the jars were standard in size, this is clearly not the case.

15.   They also claim that the CRJ was used for a long period of time, and its known assemblage represents a long period in which vessels were bought from many producers, but this is not really an explanation. We do not know that the price of the different CRJs differed, and this is based only on their theory.

considering that transportation would make the jars more expensive, and this is especially strange in the context of the 'poor' Iron I villages of the highlands. It also ignores the absence of the CRJ in Philistia, as well as the question of why the manufacture of this pottery ceased at the tenth century BCE, among others.

In sum, the fact that the CRJ did travel is intriguing, but it cannot be explained simply along economic lines. A social explanation is called for, such as that of the, albeit problematic, marriage patterns theory mentioned above (Esse 1992: 98-102; see more below).

CRJ and Symbolism

Despite the above criticism, I find Esse's observations to be of immense significance, but in need of elaboration. Although the movement of women potters through marriage cannot explain the distribution of the pots themselves, I do believe that it is plausible that marriage and the movement of women do lie behind the distribution of the CRJ. Through an explanation of this sort I will attempt to shed light on the mobility of the CRJ.

I have discussed the symbolic meaning of the CRJ and its association with the Israelites, which does not necessarily make it an 'ethnic marker' per se, but stems merely from the fact hat it was used heavily by them (a sort of 'ethnic behavior'). But why *was* it used by the Israelites? As we have seen, there is an agreement that it suited the highlanders' way of life and economic structure, but it is recalled that the dichotomy between symbolism and functionality is artificial. I would like to argue that the CRJ carried another message.

The CRJ is a very large, quite conspicuous object that contained much of the house's water, wine, oil, or grain. In many societies storage is of immense symbolic importance and could even be essential in establishing one's status (see, e.g., Sather 1980; Barnes 1974: 65-67). I believe there is a high probability that these jars were symbolically associated with the house's wealth, stability, and perhaps even fertility (e.g. Strasser 1997: 90). The symbolic association of the these jars has been suggested by London, who states that 'large collar rim store jars thus may be said to symbolize a system of storage and economics, not an ethnic entity' (1989: 44).

Although the dichotomy London postulates between urban and rural setting for the jars is unfounded, as we have seen, this observation on the symbolism of the jars is insightful and leads us to wonder whether the full CRJ symbolized the abundance of the household (see also Hodder 1991: 55). As it appears that storage was the responsibility of women here (see Faust 2002, for references), as is the case in many cultures (e.g. Kana 1989; Barnes 1974: 76-77), it can be suggested that the CRJ came to symbolize the women of the house, a full jar representing their abundance and fertility. If such is the case, then the CRJ could have been transported following the marriage of women as part of the dowry, a symbol of the future success and fertility of the new marriage. Notably, movable objects, including kitchen utensils and storage vessels, often formed part of dowries in the ancient Near East (e.g. Westbrook 1991: 143; see also Roth 1989: 8).[16] This improves upon Esse's suggestion that women potters were moved, by suggesting that the jars were transported following the movement of women. The distribution of the CRJ might therefore reflect the regions with which the highlanders 'exchanged' wives.[17]

Support for the symbolic significance of the CRJ can be found in the fact that its manufacture in Cisjordan ceased in the tenth century BCE. While this has been a well known fact used by many as a chronological tool (e.g. Finkelstein 1996b: 123-37, and additional references), the question of why it disappeared has typically not been raised (for a similar phenomenon, see Faust 2002). As we have seen above, much of the way of life common in the Iron I came to an end around the transition from the Iron I to the Iron II (see Chapter 12),[18] and it is likely that once the structure in which relatively isolated households 'exchanged' their daughters was transformed (though the society remained patrilineal and patrilocal), these pots lost much of their symbolic meaning and ceased to be used. (Note that the Iron II farmers of the highlands managed without them; a fact that seems to put a nail in the coffin of the functional explanation.) Their continuation in Transjordan (see Herr 2001; and various examples recently in Ji 1997b: 31)[19] indicates that they were still meaningful in that region, which probably underwent different processes at the time. (The reality in Transjordan requires a separate discussion; for partial treatment see Chapter 20.)

16. For an example from a very different case in which artifacts are transferred only as part of marriage, see Chernela 1992.

17. It is clear that some jars could have been moved through other mechanisms, but I would like to suggest that much of the pattern discussed here results from this behavior.

18. Note that the entire period was marked by dramatic ceramic changes, which mark the social changes. See, for a partial discussion, Faust 2002; in prep.

19. For a thorough treatment of the issue, see Finkelstein 1996b: 127-37. Finkelstein does not accept the late dating of the CRJ in Transjordan. While most of his arguments are convincing, the accumulated data (including the above data given by Ji, which were published only after 1996, and Herr 2001) seem to indicate that CRJs were still used in Transjordan during the Iron Age II (though in a somewhat different form). It might be suggested that they were used as a way to connect to older traditions (e.g. Duncan 1998: 121), but whether this be the case (thereby strengthening the symbolic importance of the CRJ) or not is of less importance. The fact that CRJ ceased to be used in Cisjordan once the traditional structure was altered seems to indicate that the two are related. For a similar and complementary phenomenon that took place at the same time and as part of the same process, see Faust 2002; see also Faust in prep.

While this suggestion is complex, it can best explain the distribution of the CRJ. Groups had different relationships with each other, so only those who 'exchanged' daughters through marriage would have 'traded' this pottery. Notably, most marriages took place in the vicinity of the settlement, but a certain percentage is expected to take place at a greater distance in order to forge or maintain alliances (cf. Lehman 2004, and references). The distribution will be further discussed later on in this chapter, and additional supportive evidence will be presented. For the time being, however, it should be stressed that the precise explanation for the association of the CRJ with the Israelites is not crucial to the present discussion, but what is important is the distribution itself—namely, its absence in Philistia, despite the region's proximity to the highlands and in contrast to its presence in Canaanite regions. This can only be explained by such a symbolic association, and by the relations of the Israelites of the highlands with the Philistines of the coastal plain, as they differ from relations with the Canaanites of the northern valleys (see more below).

CRJ Distribution: A Summary
As mentioned above, due to the presumed discrepancy between its distribution and the territories inhabited by the Israelites, there was a growing consensus that the CRJ was not ethnically meaningful (e.g. Cohen-Weinberger and Wolff 2001; Raban 2001; Wengrow 1997, and summary and references there; see also Esse 1991; but see Small 1997; Ji 1995: 138; 1997b: 32; and even Esse 1992). However, as Esse summarizes, 'Individual ceramic types are rarely ethnic indicators, especially when the type in question is primarily a subsistence marker of low innate symbolic value, rather than a vessel type ideologically charged with cultic or ritual importance. *In the case of the collared rim pithos, however, there exists a growing body of quantitative evidence that suggests that an ethnic aspect can be isolated*' (1992: 102 [emphasis added]).[20]

Although used initially to transmit messages directed toward the group itself and not toward the outside, this specific message came, as a byproduct, to be sensitive also to ethnicity (David *et al.* 1988; see also above, Chapter 6). I therefore concur with Esse,[21] Ji, and others, that the CRJ was associated primarily with the Israelites and thus could have been used to mark identity in some contexts. Therefore, in areas where ethnicity played a

---

20.   Note that in contrast to Esse, it seems that 'simple' pottery could also be loaded with symbolism.

21.   It should be noted, however, that unlike Esse (1992: 103), I do not believe there was no interaction between the Israelites and Philistines. Interaction inevitably existed, but because of competition, tension and hostility, symbols did not cross boundaries (for a more theoretical disucssion, see Bunimovitz and Faust 2001, and references there).

major role in daily life, such markers also were important and boundaries were strictly kept. In others, where competition was weaker, ethnic groups existed but symbols and markers could have crossed ethnic boundaries (e.g. Hodder 1982a).

Ethnicity in these cases (when competition was weaker) can be better learned from the analysis of ethnic behavior—such as, in our case, the construction of the four-room house or the avoidance of pork[22]—than from the distribution of objects that were more easily transported. Indeed, a former study showed that these features are useful for identifying ethnic groups even in the northern valleys[23] (where the CRJ, as an object, is 'less efficient'). But such are tentative observations, which should be explored more fully in a thorough reinvestigation of the CRJ before any final conclusions can be reached. The important conclusion to be remembered here is that boundaries between Israelites and Canaanites were less rigid than those between Israelites and Philistines. I shall further develop this observation later on.

Philistine Pottery

Another factor supporting the above suggestion regarding differences in boundary maintenance along different boundaries in the Iron Age I is Philistine pottery. In the past, scholars used the prevalence of Philistine pottery as a general indicator for the presence or absence of Philistines (e.g. Raban 1991). This simplistic attitude, typical of the culture history approach that prevailed in the archaeology of ancient Israel, became a focus of criticism (e.g. Bunimovitz 1990) and was generally abandoned. The pottery, however, appears to have at least been ethnically meaningful during the Iron Age I, as indicated by several factors.

Philistine Pottery and Ethnicity
A full discussion of Philistine pottery is of course beyond the scope of the present study, but a few notes should suffice to exemplify the ethnic sensitivity of this decorated pottery. As we have seen in Chapter 14, the absence of monochrome (local Mycenaean IIIC1) pottery at Lachish and its abundance at Ekron was an instigator for Finkelstein (1995a, 2000) in forming his low chronology; he did not believe it to be possible that some sherds would not have reached Lachish if the sites were contemporaneous. A. Mazar (1997) and others (e.g. Ben-Tor and Ben-Ami 1998) have attempted to

22. Although at such contexts behavior might change, too, it seems to be a better index of ethnicity.
23. However, this applied to the Iron Age II (see Faust 2000a); for the Iron I, see below.

explain this pattern as having resulted from segregation between Philistines and Egyptio-Canaanites. Finkelstein, somewhat cynically perhaps, referred to this idea as 'apartheid theory' and rejected it altogether (Finkelstein 1998: 167-68).

In a recent study, Bunimovitz and I (2001) have used various ethnographic examples in attempting to explain the absence of monochrome pottery at sites such as Lachish; we concluded that the absence results from interaction and competition between the newly arrived Philistines and the local Egyptio-Canaanite elite and administration existing in other parts of the lowland, as at Lachish. We have shown that societies or groups can interact with some elements of material culture not crossing social boundaries (see also Hodder 1979a, 1979b, 1982a; Graves 1994; Hensler 1998; Stark et al. 2000; Clark 2001, and references; see also various papers in Stark 1998; Douglas and Kramer 1992). Finkelstein (2003) has attempted to undermine the importance of ethnography in the present case, but I believe that his counter-arguments are not convincing. After all, it is sufficient for there to be one example of groups interacting with no mingling of some traits in order to undermine the logic behind the low chronology.

It should be noted that a close look at the archaeological evidence also supports our argument. Our understanding of the role of the monochrome pottery finds support in its absence not only from Lachish, but also from Gezer, Beth-Shemesh, and Tel Batash, all situated much nearer to Ekron. If one wishes to follow Finkelstein's argument, it must be claimed that in tandem with the first phase of Philistine settlement in Canaan the entire northern Shephelah was abandoned, only to be quietly resettled as soon as the Philistines adopted the bichrome pottery. Such took place, one must say, even though the archaeologists who have excavated these sites did not identify this settlement gap.[24] Without repeating the entirety of our arguments in detail (see Bunimovitz and Faust in prep.; see also above), it can be said here that our understanding implies that the monochrome pottery had a place in the ethnic negotiations of the twelfth century in southern Canaan. Due to its limited distribution at the urban site of Tel Qasile, we suggested that even the bichrome pottery had a similar function (Bunimovitz and Faust 2001). That is, in Tel Qasile's Stratum X, bichrome pottery is found in large quantities in one excavation area dug by A. Mazar (1980: 10; 1985a: 122-23), while in a nearby area, excavated by B. Mazar in earlier excavations, hardly any such pottery was found, leading Mazar (Maisler) to label the stratum as 'Post-Philistine' (Maisler 1950–51: 128). We believe that the

24. Finkelstein himself stressed the continuity of settlement in Gezer (1996d: 233; 2000: 171). It should be stressed that the few 'monochrome' sherds that were reported at the site date to the Late Bronze Age, and are not of the Myenaean IIICb type (e.g. A. Mazar 1998: 185; Dever 1998: 48; Na'aman 2000: 2-3).

distribution is not incidental, and that the two areas may have originally been inhabited by different groups. The area where no Philistine pottery was found is the very same quarter in which the well-known four-room houses were discovered (see Chapter 9, and more below). The ethnic significance of the four-room house has already been established, and is only strengthened by the occurrence of the four-room house in an area of Tel Qasile where bichrome pottery is absent. The complexity of Tel Qasile will be discussed in more detail below; for now, it can be used as a tool in demonstrating that Philistine pottery, both monochrome and bichrome, was ethnically meaningful.

Distribution
A new look at the overall distribution of the bichrome pottery (Fig. 19.3) can help us understand the changing nature of boundary maintenance in the Iron Age I, and complement the picture presented above in light of the discussion of the CRJ.

Figure 19.3. *Iron Age I Philistine Pottery*
(based on A. Mazar 1992b: Fig. 8.5).

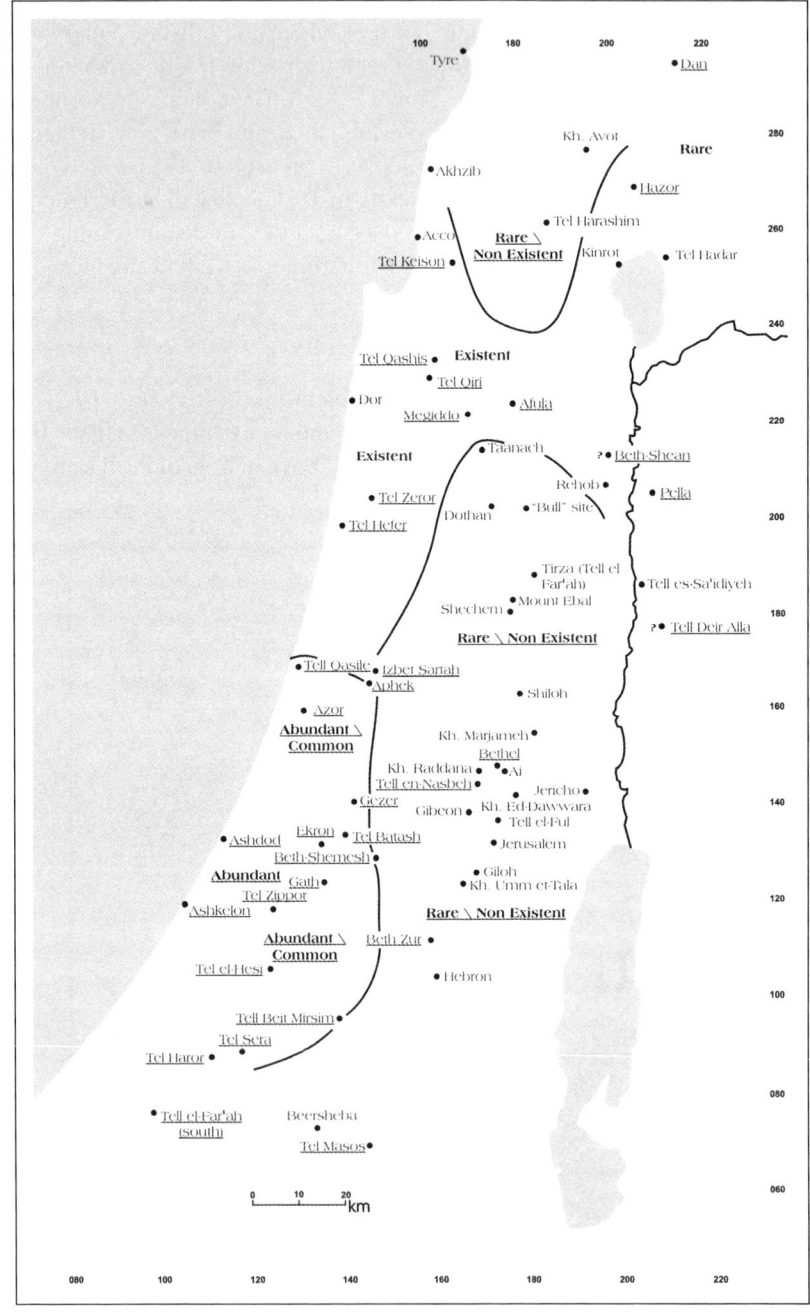

Figure 19.4. *Distribution Map of Philistine Bichrome Pottery.*

Distribution maps of bichrome vessels have been drawn by several scholars (e.g. Graham 1981a: 32; T. Dothan 1982: 26; H. Weippert 1988: 378; Dothan and Dothan 1992: 27); this pottery is found at practically every site in the southern coastal plain, and also is present in the Sharon plain and the northern valleys (see Raban 1991; S. Wolff 1998: 453; E. Stern 2000: 205-206; see also Tubb 2000). At sites in the southern coastal plain and parts of the Shephelah, e.g., Ekron, Ashdod, Ashkelon, Qasile, Beth-Shemesh, etc., it composes a large part of the assemblage (see Stager 1995: 342). At sites of the Sharon plain and northern valleys—e.g. Tel Hefer, Tel Zeror, Dor, Megiddo, 'Afula,[25] Hazor, Dan—its percentage is much smaller (e.g. T. Dothan 1982; Dothan and Dothan 1992; Raban 1991; Stern 2000; and entries of the various sites in the *NEAEHL*).

It should be noted that the maps are problematic, since they do not present the quantities of pottery found nor do they indicate the absence of finds at an excavated site. Therefore, even if there is an agreement that this pottery should be associated with the Philistines, the map cannot help us locate them, as any dot on the map might indicate an insignificant amount of bichrome pottery, which, for example, could have reached the site by way of trade.[26] But the map can still serve us here, as upon first glance one reveals a clear anomaly: while the center of production lies in the southern coastal plain and the products reached as far north as Tel Dan and Tel Hazor, hardly any such pottery was found in the nearby highlands (Fig. 19.4[27]).

Philistine Pottery in the Highlands
The appearance of Philistine pottery in the central highlands in extremely small quantities and only at a few sites is significant (note that the bichrome pottery is very distinguishable, and even body sherds are usually included in drafting distribution maps). The maps produced by T. Dothan (1982: 26, Fig. 2), Dothan and Dothan (1992: 79), and H. Weippert (1988: 378) all

25. This site had a relatively large number of such sherds. See M. Dothan 1955: 39; see also Graham 1981a: 35.

26. At Hazor, for example, very few such sherds were discovered (e.g. T. Dothan 1982: 90; Dothan and Dothan 1992: 105).

27. Figure 19.4 is a schematic map intended to show the main distribution of Philistine pottery, and is not intended to locate every single sherd found at every site. The underlined sites are those in which Philistine pottery was found. Still, in some regions even sites in which a few sherds were found are mapped, due to the nature of the discussion. Furthermore, it is likely that there were changes in the percentage of Philistine pottery over time in the very same sites, and possibly also among different contemporaneous parts of sites. Note that in order to overcome some of the shortcomings of distribution maps, this map attempts to show both the presence and absence of this type of jar. In addition, I have also commented on the frequency of the collared-rim jars in the various sites and regions. Notably, due to the many subtleties involved, the map cannot be used without a close reading of the text.

mentioned such sites. The first two mention Bethel, Tell en-Nasbeh, Tell el-Ful, and Beth-Zur,[28] while the third omits Tell el-Ful. These maps do not stress the fact that all of the other Iron I sites in the highlands, including Giloh, Shiloh, 'Ai, Raddana, and Mt Ebal, lacked such pottery entirely! While this may be sufficient to indicate that the highlands were practically devoid of bichrome pottery, I believe that re-examining the four sites where it was found will be worthwhile.

Tell el-Ful. In the final excavation report of the site it is stressed that the pottery found is post-Philistine (N.L. Lapp 1993: 447; although the excavators would have been quite happy to find Philistine pottery, as it would have supported their hypothesis regarding the Philistine fort at the site). Indeed, this site is not mentioned by Weippert, probably because of this. Thus, it should for all practical matters be omitted from the map (see also Graham 1981a: 30).

Bethel. The excavator writes that 'there is little Philistine pottery at Bethel…' (Kelso 1968: 63, see also pp. 64, 65), and notes that 'Bethel has no record of Philistine occupation' (Kelso 1993: 194). According to Dothan (1982: 54), very few Philistine pottery sherds were found in the excavations, all in unstratified contexts (she refers to four such sherds). The insignificance of these finds is also stressed by Graham (1981a: 33).

Tell en-Nasbeh. According to Dothan (1982: 54), 47 Philistine sherds were found (along with 12 questionable sherds). Graham mentions the same figure, and asserts that this is still insignificant, possibly resulting from trade (1981a: 33).[29]

Beth-Zur. The excavators note that 'Albright had stressed the fact that Philistine pottery is rarely found outside the maritime plain so that the absence of typical Philistine pottery at Beth-Zur is not surprising' (Funk 1968: 50). T. Dothan (1982: 44, 48) mentions Philistine sherds that were found at the site, claiming that 'the Philistine ceramic finds at Beth-Zur are quite meager and atypical and belong to a debased version' (p. 48). It should be noted that these meager finds were reported in the 1931 season (Sellers 1933: Fig. 31, Plate VII; also Sellers and Albright 1931: 7); apparently nothing was found in the later seasons (Funk 1968: 50, see also p. 51; Graham 1981a: 33).

---

28. Note that some such pottery was found also at 'Izbet Sartah (e.g. Finkelstein 1986). This site, however, has a complex history, and at least during some stage of its settlement it was part of the coastal economic system (see Faust 2003a).

29. Gunnweg *et al.* (1994) claimed that some of this pottery was manufactured locally. If this is correct, than it might be connected with the Philistine domination in the region as discussed in Chapter 12 (although the quantities are extremely meager).

Discussion
The above exemplifies the problematic nature of distribution maps. How should we treat these sites? Even if, let us say, all four *can* be said to have a number of bichrome sherds, their amount in the highland would still be notably insignificant. But the truth appears to be that only at Tell en-Nasbeh is any amount of such pottery found, and even there in relatively insignificant numbers.[30] At Tell el-Ful, Beth-Zur, and probably Bethel it is practically *non-existent* in consideration of the extent of these digs and the type's conspicuousness (see Graham 1981a: 33). Indeed, the distribution map published by Graham (p. 32) leaves the highlands devoid of it.

Again, we face an intriguing distribution: many of the highland sites are much closer to the coastal plain than the northern valleys, yet hardly any such pottery was found in them. This cannot be attributed to a Philistine disinterest in the region in terms of trade, for evidence suggests the contrary, as we have already seen in Chapters 12 and 14. The highly symbolic value of the Philistine pottery has already been established, and, as we shall see, explaining the absence of Philistine pottery in the highlands as a result of symbolic behavior corresponds with other lines of evidence that can give reason for other oddities in distribution, therefore strengthening this suggestion.[31]

The Distribution of the CRJ and Philistine Pottery Compared

It is worthwhile to consider the distribution of bichrome pottery alongside that of the CRJ. When the distribution maps of the two are compared (see Fig. 19.5[32] [next page]), an interesting fact clearly emerges: the central highlands and the southern coastal plain traded and exchanged artifacts and even symbols with the far away northern valleys and Galilee. Examples of sites in which *both* Philistine pottery and CRJ were found include:[33] Tel Qasile (see more below), Tel Gerisa (Herzog 1993: 483), and Tel Hefer (Paley and Porath 1993: 612) in the Sharon (in the latter two they were apparently found together); as well as 'Ein Hagit (S. Wolff 1998: 453), Tel Qiri

30. The fact that such pottery was found at Tell en-Nasbeh, and perhaps also at Bethel, can be attributed to the intensive interactions between Israelites and Philistines in this region; see Faust 2006; see also Chapter 12.

31. Such an awkward distribution was already discussed in Chapter 7; it is reiterated here that such is not a result of a lack of interaction or of chronological problems, but is quite clearly a result of cultural avoidance.

32. Figure 19.5 depicts, somewhat schematically, varying degrees of boundary maintenance in the Iron Age I, based on the distribution of several material traits.

33. Note that in some cases the quantities are small. In extreme cases, such as Hazor where only *two* bichrome sherds were found, I preferred not to discuss the site at all in this context.

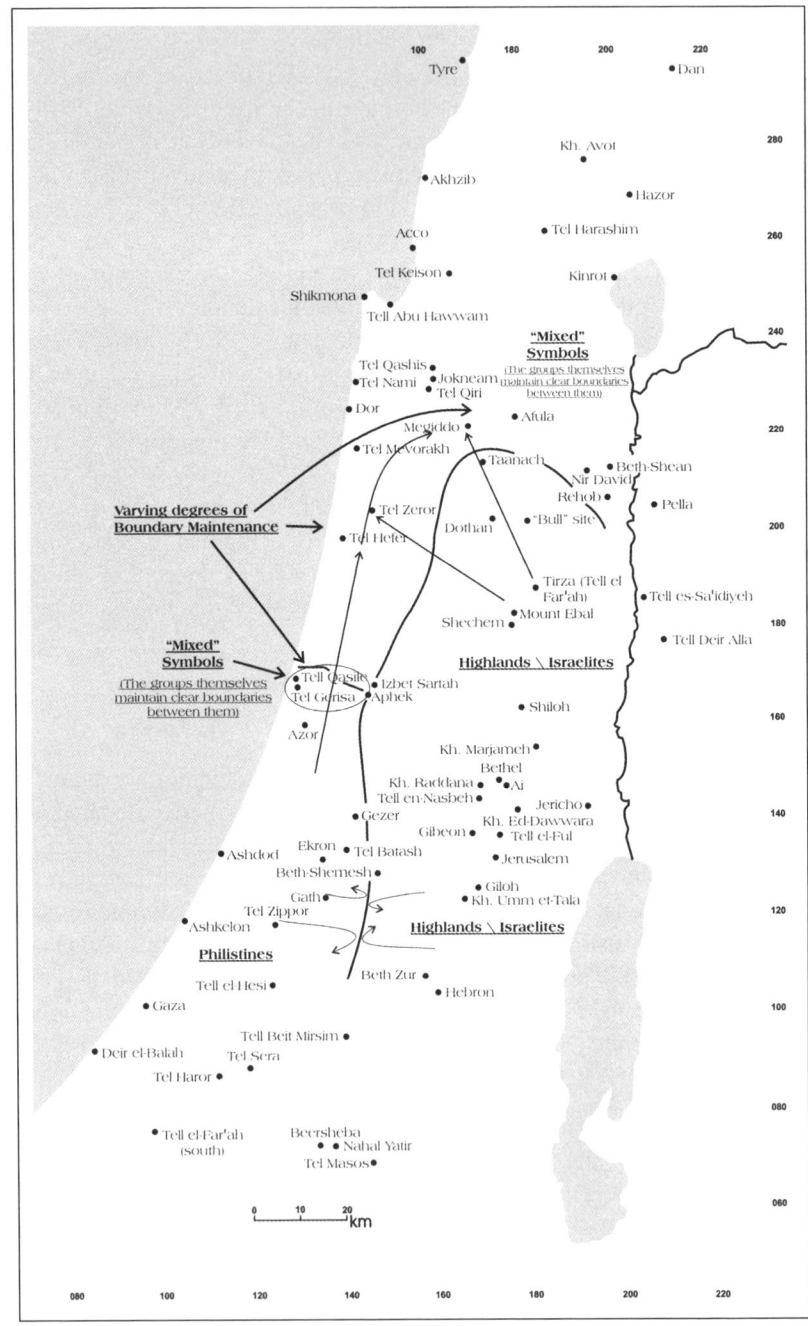

Figure 19.5. *Boundary Maintenance in the Iron Age I.*

(Hunt 1987: 200), Yoqneam (Hunt 1987: 200), and Megiddo (see more below), and some others in the north (see also Raban 1991).[34] However, despite its proximity, Philistia did not have the same relations with the highlands as it had with the north. The bichrome pottery, therefore, presents the flipside of what we saw concerning the CRJ, and together both clearly indicate that symbols did not cross boundaries between the Israelites and the Philistines: the CRJ is hardly found in the southern coastal plain, while bichrome pottery is almost completely absent in the highlands. Since both peoples interacted with areas much farther away, this trend cannot be seen as a result of isolation, but rather of boundary maintenance and cultural avoidance.

In this light the distinction between 'Izbet Sartah and Gezer, with the former containing CRJ and very little Philistine pottery, and the latter much more Philistine pottery but no CRJ, becomes significant despite the similarity of many forms (Dever 1993b: 27*; see also 1992b: 551-52). The following analysis of Tel Qasile can further demonstrate the point.

Four-Room Houses, Collared-Rim Jars and Philistine Pottery at Tel Qasile

It is recalled that bichrome pottery was found only in one quarter of Stratum X at Tel Qasile (Area C; e.g. A. Mazar 1980, 1985a), while it was almost completely absent from the other (Area A; Maisler 1950–51). The four-room houses found at the site were also mentioned; they are usually offered as examples of this house plan in a non-Israelite context, as the site after all has been regarded as Philistine. It is interesting that, generally speaking, there is a negative correlation between the presence of four-room houses and Philistine bichrome pottery at the site (Fig. 19.6 [next page]). That is, in Area A bichrome pottery was not found but the four-room house is common, while the opposite is true of Area C (A. Mazar 1980: 74-75).[35]

34. For example, Dan. Additional sites can be identified by comparing the various distribution maps mentioned above, although this should be done very carefully, as these maps are problematic. See, e.g., the inclusion of 'Afula in H. Weippert's map of four-room houses and CRJ (1988: 398) even though, as we have already seen, no examples of four-room houses have really been found there, and only one sherd of CRJ was reported. Note that the same map has many problems, e.g., the incorrect location of Aphek and 'Izbet Sartah (site nos. 21 and 22) and also, though on a smaller scale, of Tel Qasile and Tel Gerisa (nos. 23 and 24).

35. The excavator stresses the fact that the dwelling excavated near the temple was *not* a four-room house (A. Mazar 1980: 74-75). Yet the building seems indeed to have been a variant of this general type with three rooms, as one gathers from the detailed description of Mazar (1980: 43-45). At a later stage another house was excavated in the southern part of Area C, near Area A, and is probably not of the four-room type, although it has pillars (Mazar and Harpazi-Ofer 1993). The situation at Tel Qasile was complex,

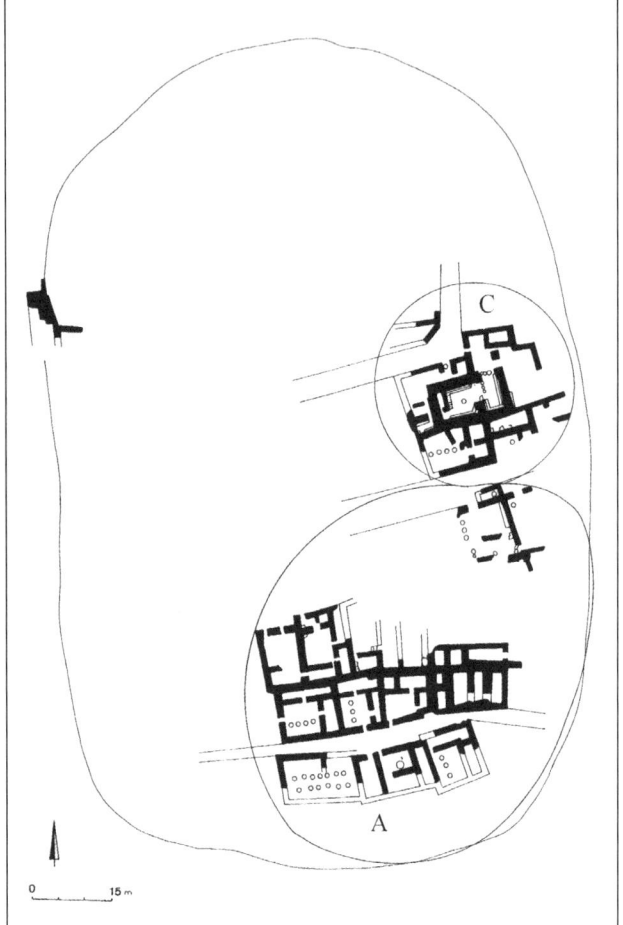

Figure 19.6. *Tel Qasile X.*
A plan of Tel Qasile Stratum X from the eleventh century BCE, showing the
two areas and the suggested different population groups, based on the
distribution of pottery and architecture.

While quantities admittedly are limited, the analysis of the CRJ at the site
is also revealing. From the final report it appears that the only complete
example of a CRJ was found in Area A, along with two complete rims
(A. Mazar 1985a: 57). Area C, however, produced 'only three small fragments of a 'collared rim' pithos' (A. Mazar 1985a: 57). This, despite the fact

and symbols were both avoided in certain contexts, and copied and manipulated in others.
Since the house was not a symbol, but rather a result of ethnic behavior, perhaps it could
have been copied more easily.

that the pottery of Area C was studied in much more detail. Since these quantities are quite small, these data could merely be incidental, but in context the comparison is important. It implies that while the inhabitants of the quarter revealed in Area A lived in the four-room house type, used the CRJ, and refrained from Philistine pottery, those in the quarter in Area C used bichrome pottery heavily but the CRJ only scarcely.[36] With this the importance of such traits in the Iron Age I is exemplified.

It is not my intention to say that the inhabitants of Area A were necessarily Israelite. Identities can vary; the inhabitants may have been, for example, Canaanites vying for power with the Philistines and consequently on bad terms with them. The pattern of distribution need not reflect a 'pure' model, as suggested for the highlands. The house excavated in the southern part of Area C, near Area A, can serve as an example of this complexity; it is most likely not a four-room house despite some similarities, yet its finds included a complete example and a few sherds of a CRJ (Mazar and Harpazi-Ofer 1993: 23-25), and virtually no Philistine bichrome pottery (p. 18). Whether Israelites lived in Tel Qasile or not, some of the inhabitants appear to have used 'Israelite' symbols, even if vesting them with different meaning in their interaction with the dominant Philistine group. Such circumstances can explain the local variations at Qasile, but most important is the evidence of non-random distribution of these ethnic traits. It suggests that symbols were played with at eleventh-century Tel Qasile.

Canaanites, Israelites, and Philistines in Megiddo VIA and the Northern Valleys

Megiddo Stratum VIA as a central focus of debate regarding ethnicity in the Iron Age I has already been discussed. Albright had suggested to identify the stratum as Israelite because of the examples of the CRJ found there (1937), then withdrew his suggestion following Engberg's criticism (1940). The Canaanite (or even Philistine, see, e.g., G. Davies 1986: 73) character of Stratum VIA has been well-accepted by most scholars ever since, Aharoni being a notable exception (1970; see more below). This acceptance has recently been reiterated by A. Mazar (2002), who, again, used the stratum as evidence *against* using the CRJ to identify Israelites.

Yet a fundamental assumption in these discussions has been that the ethnic identity of the site's inhabitants is monolithic, whether it be Canaanite, Philistine or Israelite. An exception has been Kempinski, who, on the

---

36. See A. Mazar 1985a: 124, the excavator of Area C, where he writes that 'the "collared rim" jar, a hall mark of the central hill-country sites, is represented at Tel Qasile only in a few isolated examples'. Note also that the excavator claims no four-room houses were found in Area C; see above.

basis of architectural differences (see below), suggested that 'the differences in the types of houses between areas A-A, D-D and C-C might be interpreted as an ethnic difference, with a separate group in each of these quarters' (1989: 83). Recently, the ethnically mixed nature of Megiddo VIA was stressed also by Halpern (2001: 155, 219, 376-77). Perhaps a detailed examination of the finds at Megiddo VIA will demonstrate for us the complex reality that existed there, as at Tel Qasile. But due to the extremely partial nature of the data and the many problems that accompany any attempt to use them for fine reconstructions, the suggestion below in light of this examination should be taken very cautiously, and tentatively.[37]

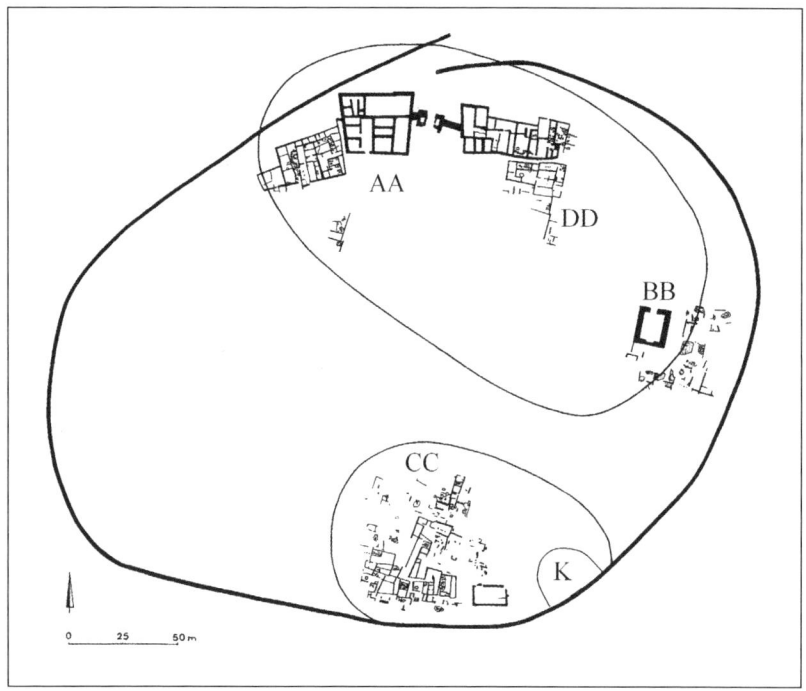

Figure 19.7. *Megiddo VIA.*
A plan of Megiddo Stratum VIA from the eleventh century BCE, showing the
different excavation areas and the suggested different neighborhoods, based
on the distribution of pottery and architecture.

A close look at the finds from this stratum indicates a strange pattern (see Fig. 19.7). The abovementioned 62 examples of the CRJ from Megiddo all come from Area CC, which, as Esse stressed, results from the fact that only

───────────────

37. It should be stressed that the arguments raised earlier in the chapter are not based upon the following.

in this area was he capable of completing the study. It is of course possible that the repertoire in other areas was similar. It is interesting to note, however, that all the examples of CRJ in the Megiddo report (Loud 1948: Plate 83; note that most of the CRJ mentioned by Esse were not reported in Megiddo's final report) also come from Area CC. This seems to support the fact that Area CC is the only (or at least the main) area where such jars were found.[38]

Upon examination of the distribution of Philistine pottery on the basis of the report,[39] however, the situation is more complex: the Philistine pottery, defined by Dothan (1982: 70-80.; but see A. Mazar 2002), has been found throughout the site, with somewhat smaller quantities perhaps in Area CC.

I would also like to look at architecture as an additional line of evidence. Let us return to Kempinski's claim regarding the several ethnic groups reflected in the architectural differences in Megiddo VIA. He asserts, 'the private houses in area C-C are of interest, since it is here that some of the architectural features of the Iron Age are best defined. In contrast to the west of area A-A, where the private houses tend to show the traditional plan of the Canaanite court house, here some three- and four-room houses could be reconstructed...' (1989: 83-84). While many of these houses are probably not of the four-room type, they differ greatly from those discovered in other parts of the tel, and while the difference may be, at least partially, attributed to wealth, it is likely that Kempinski's basic observation is correct.

Thus with caution, the complex reality reflected in Megiddo VIA can be reconstructed. Part of the population used the symbolically loaded CRJ and lived in relatively poor houses. Others lived elsewhere in a different type of dwelling and hardly used the CRJ—a situation that finds some similarity at the nearby site of 'Afula.

'Afula, it is recalled, has been mentioned in the discussion of the awkward distribution of the CRJ in the northern valleys, as the jar was found in Megiddo in relatively large quantities but is practically absent from 'Afula. According to the excavator, 'among the hundreds of jar-rims found there are none belonging to the "collared" jars. Such jars...are very common in the... hilly central region...and are present also in Megiddo, though not in large numbers. Their absence in stratum III at 'Afula, except for one (intrusive?) rim in stage B, can only be explained on the assumption that the local potters chose a particular type of storage-jar for use' (M. Dothan 1955: 36). Conversely, Philistine pottery was found there in relatively high numbers

38. Harrison (2004), in the new report on Stratum VI, identified a few examples in other excavation areas, but 'the overwhelming majority of the collared pithoi were found in Area CC' (2004: 32).

39. I accept A. Mazar's (2002) analysis of the stratification and provenance of the Philistine pottery.

compared to other excavations in the northern region (p. 39). In all likelihood, this results not from a Philistine presence at the site, but from a local
population on good terms with the Philistines, or emulating them; similarly,
the locals were on bad terms with the Israelites, thereby avoiding the CRJ.
The lack of four-room houses at 'Afula strengthens both the 'non-Israelite'
character of the population and the significance of the CRJ as an important
trait.

The historical reality behind the story of the battle between the Israelites,
under Deborah and Barak, and the Canaanites, under Yavin and Sisera
(Judg. 4–5), is not of our interest here, but the story, whether real or not, can
serve as an illustration for the circumstances evident here. A minor detail of
the story can be used to illustrate an ethnic (or totemic) reality similar to that
which emerged from the discussion of 'Afula. In addition to the two warring
parties, the Jezreel valley was also inhabited by at least one more group,
whose affiliation or extent of solidarity was not clear, or was even in the
process of evolving (or shifting) at the time. I am referring to the incident in
which Ya'el, the wife of Hever, the Kenite, was approached by Sisera.
Sisera ran to Ya'el's tent in hope of finding refuge, only to be killed by her.
It could be in this story that Hever's household sympathies toward the
Israelites were not known to Sisera, or, more likely, that Hever's group was
on good terms with Sisera beforehand, but the alliance changed following
the battle.[40] Such complexities in ethnic relations can demonstrate the situation in the northern valleys in general and in Megiddo in particular. The
conclusions presented here regarding the much-debated Megiddo VIA (see,
most recently, A. Mazar 2002) are tentative, require more data, and—it
should be stressed—are not essential to the main argument of this chapter.

But the analysis here can suggest that we are not necessarily dealing with
Israelites and their CRJ, and Philistines and their bichrome pottery; rather, it
is possible that one or even both of the groups who left behind these artifacts
were Canaanite, composed of different elements within the notably hetero-
geneous Canaanite society. This diversity is best evidenced in the Iron Age
I, a period of decline in Canaanite areas. These elements within Canaanite
society related differently to other 'non-Canaanite' groups, and probably to
each other, forging various alliances with the Israelites and Philistines. Exact
definitions are unattainable at the moment.[41]

40. I use the story, whatever its historicity, as an illustration, as I have used ethnographic parallels elsewhere. Since the story relates to the same time and region as we are
discussing here, it is tempting to give it more credibility, but this would be well beyond
the scope of the present monograph. Here it is used only as an 'ethnohistorical' source.
For a similar interpretation of biblical texts, pertaining to the same period though in a
different region, see Weitzman 2002.

41. It is interesting that the Bible often mentions several 'peoples' who occupied the
land prior to the Israelite settlement, and partially in tandem with it. There is no external

Summary

The CRJ was regarded in the past as a 'type fossil' of the Israelite settlement in Canaan, an assumption refuted in the last few decades, mainly as a result of the recognition of the jar's wide distribution, but also as part of a more skeptical approach to the issue of identifying ethnicity through material remains. While the criticism that Albright's views were extremely simplistic for our standards may be correct, I believe that the complete negation of this connection is also simplistic. The CRJ carries importance for the study of ethnicity—it is not suggested to be an ethnic marker *per se*, but an item associated with the Israelites, in a manner similar to how various items we discussed from the Baringo district were associated with certain groups. This association did not thoroughly prevent the CRJ from reaching non-Israelite hands, and it could have been used when the Israelite association was not seen in negative terms or was irrelevant. However, when relations with Israelites were characterized by competition or tension, we find their distribution among non-Israelites to be much more limited. The same is true for the Philistine bichrome vessels, an artifact with much to say regarding the nature of the Philistine's interactions with others during the Iron Age I. Philistine bichrome pottery is present in the northern valley's Canaanite centers, but not in the much nearer highlands; the CRJ is found also in the north but not in Philistia.

The distribution of both Philistine pottery and the CRJ seem to indicate that Israelites and Philistines had 'exchange' relations with at least some elements in the north (Canaanite groups), but relatively tense relations with each other. This pattern also supports the conclusion, reached earlier in this work (especially Chapters 12–15), regarding the Philistine significance for

evidence for the existence of these peoples, though for some it has usually been taken for granted (see the discussion in Chapter 22). Perhaps the biblical writer retained a vague memory of the complex ethnic reality in Canaan during the early phases of Israel's emergence.

Also insightful is a closer examination of the writings of Kempinski, who believed that Stratum VII was Israelite, and that the Israelites 'participated in turning the village into a commercial town', although, he says, the initiative for such came from the new Philistine rulers (1989: 87, 82). While his suggestion may be laden with problems, it is still appealing. Could it be, if we are to follow his ideas, that the Israelites who dwelt in the town went through a process of assimilation or acculturation during the period of Stratum VI, and adopted Canaanite ways of life? Their contacts with their 'relatives' elsewhere, including by marriage, can explain the differences between them and the other inhabitants of Megiddo. Yet we lack the data sufficient, ideally, from all the houses in Strata VII–VI at Megiddo, in order to fully tackle the issue. Thus, the above remains an enigma, until large scale excavations of these levels can supply us with more, reliable data.

Israelite ethnicity. The above discussion also demonstrates the fluid nature of ethnic symbols.[42]

And finally, contrary to recent trends in Near Eastern archaeology, but in accordance with recent attitudes throughout the world, it is clear that material culture is loaded with meanings pertaining to various forms of identity, including ethnicity. The distribution of material traits, pottery included, is affected by social boundaries, and it is clear that these are responsible for the distribution of the CRJ and the Philistine pottery.

42.   The changing nature of ethnic relations in different boundaries, where some traits might 'respect' certain boundaries while 'ignoring' others, is relevant for all other traits discussed in this book.

20

TRANSJORDAN REVISITED

One of the major practical, though not methodological, obstacles in the identification of the Israelites with some traits of the central highland's material
culture is that there is a great similarity between these finds and those in the
highlands of Transjordan (see, e.g., Finkelstein 1996a: 200, 204, 205, 208).
Though this issue was treated earlier in several places, I believe it deserves a
short discussion here on its own.

The Problem

The archaeological evidence establishes the similarity between the small
villages erected in the highlands on both sides of the Jordan River during the
Iron I. This has been discussed by many, and has also emerged from various
discussions in this book (e.g. Chapters 9 and 19). Ibrahim, for example, has
written regarding the four-room house that the examples from Ammonite
and Edomite areas 'do not fit with the conclusions of Shiloh' (1975: 73).
Regarding the CRJ, he claimed that the distribution of this type in various
parts of Transjordan 'may be disappointing for those who adopted the
Albright proposal' (Ibrahim 1978: 123). More generally, but in the same
spirit, Finkelstein has written the following:

> even if we could distinguish the highland's people archaeologically from
> Canaanites and Philistines, there remains the problem of the Iron I sites of the
> Transjordanian Plateau. From the material culture point of view, they are virtu-
> ally identical to the hill country sites west of the Jordan, though they gave birth
> to different ethnoi and national identities. In other words, from the archaeo-
> logical record there is absolutely no way to distinguish the ethnic identity in
> the highland of Cisjordan from the people of Transjordan. (1996a: 200)

Real Problems vs. False Similarities

We must first distinguish between real and superfluous similarities. In regard
to houses, for example, the number of four-room houses found in
Transjordan has been exaggerated, and the four-room house type has been

confused with houses with pillars. The house excavated by Ibrahim in Sahab is a good example, as it is often brought as an example of an inappropriate designation of 'Israelite' for the four-room house. The house is dated to the Iron II, when this area was probably Ammonite and expected to have been void of Israelites. (The problematic nature of the implicit supposition that sites inhabited only one ethnic group repeats itself here). The presence of such a house at the site—while by no means as disastrous to the ethnic designation of the house as some claim—would nevertheless be somewhat problematic, not to mention if many such examples were unearthed outside Israelite territory. However, the Sahab example has *nothing* to do with the four-room house type (Chapter 9, above). It is a large and complex structure, one room of which is subdivided by a row of monoliths,[1] and as influential as it has been in questioning Shiloh's suggestion to call the house type 'Israelite', it falls into what I called the 'false similarities' category. It is but one of many such examples (see Chapter 9; see also Herr and Clark 2001: 44).

Yet even after this kind of evidence is eliminated, we still face many genuine similarities in some regions of Transjordan. Therefore, our next undertaking is to show that the notion that these similarities can be used to disprove the ethnic label of the villages of Cisjordan is wrong.

Israelites in Transjordan

It is well known that there were Israelites in Transjordan. This is clearly attested in the period's written sources, both biblical and external, as in Numbers 32, Deuteronomy 2–3; 4.41-49; Josh. 17.1-6; 1 Chron. 7.14, among many others (see MacDonald 2000: 101-55, for a detailed treatment and various references; see also Aharoni *et al.* 1993; Aharoni 1979), and the Mesha stone, an independent external source with a clear reference to the presence of Israelites in Transjordan (e.g. McCarter 1996: 90-92; Aharoni *et al.* 1993: 97).

Several scholars have indeed stressed this fact in their addressing of some of the distribution issues; these include Ji (1995, 1997a), Herr (2000: 178), Herr and Clark (2001), Younker (1999: 16), and others. Some have rejected the abovementioned discrepancies by merely indicating that Israelites lived in this region. Others have even attempted to use new archaeological data in conjunction with the biblical texts to learn more about the settlement process

---

1. Since this house is dated to the Iron Age II, when the final form of the four-room house had been crystallized, we would expect an even greater degree of conformity in design than is to be expected from an Iron Age I house. In the present case, however, even if the house would have been dated to the Iron Age I, its categorization as a four-room house type would be unjustified. Note that in his 1997 summary, Ibrahim did not repeat his suggestion that this is a four-room house (1997: 451-52).

of the Israelites. Herr, for example (following Cross 1988), has used the early date of the four-room houses found at Tell el-'Umeiri as an indication of the early date of the settlement of the tribe of Reuben, which in turn can explain the traditions regarding the tribe's seniority as Jacob/Israel's first-born (2000). Without going into detail on these other suggestions, we have sufficient evidence to show that there is no real problem of distribution regarding the four-room house in Transjordan; rather, it is another indication for the presence of Israelites there. Outside of possible areas of Israelite settlements in Transjordan we are left with very few examples of four-room houses and CRJ.

Furthermore, most of these examples date to the Iron I (e.g. Ji 1997a: table 1;[2] Daviau 1999: 132), prior to the final crystallization of ethnic groups in the region. During the Iron Age II, the number of genuine examples of four-room houses found outside Israelite territories in Transjordan (e.g. the structure unearthed at Ghrareh; Hart 1988: 92) is very limited indeed, and can be explained, in light of their relative rarity, by a cultural connection and ephemeral influence on the peoples that lived there by their Israelite neighbors. There is also the (less likely) option that Israelites were nevertheless present in these places (as a minority, i.e., a family or a groups of families), but this cannot be inferred on the basis of the four-room house alone; Proving such should include a full analysis of the finds within the context of each house, as for example was carried out by Stein *et al.* in another case study (1996).

Although he left some issues unresolved, it would be worthwhile to close this section with the following quotes from Ji, who notes that 'central and northern Transjordan may be thought of as an extension of the highland material culture in Cisjordan' (1997a: 411). Although Ji stresses that the presence of four-room houses or CRJ are insufficient to prove the presence of Israelites, he also warns that

> Although in the past decade there has been burgeoning evidence showing cultural, material similarities between the central hill country and Transjordan, many archaeologists have ignored or minimized the potential of Israelite presence east of the Jordan valley. In so doing, they have missed the possibility that evidence of close contacts between the two regions indicates the presence of Israelite tribes in Transjordan. (1997a: 412)

Differences in Levels of Boundary Maintenance

An additional point that needs to be taken into account when discussing the distribution of Israelite traits that were actually found outside Israelite territory is that, as we have already seen, ethnic boundaries need not be kept in

---

2. While I have reservation regarding the table, it seems to be a good reference point.

the same way everywhere. While strict boundaries were maintained between the Israelites and the Philistines, as they competed for power and economic resources, and between the Israelites and the Canaanites of the valleys, although on a *much* smaller scale, the boundaries between the Israelites and the groups that contemporaneously settled in Transjordan (in addition to Israelites or those who became Israelites) could have been much more blurred (cf. Hodder 1982a), particularly during the Iron Age I. These groups came from a similar socio-economic background, and if one accepts the historicity of the core of the relevant stories in Judges, the wars between them can be seen as fighting between tribes or totemic groups, similar to the wars among the Israelite tribes themselves, and not between entirely hostile and foreign groups.[3] The much lower degree of hostility between these groups is to be expected considering the existence of more foreign, alien, and threatening groups in the background (i.e. the powerful newcomers from the Aegean world who kept many of their 'strange habits' throughout the Iron Age I).

Moreover, in light of the unclear boundaries in Transjordan in the Iron Age I (as noted, e.g., by Herr and Clark 2001: 66), and the fluidity in identity that is expected to have existed, it is possible that during the Iron Age I there were people who were Israelite or in the process of becoming so, but due to various reasons their descendents in the Iron Age II became Ammonite, Moabite, etc. This is particularly plausible considering that most of the distributional problems are dated to the Iron I. Consider, for example, the presence of the CRJ in Iron Age I Sahab. There it is possible that some of the people were Israelite or in the process of becoming so, but due to the dominance of the Ammonites at a later stage they became Ammonite. In any event, this pattern is an indication of the fluidity of identities or the blurred boundaries that existed in Iron Age Transjordan, and the fact that objects could have easily been appropriated and used by members of different groups.

Such scenarios, while by no means certain, can still undermine much of the importance given to the few 'discrepancies' that did exist at the time. But further research, and more houses excavated and published are needed in order to more confidently identify ethnic groups in Iron I Transjordanian contexts.[4]

---

3. At least the final form of the stories probably reflects the monarchic period, with its more 'advanced' states.

4. Many of the Transjordanian sites are located on top of Late Bronze Age II sites, and can be seen as continuations of them, which tentatively indicates settlement continuity (though other explanations can account for the phenomenon), so that it is possible that the settlement process started there before that in the central highland, as was suggested by Herr (2000) and Herr and Clark (2001; see also Cross 1988; see also above). This

Summary

It has been demonstrated here that finding in Transjordan artifacts or traits associated with the Israelites cannot be used to question their 'Israelite' label, for several reasons.

First, many elements found in this context were mistakenly categorized as examples of these 'Israelite' traits. The number of four-room houses in Transjordan, for example, is much smaller than typically thought. Second, there were Israelites in Transjordan, allowing for the possibility that the discovery of those 'Israelite' traits merely reflects an Israelite presence there. Third, most problems on this issue relate to the Iron Age I, a time period in which ethnic boundaries were not clear. Sites known to have been Ammonite, Moabite, etc., during the Iron II could have been inhabited by Israelites or groups affiliated with them earlier, or even during the Iron Age II. Finally, the historical and archaeological contexts clearly illustrate that boundaries between the Transjordanian groups were fluid and blurred, particularly during the Iron Age I, which is more problematic in this regard. Symbols, like people, could have crossed these boundaries.

While the proposals presented here admittedly cannot be proven until more evidence is gathered, they are forceful in rejecting those who use sites in Transjordan as examples in refuting the Israelite quality of certain traits. If such qualities had been found in quantity in Phoenicia or Egypt, for example, their association with the Israelites would rightfully be in doubt; but their discovery in Transjordan—and especially the Transjordanian highlands—can do nothing of the sort.

Notably, the dichotomy between Cisjordan and Transjordan is modern and artificial. Some parts of the latter were Israelite, and therefore more similar to Cisjordan, while others were not; this indicates that the Jordan was not a real boundary. The nature of the relationships *within* Transjordan, however, varied greatly from those within Cisjordan.[5] Perhaps the absence of the external threat of the Philistines (as discussed in Chapter 12) in this region can explain the existence and emergence of several groups and different state formation processes that took place there, with statehood evolving

might explain the 'seniority' of Reuben, but it does not necessarily say much about the process of identity formation, which may have begun in the central highlands earlier, due to the interaction with the Egyptian–Canaanite system or the Philistines. Discussing the formation of ethnic identities in Transjordan, however, exceeds the scope of the present work.

5.   Additional differences between Cisjordan and Transjordan lie in the fact that CRJ (in some form) continues to be used in the Iron Age II in Transjordan, and another in the fact that in some cases in Transjordan the Iron I settlements continue Late Bronze Age sites (see above).

only later, and the eventual emergence of more kingdoms in the region (e.g. Routledge 2004; see also Joffe 2002). This surely impacted how these groups developed their identities. A full discussion of the process of settlement and identity formation in Transjordan, however, requires its own monograph.

21

SUMMARY AND CONCLUSIONS

The scenario presented so far is very complex. Generally speaking, we have examined Israelite ethnicity going backward in time; we began the enterprise in the Iron Age II, when Israelite ethnicity is easier to establish and identify. We then analyzed the formation of those traits, and how they became meaningful in the context of the late Iron Age I and the interaction with the Philistine. This was followed by an examination of the evidence on Merenptah's Israel of the late thirteenth centrury BCE. I would like now to summarize Israel's ethnogenesis chronologically, from the thirteenth century onward.

Israel's Ethnogenesis

From the thirteenth century onward, many small, new agricultural settlements were formed in the highlands on both sides of the Jordan River. Their settlers likely came from varied backgrounds (e.g. Dever 1995a: 210-11; Kempinski 1995), but the origin of these groups, while important in itself, is of little significance for the present study.

Thirteenth-Century BCE Israel

The first highland settlers were on bad terms with the centralized Egyptio-Canaanite system of the lowland; their relations can be characterized as hierarchical or asymmetrical. As a result, these settlers, whose sites concentrated in a relatively limited region, probably formed an identity group on the ethnic side of the totemic–ethnic continuum.

Since their identity resulted from the interaction with the complex and hierarchical society of the thirteenth-century lowland, they chose elements that distinguished them from their 'other'. They developed an ethos of simplicity and egalitarianism, refrained from decorating their pottery and using imported pottery, and chose to employ a limited repertoire of vessels—all in contrast with Late Bronze Age customs, in which various types of pottery, particularly imported and decorated, were of tremendous social importance and were probably used in rites of exclusion and inclusion. The highlanders also refrained from building elaborate tombs, using any known burial type of the preceding period, and building or worshipping in the standard temples of the time. In addition, they most probably practiced circumcision, and at least some avoided pork,[1] but these did not fully function as ethnic markers at this point, as they were probably shared with other groups, including within the Canaanite society.[2]

Merenptah's stele of the late thirteenth century BCE informs us of the existence of a new ethnic group by the name of Israel, and by doing so suggests it to be a group of importance at the time. It is more than likely that this Merenptah's Israel refers to the abovementioned settlers of the highlands, both because the two appeared contemporaneously and because there seem to be parallels between the meaning of Israel in the stela and the socioeconomic structure of the highlands' villages. We also know there to be an ethnic group by the same name in the highlands a few hundred years later. The latter group exhibits a clear continuity in meaningful traits of material culture with that which preceded it; indeed, the two groups are practically the same.[3] Anyone who wishes to disconnect the Iron I highland settlers and Merenptah's Israel carries the burden of proof.

The Twelfth Century BCE

As the settlement process continued, the highland settlers became 'segregated' from the lowland centers,[4] initially as a result of the Egyptian policy, and later because of the collapse of the entire urban system, which left a sort of vacuum in terms of political authority. This segregation process was accompanied by the settlement of more sites in the highlands.[5] The two processes caused a change in the nature of the relations that characterized the settlers in the twelfth century. No more were they a small group facing asymmetrical relations with a powerful 'other'. The highlanders were now spread over large areas, and were gradually divided into several local factions.

---

1. As can be seen from the very little evidence for pork consumption found at Late Bronze Age Shiloh, for example (Hellwing *et al.* 1993: 311; this is on the assumption that there is a connection between this phase at the site and the Iron Age I settlers). Note that the finds at Mt Ebal indicate that such was practiced prior to the contact with the Philistines.

2. Circumcision, at least, was probably practiced by many groups.

3. One should consider the possibility that even during the late thirteenth century not all of these villagers were 'Israelites', but that some defined themselves differently. However, it should be reiterated that we do not possess a single shred of *evidence* for this possibility—all we know of at the time is 'Israel' (see more below, Chapter 22).

4. By 'segregation' I do not mean absolutely no contact; only that there was no large-scale regulated contact between the societies as such.

5. The establishment of new sites probably resulted from both the settlement of new people/groups, and ever-growing splintering within the existing settlers.

The absence of a powerful enemy outside the highlands enabled the relationships of various groups within the highlands to turn into a form of competition between these otherwise similar villages—the relationships that the highlanders experienced can be characterized as symmetrical, and the varied identities were therefore more totemic (cf. Comaroff and Comaroff 1992; Small 1997), that is, stressing more 'local' identity at the expense of the more complex one. It is true that we lack contemporary written evidence for other groups aside from Israel in the highlands at the time, and that the Merenptah stela mentions only Israel. It seems, however, that the biblically driven assumption that these settlers comprised various groups is logical, as maintained by scholars from all schools, e.g., Skjeggestand (1992), A. Mazar (1994: 90-91), B. Mazar (1981), Ahlstrom (1984; 1993: 356-57, 361, 369-70). Israel was probably only one of several groups that inhabited the highlands at the time. Or, more likely, if the book of Judges can serve as an illustration of the reality in the Iron I, then the totemic identity is perhaps reflected in the importance that is given to the 'tribes' and tribal identity, at the expense of the more complex 'Israelite' identity.

The Eleventh Century BCE
Gradually circumstances changed again, and following economic and social developments, these villages became more and more interconnected (on how this process worked, see, e.g., Finkelstein 1989). This familiarity between the groups in the highland may not have necessarily led to the creation of a shared ethnic consciousness at this point, but it seems to have enabled such to arise later.[6] During the later part of the Iron Age I, when the highlands came under strong pressure from the Philistines, the inhabitants of the small villages resisted the threat and moved to larger, central sites. This was a major factor in the consolidation of the group.

While living together does not necessarily eliminate separate identities—in fact in some cases it may even reaffirm them (e.g. Faust 2000a: 18, and references there)—it may when groups are not in competition with each other, which was the case for the highlanders in this period. This assumption is backed both by the fact that under discussion are not distinct ethnic groups but different clans, totemic groups, and by the reality of the shared common threat these new population centers faced. Such a threat is a decisive factor in forming ethnic identities, and this seems to have been the case here. It is also likely that the Philistine treated all those groups as one, and in so doing strengthened their 'we-ness'.

In the process of redefining themselves under these circumstances, the highlanders built upon previous markers, deemed appropriate in the new context, as those reflecting an egalitarian ethos, but also used new elements

---

6. In addition, it is likely that the various totemic groups saw themselves as related.

that became important. While circumcision and pork avoidance were probably practiced to a large extent earlier, they were now canonized in an effort
to forge a patent distinction from the customs of Israel's Philistine enemy,
who consumed large quantities of pork, and refrained from circumcision.[7]

The existing traits, such as the egalitarian ethos, the avoidance of imported
pottery, the refraining from decoration on pottery, the limited ceramic repertoire, the simple burials, and the lack of temples, while first negotiated in the
thirteenth century when they 'contrasted' key aspects of life in the Egyptio-
Canaanite city-states of the lowlands, were all reloaded with meaning in the
eleventh century as a result of the Philistine pressure. The fact that the Philistine society was hierarchical helped the highlanders reload their egalitarian
ethos with new meaning. The rich ceramic repertoire used by the Philistines,
along with their highly decorated pottery, contrasted the highlanders'
already existing practices, which were in turn redefined in their contrasting
of Philistine habits.[8]

The appearance of Israel on the historical scene already in the Iron Age I
should come as no surprise. After all, the stormy Iron I, with all its changes
in world order, is quite the suitable period for the development of new ethnicities. As Dever correctly claimed, 'anyone who thinks that such a major
upheaval—ending 2000 year old Bronze Age in the southern Levant—took
place without sweeping movements of peoples, as well as far reaching
changes in ethnic consciousness, will have a lot of explaining to do' (1995a:
206). The processes discussed can therefore be expected, and one way or
another, was perhaps almost *inevitable*.

The Tenth Century BCE (and Onward)

A full discussion of the reality in the Iron Age II, and the manner in which
the above circumstances shaped the relations during the period of the monarchy is beyond the scope of the present book, but a few exemplary notes are
in order. It is well known that most of the Israelite fortification and monumental buildings of this period were located in the valleys. In light of the
present discussion (see also Faust 1999b, 2000a, 2004a), this can be seen as
a result of the fact that the highland was populated by Israelites with a strong
egalitarian ethos, while the lowlands were populated to a large extent by
non-Israelites. The fortifications were used as symbols of power and to

---

7.   Note that at around 1200 BCE pork was consumed at Tell el-'Umeiri (Herr and
Clark 2001: 47). This shows that while the custom may have been rare, pork was consumed at the time, as its avoidance had not yet been canonized as an ethnic marker.
Admittedly, this is not the only possible interpretation, and it could also indicate how
blurred the ethnic boundaries were in Transjordan.

8.   The dichotomy which is expressed in the book of Judges between the Philistine
drunks and Samson the Nazirite (who did not drink wine), might echo a memory of the
Israelite perception of such differences.

consolidate Israelite control over the lowlands (see Faust 2000a), but without constituting a palpable contradiction to the 'egalitarian ethos,' given the ethnic composition of the region. The relative absence of monumental fortifications in the highland should therefore be viewed not only as a result of the lack of a real threat, as the area was populated by more 'loyal' Israelites, but also by the pervasive presence of the egalitarian ethos there, which would have looked down upon the erection of such monumental buildings (see also Blanton 1998: 151-52).

A Comment on the 'Longue Duree'

Some scholars have viewed the Israelite settlement process in the spirit of the *longue duree*, as part of a cyclic process of settlement in the central highlands. According to Finkelstein, the Israelite settlement is to be seen as nothing new in this process (1994; 1992: 69; 1995b; see also Finkelstein and Silberman 2001: 113-18; Dever 1994: 216). That is, the highlands witnessed a phase of settlement in the Early Bronze Age, a period of decline, then a new wave during the Middle Bronze Age, and just another wave in the Iron I. There is some truth in this observation, but it misses much of the significance of the Israelite settlement in the highlands as the last cycle of this process. Until the Iron Age, the highlands had always been on the fringe, whether relatively settled as in the Early Bronze Age, or relatively empty as in the Late Bronze Age, and the core of settlement in the region was the lowlands. From the Iron Age onward, however, with all the demographic declines that the region experienced, the highlands were never to be as empty and peripheral as it had been before. The process of the Israelite settlement and its ensuing state formation process significantly *changed* the cycle.

The *longue duree* has another dimension that has not received much attention in the archaeology of the Israelite settlement from the time of the notion's full introduction to the discipline in the 1980s (for a general criticism, see Bunimovitz 2001: 35, 44; see also Tubb 1998b: 167). It is known that events, even with all their 'unimportance' in this regard, *can* change structures (Bintliff 1991: 15). The Israelite settlement and state formation constituted just such an event (or events), the impact of which is evidenced by the ensuing revolution of settlement patterns in the Land of Israel and the relative significance of the highlands *vis-à-vis* the lowlands. Looking at the Iron Age I settlement process as just another wave in a cyclic process is therefore reductionism.

New Biblical Archaeology and the Study of Ancient Israel

Some years ago Biblical Archaeology seemed to face a dead end. Subsequent attempts to produce a 'secular Syro-Palestinian' archaeology, however, were not successful, at least as far as the Iron Age is concerned; after all, the unmitigated ignoring of a large set of data as in the Bible cannot be regarded as good scholarship, no matter how difficult and problematic this data may be. Approximately ten years ago, W.G. Dever (1993a) began to champion a new kind of archaeology, one not dependent upon the texts but not ignorant of them either. He labeled this cooperative approach 'New Biblical Archaeology'. It is a line generally pursued in this book. There are some differences of course, the major one being that the Bible plays only a secondary role here, mainly because using it as a primary source in answering the questions at hand has so far proved futile (cf. Chapter 1). By giving the archaeological evidence the primary role, new patterns were identified and new questions were raised. The written sources took a back seat here to archaeological and anthropological analysis, and they should receive more attention in future studies. But reversing the usual order seemed to be a promising line of research, and I hope it was worthwhile. Notably, the present study is innovative in many ways, and some of its arguments and conclusions will probably be controversial. Admittedly, some of the conclusions are tentative and several will probably be refined in the future.[9] I hope, however, that it will bring a fresh outlook to the old debate and will stimulate further discussion. And this brings me to my final comment.

Anthropology and the Archaeology of Ancient Israel

Israel's emergence in Canaan is a loaded issue that has occupied many scholars, as the vastness of the literature cited here on the topic demonstrates. It is, however, an excellent archaeological case-study in general, and for the study of ethnicity in particular.

The Land of Israel is probably the most densely excavated and surveyed region in the world, with hundreds of planned excavations, large-scale surveys, and thousands of salvage excavations having been conducted over the years. The Iron Age is very well represented in this database, presenting us with much information and detail. This is supplemented by historical sources, however problematic (the Bible) or fragmentary (the 'external sources') they may be for the study of ancient identities. Yet despite the great potential of Iron Age Israel for anthropological-archaeological studies, not much has been done on such in the past, due to the differing trajectory of Biblical Archaeology as compared to that of general archaeology. Here I have attempted to show that ancient Israel can serve as a good case for the study of ethnicity, and that we can trace the emergence of Israel in Canaan in great detail, an endeavor not typically possible in archaeological studies elsewhere.

---

9. Future studies should not only pay more attention to the biblical texts, but also examine additional traits. It would also be worthwhile to examine the patterns observed in the various regions in more details.

I have also attempted to learn about pre-ethnic identities, and the manner in which ethnicity evolves. I tried to decipher the way in which traits are chosen to convey messages, and how they are negotiated and renegotiated. Many of these issues tackled in the present study—especially pre-ethnic realities and ethnogenesis—are regarded in many anthropological studies as problematic, and I hope that by presenting this very detailed case-study, the archaeology of ancient Israel might contribute something to the general field. As A. Smith observed, 'the origins of ethnic differentiation...are shrouded in obscurity, even if the veil is lifted in a few cases, particularly in more recent cases' (1986: 41). I hope that here I have (partially at least) lifted the veil from a relatively old case.[10]

Endnote

Past scholars, such as Albright, have recently come under fierce attack, much of their writings discredited, their conclusions refuted, and their identifications proved wrong. Moreover, they have been labeled 'religious', 'ideologues', and 'orientalists', said to have imposed their personal beliefs on the interpretation of the finds (on various grounds, e.g., Long 1997; Whitelam 1996a), and even called racist (e.g. Whitelam 1996a: 84, 88).[11] While there may be no doubt that many of their conclusions were wrong, their work was simplistic by modern standards,[12] and their use of data may have been somewhat arbitrary, the criticisms themselves are not always justified. Not only can we not expect scholars of the past to meet our standards, but many of their ideas are not always as deficient as one might think. Albright, Wright, Aharoni, Yadin, and many others knew the material exceptionally well, which allowed for a close intimacy with the data that resulted in their use of what we may call intuition. While it might not have always been purely scientific, their judgments were in many cases implicitly based on data.

This can be seen, for example, in Aharoni's treatment of Megiddo VI (1970: 263-65). He, arbitrarily, chose the collared-rim jar—at the time seen as an Israelite marker—and preferred it as the key factor in establishing the

10. I believe that the huge archaeological database that exists in Israel, along with the detailed 'ethnohistoric' and textual information we possess, have great potential to contribute to the field of anthropological archaeology. I hope that the present monograph has shown this potential, regardless of one's evaluations of the monograph itself.

11. It should be noted that part of this criticism derives directly from modern politics (see, e.g., Whitelam 1996a as an obvious case), but it is not my wish consider these kinds of writings at any length.

12. Note that part of the devaluation of their work results, directly or indirectly, from academic trends, as is evidenced by the negative approaches to the issue of ethnicity (Chapters 2–3).

ethnic identity of the site, although he was aware of the fact that other traits regarded as important at the time, such as continuation in pottery forms, indicated differently.[13] It is clear that this approach is problematic; obviously, all the findings should be analyzed and the entire society should be studied before an attempt can be made at identifying ethnicity. Still, the conclusions of the present monograph are closer in some respects to the views of those scholars, despite the 'simplicity' of their methods, than to the opinions of several more recent scholars.[14] Their expert control of all sets of data—archaeological, historical, biblical, linguistic—led them not always astray. And lest we forget, these scholars were not familiar, for example, with Barth's 1969 work, which was slow to impact archaeological studies everywhere, or Hodder's restoration of normativism (though in a completely different manner than in the past; Bunimovitz 1999: 147; see also Chapter 2). Fair and constructive criticism is indeed in order regarding the archaeological/historical work of these scholars and its results, as well as on their background and motives (see, e.g., Dever 1993c; Silberman 1993; and now also various papers in Lewis 2002); this criticism, however, should not simply follow the trends in other fields (much criticism is clearly influenced by Said's *Orientalism* [1979]).

Finally, I believe that contrary to some recent accusations (e.g. Long 1997; Whitelam 1996a, for its transparent absurdity), they were honest scholars. They were, like us, influenced by their background and beliefs. However, a look at their work shows that they did not 'cheat'; there was no knowing and systematic distorting of the evidence. In the debate over the date of the Israelite settlement, for example, it seems that most archaeologists, like Albright, would have preferred a date that conforms with the biblical date for the Exodus and Conquest. However, they accepted a later date due to the accumulating evidence. Clearly, there was no 'squeezing' of the archaeological data in an attempt forcibly to fit a biblically derived date. Such characterizations do them injustice. We all make mistakes, and we all have biases.

We should learn from the work of our predecessors—their mistakes, as well as their devotion and passion for the archaeology of ancient Israel.

13. As already mentioned, the possibility that the site was inhabited by more than one ethnic group was not usually considered.

14. In Aharoni's case, for example, the importance he gave to the CRJ seems to be somewhat justified (though not exactly in the way he assumed), although the final conclusions, as well as some other claims, are refuted.

22

POSTSCRIPT

It appears that until the 1960s, the identification of the settlers of the high-land villages as Israelites was quite straightforward. The highland 'archaeo-logical culture', in the spirit of the Culture History school, was simply viewed as Israelite. This culture was differentiated from the Philistine of the southern coastal plain and the Canaanite of the northern valleys (e.g. Dever 1998: 47-48). The first trigger behind the questioning of the Israelite label on the settlers of the highland Iron I sites was our awareness of other groups, such as the Hivites, Kenites, etc., who were active at the time but not identified archaeologically (see, e.g., B. Mazar 1981; Finkelstein 1988: 28; London 1989: 50; Skjeggestand 1992: 165, 176, 177, 185; Finkelstein and Na'aman 1994: 16-17; Stager 1998: 136-37; note, however, that only a few of the above have used this to cast doubt on the identification of the highland settlers).

With the attempts to identify the Kenites, Amalekites, Gibeonites, etc., emerged the problem of distinguishing them from the Israelites (Kempinski 1995; B. Mazar 1981; see also Kempinksi 1981). Gradually scholars became uncomfortable with the label 'Israelite' for the 'material culture' of the highlands, as they felt it encompassed other groups as well (e.g. Miller and Hayes 1986: 85; and additional references above). In summarizing her paper, Skjeggestand wrote, 'as several different groups obviously were present in Iron Age Palestine, the social criteria presented by Finkelstein, must be left out if we are to define characteristics limited to the Israelite culture alone' (1992: 185). Earlier in the same work she wrote, 'the material culture of the new settlements in the Palestinian hills cannot, therefore, automatically be interpreted as reflecting the particular Israelite ethnic of the culture excavated. Rather, archaeologists should avoid the designation "Israelite" on those settlements, since such an identification is not warranted in the archaeological record available today' (p. 184).

The problem was not with the theoretical foundations of the equating of the Israelites with the highland material culture, but rather with the lack of sufficient or suitable archaeological cultures on record which could account for the various peoples said to have existed at the time (see also Chapter 3). Yet we know of these other groups *only* from biblical sources. If the historicity of the Bible is questioned, then these apologetic traditions, which relate to a period much earlier than the time during which the texts were written, should be among the first to be doubted. We would, therefore, have expected critical scholars, as the so-called minimalists present themselves, to discredit the existence of those groups, since they are mentioned *only* in the Bible. They are expected, however, to take the existence of Israel for granted. After all, in the case of Israel we have an external source, Merenptah's stela, which proves that Israel, of all the groups, *did* exist. It is an irony that those who use the mention of other peoples in the biblical texts[1] as reasons to doubt the identification of the Israelites in the archaeological record are the very same scholars who discredit the entire biblical corpus as a source for the history not only of the Iron I, but also of the Iron II. Scholars such as Ahlstrom, Thompson, and Lemche would be better off questioning the written traditions on peoples such as the Hivites, and sticking to the assumption that, since reliable contemporary sources reveal only the existence of the Israelites, we should treat them *only* as the Iron I highland population. And it is even more ironic that leading this trend are scholars that, due to their outright rejection of the Bible as a historical source for Iron Age Israel, were even labeled 'nihilists'. They implicitly used the texts, against whose validity they preach, in order to 'deprive' the Israelites of their identity, despite the fact that their existence is supported by external text(s) (just the proof they usually claim to be searching for). This is not, of course, because the minimalists (most of them at least) have something against the Israelites. What they begrudge is modern Israel. Their political prejudice leads them to distort both history and method.

---

1. Notably, the texts which mention these groups in the Iron Age I were written hundreds of years after that period, and should therefore be doubted by the minimalists more than many other texts which relate to later periods, and which the minimalists so easily discredit.

BIBLIOGRAPHY

Aharoni, Y.
1970   'New Aspects of Israelite Occupation in the North', in J. Sanders (ed.),
        *Near Eastern Archaeology in the Twentieth Century: Essays in Honor of
        Nelson Glueck* (Garden City, NY: Doubleday): 254-67.
1979   *The Land of the Bible: A Historical Geography* (Philadelphia: Westminster
        Press).
1982   *The Archaeology of the Land of Israel* (Philadelphia: Westminster Press).
Aharoni, Y., A.F. Rainey, M. Avi-Yona, and Z. Safrai
1993   *The MacMillan Bible Atlas* (New York: MacMillan).
Ahituv, S.
2003   'A New Moabite Inscription', *Israel Museum Studies in Archaeology* 2:
        3-10.
Ahituv, S., and E. Oren (eds.)
1998   *The Origins of Early Israel—Current Debate: Biblical, Historical and
        Archaeological Perspectives* (Beer-Sheva: Beer-Sheva University).
Ahlstrom, G.W.
1982a   *Royal Administration and National Religion in Ancient Palestine* (Leiden:
        E.J. Brill).
1982b   'Where did the Israelites Live?', *JNES* 141: 133-38.
1984   'Giloh: A Judahite or Canaanite Settlement?', *IEJ* 34: 170-72.
1986   *Who Were the Israelites* (Winona Lake, IN: Eisenbrauns).
1993   *The History of Ancient Palestine from the Paleolithic Period to Alexan-
        der's Conquest* (JSOTSup, 146; Sheffield: Sheffield Academic Press).
Ahlstrom, G.W., and D. Edelman
1985   'Merneptah's Israel', *JNES* 44: 59-61.
Albright, W.F.
1934   'The Kyle Memorial Excavations at Bethel', *BASOR* 56: 2-15.
1937   'Further Light on the History of Israel from Lachish and Megiddo',
        BASOR 68: 22-26.
1940   'Historical Analysis of Archaeological Evidence: Megiddo and the Song
        of Deborah', *BASOR* 78: 7-9.
1961   *The Archaeology of Palestine* (Harmondsworth: Penguin Books).
1966   'Some Recent Excavation Reports and Publications', *BASOR* 183: 32-34.
Alpert Nakhai, B.
2001   *Archaeology and the Religions of Canaan and Israel* (Boston: ASOR).
2003   'Israel on the Horizon: The Iron I Settlement in the Galilee', in *idem* (ed.)
        2003: 131-51.
Alpert Nakhai, B. (ed.)
2003   *The Near East in the Southwest: Essays in Honor of William G. Dever*
        (Boston: ASOR).

Alpert Nakhai, B., J.P. Dessel, and B.L. Wisthoff
     1993   'Wawiyat, Tell el-', in *NEAEHL*: IV, 1500-1501.
Amiran, D.H.K.
     1953   'The Pattern of Settlement in Palestine', *IEJ* 3: 65-78, 192-209, 250-60.
Amit, D.
     1991   'Khirbet Jarish', *ESI* 9: 157-58.
     1992   'Farmsteads in Northern Judea (Betar Area), Survey', *ESI* 10: 147-48.
     2000   'Jebel el-Habun (Alon Shevut)', *ESI* 20: 115*-17*, 156-58.
Amitai, J. (ed.)
     1985   *Biblical Archaeology Today—1984: Proceedings of the International Congress on Biblical Archaeology, Jerusalem, April 1984* (Jerusalem: Israel Exploration Society).
Anderson, B.
     1983   *Imagined Communities: Reflections on the Origins and Spread and Nationalism* (London: Verso).
Anderson, W.P.
     1990   'The Beginning of Phoenician Pottery: Vessel Shape, Style, and Ceramic Technology in the Early Phases of the Phoenician Iron Age', *BASOR* 279: 35-54.
Appadurai, A.
     1986   'Introduction: Commodities and the Politics of Value', in *idem* (ed.), *The Social Life of Things: Commodities in Cultural Perspective* (Cambridge: Cambridge University Press): 3-63.
Ariel, D.T., and A. Strikowsky
     1990   'Appendix (of "Part One: Imported Stamps Amphora Handels")', in D.T. Ariel (ed.), *City of David Excavations III* (Qedem, 30; Jerusalem: Hebrew University): 25-28.
Artzy, M.
     1993   'Nami, Tel', in *NEAEHL*: III, 1095-98.
     1994   'Incense, Camels and Collared Rim Jars: Desert Trade Routes and Maritime Outlets in the Second Millennium', *OJA* 13/2: 121-47.
Atkinson, R.R.
     1994   *The Origins of the Acholi of Uganda Before 1800* (Philadelphia: University of Pennsylvania Press).
Auld, G., and M. Steiner
     1996   *Jerusalem I, from the Bronze Age to the Maccabees* (Cambridge: The Lutterworth Press).
Avigad, N.
     1979   'Hebrew Epigraphic Sources', in Malamat (ed.) 1979: 20-43.
Avner-Levy, R., and H. Torge
     1997   'Rosh Ha-'Ayin', *ESI* 19: 40*.
Bachi, G.
     1973   'Several Kraters from Stratum II', in Y. Aharoni (ed.), *Beer-Sheba I* (Tel Aviv: Tel Aviv University): 38-42.
Ballensi, J., M.D. Herrera, and M. Artzy
     1993   'Abu Hawwam, Tell', in *NEAEHL*: I, 7-14.
Banks, M.
     1996   *Ethnicity: Anthropological Constructions* (London: Routledge).

Banning, E.B., and B.F. Byrd
   1989   'Alternative Approaches for Exploring Levantine Neolithic Architecture',
           Paleorient 15: 154-60.
Barako, T.J.
   2000   'The Philistine Settlement as Mercantile Phenomenon?', *AJA* 104: 513-30.
   2003   'How Did the Philistines Get to Canaan? One: By Sea', *BAR* 29.2: 24-33,
           64, 66.
Barclay, H.B.
   1993   'Comment on Egalitarian Behavior and Reverse Dominance Hierarchy',
           CA 34: 240-41.
Barkay, G.
   1984   'Excavations on the Slope of the Hinnom Valley, Jerusalem', *Qadmoniot*
           68: 94-108 (Hebrew).
   1989   'The Priestly Benediction on the Ketef Hinnom Plaques', *Cathedra* 52:
           37-76 (Hebrew).
   1992   'The Iron Age II–III', in Ben-Tor (ed.) 1992: 302-73.
   1994   'Burial Caves and Burial Practices in Judah in the Iron Age', in I. Singer
           (ed.), *Graves and Burial Practices in Israel in the Ancient Periods* (Jerusa-
           lem: Yad Ben-Zvi): 96-164 (Hebrew).
   1999   'Burial Caves and Dwellings in Judah during Iron Age II: Sociological
           Aspects', in Faust and Maeir (eds.) 1999: 96-102 (Hebrew).
Barnes, R.H.
   1974   *Kedang: A Study in the Collective Thought of an Eastern Indonesian
           People* (Oxford: Clarendon Press).
Barth, F.
   1969   'Introduction', in *idem* (ed.), *Ethnic Groups and Boundaries* (Boston:
           Little, Brown & Co.): 9-38.
Baruch, Y.
   1997   'Kh. el-Eid—An Iron-Age Fortress in the North of Mt Hebron', in Y.
           Eshel (ed.), *Judea and Samaria Research Conference: Proceedings of the
           6th Conference—1996* (Kedumim-Ariel: Eretz): 49-56.
Bar-Yosef, O., and A. Khazanov (eds.)
   1992   *Pastoralism in the Levant, Archaeological Materials in Anthropological
           Perspectives* (Monographs in World Archaeology, 10; Madison: Prehis-
           toric Press).
Bauer, A.A.
   1998   'Cities of the Sea: Maritime Trade and the Origin of Philistine Settlement
           in the Early Iron Age Southern Levant', *OJA* 17: 149-68.
Beit-Arieh, I. (ed.)
   1999   *Tel 'Ira, A Stronghold in the Biblical Negev* (Tel Aviv: Tel Aviv Univer-
           sity).
Beit-Arieh, I., and B.C. Cresson
   1991   'Horvat 'Uza, A Fortified Outpost on the Eastern Negev Border', *BA* 54:
           126-35.
Ben-Shamai, M.H.
   1958   'Impurity and Purity', *EB* 3: 391-94 (Hebrew).
Ben-Shlomo, D., I. Shai, and A.M. Maeir
   2004   'Late Philistine Decorated Ware 9 ("Ashdod Ware"): Typology, Chronol-
           ogy, and Production Centers', *BASOR* 335: 1-35.

Ben-Tor, A. (ed.)
  1989   *Hazor IV (text)* (Jerusalem: Magnes Press).
  1992   *The Archaeology of Israel* (New Haven: Yale University Press).
Ben-Tor, A., and D. Ben-Ami
  1998   'Hazor and the Archaeology of the Tenth Century B.C.E.', *IEJ* 48: 1-37.
Ben-Tor, A., and Y. Portugali
  1987   *Tell Qiri* (Qedem, 24; Jerusalem: Hebrew University).
Bienkowski, P., and E. Van Der Steen
  2001   'Tribes, Trade, and Towns: A New Framework for the Late Iron Age in Southern Jordan and the Negev', *BASOR* 323: 21-47.
Bietak, M.
  2003   'Israelites Found in Egypt: Four-Room House Identified in Medinat Habu', *BAR* 29/5: 41-49, 82-83.
Bikai, P.M.
  1978   *The Pottery of Tyre* (Warminster: Aris & Phillips).
Bimson, J.J.
  1991   'Merneptah's Israel and Recent Theories of Israelite Origins', *JSOT* 49: 3-29.
Binford, L.R.
  1962   'Archaeology as Anthropology', *AA* 28: 217-25.
  1965   'Archaeological Systematics and the Study of Culture Process', *AA* 31: 203-10.
Bintliff, J.
  1991   'The Contribution of an Annalistes/Structural History Approach to Archaeology', in *idem* (ed.), *The Annales School and Archaeology* (London: Leicester University Press): 1-33.
Biran, A., and O. Negbi
  1966   'The Stratigraphical Sequence of Tel Sippor', *IEJ* 16: 160-73.
Biran, A., and J. Naveh
  1993   'An Aramaic Stele Fragment from Tel Dan', *IEJ* 43: 81-98.
  1995   'The Tel Dan Inscription: A New Fragment', *IEJ* 45: 1-18.
Blanton, R.E.
  1994   *Houses and Households* (New York: Plenum).
  1998   'Beyond Centralization: Steps Toward a Theory of Egalitarian Behavior in Archaic States', in G.M. Feinman and J. Marcus (eds.), *Archaic States* (Santa Fe: School of American Research Press): 135-72.
Blanton, R.E., G.M. Feinman, S.A. Kowalewski, and P.N. Peregrine
  1996   'A Dual-Processual Theory for the Evolution of Mesoamerican Civilization', *CA* 37: 1-24.
Bloch-Smith, E.
  1992   *Judahite Burial Practices and Beliefs about the Dead* (JSOTSup, 123; Sheffield: JSOT Press).
  2003   'Israelite Ethnicity in Iron I: Archaeology Preserves What is Remembered and What is Forgotten in Israel's History', *JBL* 122: 401-25.
  2004   'Resurrecting the Iron I Dead', *IEJ* 54: 77-91.
Bloch-Smith, E., and B. Alpert Nakhai
  1999   'A Landscape Comes to Life: The Iron I Period', *NEA* 62.2: 62-127.

Bloom, J.B.
1988   'Material Remains of the Neo-Assyrian Presence in Palestine and Transjordan' (PhD dissertation, Bryn Mawr College [UMI]).

Boehm, C.
1993   'Egalitarian Behavior and Reverse Dominance Hierarchy', *CA* 34: 227-54. This paper includes comments by additional scholars.

Borowski, O.
1998   *Every Living Thing: Daily Use of Animals in Ancient Israel* (London: Altamira Press).

Bourdieu, P.
1977   *Outline of a Theory of Practice* (Cambridge: Cambridge University Press).

Braun, D.P.
1991   'Why Decorate a Pot? Midwestern Household Pottery 200 B.C.–A.D. 600', *JAA* 10: 360-97.

Braun, E.
1993   'Avot, Horvat', in *NEAEHL*: I, 122-23.

Broshi, M., and I. Finkelstein
1992   'The Population of Palestine in Iron Age II', *BASOR* 287: 47-60.

Bunimovitz, S.
1989   'The Land of Israel in the Late Bronze Age: A Case Study of Socio-Cultural Change in a Complex Society' (PhD dissertation, Tel Aviv University, Tel Aviv [Hebrew with English Abstract]).

1990   'Problems in the "Ethnic" Identification of the Philistine Material Culture', *TA* 17: 210-22.

1994   'Socio-Political Transformations in the Central Hill Country in the Late Bronze–Iron I Transition', in Finkelstein and Na'aman (eds.) 1994: 179-202.

1995   'On the Edge of Empires—the Late Bronze Age (1500–1200 BCE)', in Levy (ed.) 1995: 320-31.

1998   'Sea Peoples in Cyprus and Israel: A Comparative Study of Immigration Process', in Gitin, Mazar, and Stern (eds.) 1998: 103-13.

1999   'Lifestyle and Material Culture: Behavioral Aspects of 12th Century B.C.E. Aegean Immigrants in Israel and Cyprus', in Faust and Maeir (eds.) 1999: 146-60 (Hebrew).

2001   'Cultural Interpretation and the Bible: Biblical Archaeology in the Postmodern Era', *Cathedra* 100: 27-46 (Hebrew).

Bunimovitz, S., and A. Faust
2001   'Chronological Separation, Geographical Segregation or Ethnic Demarcation? Ethnography and the Iron Age Low Chronology', *BASOR* 322: 1-10.

2002   'Ideology in Stone: Understanding the Four Room House', *BAR* 28/4: 32-41, 59-60.

2003   'Building Identity: The Four Room House and the Israelite Mind', in Dever and Gitin (eds.) 2003: 411-23.

In Prep. 'The Date of the Arrival of the Philistines: Anthropological and Archaeological Perspectives'.

Bunimovitz, S., and I. Finkelstein
1993   'Pottery', in Finkelstein, Bunimovitz, and Lederman (eds.) 1993: 81-196.

Bunimovitz, S., and Z. Lederman
    1997   'Beth-Shemesh: Culture Conflict in Judah's Frontier', *BAR* 23.1: 42-49,
                75-77.
Bunimovitz, S., and A. Yasur-Landau
    1996   'Philistine and Israelite Pottery: A Comparative Approach to the Question
                of Pots and People', *TA* 23: 88-101.
Burckhardt, J.
    1998   *The Greeks and Greek Civilization* (New York: St Martin's Press).
Cahill, J.
    1997   'A Rejoinder to "Was the Siloam Tunnel Built by Hezekeiah?"', *BA* 60:
                184-85.
    1998   'David's Jerusalem: The Archaeological Evidence Proves It', *BAR* 24/4:
                34-41.
    2003   'Jerusalem at the Time of the United Monarchy: The Archaeological
                Evidence', in A. Vaughn and A. Killebrew (eds.), *Jerusalem in Bible and
                Archaeology* (Atlanta: Society of Biblical Literature): 13-80.
Cahill, J., and D. Tarler
    1993   'Hammah, Tell el-', in *NEAEHL*: II, 561-62.
Callaway, J.A.
    1993   ''Ai', in *NEAEHL*: I, 39-45.
Carneiro, R.L.
    1970   'A Theory of the Origin of the State', *Science* 169: 733-38.
Cassuto, D.R.
    2004   'The Social Context of Weaving in the Land of Israel in Iron Age II' (MA
                thesis, Bar-Ilan University, Ramat Gan).
Caubet, A.
    1998   'The International Style: A Point of View from the Levant and Syria', in
                Cline and Harris-Cline (eds.) 1998: 105-10.
Chambon, A.
    1993   'Far'ah, Tell el- (North)', in *NEAEHL*: II, 433-40.
Chaney, M.L.
    1986   'Systematic Study of the Israelite Monarchy', in N.K. Gotwald (ed.),
                *Social Scientific Criticism of the Hebrew Bible and its Social World: The
                Israelite Monarchy* (SEMEIA, 37; Decatur, GA: Scholars Press): 53-76.
Chernela, J.M.
    1992   'Social Meaning and Material Transaction: The Wanano-Tukano of Brazil
                and Colombia', *JAA* 11: 111-24.
Childe, G.V.
    1929   *The Danube in Prehistory* (Oxford: Oxford University Press).
    1951   *Social Evolution* (New York: Henry Schuman).
Claessen, H.J.M., and P. Skalnik (eds.)
    1978   *The Early State* (The Hague: Mouton).
Clark, J.J.
    2001   *Tracking Prehistoric Migrations, Pueblo Settlers among the Tonto Basin
                Hohokam* (Tucson: University of Arizona Press).
Cline, E.H., and D. Harris-Cline (eds.)
    1998   *The Aegean and the Orient in the Second Millennium* (Aegeum, 18; Liege:
                University de Liege and the University of Texas at Austin).

Clines, D.J.A.
   1993   'Pentateuch', in B.M. Metzger and M.D. Coogan (eds.), *The Oxford
            Companion to the Bible* (Oxford: Oxford University Press): 579-82.
Cohen, A.
   1974a   *Two Dimensional Man* (London: Routledge & Kegan Paul).
   1974b   'Introduction: The Lessons of Ethnicity', in *idem* (ed.), *Urban Ethnicity*
            (London: Tavistock Publications): ix-xxiv.
Cohen, A.P.
   1985   *The Symbolic Construction of Community* (Chichester: Ellis Horwood).
Cohen, R.
   1978a   'Ethnicity: Problem and Focus in Anthropology', *ARA* 7: 379-403.
   1978b   'Introduction', in Cohen and Service (eds.) 1978: 1-20.
   1986   'The Settlement of the Central Negev in Light of Archaeology and
            Literary Sources during the 4th–1st Millenia B.C.E.' (PhD dissertation,
            Hebrew University, Jerusalem [Hebrew]).
Cohen, R., and E.R. Service (eds.)
   1978   *Origins of the State: The Anthropology of Political Evolution* (Philadel-
            phia: Institute for the Study of Human Issues).
Cohen-Weinberger, A., and S.R. Wolff
   2001   'Production Centers of Collared-Rim Pithoi from Sites in the Carmel Coast
            and Ramat Menashe Regions', in Wolff (ed.) 2001: 639-57.
Comaroff, J., and J. Comaroff
   1992   *Ethnography and Historical Imagination* (Boulder, CO: Westview Press).
Conkey, M.W., and C.A. Hastrof (eds.)
   1990   *The Uses of Style in Archaeology* (Cambridge: Cambridge University
            Press).
Cooley, R.E.
   1997   'Radannah', in *OEANE*: IV, 401-402.
Coote, R., and K.W. Whitelam
   1987   *The Emergence of Ancient Israel in Historical Perspective* (Sheffield:
            Almond Press).
Covello Paran, K.
   1998   'Horbat Malta', *ESI* 18: 27-28.
Cross, F.M.
   1988   'Reuben, First-Born of Jacob', *ZAW* 100 (Supplement): 46-65.
   2001   'A Fragment of a Monumental Inscription from the City of David', *IEJ* 51:
            44-47.
Crowly, J.L.
   1995   'Images of Power in the Bronze Age Aegean', *Aegeum 12 (Politeia.
            Society and State in the Aegean Bronze Age)*: 475-91.
Culican, W.
   1973   'The Graves at Tell er-Reqeish', *The Australian Journal of Biblical
            Archaeology* 2: 66-105.
Dar, S.
   1986   'Hirbet Jemein—A First Temple Village in Western Samaria', in S. Dar
            and Z. Safrai (eds.), *Shomron Studies* (Tel Aviv: Hakibbutz Hameuchad
            [Hebrew]): 13-73.
Dark, K.
   1995   *Theoretical Archaeology* (London: Gerald Duckworth).

Daviau, P.M.M.
     1999   'Domestic Architecture in Iron Age Ammon: Buildings Materials, Con-
                 struction Techniques, and Room Arrangement', in Macdonald and
                 Younker (eds.) 1999: 113-36.
David, N., J. Sterner and K. Gavua
     1988   'Why Pots are Decorated', *CA* 29: 365-89.
Davies, G.
     1986   *Megiddo* (Cambridge: Lutterworth).
Davies, P.R.
     1992   *In Search of 'Ancient Israel'* (JSOTSup, 148; Sheffield: Sheffield Aca-
                 demic Press).
Davis, S.
     1985   'The Large Mammals Bones', in A. Mazar (ed.), *Tel Qasile, Part Two*
                 (Qedem, 20; Jerusalem: Hebrew University): 148-50.
     1987   'The Faunal Remains of Tel Qiri', in A. Ben-Tor and Y. Portugali (eds.),
                 Tel Qiri (Qedem, 24; Jerusalem: Hebrew University): 249-51.
Dayan, T.
     1999   'Faunal Remains: Areas A–G', in Beit-Arieh (ed.) 1999: 480-87.
De Boer, W.R.
     1990   'Interaction, Imitation, and Communication as Expressed in Style: The
                 Ucayali Experience', in Conkey and Hastorf 1990: 82-104.
De Geus, C.H.J.
     1988   'The New City in Ancient Israel: Two Questions Concerning the Reur-
                 banization of 'Eres Yisra'el in the Tenth Century B.C.E.', in M. Augustin
                 and K.D. Schunck (eds.), *Wunschet Jerusalem Frieden* (Frankfurt: Peter
                 Lang): 105-13.
De Groot, A.
     2000   'On the Dating of Terraces in the Central Hill Country', in *26th Archaeo-
                 logical Congress in Israel* (Abstracts): 20-21 (Hebrew).
De Groot, A., and D.T. Ariel (eds.)
     1992   *Excavations at the City of David 1978–1985*, III (Qedem, 33; Jerusalem:
                 Hebrew University).
De Groot, A., H. Geva and I. Yezerski
     2003   'Iron Age II Pottery', in H. Geva (ed.), *Jewish Quarter Excavations in the
                 Old City of Jerusalem Conducted by Nahman Avigad, 1969–82*, II (Jeru-
                 salem: Israel Exploration Society): 1-49.
De Montmolin, O.
     1987   'Forced Settlement and Political Centralization in a Classic Maya Polity',
                 JAA 6: 220-62.
Deetz, J.
     1996   *In Small Things Forgotten: An Archaeology of Early American Life* (New
                 York: Anchor).
Demand, N.
     1990   *Urban Relocation in Archaic and Classical Greece* (Bristol: Bristol
                 Classical).
Demsky, A.
     1997   'Literacy', in *OEANE*: III, 362-69.

Dentan, R.K.
 1993   'Comment on Egalitarian Behavior and Reverse Dominance Hierarchy',
          CA 34: 241-42.
Dessel, J.P.
 1999   'Tell 'Ein Zippori and the Lower Galilee in the Late Bronze and the Iron
          Ages: A Village Perspective', in E.M. Meyers (ed.), *Galilee Through the
          Ages* (Winona Lake, IN: Eisenbrauns): 1-32.
De Vaux, R.
 1961   *Ancient Israel: Its Life and Institutions* (New York: McGraw–Hill).
Dever, W.G.
 1985   Syro-Palestinian and Biblical Archaeology, in D.A. Knight and G.M.
          Tucker (eds.), *The Hebrew Bible and its Modern Interpreters* (Philadel-
          phia: Scholars Press): 31-74.
 1991   'Archaeological Data on the Israelite Settlement: A Review of Two Recent
          Works', *BASOR* 284: 77-90.
 1992a   'How to Tell a Canaanite from an Israelite?', in Shanks (ed.) 1992: 26-56.
 1992b   'Israel, History of (Archaeology and the Conquest)', in *ABD*: III, 545-58.
 1993a   'Biblical Archaeology: Death and Rebirth', in *Biblical Archaeology
          Today, 1990, Proceedings of the Second International Congress on Bib-
          lical Archaeology* (Jerusalem: Israel Exploration Society): 706-22.
 1993b   'Cultural Continuity, Ethnicity in the Archaeological Record, and the
          Question of Israelite Origins', *EI* 24: 22*-33*.
 1993c   'What Remains of the House that Albright Built?', *BA* 56.1: 25-37.
 1994   'From Tribe to Nation: State Formation Processes in Ancient Israel, in
          Mazzoni (ed.) 1994: 213-29.
 1995a   'Ceramics, Ethnicity, and the Questions of Israel's Origins', *BA* 58.4:
          200-13.
 1995b   'Will the Real Israel Please Stand Up? Archaeology and Israelite Histori-
          ography', *BASOR* 297: 61-80.
 1995c   'Will the Real Israel Please Stand Up? Part II: Archaeology and the
          Religions of Ancient Israel', *BASOR* 298: 37-58.
 1996   'The Identity of Ancient Israel: A Rejoinder to Keith W. Whitelam', *JSOT*
          72: 3-24.
 1997a   'Archaeology and the "Age of Solomon": A Case-Study in Archaeology
          and Historiography', in L.K. Handy (ed.), *The Age of Solomon: Scholar-
          ship at the Turn of the Millennium* (Leiden: E.J. Brill): 217-51.
 1997b   'Ceramics, Syro-Palestinian Ceramics of the Neolithic, Bronze and Iron
          Ages', in *OEANE*: I, 459-65.
 1997c   'Is there any Archaeological Evidence for the Exodus?, in E.S. Frerichs
          and L.H. Lesko (eds.), *Exodus: the Archaeological Evidence* (Winona
          Lake, IN: Eisenbrauns): 67-86.
 1997d   'Archaeology, Urbanism and the Rise of the Israelite State', in W.E.
          Aufrecht, N.A. Mirau, and S.W. Gauley (eds.), *Urbanism in Antiquity:
          From Mesopotamia to Crete* (JSOTSup, 244; Sheffield: Sheffield
          Academic Press): 172-93.
 1998   'Archaeology, Ideology, and the Quest for an "Ancient", or "Biblical"
          Israel', *NEA* 61.1: 39-52.
 2000   'Save Us from the Postmodern Malarkey', *BAR* 26.2: 28-35, 68-69.

2001   *What Did the Biblical Writers Know, and When Did They Know It?* (Grand Rapids: Eerdmans).

2003   *Who Were the Israelites and Where Did They Come From?* (Grand Rapids: Eerdmans).

Dever, W.G., and S. Gitin (eds.)

2003   *Symbiosis, Symbolism and the Power of the Past: Canaan, Ancient Israel and their Neighbors from the Late Bronze Age through Roman Palestine* (Winona Lake, IN: Eisenbrauns).

Diakonoff, I.M.

1974   *Structure of Society and State in Early Dynastic Sumer* (Malibu: Undena).

Dothan, M.

1955   'The Excavations at 'Afula', *'Atiqot* 1: 19-70.

1978   ' 'Afula', in M. Avi-Yonah (ed.), *Encyclopedia of Archaeological Excavations in the Holy Land* (4 vols.; Jerusalem): IV, 32-37.

1993a   'Acco, Tel Acco', in *NEAEHL*: I, 17-23.

1993b   'Afula', in *NEAEHL*: I, 37-39.

1993c   'Azor', in *NEAEHL*: I, 125-29.

Dothan, T.

1982   *The Philistines and their Material Culture* (New Haven: Yale University Press and the Israel Exploration Society).

Dothan, T., and R.L. Cohn

1994   'The Philistine as Other: Biblical Rhetoric and Archaeological Reality', in Silberstein and Cohn (eds.) 1994: 61-73.

Dothan, T., and M. Dothan

1992   *People of the Sea: The Search for the Philistines* (New York: Macmillan).

Dothan, T., and S. Gitin

1993   'Miqneh', in *NEAEHL*: III, 1051-59.

Douglas, M.

1966   *Purity and Danger: An Analysis of the Concept of Pollution and Taboo* (London: Routledge & Kegan Paul).

1972   'Deciphering a Meal', *Daedalus* 101: 61-81.

1975   *Implicit Meanings* (London: Routledge & Kegan Paul).

2000   'Impurity of Land Animals', in M.J.H.M. Poorthuis and J. Schwartz (eds.), *Purity and Holiness: The Heritage of Leviticus* (Leiden: E.J. Brill): 33-45.

Douglas, J.E., and C. Kramer (eds.)

1992   'Interaction, Social Proximity and Distance (Special Issue of JAA)', *JAA* 11: 103-218.

Duncan, R.J.

1998   *The Ceramics of Raquira, Colombia: Gender, Work and Economic Change* (Gainsville: University Press of Colombia).

EB (editorial)

1968   'Trade', *EB* 5: 159-64 (Hebrew).

Edelman, D.

1997   'Saul ben kish in History and Tradition', in Fritz and Davies (eds.) 1996: 142-59.

2002   'Ethnicity and Early Israel', in M.G. Brett (ed.), *Ethnicity and the Bible* (Leiden: E.J. Brill): 25-55.

Edelstein, G.
   undated   *A Weavers Settlement from the Period of the United Monarchy* (Nir-David:
              Museum of Regional Archaeology [Hebrew]).
Edelstein, G., and M. Kislev
   1981   'Mevasseret Yerushalayim, the Ancient Settlement and Its Agricultural
              Terraces', *BA* 44: 53-56.
Edelstein, G., and I. Milevski
   1994   'The Rural Settlement of Jerusalem Re-evaluated: Surveys and
              Excavations in the Reph'aim Valley and Mevasseret Yerushalayim', *PEQ*
              126: 2-23.
Eilberg-Schwartz, H.
   1990   *The Savage in Judaism: An Anthropology of Israelite Religion and Ancient
              Judaism* (Bloomington and Indianapolis: Indiana University Press).
Eisenstadt, I., K. Arabas, and Z. Ablas
   2004   'A Late Bronze Age Burial Cave at Zawata', in Hizmi and De Groot (eds.)
              2004: 77-106.
Eissfeldt, O.
   1966   *The Old Testament: An Introduction* (Oxford: Basil Blackwell).
Elat, M.
   1977   *Economic Relations in the Lands of the Bible (ca. 1000–539 B.C.E.)*
              (Jerusalem: Magnes Press [Hebrew]).
   1979   'The Monarchy and the Development of Trade in Ancient Israel', in
              E. Lipiński (ed.), *State and Temple Economy in the Ancient Near East*
              (Leuven: Dep. Orientalistiek): 527-46.
Elgavish, Y.
   1994   *Shiqmona, on the Seacoast of Mount Carmel* (Tel Aviv: Hakibutz
              Hameuchad).
Emberling, G.
   1997   'Ethnicity in Complex Societies, Archaeological Perspectives', *Journal of
              Archaeological Research* 5 (4): 295-344.
Engberg, R.
   1940   'Historical Analysis of Archaeological Evidence: Megiddo and the Song
              of Deborah', *BASOR* 78: 4-9.
Eph'al, I.
   1997   'The Philistine Entity and the Origin of the Name "Palestine"', in M.
              Coogan, B.L. Eichler, and J.H. Tigay (eds.), *Tehillah le-Moshe: Bibli-
              cal and Judaic Studies in Honor of Moshe Greenberg* (Winona Lake, IN:
              Eisenbrauns): 31*-35* (Hebrew).
Eph'al, I. (ed.)
   1982   *The History of Eretz-Israel*. II. *Israel and Judah in the Biblical Period*
              (Jerusalem: Yad Ben-Zvi).
Eshel, Y.
   1995   'Two Pottery Groups from Kenyon's Excavations on the Eastern Slope of
              Ancient Jerusalem', in I. Eshel and K. Prage (eds.), *Excavations by K.M.
              Kenyon in Jerusalem 1961–1967* (London: Oxford University Press): IV,
              1-158.

Esse, D.L.
    1991   'The Collared Store Jar: Scholarly Ideology and Ceramic Typology', *SJOT* 2: 99-116.
    1992   'The Collared Pithos at Megiddo: Ceramic Distribution and Ethnicity', *JNES* 51: 81-103.

Falconer, S.E.
    1995   'Rural Responses to Early Urbanism: Bronze Age Household and Village Economy at Tell el-Hayyat, Jordan', *Journal of Field Archaeology* 22: 399-419.

Fardon, R.
    1999   *Mary Douglas: An Intellectual Biography* (London: Routledge).

Faust, A.
    1995a   'The Rural Settlement in the Land of Israel in the Period of the Monarchy' (MA thesis, Bar-Ilan University, Ramat Gan).
    1995b   'Settlement on the Western Slopes of Samaria at the End of the Iron Age', in Z.H. Erlich and Y. Eshel (eds.), *Judea and Samaria Research Studies: Proceedings of the 4th Annual Meeting—1994* (Eretz: Kedumim-Ariel): 23-30 (Hebrew with an English abstract).
    1997   'The Impact of Jerusalem's Expansion in the Late Iron Age on the Forms of Rural Settlements in its Vicinity', *Cathedra* 84: 53-62 (Hebrew with an English abstract).
    1999a   'From Hamlets to Monarchy: A View from the Countryside on the Formation of the Israelite Monarchy', *Cathedra* 94: 7-32 (Hebrew).
    1999b   Socioeconomic Stratification in an Israelite City: Hazor VI as a Test-Case', *Levant* 31: 179-91.
    1999c   'The Social Structure of the Israelite Society in the 8th–7th Centuries BCE according to the Archaeological Evidence' (PhD dissertation, Bar-Ilan University, Ramat Gan [Hebrew]).
    2000a   'Ethnic Complexity in Northern Israel during the Iron Age II', *PEQ* 132: 1-27.
    2000b   'The Rural Community in Ancient Israel during the Iron Age II', *BASOR* 317: 17-39.
    2001a   'Doorway Orientation, Settlement Planning and Cosmology in Ancient Israel during Iron Age II', *Oxford Journal of Archaeology* 20.2: 129-55.
    2001b   'Salvage Excavations as a Source for the Reconstruction of the Settlement History of the Land of Israel'. A paper presented in a conference on *The Study of the Land of Israel*, Yad Ben-Zvi, Jerusalem (24 September 2001).
    2002   'Burnished Pottery and Gender Hierarchy in Iron Age Israelite Society', *Journal of Mediterranean Archaeology* 15.1: 53-73.
    2003a   'Abandonment, Urbanization, Resettlement and the Formation of the Israelite State', *NEA* 66: 147-61.
    2003b   'Judah in the Sixth Century BCE: A Rural Perspective', *PEQ* 135: 35-51.
    2003c   'The Farmstead in the Highland of Iron Age II Israel', in A.M. Maeir, S. Dar, and Z. Safrai (eds.), *The Rural Landscape of Ancient Israel* (BAR International Series, 1121; Oxford: British Archaeological Reports): 91-104.
    2004a   'Mortuary Practices, Society and Ideology: The Lack of Highlands Iron Age I Burials in Context', *IEJ* 54: 174-90.

2004b   'Social and Cultural Changes in Judah during the 6th Century BCE and their Implications for Our Understanding of the Nature of the Neo-Babylonian Period', *UF* 36: 157-76.

2005a   'The Canaanite Village, Social Structure of Middle Bronze Age Rural Communities', *Levant* 37: 105-25.

2005b   *The Israelite Society in the Period of the Monarchy: An Archaeological Perspective* (Jerusalem: Yad Ben-Zvi [Hebrew]).

2005c   'The Israelite Village: Cultural Conservatism and Technological Innovation', *TA* 32: 204-19.

2006   'Settlement Patterns and State Formation in Southern Samaria and the Archaeology of (A) Saul', in C. Erlich and M. White (eds.), *Saul in Story and Tradition* (Forschungen zum alten Testament; Tubingen: Mohr Siebeck).

forthcoming   'The Negev "Fortresses" in Context: Reexamining the "Fortresses" Phenomenon in Light of General Settlement Processes of the 11th–10th Centuries B.C.E.', *Journal of the American Oriental Society*.

In prep.   'The Negbite Pottery: World Order and Resistance in the Kingdom of Israel During the 10th Century BCE'.

Faust, A., and S. Bunimovitz

2003   'The Four Room House: Embodying Iron Age Israelite Society', *NEA* 66: 22-33.

Faust, A., and A. Maeir (eds.)

1999   *Material Culture, Society and Ideology: New Directions in the Archaeology of the Land of Israel* (Ramat Gan: Bar-Ilan University).

Faust, A., and Z. Safrai

2005   'Salvage Excavations as a Source for Reconstructing Settlement History in Ancient Israel', *PEQ* 137: 139-58.

Feig, N.

1996   'New Discoveries in the Rephaim Valley, Jerusalem', *PEQ* 128: 3-7.

Ferguson, L.

1991   'Struggling with Pots in Colonial South Carolina', in McGuire and Paynter (eds.) 1991: 28-38.

Finkelstein, I.

1986   *'Izbet Sartah: An Early Iron Age Site Near Rosh Ha'ayin, Israel* (BAR International Series, 299; Oxford: British Archaeological Reports).

1988   *The Archaeology of the Period of Settlement and Judges* (Jerusalem: Israel Exploration Society).

1989   'The Emergence of the Monarchy in Israel: The Environmental and Socio-Economic Aspects', *JSOT* 44: 43-74.

1990a   'Excavation at Kh. ed-Dawwara: An Iron Age Site Northeast of Jerusalem', *TA* 17: 162-208.

1990b   'The Iron I in the Land of Ephraim—A Second Thought', in Finkelstein and Na'aman 1994: 101-30 (Hebrew).

1991   'The Emergence of Israel in Canaan: Consensus, Mainstream and Dispute', *SJOT* 2: 47-59.

1992   'Response to W.G. Dever', in Shanks (ed.) 1992: 63-69.

1993   'Conclusions', in Finkelstein, Bunimovitz, and Lederman (eds.) 1993: 371-93.

1994   'The Emergence of Israel: A Phase in the Cyclic History of Canaan in the
         Third and Second Millennium BCE', in Finkelstein and Na'aman (eds.)
         1994: 152-78.
1995a   'The Date of the Settlement of the Philistines in Canaan', *TA* 23: 170-84.
1995b   'The Great Transformation—The "Conquest" of the Highland Frontiers
         and the Rise of the Territorial States', in Levy (ed.) 1995: 349-65.
1996a   'Ethnicity and the Origin of the Iron I Settlers in the Highlands of Canaan:
         Can the Real Israel Stand Up?', *BA* 59.4: 198-212.
1996b   *Living on the Fringe: The Archaeology and History of the Negev, Sinai
         and Neighbouring Regions in the Bronze and Iron Ages* (Monographs in
         Mediterranean Archaeology, 6; Sheffield: Sheffield Academic Press).
1996c   'The Archaeology of the United Monarchy: An Alternative View', *Levant*
         28: 177-87.
1996d   'The Philistine Countryside', *IEJ* 46: 225-42.
1997   'Pots and People Revisited: Ethnic Boundaries in the Iron Age I', in
         Silberman and Small (eds.) 1997: 216-37.
1998   'Bible Archaeology or the Archaeology of the Palestine in the Iron Age? A
         Rejoinder', *Levant* 30: 167-74.
1999   'State Formation in Israel and Judah, A Contrast in Context, A Contrast in
         Trajectory', *NEA* 62.1: 35-52.
2000   'The Philistine Settlements: When, Where and How Many?', in E.D. Oren
         (ed.), *The Sea People and their World: A Reassessment* (Philadelphia:
         University of Pennsylvania): 159-80.
2002a   'Chronology Rejoinders', *PEQ* 134: 118-29.
2002b   'The Philistine in the Bible: A Late-Monarchic Perspective', *JSOT* 27:
         131-67.
Finkelstein, I., S. Bunimovitz, and Z. Lederman (eds.)
1993   *Shiloh: The Archaeology of a Biblical Site* (Monographs Series of the
         Institute of Archaeology; Tel Aviv: Tel Aviv University).
Finkelstein, I., and N. Na'aman
1994   'Introduction: From Nomadism to Monarchy—the State of Research in
         1992', in Finkelstein and Na'aman (eds.) 1994: 9-17.
Finkelstein, I., and N. Na'aman (eds.)
1994   *From Nomadism to Monarchy* (Jerusalem: Yad Ben-Zvi).
Finkelstein, I., and N.A. Silberman
2001   *The Bible Unearthed: Archaeology's New Vision of Ancient Israel and the
         Origin of its Sacred Texts* (New York: Touchstone).
Fischer, P.M.
1994   'Tell Abu al-Kharaz: The Swedish Jordan Expedition 1992, Third Season,
         Preliminary Excavation Report', *ADAJ* 38: 127-45.
1996   'Tell Abu al-Kharaz: The Swedish Jordan Expedition 1994, Fifth Season,
         Preliminary Excavation Report', *ADAJ* 40: 101-10.
Flannery, K.W.
1973   'Archaeology with a Capital S', in C.L. Redman (ed.), *Research and
         Theory in Current Archaeology* (New York: Wiley): 47-53.
1998   'The Ground Plans of Archaic States', in G.M. Feinman and J. Marcus
         (eds.), *Archaic States* (Santa Fe: School of American Research Press):
         15-57.

1999 'Process and Agency in Early State Formation', *Cambridge Archaeological Journal* 9.1: 3-21.

Foster, S.
1989 'Analysis of Spatial Patterns in Buildings (Access Analysis) as an Insight into Social Structure: Examples from the Scottish Atlantic Iron Age', *Antiquity* 63: 40-50.

Fox, M.V.
1974 'The Sign of the Covenant, Circumcision in the Light of the Priestly *'ot* Ethiologies', *RB* 81: 557-96.

Frankel, R.
1994 'Upper Galilee in the Late Bronze–Iron I Transition', in Finkelstein and Na'aman (eds.) 1994: 18-34.

Franken, H.M., and G. London
1995 'Why Painted Pottery Disappeared at the End of the Second Millennium BCE', *BA* 58: 214-22.

Franken, H.M, and M.L. Steiner
1990 *Excavations in Jerusalem 1961–1967*, II (London: Oxford University Press).

Frerichs, E.S.. and L.H. Lesko (eds.)
1997 *Exodus: The Egyptian Evidence* (Winona Lake, IN: Eisenbrauns).

Frick, F.S.
1985 *The Formation of the State in Ancient Israel* (Social World of Biblical Antiquity, 4; Sheffield: Sheffield Academic Press).

Fried, M.H.
1967 *The Evolution of Political Society* (New York: Random House).

Friedman, R.E.
1987 *Who Wrote the Bible?* (New York: Summit Books).

Fritz, V.
1977 'Bestimmung und Herkunft des Pfeilerhauses in Israel', *ZDPV* 93: 30-45.
1994 'The Character of the Urbanisation in Palestine at the Beginning of the Iron Age, in Mazzoni (ed.) 1994: 231-52.
1996 'Monarchy and Re-urbanization: A New Look at Solomon's Kingdoms', in Fritz and Davies (eds.) 1996: 187-95.

Fritz, V., and P.R. Davies (eds.)
1996 *The Origins of the Israelite States* (JSOTSup, 228; Sheffield: Sheffield Academic Press).

Funk, R.W.
1968 'The Bronze Age—Iron I Pottery', in O.R. Sellers *et al.* (eds.), *The 1957 Excavations at Beth-Zur* (Cambridge, MA: ASOR): 35-53.

Gal, Z.
1979 'An Early Iron Age Site Near Tel Menorah', *TA* 6: 138-45.
1992a *Lower Galilee during the Iron Age* (ASOR Dissertation Series, 8; Winona Lake, IN: Eisenbrauns).
1992b 'Phoenicians and Israelites in Hurvat Rosh Zayit', in *The 18th Archaeological Congress in Israel* (Hebrew): 12-13.
1993a 'Rosh Zayit, Horvat', in *NEAEHL*: IV, 1289-91.
1993b 'Sasa (in "Galilee, Chalcolithic to Persian Period")', in *NEAEHL*: II, 453.

1993c   'Tel Harashim (in "Galilee, Chalcolithic to Persian Period")', in *NEAEHL*: II, 450.

2001   'Regional Aspects of the Iron Age Pottery in the Akko Plain and Its Vicinity', in Wolff (ed.) 2001: 135-42.

Gal, Z., and Y. Alexandre

2000   *Horbat Rosh Zayit, an Iron Age Storage Fort and Village* (Jerusalem: Israel Antiquities Authority).

Gal, Z., and D. Shalem

1999   'Karmi'el', *Hadashot Arkheologiyot, Excavations and Surveys in Israel* 109: 9*, 12-13.

Galloway, P.

1997   'Where Have all the Menstrual Huts Gone? The Invisibility of Menstrual Seclusion in the Late Prehistoric Southeast', in C. Classen and R. Joyce (eds.), *Women in Prehistory: North America and Mesoamerica* (Philadelphia: University of Pennsylvania Press): 47-62.

Gellner, E.

1983   *Nations and Nationalism* (Oxford: Basil Blackwell).

Gibson, S.

2001   'Agricultural Terraces and Settlement Expansion in the Highlands of Early Iron Age Palestine: Is there a Correlation between the Two', in A. Mazar (ed.), *Studies in the Iron Age of Israel and Jordan* (JSOTSup, 331; Sheffield: Sheffield Academic Press): 113-46.

Giddens, A.

1979   *Central Problems in Social Theory: Action, Structure and Contradiction in Social Analysis* (Berkeley: University of California Press).

1984   *The Constitution of Society* (Cambridge: Polity Press).

Gilboa, A.

1989   'New Finds at Tel Dor and the Beginning of Cypro-Geometric Pottery Import to Palestine', *IEJ* 39: 204-18.

1998a   'Iron Age I–IIA Pottery Evolution at Dor—Regional Context and the Cypriot Connection', in Gitin, Mazar, and Stern (eds.) 1998: 413-25.

1998b   'Philistia in Transition: the Tenth Century and Beyond', in Gitin, Mazar, and Stern (eds.) 1998: 162-83.

Gitin, S., T. Dothan, and J. Naveh

1997   'A Royal Dedicatory Inscription from Ekron', *IEJ* 47: 1-16.

Gitin, S., A. Mazar and E. Stern (eds.)

1998   *Mediterranean Peoples in Transition: Thirteenth to Early Tenth Centuries B.C.E.* (Jerusalem: Israel Exploration Society).

Givon, S.

1999   'The Three-Roomed House from Tel Harassim, Israel', *Levant* 31: 173-77.

Glass, J., *et al.*

1993   'Petrographic Analysis of Middle Bronze Age III, Late Bronze Age and Iron Age I Ceramic Assemblages', in Finkelstein, Bunimovitz, and Lederman (eds.) 1993: 271-86.

Glassie, H.

1976   *Folk Housing in Middle Virginia* (Knoxville: University of Tennessee Press).

Gluckman, M.
    1949   'The Role of the Sexes in Wiko Circumcision Ceremonies', in M. Fortes (ed.), *Social Structure, Studies Presented to A.R. Radcliffe-Brown* (Oxford: Clarendon Press): 145-67.

Goethert, R., and R. Amiran
    1996   'Salvage Excavations on the Eastern Slope of Tel-Arad', *EI* 25: 112-15 (Hebrew).

Golani, A., and O. Yogev
    1996   'The 1980 Excavations at Tel Sasa', *'Atiqot* 28: 41-58.

Goldberg, H.E.
    1996   'Cambridge in the Land of Canaan: Descent, Alliance, Circumcision, and Instruction in the Bible', *JANES* 24: 9-34.

Gonen, R.
    1992a   *Burial Patterns and Cultural Diversity in Late Bronze Age Canaan* (Winona Lake, IN: Eisenbrauns).
    1992b   'The Late Bronze Age, in Ben-Tor (ed.) 1992: 211-57.

Goody, J.
    1982   *Cooking, Cuisine and Class: A Study in Comparative Sociology* (Cambridge: Cambridge University Press).

Gophna (Gofnah), R.
    1963   ' "Haserim" Settlements in Northern Negev', *Yediot* 27: 173-80 (Hebrew).
    1964   'Sites from the Late Iron Age between Beer-Sheba and Tell el Far'a', *Yediot* 28: 236-46 (Hebrew).
    1966   'Iron Age *Haserim* in Southern Philistia', *'Atiqot* 3: 44-51 (Hebrew).
    1970   'Some Iron Age II Sites in Southern Philistia', *'Atiqot* 6: 25-30 (Hebrew).

Gordis, R.
    1971   'Primitive Democracy in Ancient Israel', in R. Gordis (ed.), *Poets, Prophets and Sages: Essays in Biblical Interpretation* (Bloomington-London: Indiana University Press): 45-60.

Gottwald, N.K.
    1979   *The Tribes of Yahweh* (New York: Orbis Books).
    1983   'Two Models for the Origins of Ancient Israel: Social Revolution or Frontier Development', in H.B. Huffmon, F.A. Spina, and A.R.W. Green (eds.), *The Quest for the Kingdom of God: Studies in Honor of George E. Mendenhall* (Winona Lake, IN: Eisenbrauns): 5-24.
    1992   'Response to William G. Dever', in Shanks (ed.) 1992: 70-75.

Govrin, Y.
    1990   'The Nahal Yatir Site—Moladah in the Inheritance of the Tribe of Simeon?', *'Atiqot* 20: 13*-24* (Hebrew).

Grabbe, L.L. (ed.)
    1997   *Can a History of Israel be Written?* (JSOTSup, 245; Sheffield: Sheffield Academic Press).

Graham, J.A.
    1981a   'Iron I at Tel el-Ful: Some Historical Considerations', in Lapp (ed.) 1981: 29-38.
    1981b   'New Light on the Fortress: Periods I and II', in Lapp (ed.) 1981: 23-27.

Graves, M.W.
    1994   'Kalinga Social and Material Culture Boundaries: A Case of Spatial
            Convergence', in W.A. Longacre and J.M. Skibo (eds.), *Kalinga Ethnoar-
            chaeology: Expanding Archaeological Method and Theory* (Washington:
            Smithsonian Institution Press): 13-49.
Gray, G.B.
    1906   *A Critical and Exegetical Commentary on Numbers* (Edinburgh: T. & T.
            Clark).
Grosby, S.
    2002   *Biblical Ideas of Nationality: Ancient and Modern* (Winona Lake, IN:
            Eisenbrauns).
Gunneweg, J., I. Perlman, and Z. Meshel
    1985   'The Origin of the Pottery of Kuntillet 'Ajrud', *IEJ* 35/4: 270-83.
Gunneweg, J., *et al.*
    1994   'Interregional Contacts between Tell en-Nasbeh and Littoral Philistine
            Centres in Canaan during Early Iron Age I', *Archaeometry* 36.2: 227-39.
Haiman, M.
    1994   'The Iron Age II sites of the Western Negev Highlands', *IEJ* 44: 36-61.
Hall, J.M.
    1997   *Ethnic Identity in Greek Antiquity* (Cambridge: Cambridge University
            Press).
Hall, R.G.
    1992   'Circumcision', in *ABD*: I, 1025-31.
Hallo, W.W.
    2003   'Introduction: The Bible and the Monuments', in W.W. Hallo and K.L.
            Younger (eds.), *The Context of the Scripture*. II. *Monumental Inscriptions
            from the Biblical World* (Leiden: E.J. Brill): xxi-xxvi.
Halpern, B.
    1983   *The Emergence of Israel in Canaan* (Chico, CA: Scholars Press).
    1991   'Jerusalem and the Lineage in the Seventh Century BCE: Kinship and the
            Rise of Individual Moral Liability', in B. Halpern and D.W. Hobson, *Law
            and Ideology in Monarchic Israel* (JSOTSup, 124; Sheffield: JOST Press):
            11-107.
    1992   'The Exodus from Egypt: Myth or Reality?', in Shanks (ed.) 1992: 86-113.
    2000   'Centre and Sentry: Megiddo's Role in Transit, Administration and Trade',
            in I. Finkelstein, D. Ussishkin, and B. Halpern (eds.), *Megiddo III* (Tel
            Aviv: Tel Aviv University): 535-77.
    2001   *David's Secret Demons: Messiah, Murderer, Traitor, King* (Grand Rapids:
            Eerdmans).
    2003   'Eyewitness Testimony: Parts of Exodus Written Within Living Memory
            of the Event', *BAR* 29.5: 50-57.
Har Adir
    1976   Har Adir, *Khadashot Arkheologiyot* 59-60: 9-10 (Hebrew).
Haran, M.
    1996   'Chapter 40: 17-32', in G. Brin and M. Haran (eds.), *Ezekiel—The World
            of the Bible* (Tel Aviv: Davidson-'Ati): 166-67 (Hebrew).

Hardin, J.W.
    2001   'An Archaeology of Destruction: Households and the Use of Domestic Space at Iron II Tel Halif' (PhD dissertation, University of Arizona, Tucson).

Harrison, T.P.
    2004   *Megiddo 3: Final Report on the Stratum VI Excavations* (Oriental Institute Publications, 27; Chicago: University of Chicago Press).

Hart, S.
    1988   'Excavations at Ghrareh 1986: Preleminary Report', *Levant* 20: 89-99.

Hasel, M.G.
    1994   'Israel in the Merneptah Stela', *BASOR* 296: 45-62.
    2003   'Merenptah's Inscription and Reliefs and the Origins of Israel', in Alpert Nakhai (ed.) 2003: 19-44.
    2004   'The Structure of the Final Hymnic–Poetic Unit on the Merenptah Stela', *ZAW* 116: 75-81.

Hassig, R.
    1985   *Trade, Tribute and Transportation: The Sixteenth-Century Political Economy in the Valley of Mexico* (Norman: University of Oklahoma Press).

Hauer, C.
    1986   'From Alt to Anthropology: The Rise of the Israelite Monarchy', *JSOT* 36: 3-15.

Hellwing, S.
    1984   'Human Exploitation of Animal Resources in the Early Iron Age Strata at Tel Beer-Sheba', in Z. Herzog (ed.), *Beer-Sheba*. II. *The Early Iron Age Settlements* (Tel Aviv: Tel Aviv University): 105-15.
    2000   'Faunal Remains', in M. Kochavi (ed.), *Aphek-Antipatris I, Excavations Area A and B, the 1972–1976 Seasons* (Tel Aviv: Tel Aviv University): 293-314.

Hellwing, S., and Y. Adjeman
    1986   'Animal Bones', in I. Finkelstein (ed.), *'Izbet Sartah: An Early Iron Age Site Near Rosh Ha'ayin, Israel* (BAR, S299; Oxford: British Archaeological Reports): 141-52.

Hellwing, S., and N. Feig
    1989   'Animal Bones', in Herzog, Rapp, and Negbi (eds.) 1989: 236-47.

Hellwing, S., M. Sadeh, and V. Kishon
    1993   'Faunal Remains', in Finkelstein, Bunimovitz, and Lederman (eds.) 1993: 309-50.

Helzer, M., and E. Lipiński (eds.)
    1988   *Society and Economy in the Eastern Mediterranean (c. 1500-1000 B.C.)* (Leuven: Peeters).

Hendel, R.S.
    1996   'The Date of the Siloam Inscription: A Rejoinder to Rogerson and Davies', *BA* 59: 223-37.
    2001   'The Exodus in Biblical Memory', *JBL* 120: 601-22.
    2002   'Exodus: A Book of Memories', *BR* 18.4: 38-45, 51-52.

Hensler, K.N.
    1998   'Social Boundaries Set in Clay: Trade Ware Patterning in the Tonto Basin of East-Central Arizona', *Journal of Anthropological Research* 54: 477-96.

Herr, L.G.
1997   'The Iron Age Period: Emerging Nations', *BA* 60.3: 114-83.
2000   'The Settlement and Fortification of Tell al-'Umayri in Jordan during the LB/Iron I Transition', in L.E. Stager, J.A. Greene, and M.D. Coogan (eds.), *The Archaeology of Jordan and Beyond: Essays in Honor of James A. Sauer* (Winona Lake, IN: Eisenbrauns): 167-79.
2001   'The History of the Collared Pithos at Tell el-'Umeiry, Jordan', in Wolff (ed.) 2001: 237-50.

Herr, L.G., and D.R. Clark
2001   'Excavating the Tribe of Reuben: A Four-Room House Provides a Clue to Where the Oldest Israelite Tribe Settled', *BAR* 27.2: 36-47, 64-66.

Herrmann, S.
1985   'Basic Factors of Israelite Settlement in Canaan', in Amitai (ed.) 1985: 47-53.

Herzog, Z.
1992   'Settlement and Fortification Planning in the Iron Age', in Kempinsky *et al.* (eds.) 1992: 231-74.
1993   'Gerisa, Tel', in *NEAEHL*: II, 480-84.
1994   'The Beer-Sheba Valley: From Nomadism to Monarchy', in Finkelstein and Na'aman (eds.) 1994: 122-49.
1997   'Phoenician Occupation at Tel Michal: The Problem of Identifying Ethnic-National Groups from Archaeological Assemblages', *Michmanim* 11: 31-44 (Hebrew).

Herzog, Z., G. Rapp, and O. Negbi (eds.)
1989   *Excavations at Tel Michal, Israel* (Tel Aviv: Tel Aviv University).

Hess, R.S.
1999   'Canaan and Canaanite in Alalakh', *UF* 31: 225-36.

Hesse, B.
1986   'Animal Use at Tel Miqne-Ekron in the Bronze Age and Iron Age', *BASOR* 264: 17-28.
1990   'Pig Lovers and Pig Haters: Patterns of Palestinian Pork Production', *Journal of Ethnobiology* 10: 195-225.

Hesse, B., and E. Brown
2000   'From Village to State: Changes in the Animal Economy during the Iron Age at Beth-Shemesh', a paper presented in a session chaired by S. Bunimovitz and Z. Lederman on *The Archaeology of a Border Community: Tel Beth-Shemesh 1999–2000*, at the Annual Meeting of the American Schools of Oriental Research, Nashville, TN, 26 November 2000.

Hesse, B., and P. Wapnish
1997   'Can Pig Remains be Used for Ethnic Diagnosis in the Ancient Near East?', in Silberman and Small (eds.) 1997: 238-70.

Hestrin, R., and M. Dayagi-Mendels
1983   'Another Pottery Group from Abu Ruqeish', *The Israel Museum Journal* 2: 49-57.

Hill, J.D.
1993   'Comment on Egalitarian Behavior and Reverse Dominance Hierarchy', *CA* 34: 242-43.

Hillier, B., and J. Hanson
    1984   *The Social Logic of Space* (Cambridge: Cambridge University Press).

Hizmi, H.
    2004   'The Excavations at el-Khirbe: An Iron Age Settlement and Byzantine Inn east of Jerusalem', in Hizmi and De Groot (eds.) 2004: 157-88.

Hizmi, H., and A. De Groot (eds.)
    2004   *Burial Caves and Sites in Judea and Samaria From the Bronze and Iron Ages* (Judea and Samaria Publications, 4; Jerusalem: Staff Officer of Archaeology—Civil Administration of Judea and Samaria and Israel Antiquities Authority).

Hjelm, I., and T.L. Thomspon
    2002   'The Victory Song of Merenptah, Israel and the People of Palestine', *JSOT* 27.1: 3-18.

Hodder, I.
    1979a   'Economic and Social Stress and Material Culture Patterning', *AA* 44: 446-55.
    1979b   'Pottery Distribution: Service and Tribal Areas', in M. Millet (ed.), *Pottery and Archaeologist* (London: Institute of Archaeology): 7-23.
    1982a   *Symbols in Action: Ethnoarchaeological Studies of Material Culture* (Cambridge: Cambridge University Press).
    1982b   *The Present Past: An Introduction to Anthropology for Archaeologists* (New York: Pica Press).
    1982c   'Toward a Contextual Approach to Prehistoric Exchange, in J.E. Ericson and T.E. Earle (eds.), *Contexts for Prehistoric Exchange* (New York: Academic Press): 199-211.
    1991   *Reading the Past* (Cambridge: Cambridge University Press).
    1992   *Theory and Practice in Archaeology* (London: Routledge).

Hodder, I. (ed.)
    1982   *Symbolic and Structural Archaeology* (Cambridge: Cambridge University Press).

Hoffman, Y.
    2001   'The Study of Biblical Historiography: History, Myth and Politics', in Levine and Mazar (eds.) 2001: 26-33 (Hebrew).

Hoffmeier, J.K.
    1997   *Israel in Egypt: The Evidence for the Authenticity of the Exodus Tradition* (New York: Oxford University Press).

Holladay, J.S.
    1992   'House, Israelite', in *ABD*: III, 308-18.
    1995   'The Kingdoms of Israel and Judah: Political and Economic Centralization in the Iron Age IIA–B (ca. 1000–750 B.C.E.)', in Levy (ed.) 1995: 368-98.
    1997   'Four Room House, in *OEANE*: II, 337-41.

Hopkins, D.C.
    1985   *The Highlands of Canaan: Agricultural Life in the Early Iron Age* (Social World of Biblical Antiquity, 3; Sheffield: Almond Press).

Horwitz, L.K.
    1986–87   'Faunal Remains from the Early Iron Age Site on Mount Ebal', *TA* 13–14: 173-89.

1989   'Diachronic Changes in Rural Husbandry Practices in Bronze Age
            Settlements from the Refaim Valley, Israel', *PEQ* 121: 44-54.
1999   'Faunal Remains: Areas L and M', in Beit-Arieh (ed.) 1999: 488-94.
Horwitz, L.K., and E. Tchernov
1989   'Appendix D: Subsistence Patterns in Ancient Jerusalem: A Study of
            Animal Remains', in Mazar and Mazar (eds.) 1989: 144-54.
Howard, M.C.
1996   *Contemporary Cultural Anthropology* (New York: HarperCollins).
Humbert, J.B.
1993   'Keisan, Tell', in *NEAEHL*: III, 862-67.
Hume, I.N.
1974   *A Guide to Artifacts of Colonial America* (New York: Knopf).
Humphrey, S.C.
1978   *Anthropology and the Greeks* (London: Routledge & Kegan Paul).
Hunt, M.
1985   'The Iron Age Pottery of the Yoqneam Regional Project' (PhD disserta-
            tion, University of California, Berkeley [UMI]).
1987   'The Pottery', in A. Ben-Tor and Y. Portugali (eds.), *Tell Qiri, a Village in
            the Jezreel Valley* (Qedem, 24; Jerusalem: Hebrew University): 139-223.
Hurvitz, A.
1974   'The Evidence of Language in Dating the Priestly Code', *RB* 81: 24-56.
Ibrahim, M.M.
1975   'Third Season of Excavation at Sahab, 1975 (Preliminary Report)', *ADAJ*
            20: 69-82.
1978   'The Collared-Rim Jar of the Early Iron Age', in Moorey and Parr (eds.)
            1978: 116-26.
1997   'Sahab', in *OEANE*: IV, 450-52.
Ilan, D.
1997a   'Burial Sites', in *OEANE*: I, 384-86.
1997b   'Tombs', in *OEANE*: V, 218-21.
1999   'Rural Archaeology—Tel Dan in the Early Iron Age', in Faust and Maeir
            (eds.) 1999: 51-66 (Hebrew).
Isaac, E.
1964   'Circumcision as a Covenant Rite', *Anthropos* 59: 444-56.
Jacobsen, T.
1943   'Primitive Democracy in Ancient Mesopotamia', *JNES* 2: 159-72.
Jacobson, D.M.
1999   'Palestine and Israel', *BASOR* 313: 65-74.
James, F.
1966   *The Iron Age at Beth-Shan* (Philadelphia: The University Museum, Uni-
            versity of Pennsylvania).
Jary, D., and J. Jary
1995   *Collins Dictionary of Sociology* (Glasgow: Collins).
Ji, C.C.
1995   'The Iron I in Central and Northern Transjordan: An Interim Summary of
            Archaeological Data', *PEQ* 127: 122-40.
1997a   'A Note on the Four-Room House in Palestine', *Orientalia* 66: 387-413.
1997b   'The East Jordan Valley during Iron Age I', *PEQ* 129: 19-37.

Joffe, A.H.
    2002   'The Rise of Secondary States in the Iron Age Levant', *JESHO* 45: 425-67.
Johnson, M.
    1999   *Archaeological Theory: An Introduction* (Oxford: Basil Blackwell).
Jones, S.
    1997   *The Archaeology of Ethnicity: Constructing Identities in the Past and Present* (London: Routledge).
Joyce, A.A., A. Bustamante and M.N. Levine
    2001   'Commoner Power: A Case Study from the Classic Period Collapse on the Oaxaca Coast', *Journal of Archaeological Method and Theory* 8: 343-85.
Kalentzidou, O.
    2000   'Pots Crossing Borders: Ethnic Identity and Ceramics in Evros, North-eastern Greece', *NEA* 63.2: 70-83.
Kamp, K., and N. Yoffee
    1980   'Ethnicity in Western Asia during the Early Second Millennium B.C.: Archaeological Assemblages and Ethnoarchaeological Perspectives', *BASOR* 237: 85-104.
Kana, K.L.
    1989   'The Order and Significance of the Savunese House', in J. Fox (ed.), *The Flow of Life: Essays on Eastern Indonesia* (Cambridge, MA: Harvard University Press): 221-30.
Katz, H.
    1979   'Iron Age "Black on Red" Pottery from the Eastern Basin of the Mediter-ranean' (MA thesis, University of Haifa [Hebrew]).
Kautz, J.R.
    1981   'Tracking the Ancient Moabites', *BA* 44: 27-35.
Kelso, J.L.
    1968   *Excavation at Bethel (1934–1960)* (AASOR, 39; Cambridge, MA: ASOR).
    1993   'Bethel', in *NEAEHL*: I, 192-94.
Kempinski, A.
    1978   *The Rise of an Urban Culture: The Urbanization of Palestine in the Early Bronze Age* (Jerusalem: Israel Ethnographic Society).
    1981   'Is Tel Masos an Amalekite Settlement?', *BAR* 7.3: 52-53.
    1986   'Philological Evidence on the Problem of Philistine Assimilation', *Archeologya, Bulletin of the Israel Association of Archaeologists* 1: 28-30 (Hebrew).
    1987   'Some Philistine Names from the Kingdom of Gaza', *IEJ* 37: 20-24.
    1989   *Megiddo: A City State and Royal Centre in North Israel* (Munich: C.H. Beck).
    1995   'To What Extent were the Israelites Canaanites?', *Archeologya, Bulletin of the Israel Association of Archaeologists* 4: 58-64 (Hebrew).
Kempinski, A., *et al.* (eds.)
    1992   *The Architecture of Ancient Israel from the Prehistoric to the Persian Period* (Jerusalem: Israel Exploration Society).
Kent, S.
    1993   'Comment on Egalitarian Behavior and Reverse Dominance Hierarchy', *CA* 34: 243.

Kenyon, K.
1974   *Digging Up Jerusalem* (London: Benn).
Kh. el-Burj
1973   'Kh. el-Burj', *Khadashot Arkheologiyot* 45: 26 (Hebrew).
Killebrew, A.
1998   'Mycenaean and Aegean-Style Pottery in Canaan during the 14th–12th Centuries BC', in Cline and Harris-Cline (eds.) 1998: 159-66.
2001   'The Collared Pithos in Context: A Typological, Technological, and Functional Reassessment', in Wolff (ed.) 2001: 377-98.
2005   *Biblical Peoples and Ethnicity: An Archaeological Study of Egyptians, Canaanites, Philistines, and Early Israel 1300–110 B.C.E.* (Atlanta: Society of Biblical Literature).
King, P.J., and L.E. Stager
2001   *Life in Biblical Israel* (Louisville, KY: Westminster/John Knox Press).
Kitchen, K.
2004   'The Victories of Merenptah, and the Nature of their Record', *JSOT* 28.3: 259-72.
Klawans, J.
1995   'Notions of Gentile Impurity in Ancient Judaism', *The Journal of the Association for Jewish Studies* 20/2: 285-312.
Kletter, R.
2002   'People Without Burials? The Lack of Iron Age Burials in the Central Highlands of Palestine', *IEJ* 52: 28-48.
Knauf, B.M.
1993   'Comment on Egalitarian Behavior and Reverse Dominance Hierarchy', *CA* 34: 243-44.
Kochavi, M.
1969   'Excavations at Tel Esdar', *'Atiqot* 5: 14-48, 2*-5* (Hebrew with an English abstract).
1984   'The Period of the Israelite Settlement', in Eph'al (ed.) 1984: 21-84 (Hebrew).
Kottak, C.P.
1980   *The Past in the Present: History, Ecology, and Cultural Variation in Highland Madagascar* (Ann Arbor: University of Michigan Press).
Kramer, C.
1977   'Pots and People', in L.D. Levine and T.C.J. Young (eds.), *Mountains and Lowlands: Essays in the Archaeology of Greater Mesopotamia* (Bibliotheca Mesopotamica, 7; Malibu: Undena): 91-112.
Kroeber, A.L.
1948   *Anthropology* (New York: Harcourt, Brace & Co.).
Kuhrt, A.
1995   *The Ancient Near East (3000–330 BCE)* (London: Routledge).
Lamberg-Karlovsky, C.C.
1985   'The Near Eastern "Breakout" and the Mesopotamian Social Contract', *Symbols* (Spring): 8-11, 23-24.
Lapp, N.L.
1992   'Pottery, Pottery Chronology of Palestine', in *ABD*: V, 433-44.
1993   'Ful, Tell el-', in *NEAEHL*: II, 445-48.

Lapp, N.L. (ed.)
    1981   *The Third Campaign at Tell el-Ful: The Excavations of 1964* (Cambridge, MA: ASOR).

Lapp, P.W.
    1968   'Review of Gibeon', *AJA* 72: 391-93.

Lederman, Z.
    1992   'Nomads They Never Were', *The 18th Archaeological Congress in Israel, Lectures' Abstracts* (Tel Aviv: Israel Exploration Society [Hebrew]).
    1993   'Respond', in *Biblical Archaeology Today—1990: Proceedings of the Second International Congress on Biblical Archaeology, Jerusalem, June–July 1990* (Jerusalem: Israel Exploration Society): 483-84.

Lehmann, G.
    2004   'Reconstructing the Social Landscape of Early Israel: Rural Marriage Alliances in the Central Hill Country', *TA* 31: 141-93.

Lemche, N.P.
    1985   *Ancient Israel* (Leiden: E.J. Brill).
    1991   *The Canaanites and their Land: The Idea of Canaan in the Old Testament* (JSOT, 110; Sheffield: Sheffield Academic Press).
    1996   'From Patronage Society to Patronage Society', in Fritz and Davies (eds.) 1996: 106-20.
    1998a   'Greater Canaan: The Implication of a Correct Reading of EA 151: 49-51', *BASOR* 310: 19-24.
    1998b   *The Israelites in History and Tradition* (Louisville, KY: Westminster/John Knox Press).
    1998c   'The Origin of the Israelite State—A Copenhagen Perspective on the Emergence of Critical Historical Studies of Ancient Israel in Recent Times', *SJOT* 12: 44-63.

Lenski, G.
    1980   'Review of N.K. Gottwald, *The Tribes of Yahweh*', *Religious Studies Review* 6: 275-78.

Lernau, H., and O. Lernau
    1989   'Appendix E: Fish Bone Remains', in Mazar and Mazar (eds.) 1989: 155-61.
    1992   'Fish Remains', in De Groot and Ariel 1992: 131-48.

Lev-Tov, J.
    1997   'Diet Urbanization and Ethnicity: Analysis of Faunal Remains from the Philistine City of Tel Miqne-Ekron', *AASOR Newsletter* 47.4: 22.

Levine, L.I., and A. Mazar (eds.)
    2001   *The Controversy Over the Historicity of the Bible* (Jerusalem: Yad Ben-Zvi [Hebrew]).

Levy, J.
    1998   'The Bow and the Blanket: Religion, Identity and Resistance in Raramuri Material Culture', *Journal of Anthropological Research* 54: 299-324.

Levy, S., and G. Edelstein
    1972   'Cinq Annees de Fouilles a Tell 'Amal (Nir David)', *RB* 79: 325-67.

Levy, T.E. (ed.)
    1995   *The Archaeology of Society in the Holy Land* (London: Leicester University Press).

Levy, T.E., R.B. Adams, and A. Muniz
    2004   'Archaeology and the Shasu Nomads: Recent Excavations in the Jabal Himdat Firdan, Jordan', in R.E. Friedman and W.H. Propp (eds.), *Le-David Maskil: A Birthday Tribute to David Noel Freedman* (Winona Lake, IN: Eisenbrauns): 63-89.
Levy, T.E., and A.F.C. Holl
    2002   'Migrations, Ethnogenesis, and Settlement Dynamics: Israelites in Iron Age Canaan and Shuwa-Arabs in the Chad Basin', *JAA* 21: 83-118.
Levy, T.E., R.B. Adams, and M. Najjar
    2004   'Reassessing the Chronology of Biblical Edom: New Excavations and 14C Dates from Khirbet en-Nahas (Jordan)', *Antiquity* 78: 863-76.
Lewis, T.J.
    2002   *The House that Albright Built* (Special Issue of *NEA*, 65/1; Baltimore: ASOR).
Licht, J.S.
    1962   'Circumcision', *EB* 4: 894-901 (Hebrew).
    1995   *A Commentary on the Book of Numbers (XXII–XXXVI)* (Jerusalem: Magnes Press [Hebrew]).
Lipschitz, N.
    1989   'Appendix C: Dendroarchaeological Studies 150: The Ophel (Jerusalem) 1986', in Mazar and Mazar (eds.) 1989: 142-43.
Lipschitz, N., and G. Biger
    1991   'Cedar of Lebanon (*Cedrus Libani*) in Israel during Antiquity', *IEJ* 41: 167-75.
Liver, J.
    1962   'Canaan, Canaanite', *EB* 4: 196-204 (Hebrew).
Lods, A.
    1962   *Israel, from its Beginning to the Middle of the Eighth Century* (New York: A.A. Knauf).
London, G.
    1989   'A Comparison of Two Contemporaneous Lifestyles of the Late Second Millennium B.C.', *BASOR* 273: 37-55.
    2003   'Four-Room Structures at Late Bronze/Iron I Hill Country Workstations', in Alpert Nakhai (ed.) 2003: 69-84.
Long, B.
    1997   *Planting and Reaping Albright: Politics, Ideology and Interpreting the Bible* (University Park: Pennsylvania State University).
Loud, G.
    1948   *Megiddo II: Plates and Texts* (Chicago: University of Chicago Press).
Loyet, M.A.
    2000   'The Potential for Within-Site Variation of Faunal Remains: A Case Study from the Islamic Period Urban Center of Tell Tuneinir, Syria', *BASOR* 320: 23-48.
MacDonald, B.
    2000   *'East of the Jordan': Territories and Sites of the Hebrew Scriptures* (Boston: ASOR).
MacDonald, B., and R.W. Younker (eds.)
    1999   *Ancient Ammon* (Studies in the History and Culture of the Ancient Near East, 17; Leiden: E.J. Brill).

Machinist, P.
    1991   'The Question of Distinctiveness in Ancient Israel: An Essay', in M. Cogan and I. Ephal (eds.), *Ah, Assyria: Studies in Assyrian History and Ancient Near Eastern Historiography Presented to Hayim Tadmor* (Jerusalem: Magnes Press): 196-212.
    1994   'Outsiders or Insiders: The Biblical View of Emergent Israel and its Context', in Silberstein and Cohn (eds.) 1994: 35-60.
    2000   'Biblical Traditions: The Philistines and Israelite History', in Oren 2000: 53-83.

Macionis, J.J.
    1999   *Sociology* (Tel Aviv: Open University of Israel [Hebrew]).

Maeir, A.M.
    2000   'Jerusalem before King David: An Archaeological Survey from Prehistoric Times to the End of the Iron Age I', in Ahituv and Mazar (eds.), *The History of Jerusalem: The Biblical Period* (Jerusalem: Yad Ben-Zvi): 33-65 (Hebrew).
    2001   'The Philistine Culture in Transformation: A Current Perspective based on the Results of the First Seasons of Excavations at Tell es-Safi/Gath', in A.M. Maeir and E. Baruch (eds.), *Settlement, Civilization and Culture: Proceedings of the Conference in Memory of David Alon* (Ramat Gan: Bar-Ilan University): 111-30.
    2004   'What's Between Gath of the Philistines and Biblical Jerusalem: Choice Perspectives and Implications for the Study of the History of the Land of Israel in the Iron Age IIA', in E. Baruch and A. Faust (eds.), *New Studies on Jerusalem*, X (Ramat Gan: Bar Ilan University): 51-62 (Hebrew).
forthcoming   'Philistia Transforming: Fresh Evidence from Tell es-Sâfi/Gath on the Transformational Trajectory of the Philistine Culture', in A. Killebrew, G. Lehmann, and M. Artzy (eds.), *The Philistines and Other Sea Peoples* (Leiden: E.J. Brill): 111-29.

Mai, N.
    1999   'Jerusalem, Giv'at Homa', *ESI* 19: 65*-66*.

Maisler (Mazar), B.
    1950–51   'The Excavations at Tel Qasile: Preliminary Report', *IEJ* 1: 61-76, 125-40, 194-218.

Maitlis, Y.
    1989   'Agricultural Settlement in the Vicinity of Jerusalem in the Late Iron Age' (MA thesis, Hebrew University, Jerusalem [Hebrew with an English abstract]).

Malamat, A.
    1997   'The Exodus: Egyptian Analogies', in Frerichs and Lesko (eds.) 1997: 15-26.

Malamat, A. (ed.)
    1979   *The World History of the Jewish People, the Age of the Monarchies: Culture and Society* (Jerusalem: Masada).

Marcus, J., and K.V. Flannery
    1996   *Zapotec Civilization: How Urban Society Evolved in Mexico's Ouaxaca Valley* (London: Thames & Hudson).

Master, D.
   2003   'Trade and Politics: Ashkelon's Balancing Act in the Seventh Century
             B.C.E.', *BASOR* 330: 47-64.
Mazar, A.
   1976   'Iron Age Burial Caves North of the Damascus Gate, Jerusalem', *IEJ* 26:
             1-8.
   1980   *Excavations at Tell Qasille*. Part One. *The Philistine Sanctuary: Architec-
             ture and Cult Objects* (Qedem, 12; Jerusalem: Hebrew University).
   1981   'Giloh: An Early Israelite Settlement Site Near Jerusalem', *IEJ* 31: 1-36.
   1982a   'The "Bull-Site"—An Iron Age I Open Cult Place', *BASOR* 247: 27-42.
   1982b   'Iron Age Fortresses in the Judean Hills', *PEQ* 114: 87-109.
   1985a   *Excavations at Tell Qasile*. Part Two. *The Philistine Sanctuary, Various
             Finds, The Pottery, Conclusions, Appendixes* (Qedem, 20; Jerusalem:
             Hebrew University).
   1985b   'The Israelite Settlement in Canaan in the Light of Archaeological
             Excavations', in Amitai (ed.) 1985: 61-71.
   1986   'No More "Philistine Culture"? A Response to S. Bunimovitz', *Archae-
             ologya* 1: 22-27 (Hebrew).
   1990a   *Archaeology of the Land of the Bible, 10,000–586 B.C.E.* (New York:
             Doubleday).
   1990b   'Iron Age I and II Towers at Giloh', *IEJ* 40: 77-101.
   1992a   'Temples of the Middle and Late Bronze Age and the Iron Age', in
             Kempinsky *et al.* (eds.) 1992: 161-87.
   1992b   The Iron Age I', in Ben-Tor (ed.) 1992: 258-301.
   1994   'Jerusalem and its Vicinity in Iron Age I', in Finkelstein and Na'aman
             (eds.) 1994: 70-91.
   1995   'Excavations at the Israelite Town at Khirbet Marjameh in the Hills of
             Ephraim', *IEJ* 45: 85-117.
   1997   'Iron Age Chronology: A Reply to I. Finkelstein', *Levant* 29: 157-67.
   1998   'Philistia, Chronology and Cultural Affinities: Discussion', in Gitin,
             Mazar, and Stern (eds.) 1998: 184-85.
   1999   'The 1997–1998 Excavations at Tel Rehov: Preliminary Report', *IEJ* 49:
             1-42.
   2000   'The Temples and Cult of the Philistines', in Oren (ed.) 2000: 213-32.
   2001   'On the Relation Between Archaeological Research and the Study of the
             History of Israel in the Biblical Period', *Cathedra* 100: 65-88 (Hebrew).
   2002   'Megiddo in the Thirteenth-Eleventh Centuries BCE: A Review of Some
             Recent Studies', in E. Oren and S. Ahituv (eds.), *Aharon Kempinski
             Memorial Volume: Studies in Archaeology and Related Disciplines* (Beer
             Sheva, 15; Beer Sheva: Ben-Gurion University): 264-82.
Mazar, A., D. Amit, and Z. Ilan
   1996   'Hurvat Shilhah: An Iron Age Site in the Judean Desert', in J.D. Seger
             (ed.), *Retrieving the Past: Essays on Archaeological Research and Meth-
             odology in Honor of Gus W. Van Beek* (Winona Lake, IN: Eisenbrauns):
             193-211.
Mazar, A., and O. Harpazi-Ofer
   1993   'The Excavations at Tell Qasile from 1988 to 1991', in R. Zeevy (ed.),
             Israel—People and Land, Eretz Israel Museum Yearbook (Volume 7–8

[25–26] [1990–1993]), Bar-Adon Book (Tel Aviv: Eretz Israel Museum):
9-34.

Mazar, B.
1964   'The Sanctuary of Arad and the Family of Hobab the Kenite', *EI* 7: 1-5.
1981   'The Early Israelite Settlement in the Hill Country', *BASOR* 241: 75-85.

Mazar, E.
1985   'Edomite Pottery at the End of the Iron Age', *IEJ* 35: 253-69.
1993   'Akhziv', in *NEAEHL*: I, 35-36.
2006   'Did I Find King David's Palace?', *BAR* 32.1: 16-27, 70.

Mazar, E., and B. Mazar (eds.)
1989   *Excavations in the South of the Temple Mount, the Ophel of Biblical Jerusalem* (Qedem, 29; Jerusalem: Hebrew University).

Mazzoni, S. (ed.)
1994   *Nouve Fondenzioni Nel Vicino Oriente Antico, Realta' E Ideologia* (Pisa:
Giardini Editori e Stampatori in Pisa).

McCarter, P.K.
1996   *Ancient Inscriptions* (Washington DC: Biblical Archaeology Society).

McGuire, R.H.
1982   'The Study of Ethnicity in Historical Archaeology', *JAA* 1: 159-78.

McGuire, R.H., and R. Paynter (eds.)
1991   *The Archaeology of Inequality* (Oxford: Basil Blackwell).

McNairn, B.
1980   *The Method and Theory of V. Gordon Childe* (Edinburgh: Edinburgh
University Press).

McNutt, P.M.
1999   *Reconstructing the Society of Ancient Israel* (Louisville, KY: Westminster/
John Knox Press).

Mendenhall, G.
1962   'The Hebrew Conquest of Palestine', *BA* 25: 66-87.

Meshel, Z.
1974   'History of the Negev in the Time of the Kings of Judah' (PhD dissertation, Tel Aviv University [Hebrew]).

Metcalf, P., and R. Huntington
1991   *Celebrations of Death: The Anthropology of Mortuary Ritual* (Cambridge:
Cambridge University Press).

Meyers, C.
1988   *Discovering Eve: Ancient Israelite Women in Context* (Oxford: Oxford
University Press).

Mienis, H.K.
1992   'Molluscs', in De Groot and Ariel (eds.) 1992: 122-30.

Milgrom, J.
1991   *Leviticus 1–16* (AB; New York: Doubleday).

Miller, D., and C. Tilley (eds.)
1984   *Ideology, Power and Prehistory* (Cambridge: Cambridge University Press).

Miller, J.M., and J.H. Hayes
1986   *A History of Ancient Israel and Judah* (Philadelphia: Westminster Press).

Miller, R.D.
2004   'Identifying Earliest Israel', *BASOR* 333: 55-68.

Moorey, R., and P. Parr (eds.)
    1978   *Archaeology in the Levant: Essays for Kathleen Kenyon* (Warminster: Aris & Phllips).
Morris, I.
    1997   'An Archaeology of Equalities? The Greek City-States', in Nichols and Charlton (eds.) 1997: 91-105.
Murray, O.
    1998   'Introduction', in J. Burckhardt, *The Greeks and Greek Civilization* (New York: St Martin's Press): xi-xliv.
Na'aman, N.
    1994a   'The Canaanites and their Land: A Rejoinder', *UF* 26: 397-418.
    1994b   'The "Conquest of Canaan" in the Book of Joshua and in History', in Finkelstein and Na'aman (eds.) 1994: 218-81.
    1996   'The Contribution of the Amarna Letters to the Debate on Jerusalem's Political Position in the Tenth Century BCE', *BASOR* 304: 17-27.
    2000   'The Contribution of the Trojan Grey Ware from Lachish and Tel Miqne-Ekron to the Chronology of the Philistine Monochrome Pottery', *BASOR* 317: 1-7.
    2002   *The Past that Shapes the Present: The Creation of Biblical Historiography in the Late First Temple Period and After the Downfall* (Jerusalem: Yeriot).
Naveh, Y.
    1962   'The Excavations at Mesad Hashavyahu: Preliminary Report', *IEJ* 12: 89-113.
Netzer, E.
    1992   'Domestic Architecture in the Iron Age', in Kempinsky *et al.* (eds.) 1992: 193-201.
Nichols, D.L., and T.H. Charlton (eds.)
    1997   *The Archaeology of City-States: Cross-Cultural Approaches* (Washington and London: Smithsonian Institution Press).
Nicolaou, K.
    1982   'The Mycenaeans in the East', *SHAJ* 1: 121-26.
Niemeyer, H.G.
    1993   'Trade Before the Flag? On the Principles of Phoenician Expansion in the Mediterranean', in *Biblical Archaeology Today—1990: Proceedings of the Second International Congress on Biblical Archaeology, Jerusalem, June–July 1990* (Jerusalem: Israel Exploration Society): 335-44.
Oded, B.
    1979   *Mass Deportation and Deportees in the Neo-Assyrian Empire* (Wiesbaden: Dr Ludwig Reichert Verlag).
Ofer, A.
    1990   'The Judaean Hill Country—From Nomadism to a National Monarchy', in Finkelstein and Na'aman (eds.) 1994: 155-214 (Hebrew).
    1994   '"All the Hill Country of Judah": From a Settlement Fringe to a Prosperous Monarchy', in Finkelstein and Na'aman (eds.) 1994: 92-121.
Olsen, B., and Z. Kobylinski
    1991   'Ethnicity in Anthropological and Archaeological Research, a Norwegian-Polish Perspective', *Archaeologia Polona* 29: 5-27.

Oppenheim, A.L.
1977   *Ancient Mesopotamia, A Portrait of a Dead Civilization* (Chicago: Univeristy of Chicago).

Oren, E.D.
1984   ' "Governor's Residencies" in Canaan under the New Kingdom: A Case Study of Egyptian Administration', *JSSEA* 14: 37-56.

Oren, E.D. (ed.)
2000   *The Sea Peoples and Their World: A Reassessment* (Philadelphia: The University Museum).

Orser, C.E.
1996   'Beneath the Material Surface of Things: Commodities, Artifacts, and Slave Plantations', in R.W. Preucel and I. Hodder (eds.), *Contemporary Archaeology in Theory* (Oxford: Basil Blackwell): 189-201.

Orser, C.E., and B.M. Fagan
1995   *Historical Archaeology* (New York: HarperCollins).

Paley, S.M., and Y. Porath
1993   'Hefer', *NEAEHL*: II, 609-14.

Parker Pearson, M.
1982   'Mortuary Practices, Society and Ideology: An Ethnoarchaeological Case Study', in Hodder (ed.) 1982: 99-113.

Parr, P.R.
1966   'Reviews and Notices: Winery, Defenses and Soundings at Gibeon', *PEQ* 98: 114-18.
1978   'Pottery, People and Politics', in Moorey and Parr (eds.) 1978: 202-209.

Pasto, J.
1998   'When the End is the Beginning? Or When the Biblical Past is the Political Present: Some Thought on Ancient Israel, "Post Exilic Judaism", and the Politics of Biblical Scholarship', *SJOT* 12: 157-202.

Pasztory, E.
1992   'Abstraction and the Rise of a Utopian State at Teotihuacan', in J. Berlo (ed.), *Art, Ideology and the City of Teotihuacan* (Washington: Dumbarton Oaks): 281-320.

Patterson, T.C.
1991   *The Inca Empire: The Formation and Disintegration of a Pre-Capitalist State* (Worcester: Berg).

Pedersen, J.
1926   *Israel: Its Life and Culture I–II* (London: Oxford University Press).

Peleg, Y.
2004   'Early Roman Farmhouse and Late Bronze Age Burial Cave East of Otniel', in Hizmi and De Groot (eds.) 2004: 260-84.

Peleg, Y., and I. Eisenstadt
2004   'A Late Bronze Age Tomb at Hebron (Tell Rumeideh)', in Hizmi and De Groot (eds.) 2004: 231-59.

Plog, S.
1980   *Stylistic Variation in Prehistoric Ceramics* (Cambridge: Cambridge University Press).
1983   'Analysis of Style in Artifacts', *ARA* 12: 125-42.

Pollock, S.
1983   'Style and Information: An Analysis of the Susiana Ceramics', *JAA*: 354-90.
Porath, Y., S.M. Paley, and R.R. Stieglitz
1993   'Mikhmoret, Tel', in *NEAEHL*: I, 1043-46.
Portugali, Y.
1999   *Space, Time and Society in Ancient Eretz Israel.* Part I. *Social Morphology* (Tel Aviv: Open University of Israel [Hebrew]).
Postgate, J.N.
1992   *Early Mesopotamia, Society and Economy at the Dawn of History* (London: Routledge).
Prausnitz, M.W.
1993   'Achzib', in *NEAEHL*: I, 32-35.
Price, B.J.
1978   'Secondary State Formation: An Explanatory Model', in Cohen and Service (eds.) 1978: 161-86.
Pritchard, J.B.
1962   *Gibeon, Where the Sun Stood Still* (Princeton, NJ: Princeton University Press).
1964   *Winery, Defences and Soundings at Gibeon* (Philadelphia: University of Pennsylvania).
1993   'Gibeon', in *NEAEHL*: I, 511-14.
Quesada, F.
1998   'From Quality to Quantity: Wealth, Status and Prestige in the Iberian Iron Age', in D. Bailey (ed.), *The Archaeology of Value: Essays on Prestige and the Process of Valuation* (BAR International Series, 730; Oxford: British Archaeological Reports): 70-96.
Raban, A.
1991   'The Philistines in the Western Jezreel Valley', *BASOR* 284: 17-27.
2000   'Collared Rim Pithoi—Ceramic Evidence for Cross-Regional Administrative System', in *Twenty-Sixth Archaeological Conference in Israel, Abstracts* (Jerusalem: IAA): 4-5 (Hebrew).
2001   'Standardized Collared-Rim Pithoi and Short Lived Settlements', in Wolff (eds) 2001: 493-518.
Rainey, A.F.
1991   'Can You Name the Panel with the Israelites? Rainey's Challenge', *BAR* 17.6: 56-60, 93.
1994   'The "House of David" and the House of the Deconstructionists', *BAR* 20.6: 47.
1996   'Who is a Canaanite? A Review of the Textual Evidence', *BASOR* 304: 1-15.
2001   'Israel in Merenptah Inscription and Reliefs', *IEJ* 51: 57-75.
2003   'Amarna and Later: Aspects of Social History', in Dever and Gitin (eds.) 2003: 169-87.
Rayner, S.
1993   'Comment on Egalitarian Behavior and Reverse Dominance Hierarchy', *CA* 34: 244-45.

Redford, D.B.
    1986   'The Ashkelon Relief at Karnak and the Israel Stela', *IEJ* 36: 188-200.
    1992   *Egypt, Canaan and Israel in Ancient Times* (Princeton, NJ: Princeton University Press).

Remini, R.V.
    1988   *The Legacy of Andrew Jackson: Essays on Democracy, Indian Removal, and Slavery* (Baton Rough: Louisiana University Press).

Rendsburg, G.A.
    1999   'Down with History, Up with Reading: The Current State of Biblical Studies', A Lecture at the McGill University Department of Jewish Studies Thirtieth Anniversary Conference, The Academy Reports to the Community, 9–10 May 1999 (an expanded text of this lecture with notes can be found on the internet at: http://www.arts.mcgill.ca/programs/jewish/ 30yrs/ rendsburgh/index.html).

Renfrew, C.
    1972   *The Emergence of Civilisations: The Cyclades and the Aegean in the Third Millennium B.C.* (London: Methuen).
    1993   *The Roots of Ethnicity, Archaeology, Genetics and the Origins of Europe* (Rome: Unione Internazionale degli Instituti de archaeologia, storia e storia dell arte in Roma).
    1994   'Toward a Cognitive Archaeology', in C. Renfrew and E.B.W. Zubrow (eds.), *The Ancient Mind: Elements of Cognitive Archaeology* (Cambridge: Cambridge University Press): 3-12.

Renfrew, C., and P. Bahn
    1996   *Archaeology: Theories, Methods and Practice* (London: Thames & Hudson).

Reviv, H.
    1993   *The Society in the Kingdoms of Israel and Judah* (Jerusalem: Bialik Institute [Hebrew]).

Riklin, S.
    1997   'Beit Aryeh', *'Atiqot* 32: 7-20 (Hebrew).

Roberts, B.K.
    1996   *Landscapes of Settlements* (London: Routledge).

Rofé, A.
    1994   *Introduction to the Composition of the Pentateuch* (Jerusalem: Academon Publishing House [Hebrew]).

Rogerson, J.
    1986   'Was Early Israel a Segmentary Society?', *JSOT* 36: 17-26.

Rogerson, J., and P.R. Davies
    1996   'Was the Siloam Tunnel Built by Hezekiah?', *BA* 59: 138-48.

Roosens, E.
    1995   'Subtle "Primitives": Ethnic Formation among the Central Yaka of Zaire', in L. Romanucci-Ross and G.A. De Vos (eds.), *Ethnic Identity, Creation, Conflict and Accommodation* (Walnut Creek: AltaMira Press, 3rd edn): 115-24.

Roth, M.
    1989   *Babylonian Marriage Agreements 7th–3rd Centuries BC* (Kevelaer: Butzon & Bercker).

Routledge, B.
    2004   *Moab in the Iron Age: Hegemony, Polity, Archaeology* (Philadelphia: University of Pennsylvania Press).
Ryman, R.L., M.J. O'Brien, and R.C. Dunnell
    1997   *The Rise and Fall of Culture History* (New York: Plenum Press).
Sacket, J.R.
    1977   'The Meaning of Style in Archaeology: A General Model', *AA* 42: 369-80.
    1985   'Style and Ethnicity in the Kalahari: A Reply to Wiessner', *AA* 50: 154-59.
    1986   'Isochrestism and Style: A Clarification', *JAA* 5: 206-77.
Sahlins, M.D.
    1972   *Stone Age Economics* (Chicago: University of Chicago Press).
Said, E.
    1979   *Orientalism* (New York: Vintage).
Sass, B.
    1990   'Arabs and Greeks in Late First Temple Jerusalem', *PEQ* 122: 59-61.
Sasson, J.M.
    1966   'Circumcision in the Ancient Near East', *JBL* 85: 473-76.
Sather, C.
    1980   'Symbolic Elements in Saribas Iban Rites of Padi Storage', *Journal of the Malaysian Branch of the Royal Asiatic Society* 53.2: 67-95.
Scarre, C.
    1998   'Traditions of Death: Mounded Tombs, Megalithic Art and Funerary Ideology in Neolithic Western Europe', in M. Edmonds and C. Richards (eds.), *Understanding the Neolithic of North-Western Europe* (Glasgow: Cruithny Press): 161-87.
Schortman, E.M., P.A. Urban, and M. Ausec
    2001   'Politics with Style: Identity Formation in Prehispanic Southern Meso-america', *American Anthropologist* 103.2: 312-30.
Schreiber, N.
    2003   *The Cypro-Phoenician Pottery of the Iron Age* (Leiden: E.J. Brill).
Schwartz, B.J.
    1999   *The Holiness Legislation: Studies in the Priestly Code* (Jerusalem: Magnes Press [Hebrew]).
Sellers, O.R.
    1933   *The Citadel of Beth-Zur* (Philadelphia: Westminster Press).
Sellers, O.R., and W.F. Albright
    1931   'The First Campaign of Excavation at Beth-Zur', *BASOR* 43: 2-12.
Seymour-Smith, C.
    1986   *Macmillan Dictionary of Anthropology* (London: Macmillan).
Shackel, P.A.
    2000   'Craft to Wage Labor: Agency and Resistance in American Historical Archaeology', in M.A. Dobres and J. Robb (eds.), *Agency in Archaeology* (London: Routledge): 232-46.
Shanks, H. (ed.)
    1992   *The Rise of Ancient Israel* (Washington, DC: Biblical Archaeology Society).
Shanks, M., and C. Tilley
    1982   'Ideology, Symbolic Power and Ritual Communication: A Reinterpretation of Neolithic Mortuary Practices', in Hodder (ed.) 1982: 129-54.

Shanks, M., and C. Tilley
    1987   *Social Theory and Archaeology* (Albequerque: University of New Mexico Press).
Shapira, A.
    1998   '"He Appointed Judges in the Land in all the Fortified Towns of Judah" (2 Chron. 19:45)—an Expression of the Separation of Powers in Israel', *Judea and Samaria Research Studies* 7: 233-43 (Hebrew).
Shennan, J.S.
    1989   'Introduction: Archaeological Approaches to Cultural Identity', in Shennan (ed.) 1989: 1-32.
    1991   'Some Current Issues in the Archaeological Identification of Past Peoples', *Archaeologia Polona* 29: 29-37.
Shennan, J.S. (ed.)
    1989   *Archaeological Approaches to Cultural Identity* (London: Unwin Hyman).
Sherratt, A., and S. Sherratt
    1991   'From Luxuries to Commodities: The Nature of Mediterranean Bronze Age Trading Systems', in N.H. Gale (ed.), *Bronze Age Trade in the Mediterranean* (Jonsered: P. Astroem): 351-86.
    1998   'Small Worlds: Interaction and Identity in the Ancient Mediterranean', in Cline and Harris-Cline (eds.) 1998: 329-42.
Sherratt, S.
    1998   'Sea People and the Economic Structure of the Late Second Millennium in the Eastern Mediterranean', in Gitin, Mazar, and Stern (eds.) 1998: 292-313.
Sherratt, S., and A. Sherratt
    1993   'The Growth of Mediterranean Economy in the First Millennium BC', *World Archaeology* 24.3: 361-78.
Shiloh, Y.
    1970   'The Four Room House: Its Situation and Function in the Israelite City', *IEJ* 20: 180-90.
    1973   'The Four Room House—The Israelite Type-House?', *EI* 11: 277-85 (Hebrew).
    1978   'Elements in the Development of Town Planning in the Israelite City', *IEJ* 28: 36-51.
    1987a   'South Arabian Inscriptions from the City of David, Jerusalem', *PEQ* 119: 9-18.
    1987b   'The Casemate Wall, the Four Room House and the Early Planning in the Israelite City', *BASOR* 268: 3-15.
Silberman, N.A.
    1993   'Visions of the Future: Albright in Jerusalem', *BA* 56.1: 8-16.
Silberman, N., and D.B. Small (eds.)
    1997   *The Archaeology of Israel: Constructing the Past, Interpreting the Present* (JSOTSup, 237; Sheffield: Sheffield Academic Press).
Silberstein, L.J., and R.L. Cohn (eds.)
    1994   *The Other in Jewish Thought and History* (New York: New York University Press).

Singer, I.
> 1988a 'Merneptah's Campaign to Canaan and the Egyptian Occupation of the Southern Coastal Plain of Palestine in the Ramesside Period', *BASOR* 269: 1-10.
>
> 1988b 'The Origin of the Sea People and Their Settlement on the Coast of Canaan', in Helzer and Lipiński (eds.) 1988: 239-50.
>
> 1994 'Egyptians, Canaanites, and Philistines in the Period of the Emergence of Israel', in Finkelstein and Na'aman (eds.) 1994: 282-338.

Singer-Avitz, L.
> 1989a 'Iron Age and Persian Period Pottery from Tel Poleg', in Herzog, Rapp, and Negbi (eds.) 1989: 375-80.
>
> 1989b 'Iron Age Pottery (Stratum XIV–XII)', in Herzog, Rapp, and Negbi (eds.) 1989: 76-87.
>
> 1996 'Household Activities at Beersheba', *EI* 25: 166-74 (Hebrew).
>
> 1999 'Beersheba—A Gateway Community in Southern Arabian Long-Distance Trade in the Eighth Century B.C.E.', *TA* 26: 3-74.

Sinopoli, C.M.
> 1994 'The Archaeology of Empires', *ARA* 23: 159-80.

Skjeggestand, M.
> 1992 'Ethnic Groups in Early Iron Age Palestine: Some Remarks on the Use of the Term "Israelite" in Recent Literature', *SJOT* 6: 159-86.

Small, D.B.
> 1997 'Group Identification and Ethnicity in the Construction of the Early State of Israel—From the Outside Looking in', in Silberman and Small (eds.) 1997: 271-88.

Smith, A.
> 1986 *The Ethnic Origins of Nation* (Oxford: Basil Blackwell).
>
> 1994 The Politics of Culture: Ethnicity and Nationalism', in T. Ingold (ed.), *Companion Encyclopedia of Anthropology* (London: Routledge): 706-33.

Smith, M.E., and L. Montiel
> 2001 'The Archaeological Study of Empires and Imperialism in Pre-Hispanic Central Mexico', *JAA* 20: 245-84.

Smith, R.H.
> 1993 'Pella', in *NEAEHL*: III, 1174-80.

Smith-Kipp, R., and E.M. Schortman
> 1989 'The Political Impact of Trade in Chiefdoms', *American Anthropologist* 91: 370-85.

Sparks, K.L.
> 1998 *Ethnicity and Identity in Ancient Israel* (Winona Lake, IN: Eisenbrauns).

Speiser, E.A.
> 1971 'The Manner of the Kings', in B. Mazar (ed.), *The World History of the Jewish People.* III. *Judges* (Jerusalem: Masada): 280-87.

Stager, L.E.
> 1976 'Farming in the Judean Desert During the Iron Age', *BASOR* 221: 145-58.
>
> 1985a 'Mernephtah, Israel and the Sea Peoples: New Light on an Old Relief', *EI* 18: 56*-64*.
>
> 1985b 'Response', in Amitai (ed.) 1985: 83-87.
>
> 1985c 'The Archeology of the Family in Ancient Israel', *BASOR* 260: 1-35.

1988   'Archaeology, Ecology, and Social History: Background Themes to the
          Song of Deborah', in J.A. Emerton (ed.), *Congress Volume: Jerusalem,
          1986* (Leiden: E.J. Brill): 221-34.
1993   'Ashkelon, in *NEAEHL*: I, 103-12.
1995   'The Impact of the Sea Peoples in Canaan (1185–1050 BCE)', in Levy
          1995: 332-48.
1998   'Forging an Identity: the Emergence of Ancient Israel', in M.D. Coogan
          (ed.), *The Oxford History of the Biblical World* (New York: Oxford
          University Press): 123-75.
2003   'The Patrimonial Kingdom of Solomon', in Dever and Gitin (eds.) 2003:
          63-74.
Stark, M.T. (ed.)
1998   *The Archaeology of Social Boundaries* (Washington: Smithsonian Insti-
          tution Press).
Stark, M.T., R.L. Bishop, and E. Miksa
2000   'Ceramic Technology and Social Boundaries: Cultural Practices in Kalinga
          Clay Selection and Use', *Journal of Archaeological Method and Theory* 7:
          295-331.
Stein, G.J
1994   'Economy, Ritual and Power in 'Ubaid Mesopotamia', in G. Stein and
          M.S. Rothman (eds.), *Chiefdoms and Early States in the Near East: The
          Organizational Dynamics of Complexity* (Madison: Prehistory Press):
          35-46.
Stein, G.J., *et al.*
1996   'Uruk Colonies and Anatolian Communities: An Interim Report on the
          1992–1993 Excavations at Hacinebi, Turkey', *AJA* 100: 205-60.
Steiner, M.
1998   'David's Jerusalem: Its Not There, Archaeology Proves a Negative', *BAR*
          24.4: 26-33.
Stepansky, Y., D. Segal, and I. Carmi
1996   'The 1993 Sounding at Tel Sasa: Excavation Report and Radiometric
          Dating', *'Atiqot* 28: 63-76.
Stern, E.
1978   *Excavations at Tel-Mevorakh (1973–1976), Part One: From the Iron Age
          to the Roman Period* (Qedem, 9; Jerusalem: Hebrew University).
1989   'Hazor, Dor and Megiddo in the Time of Ahab and the Assyrian Period',
          EI 20: 233-48 (Hebrew with an English abstract).
1996   'Tel Dor—An East–West Trading Centre in the Bronze and Iron Ages',
          EI 25: 268-73.
2000   'The Settlement of the Sea People in Northern Israel', in Oren (ed.) 2000:
          197-212.
Stern, M.
1976   *Greek and Latin Authors on Jews and Judaism I* (Jerusalem: Israel
          Academy of Science and Humanities).
Stiebing, W.H.
1989   *Out of the Desert? Archaeology and the Exodus/Conquest Narratives*
          (Buffalo: Promotheus).

Stone, B.J.
    1995   'The Philistine and Acculturation: Culture Change and Ethnic Continuity in the Iron Age', *BASOR* 298: 7-32.
Stone, E.
    1997   'City-States and their Centers: The Mesopotamian Example', in Nichols and Charlton (eds.) 1997: 15-26.
Strasser, T.
    1997   'Storage and States on Prehistoric Crete: The Function of the Koulouras in the First Minoan Palaces', *Journal of Mediterranean Archaeology* 10.1: 73-100.
Sweeney, D., and A. Yasur-Landau
    1999   'Following the Path of the Sea Persons: The Women in the Medinet Habu Reliefs', *TA* 26: 116-45.
Tappy, R.
    1995   'Did the Dead Ever Die in Biblical Judah', *BASOR* 298: 59-68.
Tchernov, E., and I. Drori
    1983   'Economic Patterns and Environmental Conditions at Tel Masos during the Israelite Settlement Period', in V. Fritz and A. Kempinski (eds.), *Ergebnisse der Ausgrabungen auf der Hirbet el-Masas (Tel Masos) 1972–1975* (Wiesbaden: Otto Harrassowitz): 213-22.
Thomas, B.W.
    1994   'Inclusion and Exclusion in the Moravian Settlement in North Carolina, 1770–1790', *Historical Archaeology* 28.3: 15-29.
Thomas, N.
    1991   *Entangled Objects: Exchange, Material Culture, and Colonialism in the Pacific* (Cambridge, MA: Harvard University Press).
Thompson, L.
    1969   'Co-Operation and Conflict: The Zulu Kingdom and Natal', in M. Wilson and L. Thompson (eds.), *The Oxford History of South Africa* (Oxford: Oxford University Press): 334-90.
Thompson, T.L.
    1999   *The Bible in History: How Writers Create A Past* (London: Jonathan Cape).
    2000   'Lester Grabbe and Historiography: An Apologia', *SJOT* 14.1: 140-61.
Trigger, B.
    1989   *A History of Archaeological Thought* (Cambridge: Cambridge University Press).
Tubb, J.N.
    1998a   *Canaanites* (London: British Museum Press).
    1998b   'Response to Israel Finkelstein', in Ahituv and Oren (eds.) 1998: 167-69.
    2000   'Sea Peoples in the Jordan Valley', in Oren (ed.) 2000: 181-96.
Ucko, P.
    1988   'Foreword', in J. Gledhill and B. Bender (eds.), *State and Society: The Emergence of Social Hierarchy and Political Centralization* (London: Routledge): vii-xii.
Uziel, J.
    2003   'The Tell es-Safi Archaeological Survey' (MA thesis, Bar-Ilan University, Ramat Gan).

Van de Mieroop, M.
  1997   *The Ancient Mesopotamian City* (Oxford: Clarendon Press).
Van Der Steen, E.J.
  1995   'Aspects of Nomadism and Settlements in Central Jordan Valley', *PEQ*
          127: 141-58.
  1999   'Survival and Adaptation: Life East of the Jordan in the Transition from
          the Late Bronze Age to the Early Iron Age', *PEQ* 131: 176-91.
Van Wijngaarden, G.-J.
  1999   'An Archaeological Approach to the Concept of Value: Mycenaean Pottery
          in Ugarit (Syria)', *Archaeological Dialogue* 6.1: 2-46.
Vickers, M., and D. Gill
  1994   *Artful Crafts, Ancient Greek Silverware and Pottery* (Oxford: Clarendon
          Press).
Waldbaum, J.C.
  1994   'Early Greek Contacts with the Southern Levant ca. 1000–600 B.C.: The
          Eastern Perspective', *BASOR* 293: 53-66.
Ward, W.A.
  1992   'Shasu', in *ABD*: III, 1165-67.
Washburn, D.K.
  1989   'The Property of Symmetry and the Concept of Ethnic Style', in Shennan
          (ed.) 1989: 157-73.
Wedde, M.
  1995   'On Hierarchical Thinking in Aegean Bronze Age Glyptic Imagery'
          Aegeum 12 (Politeia. Soceity and State in the Aegean Bronze Age):
          493-504.
Weinfeld, M.
  1979   'Literary Creativity', in Malamat (ed.) 1979: 27-70.
Weinstein, J.
  1997   'Exodus and Archaeological Reality', in Frerichs and Lesko (eds.) 1997:
          87-103.
Weippert, H.
  1988   *Palastina in Vorhellenisticher Zeit* (Munich: C.H. Beck).
Weippert, M.
  1979   'The Israelite Evidence from Transjordan', in F.M. Cross Jr (ed.), *Sympo-
          sium Celebrating the Seventy-Fifth Anniversary of the American Schools
          of Oriental Research* (Cambridge, MA: ASOR): 15-34.
Weisman, Z.
  1984a   'Israel's Genesis and its Link to its Country in the Perception of the Bible',
          in Ephal (ed.) 1984: 11-18 (Hebrew).
  1984b   'The Period of the Judges in the Biblical Historiography', in Ephal (ed.)
          1984: 85-98 (Hebrew).
Weitzman, S.
  2002   'The Samson Story as Border Fiction', *Biblical Interpretation* 10: 158-74.
Weksler-Bdolah, S.
  1999   ''Alona', *ESI* 19: 68*-70*.
Wengrow, D.
  1996   'Egyptian Taskmasters and Heavy Burden: Highland Exploitation and the
          Collared-Rim Pithos of the Bronze/Iron Age Levant', *OJA* 15: 307-26.

Wenham, G.J.
  1979   *The Book of Leviticus* (New International Commentary on the Old Testament; London: Hodder & Stoughton).
Westbrook, R.
  1991   *Property and the Family in Biblical Law* (JSOTSup, 113; Sheffield: Sheffield Academic Press).
Whitelam, K.W.
  1986   'Recreating the History of Israel', *JSOT* 35: 45-70.
  1996a   *The Invention of Ancient Israel: The Silencing of Palestinian History* (London: Routledge).
  1996b   'Prophetic Conflict in Israelite History: Taking Sides with William G. Dever', *JSOT* 72: 25-44.
Wiessner, P.
  1983   'Style and Social Information in Kalahari San Projectile Points', *AA* 49: 253-76.
  1985   'Style or Isochrestic Variation? A Reply to Sacket', *AA* 50: 160-66.
  1988   'Style and Changing Relations Between the Individual and Society', in I. Hodder (ed.), *The Meaning of Things: Material Culture and Symbolic Expression* (London: Allen & Unwin): 56-63.
  1990   'Is there a Unity to Style?', in Conkey and Hastorf (eds.) 1990: 105-12.
Williamson, H.G.M.
  1998   'The Origins of Israel: Can We Safely Ignore the Bible', in Ahituv and Oren (eds.) 1998: 141-51.
Wilson, R.R.
  1977   *Genealogy and History in the Biblical World* (New Haven: Yale University Press).
Wobst, H.M.
  1977   'Stylistic Behavior and Information Exchange', in C.E. Cleland (ed.), *For the Director: Research Essays in Honor of James B. Griffin* (Ann Arbor: Museum of Anthropology, University of Michigan): 317-42.
Wolf, C.U.
  1947   'Traces of Primitive Democracy in Ancient Israel', *JNES* 6: 98-108.
Wolf, E.R.
  1982   *Europe and People without History* (Berkeley: University of California Press).
Wolff, S.R
  1998   'An Iron Age I Site at 'En Hagit (Northern Ramat Menashe)', in Gitin, Mazar, and Stern (eds.) 1998: 449-54.
Wolff, S.R. (ed.)
  2001   *Studies in the Archaeology of Israel and Neighboring Lands in Memory of Douglas L. Esse* (Atlanta: ASOR).
Wood, B.G.
  1990   *The Sociology of Pottery in Ancient Palestine* (JSOTSup, 103; Sheffield: Sheffield Academic Press).
  2001   'Khirbet el-Maqatir (Notes and News)', *IEJ* 51: 246-52.
Wright, G.E.
  1978   'A Characteristic North Israelite House', in Moorey and Parr (eds.) 1978: 149-54.

Yadin, Y.
    1972   *Hazor: The Head of All These Kingdoms* (The Schweich Lectures 1970;
             Oxford: Oxford University Press).
Yadin, Y., *et al.*
    1958   *Hazor I* (Jerusalem: Magnes Press).
    1960   *Hazor II* (Jerusalem: Magnes Press).
Yasur-Landau, A.
    2003   'How Did the Philistines Get to Canaan? Two: By Land', *BAR* 29.2:
             34-39, 66-67.
Yellin, J., and J. Gunneweg
    1989   'Instrumental Neutron Activation Analysis and the Origin of Iron Age I
             Collared-Rim Jars and Pithoi from Tel Dan', in S. Gitin and W.G. Dever
             (eds.), *Recent Excavations in Israel: Studies in Iron Age Archaeology*
             (Winona Lake, IN: Eisenbrauns): 133-41.
Yentsch, A.S.
    1991   'The Symbolic Divisions of Pottery: Sex-related Attributes of English and
             Anglo-American Household Pots', in McGuire and Paynter (eds.) 1991:
             192-230.
Younker, R.W.
    1999   'Review of Archaeological Research in Ammon', in Macdonald and
             Younker (eds.) 1999: 1-19.
Yurco, F.J.
    1990   '3,200-Year-Old Picture of the Israelites Found in Egypt', *BAR* 16.5:
             20-38.
    1991   'Can You Name the Panel with the Israelites? Yurco's Response', *BAR*
             17.6: 61.
    1997   'Merenptah's Canaanite Campaign and Israeli's Origins', in Frerichs and
             Lesko 1997: 27-55.
Zarzeki-Peleg, A.
    1997   'Hazor, Jokneam and Megiddo in the 10th Century B.C.E.', *TA* 24.2:
             258-88.
Zerner, C., P. Zerner, and J. Winder (eds.)
    1993   *Wace and Blegen: Pottery as Evidence for Trade in the Aegean Bronze
             Age 1939–1989* (Amsterdam: American Schools of Classical Studies at
             Athens).
Zertal, A.
    1986–87   'An Early Iron Age Cultic Site on Mount Ebal: Excavations Seasons
             1982–1987', *TA* 13-14: 105-65.
    1988   'The Water Factor during the Israelite Settlement Process in Canaan', in
             Heltzer and Lipiński (eds.) 1988: 341-52.
Zimhoni, O.
    1997   *Studies in the Iron Age Pottery of Israel: Typological, Archaeological and
             Chronological Aspects* (Tel Aviv: Tel Aviv University).
Zorn, J.
    1994   'Estimating the Population Size of Ancient Settlement: Methods, Prob-
             lems, Solution and a Case Study', *BASOR* 295: 31-48.

INDEX OF AUTHORS

INDEX OF SUBJECTS

Note that such terms as Israelites, Philistines, Philistia, Canaanites, Judah, ethnicity and the like are too ubiquitous to be listed here.